SMALL
VICTORIES

To Christel, Elliott, and Eloïse—
and all the Hartes.
I care a lot.

SMALL VICTORIES

THE TRUE STORY OF FAITH NO MORE

ADRIAN HARTE

A Jawbone book
First edition 2018
Published in the UK and the USA by
Jawbone Press
Office G1,
141–157 Acre Lane,
London SW2 5UA,
England
www.jawbonepress.com

ISBN 978-1-911036-37-1

Front cover image by Dustin Rabin
Jacket design by Mark Case

Printed in China

1 2 3 4 5 22 21 20 19 18

CONTENTS | PART ONE

CONTENTS | PART TWO

CONTENTS | PART THREE

CONTENTS | PART FOUR

In 1991, there was a new, pungent taste for coffee connoisseurs in the UK. High-end beverage merchants Taylors of Harrogate imported a kilo of *kopi luwak*—and the drink proved a hit with coffee drinkers and thrill-seekers, mostly due to the abhorrent appeal of its particular production. The coffee is produced when civets in Indonesia sneak into coffee plantations and eat the choicest berries. These solitary, nocturnal, cat-like creatures cannot fully digest the coffee bean, so they excrete it—and the bean, now enriched by enzymatic reactions and musk from the cat's anal glands, is collected to make an astringent and wonderfully rare coffee. By the second decade of the new millennium, the popularity and price of the faecally fermented beans was such that production now took place on an industrial scale across Southeast Asia, with civets poached and caged in dreadful conditions and force-fed coffee beans to excrete premium coffee in commercially feasible quantities.

Since 1983, Faith No More have ingested elements of almost every musical style, and flavoured them with their own musical musk to produce seven studio albums—music like no other. Like *kopi luwak*, the peculiar production method gives their music a dark astringency, a marvellous macabre mordancy. And, as with the coffee beans, attempts since to reproduce Faith No More's music on a larger scale have resulted in horrible suffering—and some truly terrible music.

Reproducing Faith No More's music has proved impossible because the circumstances that created it are impossible to replicate. They started out burning incense and burning through singers and guitarists, out of time and out of place in San Francisco's late hardcore scene. From their early incarnations as Sharp Young Men and then Faith. No Man, the band adopted an anti-rockist ethos, playing concerts as one-off events, playing shows with no singer, playing with different band members from show to show, and playing ten-minute songs, repeating the same cyclical riffs over and over again.

Faith No More, in various incarnations, have had seven vocalists and twelve guitar players, but the band has had a consistent core. Keyboard player Roddy Bottum, drummer Mike Bordin, and bassist Bill Gould have been in place since just before the band's first show as Faith No More in October 1983.

'Mike, Billy, and I created something,' says Bottum. 'We created a style, a vision, and a sound that was different and unique and really emotional. It came from a friendship and a chemistry we had as kids.'

Others would contribute to the style over almost four decades, including Jim Martin's guitar crunch and Chuck Mosley's punk-meets-hip-hop vocals; and then, from 1988, Mike Patton's vocal versatility, Oulipian lyrics, and musical assuredness gave the band's *kopi luwak* an even greater force. But Bottum, Bordin, and Gould remain at the heart of everything they do.

From recording their first album in 1985, Faith No More always strove to do it themselves. 'We were a bunch who didn't fit anywhere else,' says Bordin. 'We were never going to find a formula and just coast.'

Conflict often ensued. Sometimes the band wanted it both ways. They were indies aligned to a major label, underdogs on the biggest rock tour of the era alongside Guns N' Roses and Metallica, and moaning about the music industry while all over MTV.

The band's all-about-the-music ethos did not preclude colourful rock'n'roll decadence and debauchery. Punch-ups between band members, sackings via fax, car crashes, scatological pranks, the hiring and firing of Courtney Love, and heroin addiction all feature in the Faith No More odyssey. Many of these incidents were provoked by a distinct absence of clarity in band communication. Band members aired their grievances in a succession of music magazine interviews, rather than speaking to each other. Faith No More's musical output could be just as obtuse. 'We had an anything goes approach. We like to surprise ourselves,' says Gould.

That approach provoked skirmishes, instability, and a constant state of crisis. It prompted sackings, a split, and a decade of silence. It produced 'Epic', *Angel Dust*, and an unlikely comeback. 'Even if it wasn't the right way to go, we used our senses as guides,' says Gould. 'We trusted the outcome, and that outcome revealed itself to us in different ways in different stages of our lives.'

The Faith No More journey takes in 1970s suburban Los Angeles ennui, the 80s music underground of San Francisco, and the 90s MTV alternative music gold rush. It is the story of Faith No More as autarkic outsiders, as buzz band, as heavy metal miscasts, as reluctant arena act, as anaphasic relics, and as comeback kings for a day, fools for a lifetime.

PART ONE

The first steps of Faith No More's journey took place far away from the scuzzy San Francisco clubs where they played their early shows. Figuratively far, but literally only a few hundred miles down Highway 101 to Los Angeles, the Faith No More story begins in the city's gilded Hancock Park neighbourhood. Bill Gould and Roddy Bottum, both the scions of successful legal families, grew up in the affluent enclave where Mae West, Ava Gardner, and Clark Gable had lived in Hollywood's Golden Age.

As his full name of Roswell Christopher Bottum III suggests, Roddy's family history was as colourful as that of his childhood neighbourhood. The Bottums arrived in the United States from England before the Revolutionary wars, shortening the name Longbottum on the way. Via the battle of Bunker Hill and spells in Vermont, New York, and Wisconsin, Roddy's branch of the clan eventually settled in South Dakota in the late nineteenth century. His great-grandfather, Joseph H. Bottum, was practising law when South Dakota was admitted to statehood in 1889, and was then the state's first register of deeds and a state senator. Roddy's grandfather, Roswell Christopher Bottum, continued the family business, enjoying a long legal career while also a member of the state legislature, where he served as Speaker Pro Tem of the House of Representatives.

Roswell Christopher Bottum II, known more simply as Ros, studied (and boxed) at the University of Notre Dame before his move to law school in southern California in the late 1950s took the Bottum name west. He later established a successful legal practice specialising in medical malpractice.

It would be tempting to see Roddy's rock music career as a rebellion against a family lineage of lawyers and legislators, but he grew up largely unaware of the full extent of this aspect of his rich genealogy, taking more pride in the even more unusual achievements in his maternal family history. In 1931, Roddy's maternal grandparents left Sioux Falls with all their belongings, and Roddy's infant uncle Billy, and pitched up in the remote 231-person town of Wall. Armed with a $3,000 inheritance, a fresh pharmacy degree, and the desire to set up on his own in a small town with a Catholic church, Ted Hustead bought the town's only drug store, Wall Drug. It was the intervention of Roddy's grandmother Dorothy almost five years later, not long after the birth of Roddy's mother Mary, that sealed the Hustead and Wall Drug names in American tourist folklore. Kept awake during an attempted afternoon nap by the incessant rumble of traffic heading to the newly opened Mount Rushmore monument sixty miles to the west, she alighted on the idea of offering free cups of water to the weary travellers. The real key to the store's unique success was marketing, and she also came up with the idea for a sign and the slogan, 'Get a soda, Get a root beer, Turn next corner, Just as near, To Highway 16 & 14, Free Ice Water, Wall Drug.'

The store became a thriving emporium and more signs followed, turning the business into a phenomenon. A family friend brought them to Europe during World War II, and they became a popular remembrance of home for US servicemen stationed worldwide. Soon the store—now run by Roddy's cousins—was attracting 1.5 million visitors a year. 'My real legacy is that my mom's family started Wall Drug, a crazy tourist attraction next to the Badlands that based its advertising structure on the concept of free water,' he says.

Roddy inherited the Bottum family names, if not the paternal interest in law or any pugilistic instincts. He may have required the latter, though, with his name proving to be a childhood burden. 'Can you imagine having that name growing up in school?' he once said. '*Roddy Bottum* read aloud in front of a bunch of kids? It was a tough one, very character-building.'

Roddy met Bill Gould in 1972 when they were both aged nine. Bill's father, William D. Gould, was also a successful lawyer. By their own telling, the pair enjoyed a largely blissful childhood, as if scripted by John Hughes and directed by Steven Spielberg.

'We lived like a mile from each other,' Roddy recalls. 'We'd ride to and from each other's houses—there was a gang of us. We hung out together, riding bikes, joined Boy Scouts together, remained friends for the most part through high school. We threw things at cars mostly, listened to music, rode bikes, made a lot of prank phone calls, built things, wreaked havoc … childhood things.'

The pair were classmates at St Brendan Elementary School, and were in the same Boy Scout troop. Their Catholic education continued at Jesuit Loyola High School. 'We went to a Catholic grammar school that was taught by nuns,' Roddy says. 'They were strict and prohibitive and horrible. They intimidated us and played mind games on the children.'

Bill Gould agrees. 'Everything else was extremely conservative about them, except they wouldn't wear the habits. They might as well have. They were sadistic; they were particularly intense and would create in our class a jailhouse mentality where we were the inmates and we stuck together. We learned to do things clandestinely. We had these little acts of rebellion.'

Overall, this early Catholic pedagogic experience had a profound effect on Roddy. 'The nuns, growing up, forced a repression on me and a sense of guilt that I can't shake. That's made me strive for and approach things in a very antagonistic way. I like to approach issues in an unorthodox way and challenge mindsets that I find to be basic and predictable. It's what drives me. Growing up with religion forced me to challenge and question authority from an early age.'

His Loyola High School experience was more rewarding. 'I was taught by Jesuit priests. The Jesuits are the intellectuals of the Catholic sect and are generally pretty cool. Though they'd taken vows of poverty, they lived like kings. That was the one chink in the armour. Otherwise, they really excelled in the teachings of history, theatre, and the arts. It was a really great high school. We didn't learn music from school, we learned it on our own. There was a record store close to our houses where a glam/David Bowie type of guy worked. That store was our early education.'

Roddy frequented A1 Record Finders almost daily in his early teenage years, with the guy who ran the store turning him on to new bands and new genres. One such recommendation was for Sparks, after Roddy had purchased a Queen record. Before that, Bottum's musical education had come at home. 'My mom is musical. She has perfect pitch and can play any piece of music in any key that she hears,' he says. 'She plays every Sunday for the mass at the men's prison in Los Angeles and sings with their choir. She was a big part of my musical upbringing.'

Roddy didn't have long to wait to make his own performance debut. 'I started playing piano regularly at the age of five. My sisters and I did improvisational duets and triads growing up. When I was six, I learned the Notre Dame fight song ["Notre Dame Victory March"], and performed it in the school talent show.' His taste quickly broadened. 'I bought Elton John's *Captain Fantastic & The Brown Dirt Cowboy*. I liked the cover, simple as that. I remember hearing his accent on the radio, and I didn't know why he was talking like that. I was that young.'

If his record-buying was precocious, Roddy had to wait until he turned sixteen to experience his first live rock performance. 'I cut summer school and went with a friend to a recording of *Don Kirshner's Rock Concert*,' he recalls. 'It was recorded in LA and Devo were on. I didn't start going to shows until I could drive. Billy had a car and started going to punk rock shows before any of us. I saw bands like X and The Plugz, but Billy saw The Germs first-hand.'

Before that punk phase, Bill's first exposure was through his father's records. 'He grew up in LA in the 50s listening to black radio stations, which was proto-rock'n'roll, so he has always been a music fan and I got that from him. When he'd drive us to school, he always played rock radio.'

Bowie was an early favourite. 'I played *Space Oddity* a lot around the house. The beauty of that was that it had a lyric sheet. Another album he had around the house was *Plastic Ono Band* and George Harrison's *All Things Must Pass*. He liked Led Zeppelin and The Beatles.'

Bill's music grounding continued when his father took him, aged ten, to his first rock concert—Bowie in his *Ziggy Stardust* incarnation at the Long Beach Arena in 1973. 'It was edgy and dark, and it freaked me out,' he says. 'I felt like I was listening to the devil's music. It was outside my white middle-class experience. I was fascinated—in a good way.'

Billy and Roddy shared both musical appreciation and iconoclasm. Roddy: 'We shared a lot musically. I remember us hating Stevie Wonder's *Songs In The Key Of Life* together. It was universally adored, and we hated it. We used the double-fold album cover on the lip of a skateboard ramp as a show of disrespect.'

❋

A shared discovery of punk intruding on peaceful Hancock helped provoke a cleavage in their teenage musical experience. On May 26 1978, the pair were cycling together to an ice cream shop in their neighbourhood when they spotted a group dressed in leather and ripped shirts, with spiked coloured hair.

Bill takes up the tale. 'We saw a bunch of weird-looking people walking on the street, and we followed them. They walked upstairs from the record store. There was a hall there called Larchmont Hall.'

Larchmont, a 1940s red brick community building, was a venue for parish council meetings, rummage sales, and Young Republican benefits. But in the summer of 1977, the hall became a suburban punk outpost, the unlikely venue for a series of fund-raising concerts for *Slash*, California's pioneering punk zine. Local punk outfit The Zeros, fresh from the release of their second single—and whose 1979 Elks Hall gig would provoke the country's first full-scale punk riot the following year—were the star attraction.

Neither the prospect of a riot incited by the so-called 'Mexican Ramones' nor support acts Clones, The Last, and Johnny Novotny were enough to persuade Roddy to linger longer, but Bill was hooked:

> I was about fourteen or fifteen, and they let us in—they didn't card us or anything, and I even got a drink at the bar. I got a beer and hung out and watched the show. It was mind-blowing. Between that and discovering the Sex Pistols, that got me into punk, and then I started going to punk shows.
>
> I heard the Sex Pistols when I was probably fifteen; I heard it at [future bandmate in The Animated] Paul Wims's house. He bought the record. I'd asked him: 'Have you heard of the Sex Pistols?' and he said, 'Yeah, I've got it,' and we put it on the record player. I was just laughing, at the time, at how bad it was, because it was so simple. But after probably eight hours,

the songs were still sticking in my head, and I had to concede that this was it.

Gould also noticed that these bands were no more proficient musically than he was, just months into his first bass guitar lessons. He recalls why he chose bass:

> There was a group of probably five of us that hung out on a regular basis. Roddy had been studying piano since I've known him, so his mother made him practise everyday. Somebody else's friend was a drummer, and he took drum lessons. Another guy was learning to play guitar. We're really young, and we're just talking about being in a group, and the only musician that we needed was bass. I didn't even know what it was. I guess that's how a lot of bass players start.
>
> I was about thirteen and rented a bass, because my mom didn't know how long I was going to stick with it. I started taking lessons from this guy in Hollywood called Pat O'Brien. It turns out that Paul Wims from the scout troop was taking lessons from Pat too. I was getting to a point where I could play a couple of songs off records, so I said, 'Let's play together.' I'd go over to his house. My mom would drop me off, and we'd play Beatles covers and other stuff like that. Then more people come—the neighbour down the street that played drums, Kevin Morgan, and then this guy Mark Stewart, who played guitar, came in. Mark's taste was a little more eclectic, and we started going from playing cover songs to trying to write music.

Punk may later have been Gould's entry point, but he had more esoteric tastes prior to that. 'I remember that when I started lessons, my next-door neighbour was into progressive rock. I went into my guitar lesson and I brought a Gentle Giant record, and I told him that I wanted to play that. The teacher said, *What the fuck are you giving me?*'

The lessons also helped forge the distinctive Faith No More sound. 'Billy is actually left-handed,' Wims reveals. 'He had to learn to play right-handed, because our teacher told him he couldn't teach him playing left-handed. That is probably why Billy has such a unique style of playing.'

The lessons were the also the catalyst for Gould's first band, one without Roddy Bottum, who recalls, 'I wasn't electric then. I just played piano. It didn't dawn on me that I could play rock music.' Gould, Wims, and some school friends started jamming. 'We practised originally with just Billy and Kevin Morgan on drums,' Wims adds. 'We played lots of cover songs— Beatles, Aerosmith, Wild Cherry. Anything with cool but relatively easy guitar parts. Mark Stewart joined us later, and then The Animated was formed. Mark Stewart brought in Chuck Mosley to the band. He knew Chuck from high school.'

Stewart and Mosley were four years older than Gould, who remembers, 'Chuck and Stew brought a much more sophisticated element into the band. I learned about bands like The Fall, The Pop Group, XTC, and Joy Division from them; to look back on it now, they probably saved my musical life! I got into more aggressive punk stuff too, maybe a bit more than them, but it created an interesting dynamic that made the music part Buzzcocks, part XTC, part I-don't-know-what. It was a very strange band compared to other bands in LA, and we really had a hard time finding anywhere to play.'

Stewart, better known as Stew, later played one show with Faith No More and inspired some of the lyrics of the *Introduce Yourself* track 'Spirit', but he achieved greater success and fame: firstly in the late 1990s, with his band The Negro Problem, and then with his musical theatre career, winning a Tony award in 2008 for his semi-autobiographical production *Passing Strange*.

Chuck Mosley went on to become Faith No More's singer on their first two albums, but when he first played with Gould, he was a keyboard player. His musical roots came from both his adopted and natural parents. 'It's weird,' he said. 'The parents that adopted me [at the age of one] were the same cultural breakdown. My mom was Jewish and my dad was black and American Indian. The people who had me, and the people who adopted me. My natural dad was nineteen, and he was a musician, and my mom worked in a record store that our family owned. Then, my parents that adopted me, my mom played classical piano, and my dad played blues and tangos and swing, just for fun.'

That background first manifested itself in Chuck playing the *Batman* theme tune on piano:

> Next thing I know I'm taking classical piano lessons for the next ten years. First, it was once a week, then it went into twice a week and I was taking piano and then I was taking composition and theory. My mom wanted me to be the first black classical pianist, but that wasn't really my plan, plus there already was one—André Watts—he already beat me to it.
>
> I wasn't really disciplined. I never learned to sight-read. I could play music, but I couldn't be like a studio musician because I just couldn't pick up a piece of music and start playing it. I played by ear a lot. My teacher wanted me to learn a song by next week, and I would get her to play it for me, and I would just remember it.

Mosley's musical outlook soon changed. 'When I was twelve years old, I would go to my piano lessons, but then I heard "Hang On To Yourself" by David Bowie. I knew then I would like to quit piano to play guitar, and I started thinking about music in a different way.'

Seeing Bowie live aged thirteen in October 1972 at the Santa Monica Civic Auditorium opened his eyes and ears to live music. 'I had a whole secret life that I was trying to keep from my parents, and they had no idea what was going on. I used to smoke a lot of weed before we went to see shows, but when I started going to see punk bands, I didn't need to get high because of all the energy.'

Mosley found a willing partner for punk shows in Gould. In 2016, he told *Fear & Loathing*, 'As soon as me and Billy met, we clicked. He was into all the same bands that I was into, so we started going to shows together. I think he liked going out to shows with me because I didn't have any limits. I always went out just to see the bands, that was all I intended to do, but it would often end up in those kinds of situations.'

Away from these adventures, the pair were also progressing as musicians. The Animated became an accomplished band. They played shows at famous LA hotspots, the Troubadour, Whisky A Go Go, and Madame Wong's. The Bangs, soon to reach superstardom as The Bangles, opened for them.

The Animated released a genuinely striking EP in 1981, simply entitled *4 Song EP*, recorded with the help of a friendly studio engineer in Silver Lake. It was a vibrant, out-of-place, and out-of-time offering, showcasing assured musicianship and clever songcraft. Opening track 'Edith C Sharp' and 'Plastic Heaven', which was a minor hit on local radio station KROQ, deserved a wider audience. These four songs that have survived convey a band with a sound that was all their own.

'Most of the influences came from The Beatles, Yes, Sparks, The Jackson Five, Blondie, Buzzcocks, XTC, etc,' Paul Wims explains. 'Lots of British influence. I was a big Jackson Five and Beatles fan. We wrote songs based on what we liked, and put it all together. If you listen to "Looking At You", for instance, those are jazz chords during the verses. Lots of minor sevenths. We just played it in a fast new-wave style, that's why it sounds so different.'

Those four songs were all that The Animated ever released—and within eighteen months the band was no more. 'All of us thought we would get signed,' Wims adds. 'As songwriters, Mark Stewart and I had some great ones. As young teenagers, we still had a lot to learn about stage presence, and, frankly, we were probably too young to realise our true potential. I believe this held us back. I also don't think we had the patience to wait and see what might happen.'

Bill Gould concurs. 'We were completely unsuccessful. We didn't fit in with anything. We were the weirdest band you could possibly imagine. Paul has a very distinctive high voice. It wasn't punk. We couldn't play a punk show, and if we did, it didn't work. It was completely incompatible with everything.'

He also suggests another reason for the band's failure to get signed: 'Everybody in the band except me was black, which doesn't mean anything except we weren't playing what anyone would think of as black music. It sounded like the Buzzcocks but up to 78rpm.'

Chuck: 'We noticed the amount of racism in the business. It didn't fit; a lot of people thought it was white music.'

The Animated apprenticeship was enough to convince Chuck that music was what he wanted to do. 'I know we all took it pretty seriously. We didn't know what we were doing. We had our buddy as our manager, but we all had the rock star fantasy. I never really took anything real seriously, but this is what I wanted to do. I was pretty hooked and knew that's where I was headed.' He was headed there without his keyboard—'I was tired of carrying keyboards around. I picked up the guitar because it was easier'—and he was headed toward punk. 'I wanted to be in a punk band. The Animated weren't a punk band, but we had a lot of punk following.'

Chuck found his punk band with Haircuts That Kill. Wims acknowledges his contribution to The Animated: 'He was an excellent keyboard and piano player. Chuck composed classical pieces when he was around ten years old. Chuck was also a very good songwriter and wrote songs with intricate chord changes. The vocal melodies were usually very straightforward (not much range variation), which might explain his success as lead singer in Faith No More.'

Bill Gould took drastic measures in a last-ditch effort to secure a deal for the band, heading to New York and London to meet record labels. 'I was eighteen, but I probably looked like I was about fifteen,' he says. 'I did the whole East Coast first, and I think a lot of people humoured me. And in London I went to Rough Trade, and they sat me down and had tea with me and acted like they were interested in what I had to say. It was a great experience. I didn't even tell my parents where I was staying, and nobody knew where I was. I was staying at people's squats, just cruising around.'

London also opened Gould's ears to even more outré music. 'I saw some groundbreaking shit,' he says. 'The one show that blew my mind was This Heat with the band 23 Skidoo at the Battersea Arts Centre. Growing up in LA, we didn't have access to a lot of stuff. There was a Tower Records that got import stuff, but imports were pretty expensive. I knew the Buzzcocks, and I knew your more garden-variety stuff. I knew the LA bands, but not the music that was more diverging from punk into different territories and different ways of playing rock music. It was just taking something that was edgy and into a new place I wasn't familiar with.'

If Gould's trips testified to his ambitions for the band, his decision to leave showcased a fierce individual drive and a frustration with others whose commitment to the cause did not match his own. 'When I left to study in Berkeley, I thought I was going to be able to commute back and forth and stay in The Animated,' he reflects. 'But that was just not going to happen. I was a pretty ambitious kid, and I felt that the band should be pushing harder and doing more things. I felt frustrated, and wanted to just branch out and do something of my own. I was really into The Animated. I was into the music. But going to the UK made me see that there's a big wide world out there.'

NEW
BEGINNINGS

2

That second act was initially a solo project. The remorseless Bill Gould had barely unpacked at UC Berkeley before he went in search of a new group to play with. His studies were never more than a vehicle to escape suburban Los Angeles for a San Francisco that promised more edge, excitement, and opportunity.

> I came from a middle-class family, upper middle-class even, so there was a push to have a career. I was the oldest of six, so I got the brunt of it. But I was living six hundred miles away from my parents. They couldn't really know what I was doing. That was a tough school. Really great academic-wise, but it's also a huge school. I think it had a population at the time of 35,000 students, so it's very impersonal and it's very easy to disappear, and I took advantage of that and put more time into music than school.
>
> I started off with, ambitiously, English and philosophy, and I realised that it was never going to happen. And I went down to Political Science because I could use the same basic

requirements, but get finished sooner. I didn't make it. I tried, but music was the only thing I cared about. I didn't want a career. I was going to be a musician. That was it.

Gould's first priority on arriving in Berkeley was to find a new band. 'There was a record store down the street. I was living in the dormitories, and I walked down the street to Telegraph Avenue to look at some records and to look at the bulletin board on the wall, where bands were always posting. The only one out of these guys that was doing something post-punk, that seemed like the closest thing I could relate to, was Mike Morris, who was looking to put a band together. And that was what became Faith. No Man.'

✦

It is entirely in keeping with the group's warped sense of time and place that the band that would eventually become Faith No More was formed in a different city in a different decade by different people under a different name. Morris formed The Spectators with Wade Worthington in 1978, then Sharp Young Men in 1980, and finally Faith. No Man in 1982.

Wade Worthington was born in March 1961 and grew up in the Castro Valley in the East Bay, about twenty-five miles from San Francisco, eventually going to the same high school as future Faith No More drummer Mike Bordin and Metallica founding bassist Cliff Burton. Taught piano by his church-organ-playing grandmother, he took professional organ lessons from the age of nine, and picked up an early taste for Bach and The Beatles. However, a short spell in a religious school that preached that rock'n'roll was the music of the devil initially inhibited his musical development.

'I felt like a stranger there and never fit in with any of the groups of students, as I was extremely shy and very socially awkward,' he says. 'Some days I'd spend my school lunch period walking to the nearby public library to see what records I could check out. I remember finding Joni Mitchell and Bob Dylan records. I also liked the San Francisco sound bands like the Grateful Dead and Moby Grape.'

In the autumn of 1978, Worthington overcame his shyness to post a 'musicians wanted' ad at a local store, Spitzer's Music. Mike Morris was one of the first to respond, and the pair agreed to meet. Despite an inauspicious and paradoxical first meeting in which Worthington effectively auditioned for the person who had responded to his ad, nervously playing some Bach on his Hammond organ, the pair, along with Morris's friend Eric Scott, began spending time together. Worthington and Morris started playing covers—Tom Petty's 'I Want To Know' and The Cars' 'Just What I Needed'—on Worthington's new Wurlitzer electric piano. They soon progressed to writing, and they recorded a Morris composition at a recording studio owned by one of his friends.

By his late teens, Morris had already played in dozens of groups. 'I got serious about playing the guitar when I turned seventeen. I've never been the hubristic sort, and knew that I was basically shite—and I told myself that I had better start taking things seriously if I ever wanted to make a proper go of it. Within a few months I did get better. The next step was to try to write songs. That took a lot longer to happen.'

Morris recalls that first meeting a little differently, but common to both versions is M. Morris taking control. 'I took the ad with me. It was a sort of pinkish-orange card hand-written in blue ink. I rang him later that day and immediately he was apologetic, saying it was a mistake. He did everything he could to talk me out of the idea. Before I managed to get a word out, he had verbally kicked himself to death. But I would not take no for an answer. We had some similar influences and worked with those. Soon enough, he realised he was perfectly able to play in a band.'

The duo became a four-piece, in time recruiting bassist Carl Leicher and drummer Larry Carter. Initially playing as Stereo, they soon settled on The Spectators and began to make an impression on the San Francisco club scene during 1980. They were rapidly regulars at the Mabuhay Gardens and recorded two singles, the Morris tunes 'Lambretta Boys' and 'I'm In Love With A Girl'. They even filmed a video for 'Lambretta Boys', which featured the band attired in thin ties, the Vespa scooters they all owned, and cheesy coordinated finger-clicking. A support slot for the Dead Kennedys at the Mab ended in violence, as Worthington recalls: 'I heard that this unlikely line-up was to antagonise the Dead Kennedys fans by putting a mod band in with the mix. It worked, because one obnoxious member of the audience grabbed Mike's guitar strings while he was playing. Mike booted him in the face.'

Not long after, Worthington chose to quit. 'At some point, I became dissatisfied with The Spectators. It was the first time I had quit a band of Mike's—and it wasn't the last. My musical tastes were changing, as there was so much to explore in music that to be a teenager and to stay stuck in one genre for too long was like a crime.'

The band played on, and even played support for XTC at San José State University on Halloween night 1980. 'I have few memories about that particular gig,' Morris recalls, 'because it was marred by girl issues which, to a large extent, led to the demise of the band. But I remember the real Andy Partridge telling me that he was quite impressed with my songs. We got as good a response as anyone could expect considering everyone, including me, came to see them.'

It proved to be The Spectators' penultimate show: band tensions became too much, and the group disbanded. Worthington and Morris reunited the following year after the former had again advertised for band members but found himself asking Morris to attend an audition to lend advice. 'Morris and I had remained friends, and he agreed to help me out,' Worthington recalls. 'Before long, it became apparent that we shared a lot of things—friendship, musical ambition, and now even direction. It didn't seem like a gamble this time, and he was accepting of my contribution as a singer and songwriter.'

Worthington and Morris were reunited, but the auditioned drummer did not work out. Then, later in 1981, a friend called Rick Clare recommended another drummer.

'My first impression was that he was fairly quiet and polite, and seemed quite sane,' Morris recalls. 'Not the attributes you generally expect of a drummer. But after he started playing, I definitely wanted to pursue more with him. He told me that he used to be in a Ramones-type band. I was worried that he might not be open to what I wanted from a drummer. I told him I was looking for someone who was powerful and primarily used his toms to provide beats. He just embraced his role and kept getting better and better. And talk about stamina—he was, and still is, a machine who really doesn't tire.'

That drumming machine was Mike Bordin.

When life betrays, music soothes and saves. The healing power of music has become a trite trope, but it was sadly true for Mike Bordin. In 1972, when the nine-year-old Bordin sought sanctuary and solace in his East Bay bedroom after the sudden death of his mother, his father brought him a radio. The sturdy dark brown Bakelite Emerson tube radio became his constant companion in the difficult weeks that followed. And, even limited to AM, he sought music. Up the dial a little for The Temptations ... down the dial and there was the heavy organ intro and fire, pyre, mire rhyme of The Doors' 'Light My Fire' ... then to KYA 1260 and Smokey Robinson's 'Tears Of A Clown'.

'The radio and music popped into my life then like a life vest or a beacon,' Bordin says. 'And, once it came in, it never left. That's why music is so important to me, because from the beginning, it was something I could relate to.'

The Bordin household had always been musical. Mike's doctor father, Edward, was a classical music devotee, and the Bordins regularly went to the opera and the symphony. Even Bordin's first forays into buying music came with parental approval as a consideration. 'The first record I bought myself was Creedence Clearwater Revival's *Cosmo's Factory*,' he recalls. 'That was something where my parents would have said, that's OK.' And Bordin, aged ten, went to his first concert soon afterward— Elton John touring *Goodbye Yellow Brick Road* at the Oakland Coliseum in September 1973.

But Bordin had to fight for the right to see his favourite bands, with his father barring him from unsuitable venues in unsuitable parts of town, and from unsuitable bands:

I was beating him up every Sunday. The *Sunday Chronicle* had the pink section, the entertainment section. And in the pink section, in the first page or two, Bill Graham always had a massive ad about what concerts he was promoting at the time. Every single week I'd beat my dad up: 'This guy is coming, that guy is coming,' and he'd be, 'No way, no way, it's a school night,' or, 'No way, no way, not safe.' It took me six months of beating him every Sunday for him to finally decide that there was a concert safe enough for me to go to. He allowed me to go for my sixth-grade graduation, and my cousin took me to see the Grateful Dead. It was Bill Graham's second Day On The Green in June 1974, and I hung out all day with Hell's Angels!

Music became the teenage Bordin's life. He listened to AC/DC, Lucifer's Friend, and Sir Lord Baltimore. He listened to ZZ Top, Captain Beyond, Van der Graaf Generator. He listened to Robin Trower, Thin Lizzy, and Blue Öyster Cult. And then he heard Black Sabbath. 'Once I heard Sabbath, everything else was in second place,' he says. 'The first album I bought was *Sabbath Bloody Sabbath*, and to me it was wow, wow, wow.'

Bordin also found a deeper kinship with Sabbath. 'In some ways I was so lost, and Ozzy was singing about all dour and depressing down stuff, and I realised that there are other people like me, other people like that.'

Later, the teenage Bordin's regular brother-in-arms for gig-going was future Metallica bassist Cliff Burton. The pair met when Bordin was eleven years old on the first day of sixth grade at Castro Valley High School. They hit it off immediately. 'His brother died within six months of me meeting him, so we had things in common there and then. And for him, music was it. For me, music was it.'

With Bordin Senior long since on board with Mike's concert-going, Bordin and Burton would travel far and wide for concerts.

Cliff's dad used to take us. Cliff and I would take the bus from the East Bay into San Francisco, to Winterland or wherever, and after the shows Cliff's dad would pick us up.

It wasn't just rock. Cliff and I saw Andrés Segovia together—

that's about as far from rock as you could get. We saw The Tubes a bunch of times. It was music, just music. That was the thing. Metallica listened to the Misfits because Cliff turned them on to them, and he liked R.E.M. and Devo and Johnny Cash and Bach. It's good music or it's not. I wanted all of it. I loved Black Sabbath, but I loved Sparks too.

The pair graduated from listening and watching to wanting to play. 'We were in Cliff's bedroom, and out of nowhere Cliff says he's going to play bass—and I said, that's cool, I'll play drums. I don't know why. Maybe it was support. I couldn't tell you. It was pure reflex, like when you karate chop your kneecap and your leg kicks. I've said some stupid things in my life that were pure reflex, and I couldn't explain why—but that wasn't one of them.'

Prior to that life-changing show of solidarity, Bordin's focus had been more on guitar-playing and guitarists: Rory Gallagher, Tony Iommi, Billy Gibbons, Angus Young, Michael Schenker. But like his previous childhood ambition to be an ice hockey goaltender, guitar hero wishes were soon set aside. 'I can look back on it and say it was because it's saying, *I'm not going to be the alpha male of the pack and put things down my trousers and everyone is going to worship me, I'm not going to be the superstar of superstars. I just want to play music, and it will be great.*'

True to his word, Bordin immediately set about becoming a drummer. 'I went home and told my dad I was going to be a drummer, and he said, No, you're not. And I said, Yes I am—and I did. I kept practising, I practised a lot, and I didn't do anything else for almost five years from aged thirteen to eighteen. Which is a good time to stay out of trouble, because in my area, in the East Bay, there was plenty of trouble to be found.'

Bordin's new focus on drumming proved a salvation. 'I was being a rotten reprobate kid with my mom having passed. It was hard, and my dad just said, You got to go, and I got sent to a boarding school.' A one-year exile at Menlo School followed. 'I went to school and became a better guy, stopped running wild, and it was all because I had something I was interested in.'

Bordin set about finding gear and finding lessons. He bought a set of old Camco drums piece by piece, turning them from mahogany to streaky blonde in a misguided customisation effort. They would do for starters but, three years later, he upgraded and upsized. 'My friend had a pickup, and we loaded up all the drums in that and took them down to this super music store in Oakland, Leo's Music, and I traded them all in for this Yamaha set. It had fifteen-inch and sixteen-inch rack-toms, an eighteen-inch floor-tom, and a twenty-six-inch kick drum. They were the biggest drums I could find.'

These were the drums he would use on Faith No More's first three albums.

Bordin didn't have to look far for a teacher, hooking up with Jim Eaton, the older brother of a school friend, who lived in the neighbourhood. Eaton was a student of Bay Area drum mentor Chuck Brown and was teaching his techniques. 'I went to see him, and I said I played drums,' Bordin recalls, 'and he asked me, What do you like? I said Robin Trower and Thin Lizzy and Black Sabbath and UFO and Blue Öyster Cult and Deep Purple, and he says, Go back and buy this record and listen to it, and then I'll teach you.'

The record wasn't metal or hard rock, or even rock. It was *Believe It*, the first album by The New Tony Williams Lifetime, the new project from the jazz-fusion pioneer who had been part of Miles Davis's band. 'That album wasn't what I expected. It was so monumentally powerful. Tony Williams was such an incredibly forceful drummer when he wanted to be—John Bonham in a fusion band. You had such finesse as well and such feel and such dexterity, yet still you've got your sticks turned around backward, and you're breaking cymbals.'

Under Eaton's guidance, Bordin set about learning that forceful finesse. 'He taught me the basics of how to hold sticks and he was real, real hard on that stuff, the proper technique. The watchword for me, what I had in mind, was that portrait of Black Sabbath's Bill Ward on the inside of *Vol. 4*—that's where I was heading.'

When he wasn't having almost daily lessons with Eaton, Bordin was spending every other spare minute practising. 'I had a little one of those practice pads, and it took me years to be able to swing the stick right and get it to bounce right, and to have enough strength in my arms. I worked hard. If it's something you want to do, you work really hard at it.'

Bordin also practised daily with Cliff Burton. The pair would go straight from school to Bordin's house and jam all evening. 'We'd play right there in the living room. We drove my neighbours nuts, absolutely out of their tree.

But we never stopped. We had such a thirst for experience or knowledge or whatever.'

The first songs they jammed on together were David Bowie's 'The Jean Genie' and The Kinks' 'You Really Got Me', and the first record Bordin played along to was Roxy Music's *Stranded*. All of their sessions were taped on a standard cassette recorder. Of Burton, Bordin says, 'He was good, and I was crummy. I was just learning. I wasn't strong, and I needed strength. And he was really good, very early.'

The pair graduated to their first band and a first live show. They were called Fry By Night after a typo on a flyer had mangled their original moniker, Fly By Night. The band comprised Bordin and Burton and a friend, Eddie Chacon, who went on to find success as one half of the pop-soul duo Charles & Eddie, who had a worldwide smash hit in 1992 with 'Would I Lie To You?' Chacon recalls:

My family moved just a few houses down from Mike Bordin's house when I was about thirteen years old. I can't remember exactly how we met, but I remember going up to his house and him cooking breakfast for me—eggs in a hole—which struck me as funny because of how young we were. He was like a super-articulate adult in a kid's body. I remember him being crazy passionate as he told me everything he knew about a brand new band out of Ireland called U2. I was taken aback by how loud he was playing this song, and a sound I'd never heard in my life. As 'I Will Follow' played, Mike was yelling over the music, saying this band was going be the biggest band in the world. I'd never met a kid like Mike before.

Even at a young age, he adds, Bordin and Burton took their musicianship very seriously.

Shortly after that first meeting, he introduced me to his bass player friend, Cliff Burton. Cliff was a lanky kid with long red hair all over the place. I was dreaming of being a rock singer at that time, but hadn't really begun the journey yet. I think the clincher that got me the singing gig in the new cover band they were starting was that my dad, who owned a trucking company, had said I could use his offices in the industrial part of San Lorenzo as a rehearsal studio. I wasn't really the right guy for the frontman position in their heavy metal cover band, but I was up for anything. Up until then, I had cut my teeth mimicking polar opposites Robert Plant and Al Green. The first few rehearsals, I was the guitar player as well as the singer. We were running through [Rick Derringer's] 'Beyond The Universe' and [Black Sabbath's] 'Iron Man'. I remember thinking, *Jesus, how the hell can these guys already be insanely consummate musicians at such a young age?* I was serious, but I was like a student that didn't know how to study until I met them.

They were meticulous and critical of every creative choice I made. Up until then, it had not occurred to me that there were creative choices to be made. I was all on instinct. I remember specifically Cliff telling me at one point, 'Your guitar solo isn't going anywhere. Your solo needs to have a beginning, a middle, and an end.' As a singer I lacked confidence. It didn't discourage Mike, but he was not going to tolerate it either. I'll never forget him getting up in my face and screaming, 'Just sing, man!' It wasn't mean-spirited. On the contrary, it actually felt like he was giving me permission to go crazy. I was learning fast from these guys.

Fry By Night certainly did not come across as three future rock and pop stars at their debut show in 1976, at a rented movie theatre in San Lorenzo. Bordin: 'Cliff was running around and plugged the chord out of his amp, and the first thing that happened to me was that I catch my index finger on my left hand on my rim. I ripped my knuckle open completely, and there's blood everywhere. My teacher came along—he bought a really good-looking girl along with him—and he was horrified.'

Constant practise and jamming with Burton and others continued, and Bordin's tastes were also broadening. 'As soon as I heard Motörhead, I knew that I didn't have to listen to Ted Nugent anymore. The next thing for me was punk and metal. It was Motörhead and AC/DC. Those were my escape hatches, because they took me straight into anything else. After that, I was all too happy to listen to Devo and The Stranglers, and the Sex Pistols and The Vibrators, and The Dils.'

Mike went to the Sex Pistols' last-ever show, at the Winterland in San Francisco, with Burton. And soon the pair had put together another group, EZ Street, along with mutual friend and future Faith No More guitarist Jim Martin. 'Cliff and I both met Jim at the same time,' Bordin says. 'There was a band in Hayward, the next town over from us that needed a bassist and a drummer. Cliff said, Let's go check them out, so we did. We ended up in Jim's band. That didn't last very long. I probably didn't play very well; it wasn't what I was trying to do.'

The band played covers mostly. The Rolling Stones' 'You Can't Always Get What You Want' was one, and Bordin soon wanted out. He and Jim Martin got on each other's wick from the start. 'We never hit it off. I don't know why. He's a very unique dude, and he was, even in high school.'

Jim Martin's memories of this are slightly different. 'By that time, we were writing original stuff,' he said in 1992. 'We had a song called "Retarded Guys" that sounds similar to Nirvana's "Come As You Are". That band was together for over five years, but Bordin didn't last too long, because he talked too much shit. He joined some pop-punk band.'

One legacy of that time was Bordin's nickname, Puffy, which came from his teenage hairstyle. 'I really didn't like short hair particularly,' he explains, 'and that's how it grew out. I just never cared for it, being a dirt-head rock kid.'

With patience, nature, and judicious combing, his hair grew, and grew up, and grew out, so much so that he looked bald on his first driving licence photo, with his hair too big to get in shot. 'What happened was that hair would break away at the side, and it ended up being thin on the side and big on the top. Cliff thought it looked like a microphone windscreen, and he started calling me "Mike Rafone, one of the West Coast band, the Rafones". But then Puffhead came from Jim, and then it was Puffy, and that stuck.'

The pop-punk band referred to by Martin were Fun Addicts, more precisely a power-pop outfit led by Rick Clare and fronted by Debra Knox, which had been going since 1979. Bordin was recruited as their fourth—and final—drummer in 1981. 'I probably didn't do a very good job,' he says. 'It wasn't the right fit for me; they wanted to look good and sound good and be pop. But I didn't have any other options to go and do what I wanted to do.'

Rick Clare helped him with the next step of that quest. 'At this time, I was listening to all this amazing music like XTC and Squeeze, and one day Rick Clare said to me, "You like all this really weird music. You've got to go and meet this guy I know, because this band isn't the right band for you. Go and talk to this weird dude I know. He's putting together a trench-coat band."'

The weird dude was M. Morris. And the trench-coat band was Sharp Young Men.

'I met Morris in Wade Worthington's garage before we started playing together,' Bordin continues. 'And along with those two, there was this little scrawny kid from LA, who had a really funny punk rock haircut and a big giant bass that was way too big for him. And his amp was one of those old acoustic research cabinets with the big horn and the big bin. And it was Bill. And he just started playing.'

4

SHARP

YOUNG MEN

In the same week in the autumn of 1981, Bordin and Gould both ended up joining the band that Morris and Worthington were putting together, the band that would become Sharp Young Men and then Faith. No Man. Gould's search for a band as soon as he arrived in San Francisco had led to several dead ends before he happened upon that ad posted on a bulletin board in Rasputin Records on Telegraph Avenue in Berkeley. On this occasion, Worthington did not get cold feet, and a meeting was arranged at Bill's student residence.

'Bill was first to respond to my ad,' Worthington says. 'He was a freshman at the university there. Morris and I went to meet him in his dormitory. Bill was a charming young guy—he must have been at least seventeen, although he looked twelve. Bill came from LA and had dyed hair. Morris and Bill did all the talking. Bill had a lot of energy, and seemed eager to get together with us.'

Morris has similar recollections. 'At that point we were very much in need of a bass player,' he says. 'I don't think I ever saw the actual ad. My very first impression was *how old is this fellow?* He looked so young—you could have told me he was fifteen and I wouldn't have argued with you. But he told me that he was eighteen and had enrolled at Berkeley. But he could play the bass and understood the sound. And he always had big amps. I played through small amps because, to me, the guitar was secondary in the band. It was all about the drums and bass. Not just hearing them but feeling them.'

A shared affection for the English art-rock outfit Be-Bop Deluxe helped Morris and Gould bond. 'Mike Morris came over to my dorm and we talked,' Gould says. 'Him and this guy Wade Worthington. And Mike liked me immediately because I was a big fan of Be-Bop Deluxe, and I had a picture of Bill Nelson [their lead singer] on my wall, so I got points with him for that.'

Bordin joined days later. While he remembers his first meeting with Morris and Worthington taking place at Wade's parents' garage, Worthington himself remembers the trio meeting at Bordin's Castro Valley home:

> Mike Bordin lived up a dead-end court full of nice homes—the same street that Cliff Burton lived on. Bordin's dad was a doctor, and kept a classic Porsche in the garage. Bordin let us into his home and into his bedroom. There was a poster on the wall of Motörhead—I had never heard of Motörhead at that stage. Again, Morris and Bordin did the talking as I listened to the reggae music playing in the room. Like Bill, Bordin was a college student. He was a good listener and struck me as an intelligent guy. While passing by the living room, I spotted a

framed photo of a much younger Bordin with a full-on Afro. This image has stuck in my head, and I think of it whenever I hear of Bordin's nickname, Puffy.

Gould and Bordin hit it off straight away. 'The guy I met is really different than the guy now,' Gould says. 'He was a hilarious guy, but he really had a devil-may-care attitude. He'd say very audacious things. This music that we were playing was really new to him, so he was also extremely enthusiastic. We became very close. We hooked up on the same wavelength very quickly. It wasn't just music; you find kindred spirits, and music is just one of those things that you do.'

Meanwhile, the Worthington family home became the band's base from late 1981, and Morris christened the band Sharp Young Men. 'I was being completely tongue-in-cheek, as in *respectable and well-groomed young men*. The Protestant ethic which formed so much of the West, I thought was shit.'

The Worthington garage actually became quite a sophisticated practice space for the band, as Worthington remembers. 'It was a great space, and we shared it with some of the Worthington Photography [the family business] backgrounds and supplies. It even had soundproofing of an inner wall built by me and my friends back during The Spectators days. And soundproofing was needed to keep a couple of yelling neighbours at bay.'

Morris was the bandleader and the main songwriter. Gould and Bordin were content to hone their craft. For now. 'We all got to put our parts in,' Bordin states. 'Morris suggested a few things to me at the very beginning, and then I felt that I was off and running as far as I can do things I want to do. We all had itches that weren't being scratched by other, easy-to-find stuff. That's what got us to that garage in Castro Valley.'

'The music was almost as new to me as everyone else,' M. Morris adds. 'It was not something that just flowed out naturally. I had to really mould the songs. Build them up, tear them back down to see if there was a better combination of chords and beats.' He had a clear vision for the band: 'Early on, I saw XTC, Killing Joke, Gang Of Four, so many other seriously unique bands. My first love will always be pop and soul music. But I also love power and drive and things where the music just takes you up and surrounds you.'

The post-punk influence was also keenly felt by Bill Gould, who wore his devotion on his sleeve—almost literally. 'I remember Bill showing up to practice once with his arm autographed in heavy black marking pen by Siouxsie of Siouxsie & The Banshees,' Worthington says. 'I think he had attended a promo event at one of the Berkeley record stores. He avoided washing that arm for the longest time.'

According to Worthington, such earnestness was unusual for Gould. He detected early signs of the post-modernism or irony, even inauthenticity that would later define Faith No More. 'Bill had an appreciation for the ironic,' he says, 'It was the first time I met someone who I didn't know whether he really liked something, or whether he thought it was cool because it was silly. I know a fondness for things ironic became common in subsequent generations, but Bill was the first one to embrace this that I knew. I think he liked KISS, but I was not sure if he really did. Bill also had a jacket with its backside displaying a low rider car along with the words *Puerto Rico*. This contrasted with Morris and me, as we would frequent the thrift store looking for serious post-punk uniforms like long black overcoats.'

Sharp Young Men recorded a three-song demo with future Faith No More producer Matt Wallace at his Dangerous Rhythm studios in 1982. It was a fair approximation of Joy Division fronted by Public Image Ltd.-era John Lydon. Gould had met Wallace when he took a band he was producing called Your First Born to his studio for a session.

'I "borrowed" my parents' two-car garage and built a control room and studio and set up an eight-track, reel-to-reel, semi-professional studio,' Wallace recalls. 'Our house was located about forty-five minutes north and east of San Francisco in a town called Moraga. Bill picked up a studio flyer at the Rather Ripped Records store and came to see me. I remember the first time I met him, because he and the band had taken the BART [local train network] to a town near my parents' house and I drove down to pick them up. As we were driving up the hill toward my studio, Bill was flipping off all of the cars that were behind us.'

Otherwise, Wallace's first impressions were positive. 'Bill was always very determined and actively pursuing his musical goals. He always seemed to have a vision as to what it was that he wanted for the end result of our recording. He was the first person whom I worked with that worked in the capacity as a producer. It was unique for me, as an engineer at the time, to see someone who wasn't a part of the band, working with them and me.'

The band played a number of shows throughout 1982, locally in Hayward and at On Broadway, Mabuhay Gardens, and Sound Of Music in the city. According to Worthington, Sharp Young Men had their first live performance at San Francisco State University on Friday March 19 1982. 'This came upon us suddenly, but was welcomed, as we were nervously preparing for a show at a club in Hayward called Frenchy's, which was scheduled for the following week. It was a band showcase, where many bands were given twenty minutes each to play. It was my debut show as a singer for one song I wrote called "A Life". I found I could help divert my onstage nervousness by my moving around behind my keyboard and screaming into the mic.'

Sharp Young Men changed their name to Faith. No Man later that year. 'Bill hated the name,' Morris states, 'and rallied the others against it. I tried to explain, but it fell on deaf ears. It even looked good written. Well-formed. But no one was having it. I could have fought to keep it, but I am not unreasonable or a fascist. I let it go.'

Morris came up with the replacement himself:

I thought about it, and one of the things going on in my mind was centred around trust. Trusting other people. I eventually came up with 'Faith In No Man'. But Mike Bordin pointed out that the name was a bit wordy. I had to agree. After a while, he said, How about 'Faith. No Man'? I had no objections, even if it is a bit too mystical for me. Faith asks irrational things from otherwise reasonable people. I am pretty sure we all liked it better with the full stop rather than without. It both put the emphasis on the general nature of men and the fact that none are completely trustworthy. Faith? No man! It also added something to the words when it appeared on paper.

The newly monikered quartet gigged extensively in early 1983. Their show at the Valencia Tool & Die was recorded for posterity by an audience member with an early camcorder, and the five tracks played—'Quiet In Heaven', 'Life Is Tough For Me', 'Decay', 'Song Of Liberty', and 'Under

The Gun'—show a purposeful and polished outfit with the peroxide-blond Morris up front and centre. The novelty of being captured on video was enough to get each band member to fork out $10 for a VHS tape of the show.

Soon after, the group again repaired to Matt Wallace's home studio to record a seven-inch single. Those songs saw the band and Morris as a songwriter really finding their sound and voice. According to Morris, 'Song Of Liberty' and 'Under The Gun' were 'me hitting my mark, which wasn't consistently enough as far as I was concerned. I needed to be better, become more consistent.'

'They were a serious band with focus, intent, and talent,' Matt Wallace recalls of the record session. 'Each member fulfilled an essential role and, as it was a relatively lean musical group, they created some solid, focused, and exciting music. They were obviously influenced by other bands, but they were carving out their own, distinct, sound.'

The 'Quiet In Heaven' / 'Song Of Liberty' single, released on the band's own Ministry Of Propaganda label, was a highly impressive, ambitious record, brimming with energy and vitality, and showcasing an already keen musicianship. A press release declared, 'This single was produced on a minuscule budget in a minimum amount of time, as we feel it important to get this product out to you, the public, as soon as possible to emphasise its validity. … Good or bad review, we would appreciate a reaction.'

One such review was forthcoming, from Jeff Bale in the September 1983 edition of San Francisco punk bible *Maximum Rocknroll*: 'Heavy bass- and drum-orientated post-punk with rich guitar frills. "Quiet" inexorably advances like a slow-moving freight train, whereas the flip is more up-tempo and guitar-heavy. Thought not as abrasive or as reminiscent of Killing Joke as their live show, this record is quite good.'

The band also flirted with record label and radio station attention. The single was distributed by Rough Trade, but other labels expressed interest, as Mike Morris explains. 'There were rumblings based on the single. Initially, the collective Crass were said to be interested in us, but weren't offering any money. I said, Fuck that. If I'm going to be in a band I need to make money from it. At the very least to eat. I remember Bill getting extremely pissed off at me for not jumping at it.'

Soon after that, word came that Adrian Sherwood—founder of the

UK On-U Sound Records label, which specialised in dub, reggae, and electronica—was interested in the band. But by the time the *Maximum Rocknroll* review was printed, Faith. No Man were no more.

First to leave was Wade Worthington. His departure had already been noted in the liner notes of the single: 'Passing the faith to Roddy. Play this as loud as equipment permits.' The replacement was Bill Gould's childhood friend Roddy Bottum, who had also moved from Los Angeles to study at San Francisco State University. Eventually, he would meet up with Gould again. 'I lived for the first semester in the dorms, and then got a place together with Billy and a bunch of friends on 16th Street. We called it the Island of Human Kindness. Billy had bought a four-track recorder, and we started making music on that. Suddenly, recording music was an option, something I hadn't really considered. All of us in the apartment were musicians, and we all made music together, not just band music.'

In May 1983, Worthington informed his bandmates that he did not want to play any more. 'I can't blame the other members,' he says, 'as it really was my responsibility to set my boundaries—something I had trouble doing. But my resentment, along with the other ingredients such as being embarrassed about my performing, feeling frustrated with my songwriting, and feeling physically ill from my stressful load of college courses—all this caused me to reach my tipping point.'

Worthington could not resist a few more favours for the band, and, as well as allowing the band to continue practising in his garage and lending his successor his Prophet-5 keyboard, he agreed to postpone his retirement for half a show, as Roddy had not learned the full repertoire. 'I started the set and Roddy finished it,' he recalls. 'For some reason, I felt calm and relaxed for this performance. I thought I could actually sing and have the stage presence thing happening. I felt this show was a good way for me to conclude my involvement with the band.'

Worthington ceded the stage to Bottum seven songs into the show at the Sound Of Music on May 13 1983. Bordin: 'I met Roddy when Wade left the band. Bill said, I have a friend here from high school who plays keyboards. We got along right away.'

Roddy jumped at the chance to play in his first band. 'Wade didn't want to be in the band anymore,' he recalls, 'He had a Prophet-5, and we shared his keyboard for that show. It was understood that he was *passing the torch*. It was a no-brainer. Billy and I lived together at the time, and had such a history of friendship and sensibility, and I loved Faith. No Man.

'The Sound Of Music was super-down and dirty,' he adds. 'In the epicentre of the Tenderloin, lots of drugs and sex workers. And, for some reason, I did speed that night—I'd never done it before—and it was just this overwhelming crazy mix of a lot of things coming together.'

✦

Bottum's arrival brought into sharper focus divisions within the band, in particular Gould and Bordin's frustration with Morris's creative control. 'When Roddy joined, it became obvious we were going in a different direction,' Bordin recalls. 'We just wanted to play and explore. Maybe Sharp Young Men/Faith. No Man had just ran its course. Evolution happens. At that time, there were so many insane things happening musically and culturally. Everything was moving, we weren't going to stand still either. We rehearsed a lot for just a few gigs, and it didn't feel like it was really working out. Sharp Young Men was definitely his baby, but once we figured out there was something we wanted to do, we wanted to do it.'

There was antipathy between M. Morris and Bill Gould almost from the start. Morris was so peeved at one stage that he went so far to audition for a replacement bassist. The chosen replacement was Crucifix's Jake Smith, who would go onto to be Faith No More's first guitarist. 'I was a big supporter of Faith. No Man,' he says, 'and would go to their shows and even tried to help them get distribution through my Rough Trade contacts. Billy and Morris didn't get along, and I tried out on bass once. I sucked.'

Gould might have sucked at the time, too. 'Apparently I was not such a good bass player then, which I found out later,' he says. 'Some people were saying what a shitty bass player I was. And I've since heard that there was a point when they were auditioning bass players and I never knew about it.'

'It was basically Mike Morris's band,' he adds. 'He was probably twenty-six and we were eighteen. He was the guy who called the shots, so it was called Sharp Young Men, and I never liked the name. Then he changed it to Faith. No Man, which I hated as well. But it wasn't my band.'

Bottum is more direct on the cause of the problem. 'Mike Morris had a real strict vision of what he wanted the band to sound like. Mike Bordin and Billy and I had more of a personal connection between the three of us and felt a little bit talked down to, the way I remember it. Mike Morris was extremely bossy, and we weren't into being involved in that kind of hierarchy.'

Morris's recollection of the Faith. No Man implosion is a little different.

> I detected something coming from Bill, but I tried to ignore any possible negative vibes, because he was a member of the band. We were partners in creating this amazing thing. He was not supposed to be my enemy. Because there is nothing worse than band discord for any musician. But at no time did I expect him to love me, just to love the music.
>
> I was trying very hard to make something work for all of us. At no time did I ever refer to it as 'my band'. It was a group effort from four individuals. I have never had illusions about being a solo artist. That has never appealed to me. To me, being in a band is just like being in a gang. I need that shared experience to work to the highest standard possible.

Gould cites disputes over the image of the band as typical of his and Morris's irreconcilable differences.

> I just felt completely crushed and voiceless in that band. When I made suggestions, they were belittled, and he made me feel like I wasn't very good at doing much. I also thought he was image-conscious in what he wanted the band to be, and how they wanted to look. I listened to a lot of the same music as him, but I also grew up as a southern California guy who surfed. I didn't want to conform to something that was happening 5,000 miles away. It didn't need to sound like it looked, all dark and trench coats. I wanted to be myself and play music and express myself. At a certain point, it was going to separate, and then it just did.

In the late summer of 1983, the Bordin-Bottum-Gould trio simply broke away. 'What happened was that I quit a band, which you'll see is a very familiar pattern,' says Gould. 'I quit the band, and everybody else quit, too. We never saw him again, and that was just the end of it. It was very non-confrontational. It wasn't a big blowout—we just stopped seeing each other. Suddenly we didn't have a singer, we didn't have a guitar player.'

Morris recalls a short phone call to dispense with his services. 'I was not especially surprised, because I knew there was friction. My only regret is that it never had the chance to become a bigger, well-formed band. We were around for such a short time—just a single, no album on which to be fairly judged. But I dare say that Faith. No Man is bigger now than it ever was when we were active. And for that I am extremely grateful.'

❋

M. Morris continued to make music but retreated from public performance. 'I could have joined countless other bands if I had so chosen,' he says, 'if all I wanted to do was be a semi-famous musician. I know that very few just fall into longevity. It takes a certain something that few actually have. Many years later, Mike Bordin told me, "You know, it just occurred to me that you're like Brian Jones. You are the one who started the band, and it went on without you." And he was exactly right. We thought more about it, and realised that it's not that common a position to be in. Few bands who go on to fame have the founding member being left behind completely.'

Morris was an accomplished musician and composer with a singular vision—an important component of Faith No More pre-history. Matt Wallace states, 'Morris probably provided the essential motivation and direction for the genesis of Faith No More, and it can be argued that the band wouldn't have happened if it weren't for Mike.'

Mike Bordin is similarly respectful, but takes a different conclusion. 'He had a bass player and a drummer playing behind him, and he allowed them to find themselves and to define their own sound. He allowed us the space to have rhythms that have contour. He allowed us the space to find ourselves. There should be credit for that. But there is no way that Faith No More would have been Faith No More if he had been still in the band. We had to move on.'

❋

The embryonic era of Faith No More was almost over. As well as a singer and guitarist, however, the new band needed a name. That would come courtesy of Will Carpmill, whom Bill met in the UC Berkeley dorms. He was classically trained in piano, and was a synth and keyboard pioneer in his own right. One of the first musicians to hook up an Apple Mac and keyboard onstage, he later played in the band Systems Collapse with future Faith No More guitarist Jon Hudson. The trio bonded through music, pranks, and airgun shooting.

Carpmill recalls the band's christening: 'I was an electrical engineering major, Billy was studying political science, Mike Bordin was an English major. Mike and I were in rhetoric class, trying to come up with a new band name. We were passing a sheet of paper back and forth with our ideas, riffing on Faith. No Man. I think I suggested Faith. No Morris with a laugh, and then a few seconds later, one of us had Faith. No More.'

Faith. No Man was dead. Long live Faith. No More.

5

FAITH.

NO MAN

Before Faith. No Man became Faith No More, the band needed to find a singer and a guitarist. Neither was an urgent priority. Freed from the constraints that they felt while working with M. Morris, the trio were keen to explore and create without outside interference.

That outside interference should have included their studies. Bordin's English literature degree had seen him work hard to transfer to UC Berkeley from California State. 'I got my degree to make my parents happy. I was still turning in term papers even when I was going on tour. My two real specialities were Middle English like Chaucer and Edmund Spenser, and I even liked Shakespeare a lot. To graduate, I did a thesis on Richard Wright, the African-American novelist. I read literally everything that he wrote. I can't do maths and I can't do science, and when the numbers start building up, my mind just shuts off, but I felt I could read a book and have an opinion on it.'

Bordin was the only one of the Faith No More students to graduate but, even for him, college was more an important milieu for musical development. 'School was not that important to us. The real truth is that much of Bill's and my time together at Cal was spent cutting class and going to the record store, and finding crazy rare reggae records or weird stuff that came from England, and drinking coffee and talking about the music we wanted to play.' He soon moved from Berkeley. 'I lived there for one year. Hated living there and decided to move to San Francisco and I'd commute to Berkeley, which meant I never went.'

Roddy was still technically a film student, but he remembers, 'We mostly made music, and stayed up all hours causing trouble. We didn't study that hard, but we spent lots of time at school making friends and creating art. I made films, and we'd all make music to the films. We strategised what to do with Faith No More constantly. Every show we played was treated with utmost sincerity and seriousness. We took a lot of care on the posters and flyers, as well as on the presentation.'

Those films were the first time that childhood friends Bottum and Gould had worked together on music. The teenage trio were finding their feet. As musicians, as artists, as kindred spirits. Bottum: 'The scene wasn't so pigeonholed back then. Any kind of expression was fair game. Kids sniffed through the bullshit astutely in this era. If your heart was in it, if you were making something different, it rose to the top real quickly.'

As he later noted in the liner notes to the *We Care A Lot* reissue, 'The hippies mingled with the punks, the artists hung out with the musicians, the dance people and the punks were one and the Satanists and the sexual pioneers … all part of the same scene.'

'We all hung out and created together,' Roddy explains. 'It was really a homogeneous mix of people doing different things. We were really respectful of any forms of art that were being made at the time. We weren't

specifically music. Some of us did photography, some film, some dance …
it was a really healthy community.'

For Bill Gould, this scene also had a maturing effect. 'All the people
we hung out with were really between eighteen and twenty-two, but
they seemed very adult at the time. I felt like an adult. There was lots of
parties, lots of gigs, lots going on every night of the week. San Francisco,
economically, was pretty depressed, there was a lot of crime, but there was
also not a lot of enforcement of underground parties. It reminded me a lot of
London, as far as people were listening to all kinds of different things.'

Mike Bordin also took the chance to fly the coop from the East Bay, first
hunkering down on a floor with Bottum and Gould, and then finding a place
to live with his girlfriend. He also found stability and fellow feeling in the
band. 'Bill and Roddy and I, we all looked at things the same way. We were
driving in the same direction, and we were in agreement with what we were
doing, and we were up for it.'

For rehearsals, the band moved on from Wade Worthington's garage
to the Vats, an old abandoned Hamms brewery building on 4th Street at
Bryant. The brewery had closed in 1972 and, in 1981, it was broken into and
squatted. It soon served as living quarters, party venue, and practice space
for hundreds of local bands, as well as several visiting from out of state. The
likes of MDC, Dicks, and The Rhythm Pigs set up their bases there on their
arrival in the Bay Area.

The Vats contained around thirty or forty huge beer tanks spread across
its four floors. Each vat—a huge rubber-coated tank with a chained
manhole serving as a rudimentary door—could house around ten people.
They were initially occupied by squatters, before a crude rental system
developed: $200 for a vat per month. Soon, bands that did not live there
were able to use the huge spaces to store equipment and practise morning,
noon, and night. The vats on the first floor were converted into rough-and-
ready rehearsal studios.

'You could get a room there really cheap,' Gould explains. 'We just put
our gear in there. We shared with another band, and we didn't really have
a plan. At the time, Mike Bordin and I had just broken up with girlfriends,
so we were going through this life-change thing where everything was an
open slate. We decided to just start making noise without any goal in mind.

The rehearsals were long jam sessions of skips, loops and rhythms, played very, very stoned.'

'The instruments and the loops that we were making were always the priority,' Bottum adds. 'Looking back on it, it was a pretty audacious perspective ... the music came first. I think it was because we had such a strong core unit with the bass/drums/keys sound. We were all very much on the same page conceptually, and really into what we were doing.'

The trio would meet up three or four nights a week, load up on forty-ouncers of beer and hit the Vats. According to Gould, there was no particular end or objective for the music-making. 'We just started doing things that we thought were cool. There wasn't even any thoughts of what kind of gigs were we going to do, we didn't even think about that. We were just doing it for ourselves basically. But people in the Vats would come in and hang out in the room because it was almost psychedelic, like Pink Floyd stoner stuff that we were doing.'

The first of those Vats sessions proved particularly productive, spawning the initial riff from 'Zombie Eaters', a song that would not be recorded until six years later, on *The Real Thing*. All such sessions were taped on Gould's new four-track recorder, which became a repository for what Bottum refers to as 'a lot of repetitive, moody recordings'.

The music marked a departure from the Sharp Young Men/Faith. No Man era. Shorn of guitars, there was certainly less focus on melody and structure. The band later dubbed the cassettes that circulated from these sessions 'rhythm exercises', and here we find the base of the band moving away from the cool and controlled pastiche of new wave of the Morris era to something undoubtedly their own—something rawer and more rhythmic.

Gould: 'At first, they were just these long, repetitive loops and skits that just sounded cool, and the keyboards just provided this atmosphere on top of them. Then we started putting different parts together. They started becoming verses and choruses, and they then became songs. And because we weren't trying to force our instincts, we discovered them.'

The African drumming philosophy and techniques that Bordin learned at this time from Ghanaian drumming guru C.K. Lapzekpo at UC Berkeley helped inform this shared musical development. Bordin: 'Once you break the real heavy metal bond—*If it's not metal, it sucks*—then you open up to everything all of a sudden, and you can listen to everything and metal as well. The African deal was a big deal. It was someone teaching me something that was a different way of looking at things. It was the rhythmic approach, it was the rhythmic philosophy. The downbeat was really important. The way Lapzekpo described it was that it was the central thematic unifier of West African culture.'

Gould: 'I went to a couple of classes with him. It wasn't the linear way of looking at music; it was circular, and we started doing things together, figuring out how to do things in that. It became this toolbox we got, where we started approaching things more from this African-type perspective, and that's how we started writing our songs.'

Bordin: 'We all learned a language together, and we were the only ones who really spoke it. I think Roddy, at the beginning, his melodies were very syncopated, pretty simple but very syncopated, but we were all playing percussion to each other, all syncopating with each other around the rhythm.'

'He can be the nicest guy in the world,' Bordin says of his rhythm partner, Gould, 'but he can also be very inscrutable in some ways, so you don't know what he's thinking. But the musical communication has always been there. It feels very instinctive and natural to me, and it has since the beginning.'

Gould acted as a conduit between Bordin's pure rhythm and Bottum's melodies. 'He was the guy in between,' says Bordin, 'and, all of a sudden, you've got free communication going back and forth to all the different elements.' The band weren't just developing musically: they were also metamorphosing into a physical unit. This was kinaesthetic training, the building up of shared musical muscle memory. These exhaustive, formative months in the Vats built the foundations of Faith No More.

On the extant recordings from that period—the unnamed songs, or, to be more precise, musical excursions, that feature on Side B of their first cassette, released in late 1983, with Side A comprising a recording of their show—the experimentation is evident. So too are curiosity, relentlessness, and a sense of something clicking into gear. The clean and cold new-wave sounds of Faith. No Man had been supplanted by something grimier and grittier. There are hints of an industrial noise approach on later tracks on the recording, with any vocalisations seemingly provided by the rats in the

Vats rather than anything human. But that track then segues abruptly to some purely funky slap bass, underpinned by repeated drum loops. Bordin, Bottum, and Gould may well have known where they were going but, on this evidence, it is not that surprising that no one else did. Soundscapes, loops, drones; absent or indistinct vocals; this was post-rock *avant la lettre*.

The band were also walking before they could crawl, and running before they could walk. This was Bottum's first band, while Gould and Bottum, for all their individual playing and practising, as well as the occasional guest spots in other bands such as the Pop-O-Pies and Police State, were not seasoned songwriters or performers. That weakness became a strength, as the trio—three flowing stones without a Mick and Keith—created music the only way they could.

Bordin: 'When you don't know how to write songs and you don't know what type of songs you are going to write, anything can happen.'

THE FIRST FAITH
NO MORE SHOW

6

'These guys up here, they are not like trendy art faggot-type people. They're really good people. These people have paid some dues. They're not, like, on some sort of trip, man.'

On October 7 1983, Faith No More were playing their first-ever show— billed on their self-made posters as 'a one-time only performance'—as Faith No More. They were introduced by this inelegant tribute from guest vocalist Joe Callahan, aka Joe Pop-O-Pie from local punk outfit Pop-O-Pies. The venue was San Francisco's pink punk palace On Broadway, upstairs in the garishly beautiful Mabuhay Gardens building in North Beach. Around fifty punk veterans and underage opportunist drinkers thronged the former home to beat poets and beat-up boxers.

Faith No More's founding trio of Mike Bordin, Roddy Bottum, and Bill Gould were bolstered on this occasion by Callahan and guitarist Jake Smith, who had just finished recording *Dehumanization* with the band Crucifix. Friend and future producer Matt Wallace taped the show, which was later released as part of the band's first demo cassette.

They came to the stage billowed in clouds of burning incense and sage, and were turned out variously in dashikis, dreadlocks, and even flared jeans.

'We had incense,' says Bottum. 'It was part of that neo-hippie vibe we were pushing. Incense, dashikis, dreadlocks. We were super ramshackle hodgepodge fashion. We wore dashikis for sure. We had gotten into Last Poets, and we loved fucking with all the punkers who were wearing the traditional Doc Martens. It was so uncool to be a dirty hippie at that time. It was our main intention to set ourselves apart from the scene that was going on at the time. And we just found it all really provocative and hilarious.

That came through in the music, too. Hunched over his keys, bleached blonde dreadlocks obscuring his face, Bottum played tarry synthesiser sounds, almost nausea-inducing in their thickness, with haunting E and A chords punctuated by repeating minor key brightness. The keyboard sounds dominated, with Bill Gould adding restrained distorted bass accompaniment.

The song 'Intro' signifies a lot. Firstly, it is a statement of intent. 'We wanted to set a beautiful tone and then smash it all down,' Bottum says. 'We knew people expected a hard, hard sound from us, so we wanted to break down those expectations.'

'Intro' also showed that, even in their music of gothic darkness, there would also be light and humour. Inauthenticity, even. 'We found that keyboard in Los Angeles,' Bottum adds. 'The man who did the music for *Flashdance*—his name was Duane Hitchings, I believe—he sold it to us. We thought it was hilarious that it had that history. It was the synth used on Rod Stewart's song "Da Ya Think I'm Sexy?" That always made us laugh.'

'Intro' is also a statement of the band's inchoate philosophy. 'The contrast between classic beauty and big drama were really important to us,' Bottum states, 'so that initial piece we played at the On Broadway that night was meant to be classic beauty set up for the big drama that followed.'

Finally, 'Intro'—if we cheat by fast-forwarding the concert another ten seconds, until Bordin literally kick-starts the second track, 'The Jungle'—immediately puts on display the beating heart of Faith No More: Bottum's keys, Gould's rhythm, and Bordin's beat. 'The Jungle'—which would appear complete with vocals on the band's debut album, *We Care A Lot*, in 1985—saw Faith No More up the tempo and largely succeed in stifling the incipient conversations among the crowd. Bordin's distinctive downbeat, as he hits so hard to almost register two crashes each time, is matched by Gould's insistent groove, with Jake Smith playing a crunching, repetitive riff over the top.

Gould's thumping bass and Bottum's synth washes highlight a more mid-tempo, cyclical song in 'Why Do You Bother?'—another track that, fully realised and with proper lyrics and vocals, would appear on *We Care A Lot*.

With the assiduous Gould acting as manager and booking agent—his hair shorn to near respectability, save for a post-punk rat tail—the band as Faith. No Man and now as Faith No More sought gigs where they could. 'Getting onto the established club circuit was difficult,' Gould explains. 'Bill Graham still ran the local scene, and was pretty hardcore about shutting down punk clubs, even though that scene represented no threat to his world. It was hard for us to find our place initially; we were invisible in the media, and if we played to forty people, that was a good crowd for us.'

Graham—the Bay Area impresario who monetised the 1960s counter-culture and invented the modern rock show, the arena tour, and the promoted rock festival—had also been a *bête noire* to the San Francisco punk community since he promoted The Clash's first show in the city, and cracked down on plans by The New Youth Movement to hold a free alternative show by the London outfit.

San Francisco did have considerable advantages for an underground music scene. Punk zines, first *Search & Destroy* and then *Maximum Rocknroll*—which promoted many On Broadway gigs—provided exposure, promotion, and a left-wing ethos. The campuses of Berkeley and the San Francisco Art Institute brought young people, the raw material of the bands and their audiences.

While San Francisco had Graham, it also had his punk equivalent in Dirk Dirksen, who brought local punk to the city when he took over the music management of the Mabuhay Gardens in 1977. The club and the upstairs

On Broadway were owned by Ness Aquino, but it was Dirksen who, as promoter, transformed both venues into punk meccas. Dubbed the Pope of Punk, he shared Graham's abrasive edge. His rants from the stage, violent clashes, and hectoring of bands and audience alike were as much part of the Fab Mab and On Broadway attraction as the shows he put on from the Damned, Devo, Dead Kennedys, Ramones, Flipper, and Black Flag among many more.

Not for the last time in their career, Faith No More found themselves in the right place at the wrong time. By 1983, the first wave of punk had long since peaked, and live music was in the doldrums in the city. A show at Dirksen's On Broadway was as good as it got for a new band. 'Our crew was all there,' Bottum reflects. 'It was not well attended, but we treated it like a very big deal.'

'At the time, very few people had heard of Faith No More,' says Joe Callahan. 'Up until 1985, Faith No More and the Pop-O-Pies were pretty much the same band. The deal was, I needed a great group of instrumentalists to work with, and they wanted some experience before committing to doing their own thing exclusively. It was a symbiotic relationship. My role was almost that of a mentor to the Faith No More guys. We knew that we'd only be working together for a while until they felt ready to go it on their own. In the meantime, I would take every opportunity to help get these guys noticed.'

Smith, too, only played one show with Faith No More. 'I was sneaking the FNM thing, as the other members of Crucifix were uptight and judgmental about nearly everything, so I just never mentioned it.'

Smith was introduced to the band by Mike Bordin. The pair had met in 1981, in a Sacramento club where a sixteen-year-old Smith was playing—drums—with Bad Attitude, a band fronted by Chuck Prophet, later of Green On Red. He recalls:

> Mike and I hit it off, realised we were both East Bay residents, and started hanging out as friends after that. We'd smoke weed and bond on our mutual love of the Stranglers and Killing Joke. Mike ended up replacing me in Bad Attitude when I left to do whatever it was at the time. Then I met Billy Gould, after he moved up from LA.

I was never really happy in Crucifix, as they were very dysfunctional and humourless. Faith No More were new, but already solid, so from a musical standpoint, it would have been a cool band to play in. As a drummer, I loved Mike's playing, and it was fun to make music with him involved. The others were all talented too. I thought they were a great band, but it was still very formative.

Bill seems like a super-chill guy now, but he was an obnoxious instigator at the time, and we were never going to be friends like Mike and I were back then. I found him hard to be around, because he was always drawing attention to himself, and trying to be offensive and confrontational. And I was a stubborn, hot-headed young guy myself.

When Smith heard the cassette recording of the On Broadway show, that tension reached boiling point:

The guitar was barely audible. It was a board tape, and my amp was so loud, it wasn't miked through the board. I was pissed that we didn't take the extra care to sound-check with the recording in mind, if it was going to end up being an important recording. My second issue with the recording was that they released it without asking or telling me of their plans. It's a shame, because the rest of the band sounds great. Bill and I had a phone conversation, where he asked what I thought of the tape, and I gave my honest opinion: 'Sounds good, except there's no guitar.' Bill was quite offended by my opinion, and we parted ways musically at that point. At the time, it seemed so important. I can't speak for Bill, but I was certainly opinionated and very passionate about my opinions at the time, and kind of a hardhead. I never ran from a musical fight.

Before the end of 1983, Faith No More—still stylised on the label as 'Faith. No More', a designation they would keep until early 1984—released their first demo tape, limited to around 200 copies. Side A comprised the entirety of the debut On Broadway show. Side B was twenty minutes of instrumental music, what the cassette notes termed as 'an attempt to sum up the feelings of FNM during the time period surrounding the live show'.

'Band members consisted of Faith. No More, along with appreciated assistance from Joe Pie (vocals) and Jake Smith (guitar),' read the cassette notes. In the only review of the tape, *Unsound* magazine, in its third edition in late 1983, compared the updated band to Faith. No Man: 'The live show seems very linear with heavy metal guitar and poetry that is hardly reconcilable, and the core of the group i.e. bass, drums and synthesiser, seem the same as before, except less interesting when combined with the improvisational mess of Joe Pie poetry and heavy metal guitar.'

Faith No More's varied discography and rotating cast of guitarists and singers lends itself to Heraclitian analysis. Depending on whenever you dip your feet into the band's oeuvre, the band is never the same. But the enduring presence of the band's core—bass, drums, and synthesizer; Gould, Bordin, and Bottum—offers an alternative Parmenidean explanation. There is change, since change consists in things coming into being or ceasing to be; once Faith No More came into existence, 'unbeginning unending', on that October night, it did not change.

As well as cod philosophy, we can also lean on pseudoscience here. Faith No More's genesis was not so much intelligent as inelegant design. To borrow further from creationism, it was when Bottum, Gould, and Bordin came together that Faith No More acquired its irreducible complexity—a system of interconnected parts that perform the basic function, where the removal of any one of the parts causes the system to effectively stop working. For Faith No More, the journey to achieving that complexity was far from straightforward.

SEARCH FOR A SINGER, SEEKING GUITARIST

After their opening show at On Broadway in October 1983, Faith No More did not play live again for another two months. But their debut show in Los Angeles, at the Fiesta House—a small punk club that had previously played host to Hüsker Dü, The Minutemen, and the Red Hot Chili Peppers—was pencilled in for December 30.

Faith No More—Bordin, Bottum, and Gould, that is—had spent the intervening months in continued practice and rehearsal at the Vats. They were primed for action, but, yet again, they needed a singer and a guitarist.

Bottum: 'It was our intention to have a different singer and guitar player for every show. We wanted to keep people guessing, and to keep our sound and presentation fresh and challenging. Anything we could do to set ourselves apart from other bands worked for us.'

Bordin: 'We had a different singer and a guitar player for the first half-a-dozen shows we did. That should say something about the core of the band, or what the approach was.'

Gould: 'The set we were doing was very loop-based. It was very hypnotic. It wasn't the kind of thing that seemed it would have any singing over it. My original idea was that people would do speeches over it, and it would be some weird subliminal type of event.'

The guitarist for the Fiesta show was a familiar figure, Gould's former Animated colleague, Mark Stewart. 'He turned me on to a lot of stuff that I would have never discovered on my own,' says Gould. 'He was very open-minded, and he just knew a lot about different things.

The singer had to be a character in him or herself; had to be able to provide melody and words to their pre-existing music; and had to be a kindred spirit. Actual vocal ability was low on the list of requirements.

Enter Walter O'Brien, a former fellow San Francisco State student with Roddy, whom the band offered the chance to sing at the Fiesta show.

Bottum: 'I'd gone to school with Walter, and he was a commanding persona. He hadn't sung in a band before, and we liked that about him.'

Bordin: 'He was a real inscrutable dude to me; he was as mysterious as hell. He was an artist, I think he was a good artist.'

O'Brien: 'I always had a fantasy of being a rock star, so when Roddy suggested singing for Faith No More, I took up the opportunity.'

In their seven-song set, the band played two instrumentals, 'Intro' and 'Spirit', also the only two songs repeated from their first show at the On Broadway. 'Death Disco'—a very early version of 'Death March', which appeared on *Introduce Yourself* in 1987—and 'Mike's Disco'—whose percussive riff would later be used in *The Real Thing* cut 'Zombie Eaters'— were effectively instrumentals as well.

O'Brien never played with Faith No More again, and that twenty-five-minute set was the sum total of his music career. 'Even at that time,' he says, 'those guys had a musical sophistication that set them apart from other bands, and the drive to be a great band.'

Faith No More started 1984 as they ended 1983, with a gig in Los Angeles, at the Lhasa Club, on January 2. The core trio were both support act and headliners, providing the music for Ron Dumas & The Attack Group. Faith No More played a largely instrumental set for the fifty or so paying customers.

There was more blurring of band membership for Faith No More's next concert in February. Back at On Broadway, they were bottom of a bill featuring Christian Death, Frightwig, Brain Damage, and Paranoid Blue. Frightwig shared rehearsal space with them at the Vats, and, for this show, the bands shared a guitarist and singer in Paula Frazer.

Raised in Georgia and Arkansas, Frazer moved to San Francisco in 1981, aged just eighteen. Growing up in a musical family, the daughter of a Presbyterian minister and a school teacher, she started playing guitar aged nine, sang in the school choir, and started fronting her first band, a rock outfit called Straye, aged thirteen. By the time she was sixteen, she had graduated to making her own demo cassettes, folk compositions heavily influenced by Joni Mitchell and Fleetwood Mac. Invited to visit the Bay Area by a friend, she quickly settled, finding a home, a job, and punk in her first week in the city. There she met and joined Frightwig, a group founded by Deanna Mitchell and Mia d'Bruzzi a few months before in 1982. Frazer's first contact with Faith No More was with Roddy, with the pair both working at the art-house Cedar Cinema.

Frazer stepped in at the last minute as both singer and guitar player. The result was an improvised Faith No More set, and a sound unlike any of their shows before or since. A recently rediscovered recording of a portion of that show testifies to that, with wailing largely wordless vocals and melodic and plangent guitar tones matching Roddy Bottum's dominant keening keyboard chords. The rock-trance snippet that remains fails to do justice to Frazer's cough-syrup voice, which brought her critical acclaim and success both with her band Tarnation and as a solo artist. 'I just showed up with my guitar,' Frazer recalls, 'and I think I just sang spontaneously. It was purely improvisational. That's why my singing was so bad. Who knew it would ever be heard again?'

There was never any prospect of Frazer joining the band in a permanent capacity, as, in addition to Frightwig, Frazer was juggling her two other bands, Trial and Plastic Medium, plus college and work. Bottum: 'She has an amazing voice, and played really weird guitar parts. She was also a really good friend.'

Faith No More's next singer also came with an attitude: Courtney Love. The story of how she came to join the band remains suitably muddled for an artist who exceeded even Faith No More's own capacity for misinformation and mythmaking. Love played with Faith No More for approximately four to five months in 1984. Bottum and Love also had a romantic relationship for a time, but Love had joined the band prior to that.

'We met Courtney through our friend Deanne Franklin,' Roddy explains, 'She moved into our circle and basically demanded to sing. She, again, was a really strong personality; she wrote intriguing dark poetry; she was hilarious and someone we all really connected with. More than anything, she had conviction, and a presence that was undeniable.'

Love was in the audience at that Fiesta Paula Frazer show, and she made it known in her own way that she was what the band were missing.

Bordin: 'It was like Keith Moon joining The Who, turning up at a gig and saying, Fuck, that guy sucks—I'll play. And Courtney said, Fuck, those guys suck—I'll play.'

Courtney Love's own recollection may contain some mythmaking, but it goes like this: 'It was the summer, I was eighteen in San Francisco. Faith No More were playing, and they had a crap singer. I had a wedding gown on, and I looked fucking cool and I knew it, and I demanded to be in their band. And then I broke a bottle over my head, or that is the legend.'

The bottle-breaking probably came later, but the fact was that Love was in the band—not in the summer of 1984 but from February that year. Her first show with Faith No More was on February 27 at the Mabuhay Gardens, and she played several more shows in San Francisco in March and April that year. Her final show was also at the Mab on June 17. As Roddy states, 'She was really good. She did a lot of screaming stuff, and we had a lot of slow melody stuff too. When she sang with us, she was punk rock.'

Gould: 'She was really engaging with people, and she pissed a lot of people off. It's the aesthetic we had. But when she was there, it was probably the first time it felt like a band, and she thought of us as her band. That's the most significant part of her involvement: that we started becoming a band at that point.'

Love also took part in the band's first television appearance, on a local public access channel. 'She went to the flower mart early in the morning and brought bags and bags of flowers for the shoot,' Roddy remembers. 'We covered the stage with flowers and wore dashikis and burned incense. In the punk scene of San Francisco, this was completely audacious.'

But otherwise, according to Bordin, it was a fraught few months. 'The bad of Courtney was the drama that was around—a tornado of shit the whole time. She was the only person who had the balls to get up and sing. She wrote some lyrics, and she sang what she wrote. It was nascent Faith No More, and still a little trance, a little bit unformed.'

That intensity became too much, and the band fired Love after that June 17 show. Love's explanation has always been that this was due to the band, who had had two female singers in a row, not wanting a female singer: 'Faith No More did not want to have the image of a chick singer any more, and I was as unhappy as hell.'

Bottum concurs. 'I think our musical voice is way more sort of male-driven. We're way more of a dude band. Courtney is awesome and she's powerful, but I think having a male singer was the route we needed to go.'

'She's got to lead and tell people what's what,' says Gould. 'She was the dictator, and in our band, things were democratic.' There were other factors, too: 'I felt like she was a bit of an actress. She had a persona onstage. That rock star thing offended me. And there were a lot of people in the city that didn't like her, and that started to get on us a little bit. Some things that she had done that we became associated with.'

Love did not go quietly. She again tried to storm the stage when the band, playing as The Chickenfuckers, with Gould on vocals, played the Mab on June 26. But by the end of the night, she had agreed to join Allin Black's band Our Lady Of Pain, only to leave San Francisco the following day.

The band had not moved completely away from performance art, and, during Love's tenure, a friend of the band, Jim Pasque, performed some of his poetry onstage with the band. 'I wrote a poem that Billy liked, and he insisted I perform at Mabuhay Gardens,' he says. 'I borrowed full ceremonial robes from Hamilton Methodist Church and performed the poem. I was inseparable from Roddy for two years, and considered him my best friend through film school. I was friends with Billy, and will never forget his passion for the band and hard work on their behalf.'

The band were churning guitar players as much as singers. Scott Culbertson was the next guitarist, but he never played a live show. 'Scott had a great sound,' Bottum remembers. 'We might have played a couple of shows with him, but mostly just jammed in the studio with him.'

Next up was another friend of the band. Mark Bowen's girlfriend shared an apartment with Bill and Roddy, and he had also played alongside them and Mike with Pop-O-Pies. He also played with garage punk outfit Tanks, and later drummed with Three-Day Stubble, who often shared bills with Faith No More.

'I don't think I actually joined Faith No More,' he says. 'I was friends with them, particularly Billy and Roddy. They had demo tapes, but no regular singer or guitar player at the time, so when they got gigs, they asked me to play. I rehearsed with them and did the gigs with a couple of different singers. I'm not sure I was ever asked to join, though I played with them somewhat regularly. I felt I was in the band, but not quite.'

In 1985, Faith No More titled one of the tracks on their debut album after Bowen, whose time in the band saw him play with both Courtney Love and Chuck Mosley. Bowen recalls:

> They were all a few years younger than I was, and were very excited and energetic. I felt especially close to Bill, as he shared the apartment with my girlfriend, so we hung out together. Bill was always popping up with an eclectic assortment of cool music, from Yellowman to Kukl, to Killing Joke. Same with Mike, but I spent more time with Billy. They were all great to play with, because they were so good and rhythmically tight. They got down to business at rehearsal, which I found refreshing, but they played so well, and we had a lot of fun.
>
> They were different than most of the bands on the scene. Most of those bands were either hardcore punk, or arty and weird. They had some struggles, because they didn't exactly fit in, but it seemed apparent that they would succeed.

Bowen was almost the final step in the band's early guitar evolution. 'We wanted that aggressive rhythm playing and tonal structure,' says Bordin. 'Mark Bowen wasn't that guy. He was more than we had before, and in the right direction. We needed to keep evolving and improving.'

The next guitarist up to the plate was Desmond Shea, a friend of Paula Frazer, who became Faith No More's seventh guitarist in early 1984, aged just fifteen. He knew Bill and Mike and Roddy, having played with the latter two in other bands. 'Roddy was an occasional collaborator as keyboardist in Trial, perfectly adept at arriving without rehearsal, Oberheim Matrix 12 in hand, ready to provide an ethereal if not oozing and organic addition to our minimalist post-punk throb,' he later recalled. 'Mike Bordin was also a frequent member of my other band, Rhythm & Noise, providing a most cohesive and coherent "rhythm" to our "noise".'

Shea's time in Faith No More coincided with Chuck Mosley's transitional period in and out of the band. 'I believe most of the set would have been instrumental at the time,' he said. 'There was discussion of getting some guy from LA in the band Haircuts That Kill to audition as a vocalist. I did play one gig with Chuck in the band, though his approach was not as refined as it would become.'

The teenage Shea was also particularly impressed by the band's flow-like rehearsals:

> [They were] the epiphany of coalescing musically to the point of meditation—an actual Zen-like experience where instruments would seemingly mechanise, their characters shifted. Overpowering frankincense at gigs was regular. I smoked opium for the first time at the Mabuhay Gardens before a show with them.
>
> Mike and Billy as a rhythm section and as composers were, in a word, unimaginable. Billy's conceptual reinvention of the role of a bassist—both percussive and harmonic, and rhythmically contrapuntal—was fascinating. They were a dynamic, machine-like system, and I had never heard anything like them. Incorporating minimal, industrial and dub elements into what might be called 'new metal' or 'rap rock' or 'alternative metal' ten plus years later.

The Chickenfuckers show on June 26 that marked the end of Courtney Love's time also brought the band's long search for a guitar player to an end. It was the first time that Jim Martin played with Bordin and Gould.

Martin had previously played with Bordin in the band EZ Street, and he also hailed from the East Bay area. Born in Oakland in July 1961, he was already playing with a toy guitar aged four or five, but his first serious music exposure did not come until he was twelve. 'I started jamming on my cousin's old Rickenbacker through a little Fender Champ amp. Before that, I played on my mom's Harmony Patrician, a great old guitar. Eventually, my folks got me a Japanese Epiphone and a piece-of-shit Yamaha amp for Christmas, and I started playing Black Sabbath tunes. The first song I learned was "Iron Man", then "War Pigs".'

At a similar early age, hearing The Beatles put him off listening to the radio, but he soon discovered Jimi Hendrix, Lynyrd Skynyrd, and early

Aerosmith. But it was Sabbath that became his touchstone. He devoured *Paranoid*, and it was only when it had exhausted his curiosity that he moved on to *Black Sabbath*. That album was the record of choice in his teenage years hangout, the Shack, a friend's shed, where most of his early music listening took place. But it was in another shed that Martin honed his playing. 'We had this property that my folks bought. It's up in the Coastal Mountain Range, in California. It's well off the beaten path. That's where we did most of our exploratory music projects. We recorded them on the spot as they happened. Tapes and stuff of just whatever was coming right off the top.'

Martin's playing partners were usually Cliff Burton and Dave DiDonato, another close friend and drummer. Burton was also friends with Mike Bordin, and the trio had played together as EZ Street for a short time. The band's high point was finishing fourth in the 1979 Hayward Area Recreation District's annual Battle of the Bands at Chabot College.

While Bordin moved on to Fun Addicts, EZ Street continued briefly and morphed into Agents Of Misfortune, a band formed out of those jam sessions with Burton and DiDonato. That largely instrumental trio allowed Burton and Martin to indulge their creative sides. Burton refined his classical-and harmonics-influenced bass style, with Martin even occasionally playing his guitar with a violin bow. When Burton moved on to his final pre-Metallica band, Trauma, Martin was left in limbo. But he was still picking up new influences from his friend and musical kindred spirit. 'I didn't get into punk until Cliff turned me on in the early 80s. I was still listening to Sabbath, Zeppelin, and Floyd, and Cliff introduced me to bands like Fear, GBH, Black Flag, and The Exploited. That stuff was pretty wild; it was exciting and new for me. Cliff turned me on to a lot of cool stuff when he was in Trauma, though I can't say I was a big fan of theirs.'

Martin was initially against Burton's next move, too. 'I told him not to join. I said, Fuck those guys, they suck. I just thought they were stupid. When James Hetfield called up Cliff and said that they wanted him to join, I went with him to see Metallica play with Bitch at the Stone in San Francisco. Cliff was saying, Geez, this is kind of weird—these guys want to talk to me about joining their band, and their bass player's still here.'

Soon, Martin found his new band as well. Bordin recalls, 'Billy and I were sitting at Cliff's favourite Mexican restaurant having lunch one afternoon in

Hayward in the East Bay, and Cliff was back from tour with Metallica. He wanders in and he sits and has lunch with us, and he says, "Jim has a regular job and it's killing him, he needs a band. You should put him in the band. He can do it." And I said, "Yeah, but we didn't get along then, Cliff, how are we going to get along now?" Cliff said, "Don't worry about that, he needs a job." So I said, "OK, we'll try it.'"

The band had a show lined up supporting 45 Grave at the Mab that they had cancelled due to the lack of a singer and a guitarist, but they managed to get the gig back and played as The Chickenfuckers, with Gould and Bordin joined by Martin and Burton. 'I'd never sung in a band before,' says Gould, 'and I've never sung in one since. I drank a half a bottle of whiskey during that performance. It was an "anything goes" jam, just try to go as "out there" as possible.'

'CHUCK'S COOL, CHUCK DOESN'T GIVE A SHIT.'

8

Even with a new guitarist unearthed and debuted, the evolution of Faith No More, like their early music, continued to deviate from the linear. The band was on hiatus for much of the summer of 1984 as Billy, Mike, and Roddy joined up with Joe Callahan on a nationwide Pop-O-Pies tour. The characters contained within ensured that Faith No More could only be a contrarian band, but the core trio honed their audience antagonism, appreciation of unpopular covers, and disdain for genres and genre conventions in this intense spell with the Pies. While Faith No More was the main attraction for Bordin, Bottum, and Gould, the Pies came a close second. And it was with Joe Callahan's project that the trio had their first proper recording and touring experience. The tour took them as far as Texas, and almost brought both bands to a premature end.

Before a show in Dallas, Bordin wiped out skateboarding on some steps and ripped a hand open on some loose nails. He was rushed to Baylor University Medical Center, but dreadlocked, dirty, and dishevelled from touring, he was initially refused admittance and sent in the direction of another medical facility that treated local down-and-outs. Bordin was forced to invoke the name of his doctor father; phone calls were made and surgery arranged. Bordin: 'I was going to lose the use of three fingers on my left hand. But the surgeon said that the muscles on my hand were so tight from playing that they were protected from the bone, so they could save it.'

Bordin was out of action, which meant that the Pop-O-Pies needed a replacement drummer. Gould: 'I stayed behind in Houston and met these girls there, and we ended up driving up to Dallas. The car broke down, we ended up having to hitchhike to the gig and the band was going onstage right at the time I showed up. Then I found out about Bordin's hand, so I played drums at that gig. The one and only time I've ever played drums— apart from in a wedding band once—and I'm a terrible drummer.'

✸

Later in the summer of 1984, Faith No More regrouped in San Francisco. They needed a singer. Again. And, after exhausting all options in the Bay Area, they returned to Los Angeles and a familiar figure. Chuck Mosley, the keyboard player from Bill Gould's LA band The Animated, had continued to make music with a punk outfit called Haircuts That Kill. Like Faith No More, the band struggled to recruit and keep singers—so much so that Mosley himself took over vocal duties. 'I started singing because we didn't have a singer,' he said, 'and I didn't really consider myself a singer.'

Mosley was in the audience for Faith No More's Fiesta House show in December 1983. 'We'd always be in touch,' he recalled. 'Every time he came down for holidays and stuff, like Christmas or whatever break, he'd call me up and we'd go out. We'd fill each other in on what we were doing—"I'm playing in this band Haircuts" and "I'm with a new band Faith No More"—and that was pretty serious for him.'

Asked by Gould to try out as singer for some dates booked in Los Angeles, Mosley said, 'Three shows turned into five turned into ten turned into a few years.' The low-key nature of the recruitment was summed up by Mike Bordin, who recalls, 'Bill said, "This is Chuck, Chuck's cool, Chuck doesn't trip or give a shit. He'll try to sing."'

Mosley joined Faith No More around August 1984. He had briefly stepped in to sing when the band played the Lhasa Club in Los Angeles in January as well. But his first full show as singer was on September 22 at the Club Foot in San Francisco, where Faith No More played until almost two on the morning. Faith No More wanted a presence for live shows, rather than a voice for recordings. Mosley fit the bill perfectly.

The quintet regrouped in September, but dates were few and far between before the end of 1984. Shows in Club Foot and the Mab on home turf in September and October allowed the group to focus on getting their sound down. Not long after Chuck joined, the band recorded a track for Doug Moody's Los Angeles-based Mystic Records label. The session was organised by Phillip Raves, a friend of Chuck's, and the label's in-house engineer and producer, who had helmed the debut record by NOFX and other releases from the likes of The Mentors and Dr Know. 'I invited the band to record,' he recalls. 'They were friends of mine, and at the time they were unknown, and I thought it would be helpful. We had no plans to sign the band, as we were primarily a hardcore label.'

The song was entitled 'You're Gonna Die'; it was also known at various times as 'Surprise! You're Dead' and eventually became 'Zombie Eaters'. The compilation, a follow-up to the 1984 release *Copulation*, which had featured Black Flag, White Flag, and Ill Repute, never saw the light of day. It was never mixed and remains largely unheard, with the two-inch master tape in need of restoration.

Undeterred, on October 27, the band headed to Matt Wallace's Dangerous Rhythm studios to record their most advanced demo up until that point, and a cassette was subsequently distributed featuring 'Mark Bowen', 'Greed', and an alternative dance mix of 'Greed'. The recording session lasted one day, from eleven in the morning until seven in the evening, and the band paid $148—including four bucks for a Maxell C90 tape—for the privilege. The demo was reviewed the following year by the *Wiring Department* zine:

Here is a parade of uncanny drums, bass rhythms, melancholy keyboards. All the excitement of Killing Joke. The sound is original in treatment. To give authenticity, the music has been based in varying degrees upon well-recorded incidents or experiences in which the members sincerely believe. The excellent recording puts Faith. No More's music where it rightfully belongs—in our minds.

'Mark Bowen' and 'Arabian Disco' from the same session also featured on the *Numb Tongue, No Taste* compilation released by German label Masking Tapes on December 20 1984. One day later, the band played their biggest gig to date—and their last styled as Faith. No More—back at the Anti-Club in Los Angeles. In an apparent attempt to goad the LA crowd, Bill Gould was attired in a ball gown, and Jim Martin had his hair in curlers. Significantly, the band were now getting media attention, with the *Los Angeles Times* reviewing that show: 'On its first Los Angeles visit in a year, the boisterous band played music as disruptively oddball as that period in the middle of their name. It was how Captain Beefheart might sound if he went punk-metal.'

9

WE CARE

A LOT

In 1985, the band set their sights on making their first album. They knew what they wanted to do and why, as Gould and Bottum explained in an interview published in June 1985 by San Francisco music zine *Wiring Department* (which featured occasional articles and reviews written by Roddy).

'On the twenty-first of this month, we're going for a three-day recording marathon in Cotati,' Bottum stated. 'We're working with our producer, Matt Wallace, to get these twenty-four-track recordings where we want them to be. These recordings are what we hope to be putting out on an EP. We're looking for financial support in the pressing and distribution, but the recording and mixing will be finished in two weeks.'

'This is the first step,' Gould added. 'We just got tired of waiting for people.'

Frustration with a lack of interest from record labels was a key factor in provoking the band to do it themselves. In that same interview, Gould mentioned Enigma as one frustrating label, and Bordin lists other labels who didn't get them: 'We were ready to commit our songs to tape. We felt it was time, we felt we weren't getting anywhere just kicking around hoping that Howie Klein [then of San Francisco-based 415 Records and a KUSF radio DJ; later president of Reprise Records] or the dude from Subterranean Records or Rough Trade, who had a big profile in San Francisco, would sign us. We felt that we weren't going to get any further, and we may as well record good versions of these songs and get good versions out there.'

The band had received one rejection letter in October 1984 after sending out the cassette of their opening show and initial recordings. The writer was Bruce Licher, owner of Independent Project Records and former Savage Republic guitarist. His IPR label was famed for its striking and Grammy-winning album artwork, designed by Licher himself, and had released Camper Van Beethoven's debut album in 1985. It could have been Faith No More, but Licher gave a reasoned rejection in his letter to Gould:

I found the live at On Broadway stuff the most interesting, in the sense that I would want to return to it to listen again and again ... you have created a definite sound that is quite good. The one part that needs the most work, and I say this at the risk of offending one of you, though please realise that it is meant positively, is the singing. I find myself almost wishing that the songs were instrumental. Some of your material would make very good soundtracks—the first instrumental, and perhaps you could think of moving in that direction if it interests you ...

If your vocalist could work on what he does and could develop his 'singing', then your music would ultimately be more powerful and satisfying. Your music demands more than a sort of post-punk shout, and if your vocalist could work on experimenting with his voice a bit, he might come up with something quite interesting.

Still without a label, band and producer decamped to Prairie Sun Studios on Friday June 21. Cotati is an hour or so north of San Francisco in the Sonoma County wine country, and sits on a ten-acre ranch that was mostly populated by chickens during the band's stay. The band were recording commando-style: getting in, getting the songs down, and getting out; spending two nights together in a converted loft.

Gould: 'There was zero fun: we just worked, slept on the floor and started recording again as soon as we woke up. We recorded everything in two days and mixed it on the third day.'

Bordin: 'To me, that was fun. We were doing something for ourselves, and so to me that was total fun. But we didn't fuck around. We worked really hard, and I remember at the end of it we were wiped out.'

For Matt Wallace, this was not the only novelty. He had never previously worked with two-inch tape or twenty-four tracks. Of the band, he says, 'Their "signature sound" came into being during the making of *We Care A Lot*. By having access to a larger studio to record in, a live acoustic chamber to send Mike Bordin's drums into, as well as using that same acoustic chamber to put Bill's bass amplifier in, this helped to shape and create the "FNM sound", which, at least for me, is punchy drums with ambience and distorted/driven bass with some room sound.'

The band had around fifteen songs written and mostly ready. They brought in banners featuring their eight-pointed star logo. The band designed all their early posters, banners, T-shirts, and logos themselves. The logo was inspired by a symbol-of-chaos design that Gould and Bottum had spotted in a book of tribal tattoos belonging to Gould's then girlfriend. 'We thought that was cool, because our shows were chaotic,' he says. 'It was just a cool, fucked-up, chaotic symbol to throw out there with flyers for our shows.' The Star of Lakshmi in Hinduism and the Rub el Hizb in

Islam, as depicted on the coats of arms of Turkmenistan and Uzbekistan, and, until 1659, the national flag of Morocco, are very similar octagrams. 'It ended up having a little more meaning as we went on,' he adds. 'We realised that a lot of cultures use it for different things, and it took on a life of its own after that.'

As well as hanging the banner, the band burned incense prior to their sessions to create an atmosphere akin to their live shows. There was so much incense that the main recording room was obscured by clouds and Wallace went into a panic, fearing that sensitive microphones and recording equipment would be damaged.

The band laid down four tracks on that June Solstice weekend. 'Greed' was the first song completed. The music had largely been put together by Bill Gould and honed in rehearsals. Gould even provides much of the melody, his bass stretching out midway through the track. The track is a prime example of Faith No More's percussive approach to songwriting, with Bordin's very busy drumming—even toned down as it is from the demo version—and Martin's insistent and persistent major chord. Bordin states, 'Jim playing that counter rhythm—that suggestion would have come from Bill. But it is guitar-playing percussion. We had that in a lot of songs. It is percussive—it is not smooth and figurative—and a lot of times that's what we needed to do.'

The song seems simple, but it took a lot of work to get Gould's exact idea down pat, according to Bordin. 'We worked on that song a lot, the drums are very busy, but they were even more tribal in the demo version [included on the 2016 reissue]. I think they did a really good job getting that weight back, but I always felt like whether it was just we didn't have enough space on the tape because the drums are so large and loud and big, I never felt like we got exactly how I always heard them until much later, much later.'

Lyrically, the song shows that the band were post-modern, self-referential, and even *meta* long before Mike Patton joined the band:

> *Over the hills they came from the valley*
> *Making innuendos about my lack of talent, oh well ...*
> *They say that when I'm supposed to be singing*
> *All I'm really doing is yelling.*

The yelling reference was to Mosley's earlier 'screamo' vocal style, which had since been smoothed out. 'In early versions of the song, he doesn't sing and croon, he just screams,' Bordin states, 'which I thought was really aggressive and really cool. It's like, *Yeah, fuck you, you're all fucking valley assholes anyway*, which is so funny. That's Chuck at his best.'

Mosley: 'I was really nervous. And I remember being in awe of this sound because I hadn't heard anything like it before. It made me nervous, because I didn't know what to do with it. That was where the rapping stuff came from. I couldn't really understand the music. It was complicated and different to me, so I was just screaming to the beat, like ranting. Not rapping, but ranting.'

Mosley's contributions prior to recording were limited to him receiving tapes of music from the band down in San Francisco, adding his vocals, and sending them back from Los Angeles. Often, the tapes got lost in the post. 'I sent and got sent demos, and would say, This would sound good. But I didn't know I could sing. I could imitate it, but not do it. David Bowie was my hero, and I tried to sing like him and croon. I tried to stay in tune, and when they did melodic stuff, I'd find something to sing to. But there was other stuff I didn't understand, and I would rap and rant over it. I was black and white. So it was my two worlds together.'

That was the origin of rap-rock. Punk attitude, unfamiliar music, rap background, and little chance to rehearse led to chanting and ranting and—when things calmed down in the studio—to rapping.

There was another problem, however. 'I wanted to get it right and I was really nervous,' Mosley recalled. 'But I got a cold. It happened almost every time I went to the studio. I think it was because of the stress.'

Less than a year into his Faith No More tenure, Mosley was already sensitive to criticism. 'I was hearing all the naysayers. People saying that I couldn't sing. I knew I wasn't a singer, but I wasn't going to let that stop me. "Greed" is just me talking shit to all the people that are talking shit about me.'

The band also got self-referential on a track named after previous guitarist Mark Bowen. The track was originally so named as a working title, because an early version began with Bowen's guitar. But Mosley took the working title and ran with it, and thus a former member of the band achieved musical immortality. Musically, the song is the most developed example of the dub sound that the group were exploring at this time. That was achieved mostly by Bordin's use of a chrome timbale, an effect that the band would use only once more, on 'Surprise! You're Dead' from *The Real Thing*.

'Mark was a really nice guy,' Mosley recalled. 'Quiet and unobtrusive. Everything before that is about everybody in the world except him.'

According to Bowen himself, the name came about as a result of him coming up with the intro:

> I'm told by Mike that I created the guitar intro to the song. I think the song is a bit of a fluke. When we practised, there was no official singer, and no singer present. The songs were often named after an object, person, or situation that was present at the time. I apparently created some part of the composition of this song, so it became the 'Mark Bowen' song. Chuck didn't really know me all that well, but we had met and spent some time together. Billy sent Chuck a tape of songs, and one was called 'Mark Bowen', so he created lyrics based on his impression of me. Most of the things he says about me in the song could also be said of Chuck. But I am a pretty damn nice guy anyway.

Another song from the session, 'Arabian Disco', was just one of Faith No More's large suite of 'Disco'-titled songs. 'We called it our disco phase, but we weren't even playing disco music,' says Bordin. The band had released a demo version of the track on the *Numb Tongue, No Taste* compilation released by Masking Tapes in December 1984.

By the end of this first weekend session as recording artists, the band had upped the ante again to deliver a genuine pop classic. On 'We Care A Lot', the third track from the sessions, Faith No More's complexities—their complementary and clashing heaviness and hookiness; their gift of melody; and their refusal to sound like anyone else, or like was expected of them—is already thrillingly on display.

If 'Mark Bowen' was Mosley talking shit to people talking shit about him, the eventual album's title track is the whole band talking shit to the whole world. So forward-thinking that it was actually recorded one month before the Live Aid concerts that it references took place, 'We Care A Lot' is a punkish middle-finger salute to the 'rock star as saviour' moment, a deadpan and deliberate deconstruction of rock dinosaur do-goodery. Though his lyrical contributions were infrequent, Roddy Bottum was always direct and to the point, and always the most likely to tackle topical and political issues. His four snappy verses here deal with Live Aid and AIDs; street suffering and saving the world; the police, the military, and perpetual war; and child commercialisation and pop culture. All over a swinging beat, crunchy guitar, barely there keyboards, and all in around four minutes and little more than 140 words.

'We were heavily into Run-DMC at the time,' says Bottum, 'and the beat and the bass line of "We Care A Lot" felt like a heavy proper rap song to us. It made sense that we do a rap type of vocal. We were very sarcastic kids, and we really were just aiming to make ourselves laugh. I remember writing the lyrics at my parents' house in LA. The sound of the song was really the quintessential FNM sound. Heavy drum rhythm, punctuated bass and floaty keyboards.'

Mosley chimed in with the killer melody and chorus—'*It's a dirty job but someone's gotta do it*'—giving the song two catchy hooks. Beat-driven, it invites Mosley's snotty rapped verses, perfectly distilling the band's post-adolescent arrogance and us-against-the-world stance. There is also room for Jim Martin to insert apposite riffs, his tone at its crunchiest, and a harbinger of *The Real Thing*'s crossover appeal.

The song began life in late 1983, with Bordin and Gould making beats together. Bordin: 'Me and Bill were just jamming, doing pulses, little chunks of rhythmic framework. It just came out. It could not have come out more naturally than that.'

'We played "We Care A Lot" as an instrumental for a year before Roddy wrote the lyrics,' Gould recalls. 'We got all excited when Chuck sang it, because it was the first thing we ever did that sounded like real music.'

As soon as the band had recorded the track at Prairie Sun, they knew they had captured something special. They barely had time to assess their progress, having to pack up quickly as their time at the ranch expired. Exhausted, they returned to the city.

Within a month, Gould's calculated gamble that better-recorded versions of their songs would lead to record company interest paid off. For a band like Faith No More, college radio was the only likely outlet for their music. And the king of college radio in southern California in the early 1980s was KXLU, which had been broadcasting out of Loyola Marymount University since 1957. The student-run station—later the first to air Nirvana's 'Smells Like Teen Spirit'—was the only outpost for late punk and hardcore, and was the first station to play Black Flag and The Minutemen.

In 1984, one KXLU DJ in particular wanted to expand further on this focus on the new and the unheard by playing demo tapes of unsigned or undiscovered bands. Solana Rehne was known as Bunny Bouffant when she first started on the AM section of KXLU in 1982. She'd initially gone to the station studio to interview people for her journalism class, and ended up cutting hair at the studio before practically moving in. From Orange County, and a fan of the South Bay band Agent Orange sporting bright orange hair, she changed her on-air name to Agent Ava when she moved to the KXLU FM station in 1983. Soon she had the idea for her own programme showcasing demo recordings, *Demolisten*. 'I would hear the first few notes of a song and know which bands would be the most powerful and loved,' she explains. 'Faith No More was one of those bands … the first few notes. A lot of bands started recognising me as Agent Ava from KXLU and gave me demo tapes of their sounds.'

Demolisten later paved the way to record deals for The Offspring and Beck, and gave early exposure to Guns N' Roses and the Red Hot Chili Peppers. But it was Faith No More and Jane's Addiction who inspired the *Demolisten* show initially:

By 1984, I had seen Faith No More live several times in the LA clubs, and was anxious to get their sounds on *Demolisten*. Their live shows had a lot of power with the fusion of funk, punk, rap, soul. It was a new genre that was moshable and danceable. Chuck personally brought up a test pressing of some of the songs from the eventual *We Care A Lot* release—'Greed', 'Mark Bowen', 'Arabian Disco', and 'We Care A Lot'. I carted up Faith No More and the other top songs from *Demolisten* for regular airplay on KXLU.

There was a huge positive response, and lots of listeners called in saying, 'Finally we get to hear these guys on the radio.' I'm happy the band's music reached the multitudes; that was always my intention with any band featured on *Demolisten*.

The band also got heavy airplay on KXLU from DJ Adam Bomb, aka Pat Hoed, who hosted the *Final Countdown* show featuring otherwise largely unheard hardcore and thrash metal. On San Francisco college station KUSF, future Reprise/Warner Bros president Howie Klein also gave Faith No More early airplay.

With the music out there and attracting attention, Faith No More just needed a record label ear to take notice. Faith No More folklore has it that one such record label representative, Ruth Schwartz, who had left Rough Trade to form her own Mordam distribution company in 1983, heard the four tracks from the Prairie Sun session being played by a friend of the band, Will Carpmill (who had earlier came up with the band's name), at the Rough Trade Records distribution centre in San Francisco, where he worked as a bookkeeping assistant. According to Schwartz herself, though, she first heard the demo through another Rough Trade employee, her roommate, Kent Jolly.

'I went to see them at Club Foot in San Francisco, as I knew the guys,' Jolly explains. 'I'd known Mike Bordin since before I was ten years old—our families went camping together. So I bought the cassette there. I remember "We Care A Lot"—it was their signature tune. I loved them and always have. The demo was great, so I brought it home for Ruth.'

Schwartz had already built Mordam up into the most important punk record distributer in the city. She had started out working for *Maximum Rocknroll* as a record reviewer, then as an editor—her record reviews even appeared on the same pages as early Faith. No Man reviews—and as a radio show presenter on MMR Radio. She set up Mordam in 1983, hitting on the idea of setting up an independent distribution company for the city's many punk labels. After the collapse of Faulty Records, she helped her friend Jello Biafra of the Dead Kennedys to rescue his Alternative Tentacles stock from the pressing plant, and soon other relatively big punk labels Maximum Rocknroll and Social Unrest came on board. In *We Owe You Nothing*, a collection of interviews from the magazine *Punk Planet*, editor Daniel Sinker declared Mordam 'the cornerstone upon which much of the modern punk scene was built.'

In 1985, Mordam was a distribution company, not a record company. Faith No More changed that. The unique situation Faith No More were in at this juncture, with music recorded but no label on board—plus the prompting of Jolly, the quality of their music, and Schwartz's astute judgement and eye for an opportunity—invited this deviation from the Mordam model.

Schwartz: 'Kent brought their demo home and told me that we should go see them. The record was already recorded, and they just wanted someone to put it out and distribute it, which I did. The rest is history.'

Bottum: 'I think she made her decision based to a large extent on "We Care A Lot", the song. She was really into punk rock. Punk rock was her life—[she was] really a *Maximum Rocknroll* person. It surprised us that she'd be into what we were doing, because we really were not into that scene.'

Schwartz also offered to finance another recording session to get an album's worth of material, and she was prepared to release the record directly on Mordam—the first record to be put out on Mordam, rather than just distributed by the company.

Bordin: 'There were possibilities; we could do what we wanted. We were checking things off the list: get a demo, get a record. People tied themselves to us, and they were willing to take a chance with us. She was somebody on your side, somebody who believes in you.'

❖

The band now had the finances and the support to finish *We Care A Lot*. A second three-day weekend session in Prairie Sun was duly booked for later in the summer. The songs, painstakingly pasted together over the previous two years, were primed—and so were the band. Lyrics were only added at the last minute, as was to become Chuck Mosley's fashion, and the singer's renewed bout of 'flu and improvised approach were the only slight bumps on another smooth recording session.

Most songs were again the products of collective effort and repeated redefining, but Jim Martin did bring his own composition, 'Jim', one of two instrumental pieces on the album. 'Jim'—which never graduated from working title to actual title—is a contender for the oddest song in the band's oeuvre, a seventy-six-second slice of pastoral acoustic expressionism. Martin brought the song to the session complete and ready. The fact that he could do so and the fact that the otherwise unadorned track made the final album cut belies any notion that Martin's creative input was not appreciated. Of course, this being Faith No More, the song also puts on display some band personal friction for all to hear with the inclusion of an impromptu pre-song exchange between Martin and Bordin, who recalls, 'That was totally off the cuff—me being a total asshole, and Jim being his normal crabby self.'

'That song was Jim's deal entirely,' says Bottum. 'It was something he had played since he was a kid. It was preposterous to include it; thus, it worked!'

Chuck Mosley also brought his self-penned 'New Beginnings', the album's closer, to the session, with Martin's acoustic opening and his choppy guitar work throughout becoming highlights of the song. It is also one of Mosley's finest moments as lyricist and as a vocalist. According to Mosley, the song was inspired by the 1971 film *Johnny Got His Gun*—which also inspired the music video for Metallica's 'One' four years later—about a soldier who returns from World War I a quadruple amputee. Mosley gave it his own interpretation: 'He died, but he didn't know he was dead. It's about his life flashing by, and not really realising until the end that he's actually dead.'

Some songs did require work in the studio, as well as the engineering and production skills of Matt Wallace. 'The Jungle' was a case in point. A song Faith No More played at their first show in 1983, it developed over time but never grew. Wallace cut and pasted sections together in such a way that the middle eight became the introduction. As for Chuck Mosley's lyrics, he said, 'I equivocate the deepest part of the jungle with God—just like a scary, sacred place, but then I also liken it to places you've never been before with a girl.'

Played at their first show, attitudinally antithetical to the album's title track, and a circular rhythmic *tour de force*, 'Why Do You Bother?' was the quintessential proto-Faith No More song. Despite being a live staple for almost two years, it was not quite finished when the band entered the studio. Bordin: 'It was super-vague and nebulous. That same part just keeping playing and playing until the wheels came off. It was big and open and mean and extremely repetitive, very trance-like.'

In contrast to that song's repetition, 'Pills For Breakfast' pointed the way forward to future Faith No More. It would have sounded right at home on *The Real Thing* and serves as a precursor to 'Woodpecker From Mars' from that record. Taking its name from a catchphrase of Jim Martin's, the song was written by Martin and Bordin, whose propulsive style is to the fore.

Apart from the title track, the song from the album that would make the most prominent entry into the Faith No More live canon is the exhilarating 'As The Worm Turns'. Like the album's title track, 'Worm' is an anti-protest protest song. The lyrics largely read as a mood-booster to the unemployed, but according to Mosley, 'It's my take on a San Francisco mentality; vegetarian and peace-loving hippies. My take about people that are protesting and complaining. If you want to do something, don't sit around—just get off your ass, and choose family.'

Even with a label behind them, the production and packaging of the record was a band-and-friends effort. Joan Osato was a talented photographer who lived with Roddy Bottum, and she provided the band portraits. The album graphic design was produced by Olga Gerrard, sister of band-name originator Will Carpmill, and one half of the group's management team along with husband Gerry.

We Care A Lot was released on November 25 1985. Mordam had paved the way for *We Care A Lot*'s release with a stealth campaign, primarily through Ruth Schwartz's *Maximum Rocknroll*. In the magazine's November edition, Kent Jolly picked the band's test pressing as one of her 'Top 15' records alongside Hüsker Dü's *Flip Your Wig* and Green River's *Come On*

Down. In the same issue, Jolly waxed lyrical about the band in her regular Northern California round-up: 'Oh, yes stay tuned for Faith No More. I heard an incredible demo. How to describe it? Kind of "gothic rap". You just have to hear *We Care A Lot.* Great music and hysterical lyrics. And live, they are so powerful it's incredible.'

In the following month's edition, both Jolly and Schwartz, as well as Martin Sprouse, had *We Care A Lot* among their 'Top 15' lists. Jolly again gave the band a prominent mention in her column: 'Just last issue I raved about Faith No More and their demo tape—well, I'm ecstatic as hell to report that they've been snapped up by our local Mordam Records (our very own Ruth Schwartz's very own label). I've heard the test pressing, and it's intense.'

Martin Sprouse, who had founded the *Leading Edge* fanzine in San Diego in 1983, and then moved to San Francisco in 1985 to take a leading role in running *Maximum Rocknroll* at the tender age of nineteen, had the distinction of giving *We Care A Lot* its first review. 'Take the necessary ingredients to produce hard-hitting raps in the vein of Run DMC, add slow, flowing keyboards and you will have a good idea of what this band has struck upon,' he wrote. 'The title track is by far the standout, and I see no reason why the remaining tunes wouldn't become popular with a lot of underground dance clubs.'

The band played a release party at the VIS in San Francisco five days later. The Mordam press release was a paragon of understatement: 'These guys are definitely happening. I mean they are unusual, interesting and ready for their first LP.' *Billboard* was even more understated in its assessment in January 1985: 'Nihilist rockers from San Francisco. Worth a shot if you like that sort of stuff.'

The album's title track was soon picked up by college radio stations in California and, by early 1986, local San Francisco dance clubs were also playing the track. By February, *Ward Music Monthly* was reporting in its album review that 'already the title track is filling the dance floor with its postpunk beat' and had the album entering its college radio airplay chart at #39. It took until May for the album to appear as a new entry in the *Rockpool* College Radio charts. But while college radio was a springboard for success, it was the live shows that would drive Faith No More forward.

Within eight months of the release of *We Care A Lot*, Faith No More had completed their first national tour, signed a record deal, and recorded their follow-up album. Buoyed by industry attention and an album that showcased their abilities, the band and managers Olga and Gerry Gerrard and booking agent Jim Dunbar were able to put together a rough-and-ready first national tour, which ran from February to April 1986. For Bill Gould, that was the most important thing. 'Holding the test pressing for the first time was pretty cool. And it was extra cool, because it was Mordam's first record too, so Ruth Schwartz was as excited as we were. Having a record meant that we could tour, so we were off and running.'

Running might actually have been a more efficient mode of transport than the '66 Dodge van and initially hired and then 'purloined' Jartrans trailer that the band were provided with for the tour. With a roadie that didn't drive, Mike Bordin largely ruled out of driving after another in a series of accidents, and Jim Martin driving according to his own schedule, the tour was an exercise in logistics and group dynamics as much as stagecraft and musicianship. The plan was to start in California, drive as far south as possible, play shows there, move to the East Coast, and then drive back north. Bordin: 'As soon as we could, we got the hell out of there and tried to get gigs at colleges across the country. That was the start for us. That was us figuring out who we were and where we were going.'

Where they were going initially was to Tucson. After a show in Los Angeles in February, the band embarked on the seven-hour journey to Arizona for two small gigs. A mid-tour interview in Austin-based zine *Your Flesh* revealed the band's frustrations. 'Tucson is a weird scene,' Gould said. 'I've heard that people there don't go to shows until the band comes their second or third time around. We are a really hard band to hear sometimes for the first time, if you are not used to our sound. We just want to play better clubs, so we can play for better sound systems. It has nothing to do with greed or money.'

The band kept going south, and shows at the Beach in Austin, and in Jacksonville, Mississippi, were better attended. But the band learned a harsh lesson in the realities of college touring at the next stop, Athens, Georgia, as Gould recalls:

> We stopped for gas about five hours into the drive, and I called the club to get the load-in time, and they said, 'School spring break started today, so there's not going to be anybody at the show. You might want to think about cancelling.' We decided to keep going.
>
> Somebody from Jacksonville gave us a number of somebody in Athens and I called him up. Ron Hargreaves was his name. He came to the show, and I put him on the guest list, and he bought a beer. Because he bought a beer, we got paid two dollars. There was only Ron and his friend and the bartender watching, and we got into a fight onstage because Roddy was saying after every song, 'Thank you everybody, it's such a pleasure to be here, this is a real wonderful audience.' He just kept doing it over and over, and finally I snapped, 'Shut up, shut the fuck up, will you!'

'I got really frustrated after the show,' Bordin adds. 'Normally, no matter what, if it's five people or ten people, you're doing a show and you're working and you're learning. But I remember that one—I felt mad.'

Frustration would grow into stoicism when the band were left stranded for ten days in Atlanta after more shows were cancelled, and with money running low, the quintet, plus roadie Jim Olson, had little choice but to live at their next venue, the Metroplex, a former blood bank that became the epicentre for the city's hardcore scene when it opened in 1983.

Bordin: 'We showed up but had no gig. They said, We can give you a gig in a week if you flyer the town for us, so we did, because we had nothing better to do.'

The Metroplex already served as a sanctuary for troubled local youths, who would use the upstairs room to crash, and the club was happy to let cash-starved bands stay as well. Bottum: 'We ran out of money and a bunch of shows got cancelled, so we just stayed put. There were rats in the club, and we slept for the most part on old sofas. I remember practising there too, and working out "Greed".' The quintet also spent some nights in a downtown rehearsal space that was in such a dangerous area that the band had to be padlocked in overnight and let out from the outside again in the morning.

Atlanta was also the scene of a coming-out of sorts of Roddy Bottum. Bill Gould and Jim Martin were making their way from the venue to the tour van, both having just done ecstasy for the first time, when they happened upon Roddy and Jim Olsen in the back of the truck. Gould and Martin exchanged looks that said, 'Are you seeing what I'm seeing?' and beat a hasty retreat. In typical Faith No More communication style, nothing more was spoken of the *coitus interruptus*. Of the tour itself, Roddy recalls, 'I slept in the back of the Dodge the whole tour with my then-boyfriend, Jim Olson, who was our inept roadie.'

Otherwise, the band made the most of their downtime in Atlanta, and wrote 'Chinese Arithmetic' on the venue's stage. Eventually, they played support to the Misfits on March 22 1986 at their adopted home.

Gould: 'Glenn Danzig was one of the first people we ever sent our tape to when we were making demos. I was really into the Misfits back then, and Roddy got his address and we sent it to him. We got a fan letter back from Glenn, which was pretty amazing. They really liked it. That was the first feedback we got from anybody. When we went to the Metroplex, they were playing, and Danzig said to Puffy, "Bordin! You sent me that tape!"'

The tour could not go on like this. An SOS call was put out via the Gerrard management team to Steve Blush—who, before he became the chronicler of American hardcore and New York rock, was a club promoter. Blush put up a $500 guarantee to bail out the band and set up a series of lucrative dates on the East Coast.

Reprieved, the band were in their element, and, according to contemporary accounts, went on to put on a series of explosive shows. First up was the Cook Campus Center at Rutgers University in New Brunswick. The band then succeeded in inciting a riot and getting thrown out of the venue on their next stop at City Gardens in Trenton, New Jersey. Ministry were the headliners.

Bordin: 'That was before Ministry became what they became, they were more like Depeche Mode. And the guy who owned the club said, "My God, I can't believe I found a band that will work with Ministry." And we were thinking, *We're going to book tours together. Fuck yeah, we've made it out of the wilderness.*'

Bottum: 'We thought Ministry were hilarious. It was in their disco phase, before they got "dark". We thought they were English. They were such assholes.'

Ministry had already set up their stage, with their huge $50,000 Fairlight synthesizer taking up much of the space where Faith No More were performing their support slot. 'We were really psyched,' Bordin recalls, 'and, in his enthusiasm, Chuck knocked over a beer. He might have put his beer on the Fairlight, but it was not malicious.'

Mosley: 'Ministry had all this gear set up on the stage already. They had their monitors right by my feet and the mic stand. The whole stage was congested. I am an uncoordinated klutz, and I was doing what I normally did when we played, I was really into it, jumping around and stuff. Ministry had some computer thing set up as part of their act, and I did everything I could to avoid it. I didn't smash anything, I didn't destroy anything, and I didn't break anything. The one thing I might have done was spill some beer or water on something that was at my feet, and that would be the extent of it.'

Then, according to Bordin, the promoter intervened. 'The promoter went through the PA, which I'd never heard before, and he was yelling at us between songs: *Don't fuck with Ministry!*'

Chaos reigned, with bottles smashing, and the stage rushed by fans, security, and Ministry road crew. The topless Mosley was unceremoniously removed from the stage by a bouncer grabbing him by the waist of his shorts. The clashes spilled over to the parking lot outside; the band's equipment was brought out and dumped alongside them, and they were summarily dispatched—without their $125 appearance fee—and banned from the venue.

But Ministry bore no grudges, with Al Jourgensen recalling, 'We were playing this pop music then, at Clive Davis's instruction, we were like Milli Vanilli. And Faith No More wanted no part of that—and good for them! Even though they destroyed my $50,000 synthesizer. We weren't sure how it was going to last on tour, and it certainly didn't last with Faith No More spilling beer on it. Either way, good for them.'

Once more, the band were saved by Blush's connections as he conjured up their biggest gig to date, at New York's the World, where they played a late-night show on April 5.

Bottum: 'Steve was an early fan and reached out to us. That whole tour hinged on the amount of money that we'd be paid to play The World. He got us lots of college shows in the vicinity too, like Rutgers, and a couple of other shows. It was all based on "We Care A Lot". There was talk that Run from Run-DMC was at the World show. The crew we met on that trip stuck with us. We stayed on couches and floors in Alphabet City mostly. We're still friends with all those people. Most of the cast from [the band's 1987 song and video] "Anne's Song".'

The tour had highlighted that the band had momentum and support, but they were frustrated that *We Care A Lot* proved hard to find in most of their tour stops. Now there was more label interest than before: Australian label Big Time had handled distribution for *We Care A Lot* outside the USA and was keen to sign the band to a more conventional deal. But the label, which released albums by Redd Kross and the Hoodoo Gurus, among others, declared bankruptcy later in 1986. That left Slash—the label owned by Bob Biggs, and a spin-off of the magazine that chronicled West Coast punk—as the leading contender to release new Faith No More music.

Although Biggs, a visual artist, was far removed from punk both aesthetically and commercially, he largely kick-started San Francisco's punk scene when he put up $1,000 to finance The Germs' first single, and, in doing so, bought his first chunk of Slash. Biggs and Slash went on to sign and break a number of hugely influential bands in the early 80s, including X, Dream Syndicate, Violent Femmes, and Gun Club. And, in 1982, Slash became the first indie label to go into partnership with a major label when it entered into a distribution deal with Warner Bros. Effectively, the deal meant that Warners distributed Slash products through WEA (Warner

Elektra Asylum), and had the option of picking up any of Slash's releases and assuming the license.

In a later interview with the *Los Angeles Times*, Biggs responded to claims that such a deal was a sell-out from the one-time punk outlet: 'I've never felt that the label stood for a specific set of ideals that I was obliged to uphold. It might stand for honesty of expression and artists who are concerned with integrity in their own work, but the label itself is not about those things.'

Biggs also had a clear vision of what type of artists he wanted on his label—a vision that might as well have spelled out the letters Faith No More:

> We tend to get involved with the bands for which there is no market. Something good by definition, it seems, has no market. So we develop the market. The first thing we try to do is put soap in a soapbox, try to make them identifiable, so people can segregate them from the rest of the environment. And make sure that what you present is what they actually are, and give people a reason for wanting it, to make it a part of their lives, whether it's the clothes, music, or lyrics. A band comes to us with an image, and we try to make it desirable. For us, 'mystique' and 'aloofness' is not for a first record—you need to get out and play live.

The task of identifying bands for Biggs fell to Slash A&R rep Anna Statman, and she quickly made it her mission to sign Faith No More. Statman had started in the Slash mailroom in 1979, before graduating to marketing and then to A&R upon enticing The Blasters and, later, Violent Femmes to Slash. She had been sent a Faith. No Man demo by Bill Gould some years previously, but it was only in 1985 that she first heard Faith No More on KXLU, thanks to Adam Bomb. 'I just really immediately fell in love with the band's music, and became a big, fat, superfan,' she recalls. 'I was telling everyone at Slash, "This is like the greatest band in the world, we've got to sign these guys. Listen to how great this is."'

Gould: 'I met Anna when we played a club, Raji's, and Anna had the Slash credit card out. She was buying drinks that night, and it was the first time I'd ever seen that. And she said, Come on over tomorrow, Bob wants to meet you. We went to Slash and we met them in this little office. That's where we really got to know Anna, and she became like our godmother. She knew her way around; she knew things, and she gave me perspective. I was still very much a hands-on guy with the band, and I didn't know what the fuck I was doing. She really set me straight.'

Before Big Time went out of business, there was still a low-intensity bidding war, he adds:

> Slash took us out and they bought us drinks and they bought us lunch, and we were like, 'Holy shit, that's the first time that ever happened.' Then we go to Big Time and they'd take us for lunch and drinks. We strung them both out as long as could to get all these free lunches and free drinks. I mean, Puffy was even asking the Big Time guys, 'Hey, do you know any place I can get some weed?' The guy said, 'Hold on,' we drove to his house, and he gave us his weed. So we were, 'We got to work this, I don't know what we've stumbled into but we can't let this go.' It was only going to be Slash, because we liked what they represented and who they were. It was a logical fit.

Statman was able to persuade Biggs, and, in early 1986, a deal was signed. 'The chance to work with Bob Biggs—the guy who built his company around The Germs, X, *Slash* magazine, Gun Club, etc—was definitely a cool thing, but only a small component,' Gould explains. 'The largest, single reason was distribution. We loved Mordam and Ruth Schwartz, but we also experienced touring across the country in tough conditions, learning that our record was not easy to find anywhere. We needed that support, and the Slash route seemed like a good path to take in that regard.'

Bordin: 'Anna took a chance on us and put her money where her mouth was. Anna was saying, I believe in this band and I think we should sign them and I think we should invest our money. And if the band fails, she's probably going to get fired.'

The band also had no punk-attitude qualms about Slash's tie-up with Warner Bros. 'It was an enticement, because it was built-in promotion within the companies,' Bordin adds. 'If you do well enough or there's enough interest, you can go straight across the hall to Warner Bros. Then, all of a sudden, you have their staff, you have their distribution, you have everything at your disposal from them.'

Gould: 'Technically, we considered Slash an indie. I loved the people who worked there—they were accessible and behind us. There's always been an "indie equals good, major equals bad" prejudice in music, but, at the same time, I always thought that our music was unique and universal enough to operate successfully within a major apparatus, given the right team. We did have a choice, but we chose to take our chances and see if we could do some real damage.'

In May 1986, Faith No More—after some further complications—signed a standard minimum five-album deal with Slash, with the label retaining the exclusive right to drop the band before that. 'We just didn't have any choice,' Bordin adds. 'We didn't have any other options. It was just that simple. Whether it was a good choice or a good deal or bad deal, we were a new artist, and a new artist generally got nothing. I wasn't going to think about that, because I couldn't control it.'

An article in *BAM* magazine on October 31 1986 carried the news and more: 'Faith No More have officially signed with Slash and will begin recording their second LP in November. Among the producers being considered are Ted Templeman (Van Halen, the new Cure LP), Bob Nusso (PiL, Big Country), Gene Simmons (the KISS dude) and local whiz Snakefinger.'

Slash was keen for Steve Berlin, multi-instrumentalist with the label's most successful band of the time, Los Lobos, to produce. Philadelphia-born Berlin had been saxophonist with The Blasters, moving into production as co-producer on the Los Lobos EP ... *And A Time To Dance* before becoming a full-time band member. He was keen to return to production, should the opportunity arise:

I used to just hang around the Slash office, because it was a fun place to be in those days. I remember Bob Biggs mentioning Faith No More as a band they were considering, and I flipped out over the demo, so I think my enthusiasm about it enhanced my portfolio for the job. It was life-altering to hear that music before almost anyone else.

Even in an era when there was so much amazing music everywhere, they clearly stood out. It just seemed to be more developed and evolved in a way that was just really unusual for that moment. I'd heard a demo first, I still have the cassette with Mike's scrawl, 'FnM FoR StEvE'. I heard the Mordam record later, but it was the cassette that rang my bell. Bob then said they would fly me to San Francisco to meet with their managers to talk about it first. It just happened after that. I was pretty green in those days, having produced all of about three records prior to that.

Berlin was also soon aware that the band would, as ever, have significant input into the record's production in any case—especially their musical alchemist, Bill Gould. 'He is just a super smart and curious guy,' he continues, 'so it wasn't as if he was manning the controls, but he was certainly interested in what and how things were being captured. None of us had much of a track record at that point, so it wasn't like Matt and certainly I had a bunch of hit-making experience to impart. We all just knew we had something super-special and cool, so lets not fuck it up—not that they would have allowed that to happen.'

Slash did have an eye on making a hit—or, at least, remaking one—when the band turned up to record at Studio D in Sausalito, a few miles north of the city over the Golden Gate Bridge, in July 1987. Part of the band's deal specified that their breakout track, 'We Care A Lot', would be re-recorded. 'We Care A Lot' had become a minor hit on college radio, and, in testament to the band's appeal beyond the rock demographic, in dance clubs and among DJs. In June 1986, the *San Francisco Chronicle* reported, 'Even major commercial rock stations in the Boston (WBCN) and Washington, D.C. (WHFS) markets are playing the title song from the San Francisco band's first album, *We Care A Lot*. But a far more intriguing crossover is occurring, courtesy of Bay Area club DJs. With its lumbering, deliberate beat, staccato guitar riff and a sarcastic vocal delivery reminiscent of Run-DMC's hard-rock rap music, "We Care A Lot" actually is becoming a dance floor hit.'

Chuck Mosley: 'Slash felt it hadn't fallen on enough ears. They thought it was a hit. Hence the second version. There were two years between the two versions, and we updated the lyrics. I had a habit of ripping off parts of songs—including my own. It made sense to have a second version, where we were biting off of our own song.'

The lyrical changes to the reboot were more or less a straightforward update for topicality, although replacing 'freaks' with 'geeks' was a more arbitrary, editorial alteration. New lyrics included the addition of '*NASA shuttle falling in the sea*', Madonna and Mr T. dropped in favour of *Transformers*, and '*Cabbage Patch, The Smurfs, and DMC*' deferring to the Garbage Pail Kids.

'They wanted to smooth it out,' Mike Bordin explains. 'I was told, "The DJs when they're going to be cutting your songs, live mixing, two snare hits that flam [like in the original version], they can't cut it. So it has got to be one snare hit." And that was one of the very few things we let an outside force drive.'

Gould, meanwhile, had heard that the label wanted the record to sound better. 'Maybe they talked to us in the language they thought each of us could understand. They said, "We want to re-record it. We want to own the recording." I guess the Mordam version—we were all happy with how it sounded, but on the level that Slash was looking, it probably could have been recorded better. The production could have been improved, which, when you hear the two back to back, you can see that. I don't think anyone had great objections having to do it. It was just something you had to do. It's a tug of war. You pick your battles and you try to maximise what you can.'

'I can understand it,' Bordin adds, 'because we already did it the other way, why would you do it exactly the same way? And honestly, the song did get a ton of spins in fucking discos everywhere.'

The band were willing to both embrace the dance floor and not reactively recoil from commercial considerations. Right from the start, Faith No More were unambiguous in their attitude to selling records and selling out. A band exchange in a 1986 interview with the *Your Flesh* zine summed up this early ethos:

> BILL: There's no such thing as selling out, because if you're doing something yourself, it's real easy. It's like people have

a fear to develop and if anybody else develops they like to put a label like 'selling out' on them because they're reinventing themselves.

CHUCK: Selling out is when you work hard enough to get famous. For me, selling out has been doing other jobs that I hate and getting paid for it.

JIM: That fucking regular guy who goes and gets a job is selling out.

This was a practical consideration for the band members. The tour had seen them break decisively with being that regular guy, and they often found themselves living hand-to-mouth on the road. So, while a potentially more lucrative life had been left behind for the sake of music, they were not choosing music and penury on principle.

They could even joke, as Chuck did in that interview, 'Our main goal is to have our original fans call us sell-outs in the near future.'

THE MAKING OF

INTRODUCE YOURSELF

12

With 'We Care A Lot' revamped, there was little chance that anyone would be alienated by a sell-out follow-up. 'Nobody really knew what the fuck we were doing,' Bordin explains, 'so how's somebody going to tell us what we're supposed to do?'

Armed with a $50,000 budget, Faith No More had much more time to prepare. They again went into the studio with their own vision. Despite the reboot of its title track, they were keen to avoid making *We Care A Lot*

Take Two, and the band had written, arranged, demoed, and rehearsed every track before they entered Studio D. They also had an extra pair of ears and the expertise of Steve Berlin. 'Slash trusted him,' Bordin adds. 'He was an excellent go-between for a first-time unknown bunch of knuckleheads, and he kept the business people off our back. He was very helpful.'

Matt Wallace was also back on board, as Berlin recalls. 'I had only heard that there was an engineer attached to the project that the band was close to. I didn't get the specifics until I hung out with Matt a little later, and, then, in the first rehearsals, I realised he had done so much groundwork.'

'Steve was in a no-win situation,' Wallace explains. 'I think he was brought in as insurance that we made a record, and that we didn't just spend it on drugs and women, which we were never going to do anyway. We were too driven for that. I think it must have been a difficult situation for him, because he's obviously really talented. He's got great ears, but the kind of music that he was working at was more like The Blasters and Los Lobos. He was a saxophonist, so it was just a different aesthetic. I don't think there was anybody who could have given us input, because we were so insular. After a time, I think he finally gave up and hung out and babysat us.'

'They seemed to have a process that resisted input from anywhere, really,' says Berlin, 'including Bob Biggs. Matt was there from the conception, so it was his ideas along with theirs that were already baked in. I just recall throwing a few things at them that they tried somewhat half-heartedly, and went back to what they wanted to do. I realised that their process was like forging a knife blade. They'd hammer and hammer until it was sharp, so it was initially daunting, and, then ultimately, futile to hit them with a lot of my ideas.'

Berlin remains good friends with members of the band, and there was no deep-seated resentment. The Los Lobos man even had the good grace to give Wallace a production credit, which Wallace appreciates to this day: 'I will forever be indebted to Steve for sharing the production credit, because he easily could have kept the entire credit and credited me solely as engineer. He was a good guy with his heart in the right place, and was already a talented producer in his own right.'

❦

The one older track on the album is 'Spirit', a rudimentary version of which the band played at their first show, with Joe Callahan from the Pop-O-Pies on vocals. It was also known as 'The Words Of Jamal', and appeared under that title on the Pop-O-Pies' *Joe's Second Record* (which featured Bordin, Bottum, and Gould as instrumentalists) in 1984. Some of the words from that earlier version remain in the opening refrain; the rest, all slithering beats and crushing guitar, was written by Gould.

Mike Bordin was the inspiration for 'Chinese Arithmetic', a song conceived in the band's refuge in Atlanta's Metroplex the previous year. It is the perfect encapsulation of mid-1980s Faith No More: martial drumming, percussive guitar, eldritch keyboards, bombinating bass, and crooned and rapped vocals, with lyrics equal parts silly and sapient.

'I wrote it on the stage at the Metroplex,' Bordin explains, 'just one afternoon when there was no show. My drums were up, and I started playing that intro to it. I just started playing the drum beat because it sounded so good there. It was a room like the On Broadway, like a miniature Brixton Academy, with a little balcony and a high roof, and naturally sounds big. There's natural ambiance—stuff like rims and clicking aren't lost. It's got every element of Faith No More.'

Those elements included a fair amount of the puerile and flippant, such as in the song title. Mosley: 'The title "Chinese Arithmetic" was born when my friend George used the phrase to describe how hard a certain body part was, and I thought, *How wonderful a description.* I decided then and there that that would be the title of the very next song that needed one. It just so happened that it fits the lyrics and subject matter of that particular song to a tee.'

While the rest of the band honed their playing to perfection, Mosley was happy to leave his singing for the stage and studio. The Mosley factor was something that outside producer Berlin noticed straight away:

> Chuck was very clearly in the throes of a serious psychiatric malady, which was initially indistinguishable from the way a lot of my friends and fellow musicians behaved really, but, as we went along, it was clear he was wrestling with some major demons. The casual level of drink and drugs around—which was never much with these guys—would sometimes just send

him off into a fit. He didn't direct all of it at me, but the times he did were pretty terrifying, but then the next day it would be as if nothing had happened. Much of the time he seemed to be as dedicated as the rest of the guys, but, as the record went along, he seemed to be pulling away—like he was afraid of what it could become.

'We were trying to strongly evolve, and strongly move forward,' Bordin adds, 'and I'm not so sure that Chuck was there.'

'Everyone was on my case,' Chuck later recalled. 'I was a crabby person at the time. Everyone acted accordingly. When a young band starts to get major attention, money is thrown—not at them, but in their direction.'

Chuck's absences were such that Wallace and Berlin were not able to capture all vocal tracks at Sausalito, and they had to be finished along with the later overdubbing in Los Angeles of an extra five sessions of vocal work. The problems between Berlin and Mosley were compounded by the fact that they both had the same girlfriend at the time. 'That was a little weird, to say the least,' Berlin explains, 'but she wasn't the root of any of the issues with Chuck—it was all the thunderstorms in his head.'

Those thunderstorms could occasionally subside to allow moments of musical sunshine. Mosley hit his lyrical and vocal peak on 'The Crab Song', probably the most personal and romantic song in the Faith No More canon. The song was another joint effort by Gould and Bordin, and it dated from when Jim Martin joined the band. The early live versions were skeletal compared to the muscle-bound stomper it became when recorded in Studio D. Lyrically, Mosley evokes every emotion in a doomed relationship arc: love, yearning, frustration, anger, hatred, and regret. Or as Chuck himself put it, 'Getting broken up with, thus turning from a sad little love monkey into a raging psychopathic, blood-lusting, sociopath of a serial killer, inflicting the pain in your heart upon everyone who has the misfortune of crossing your path. Then, turning back into a sad little love chimp regretful of what you've done.'

'Chuck had one of his finest moments there,' says Bordin. 'It's aggressive in the right parts, and croony in the right parts.'

The song was also the sound of the band coming together with Jim

Martin. Gould: 'Mike and Roddy and I wrote that song without a guitar. It was the early days when Jim first joined the band, and we had to work how Jim would fit in. He had the chords—that part he got really good. Technically speaking, Jim was a really good guitar player. He had great tone, and he had a great ear. Even if we gave him ideas, he took them and did very good work with them. But the riff here, Puffy actually wrote that riff, and Jim played it.'

'I liked the way he took that riff and embellished it and messed around with it a little bit,' Bordin adds.

As on *We Care A Lot*, Martin busied himself in the studio in an almost quixotic search to find the perfect tone. Steve Berlin sympathised with his place in the band. 'The way the songs were put together limited the scope of what was expected from the guitar parts, and not a lot of guys can do that without getting frustrated,' he says. 'I loved what Jim did, but it didn't seem like the rest of the guys were ever open to new ideas on the guitar parts from anybody. They wanted the guitars to sound like a giant steamroller. I don't recall any solos that weren't studiously composed like everything else. Jim was a team player for the most part, though. Even when the other guys shot his ideas down, he just went back to doing what they rehearsed.'

Martin was allowed one notable solo on the otherwise Gould-and-Mosley-penned 'Anne's Song'. It existed as a rough-and-ready demo for several months, but was perfected and polished beyond all recognition in the studio. 'It just didn't work right,' Mike Bordin explains, 'and we just kept playing it and playing it and, finally, the snare beat smoothed out. We always thought it would sound good on the radio.'

The best pop music is about vulnerability and about communality; but the very best expresses swagger and exclusion. 'Anne's Song' is the sound of the party you're not invited to, the too-cool club you can't get into. Typically for Faith No More, it was only when they were at their most pop that they allowed an unabashed guitar solo to intrude. The original demo contains a guitar interlude, played by Gould, but the solo here is all Martin. It was hotly debated. After hearing the demo, Martin told the rest of the band that he wanted to write a solo for it, later playing his bandmates an updated demo at a band meeting. 'He had this three-part solo that sounded like Iron Maiden,' Gould recalls.

When he played it, Bordin immediately interrupted, shouting, 'That's not going on. That's off. That's forbidden.' Gould's reaction was a slightly less shocked 'What the fuck!' that softened eventually to, 'Well, it sounds like Jim, put it on.' Thus, one of the few solos in the Faith No More canon was committed to tape.

The eponymous Anne was New Yorker Anne D'Angillo, a friend of the band whose Big Apple base provided a home from home while they were on tour. The song was based on one night in Anne's apartment, and all the names mentioned in the song are those of her friends. She first heard a demo version of the song between Christmas and New Year's Eve in 1986. 'I loved it because all my friends are in it too,' she says, 'but I love other songs on that album more, musically speaking.'

If 'Anne's Song' sounded effortless but was not, another song, 'R n' R', took even longer in the studio. 'That song we worked on for so long,' Bordin explains. 'Different parts, different speeds, different patterns. I never felt like we really nailed it.' Gould adds, 'It could have been more pile driving, and we never quite got it to slam the way we wanted it to.'

'Death March' was another song that the band had worked on for more than a year, but Mosley's spoken-word introduction was opportunistically recorded, and it captures their early spirit. The intro rant was actually taped at the second set of sessions in LA. The catalyst was Chuck again showing up for the session intoxicated, and not in a fit state to sing. Gould: 'He was just wasted and wouldn't stop talking. We turned on the tape. There's about thirty minutes of it. I was so pissed off at him—we all were—so we put it on the record just to piss him off. Chuck got real mad, but that was our way of fighting back.'

The rant is accompanied by Jim Martin on congas, though it is his guitar riff that elevates the song. The riff mimics the Black Plague nursery rhyme 'Ring A Ring O' Rosie' to such an extent that Matt Wallace suggested that Mosley sing some lines from it in the song.

Roddy Bottum's melodies continued to be the genesis of many of the album's tracks, and his subtle tones underpinned the rest. 'Faster Disco' is where his still gothic touches coalesce most perfectly with Martin's choppy guitar and the downbeat from Bordin and Gould. Steve Berlin recalls, 'Roddy's parts were so integral to what made Faith No More special—they were just so beautiful and melodic all the time. It was that contrast between this brutal kill-the-hostages approach in the rhythm section and Roddy's incredible melodicism that defined them, and he really understood synthesizers—he crafted those sounds like a sculptor.'

The song was initially written by Gould on acoustic guitar, but it only came together in the studio, as Bordin explains. 'That was the sound of the future. It still had strong rhythm, and it still had a jagged, powerful underpinning, but there was a good melody to it.'

Or, as Bottum himself, put it, 'We fancied our songs as danceable. I remember wanting it to sound like Simple Minds.'

A sister to the title track, 'Introduce Yourself' had Roddy's distinctive call-and-response lyrical trademark. Unknowingly foresighted in introducing the whole band except Chuck Mosley, the song captures the band's youthful swagger. Roddy wrote it on the band's first nationwide tour months before. They were driving from Wall, South Dakota—from where Roddy's maternal grandparents had migrated, half a century previously—to Portland, Oregon, and were going through Missoula, Montana, when, after a truck stop for coffee, Roddy was inspired to write what he called a 'cheerleader song'. He jotted down the lyrics during the next leg of the journey, while sitting in the passenger seat of the Dodge, with Gould driving alongside.

In contrast to that snotty, ninety-second track, 'Blood' shows off the band's gothic side to its truest extent. It is another song that displays Bordin's accomplished playing style. Steve Berlin recalls, 'Besides being one of the hardest hitters I've ever seen, Mike innately understands where things should go to achieve maximum momentum from his parts. He was interested in making the whole engine go—how all the parts interact, and not just his own. He was so consistent—everybody wears down over the course of a twelve- to fourteen-hour session—but I remember Matt pointing to the meters on the snare channel, and noting that the levels hadn't changed a micron from beginning to end every day.'

Toward the end of the studio session, Berlin heard the band playing a distinctive chord sequence, and quickly interjected, 'Wait what's that one? Can we work on that?' He was shot down by Bill Gould: 'Nope—it's not ready yet.' According to Berlin, the band were working on what would become 'Epic', though Gould and Bordin recall that it was more likely a similar-sounding riff.

'I honestly doubt it would have been a hit without Patton's contribution,' Berlin reflects, 'but I would have loved to hear Chuck's take on it.' More generally, he adds, 'There were bit and pieces of what would become later hits in the demos they shared, but they kept saying that they weren't ready yet. Even as effectively a baby band, they had a deep process they were fully invested in and committed to, which was impressive to see, even as it was frustrating for me to not get my hands on some of these ideas.

'What was unique was this almost military ethos they developed—pretty much every other band I went on to work with had a concept of themselves that allowed some sunlight and openness in, when merited. Faith No More went about their business like Navy SEALs—like they had a mission to complete.'

After the six-day session for *We Care A Lot*, Faith No More had more time to complete their *Introduce Yourself* mission. Rehearsals and initial tracking took place at Prairie Sun, and despite the time at their disposal, all the instruments were tracked in little over a week, with mixing taking another week. Then they decamped to Los Angeles for overdubbing, and those extra Chuck vocal sessions at the Ground Control studios in Santa Monica in late summer. Wallace, Gould, and Martin stayed at the Tropicana motel, which was cheap but characterful, and something of a magnet for musicians, with Iggy Pop and Alice Cooper among its regular visitors. It was demolished later in 1987, and Faith No More played their part in getting that process started during their stay. With Gould as ringleader, the band shorted the hotel's electrics and exploded a television by pouring water inside the cabinet. The antics were hardly Mötley Crüe *The Dirt*-level debauchery, but the band were cutting loose.

Otherwise, the band got their work done in LA. The record was finished, with only two weeks of mixing left back at Studio D. But Slash had reservations with the final sound. Wallace recalls, 'I remember Anna Statman being supportive and on board with all of *Introduce Yourself*, and it was only just after I'd had the album mastered, that she said that it didn't sound good. Maybe it was too polished for her tastes.'

The rebuke was a stinging one for Wallace. 'I love Anna, and honestly think that she had one of the best sets of ears in the Los Angeles recording industry. She was onto Green River before they morphed into Mother Love Bone, and then Pearl Jam. She was into Soundgarden well before other folks.'

Statman also advised on sequencing and, while it is not completely front-loaded, the album's more melodic and groovier tracks—'Faster Disco', 'Anne's Song', 'We Care A Lot'—were up front, with the moodier, gothic tracks 'Blood' and 'Spirit' at the end of the record.

The band got their first introduction to the concept of record industry control in what was the first of many disputes over album imagery. 'The cover was a compromise,' says Gould. 'Slash asked what we were going to do, and I said, "Why don't you just get some big thing splattered against the wall? That's like our music—just a big splatter." Like a bird or something that crashed into the wall with the blood dripping down.'

Label president and artist Bob Biggs worked with Gould on the concept, but Gould was not happy with the final outcome. 'When I saw it, I said, "Bob, it's green. I wanted a red one,"' he recalls. 'And he said, "That's so obvious. It's so trite." I was telling everyone, "That's not what I wanted to do." But now I think a red blood splatter is pretty simple-minded. In retrospect, it was a good call.'

◆

The band spent the interregnum between recording and release with another series of dates in the autumn of 1986, a short tour that also included their first show outside the United States. That show, at the Town Pump in Vancouver on October 6, provided a taste of the future, as the band were without Chuck Mosley, not allowed entry into Canada due to an undeclared driving-under-the-influence offence. The set was largely instrumental, though Jim—not Bill or Roddy—stepped up to sing on a couple of songs. Another glimpse of the future was the band's pairing with Soundgarden for the show—the first of many times over three decades when the groups would share the same bill.

They really went back to the future two days previously—on October 4—when they played at Humboldt State University Depot in Arcata. Future members Mike Patton and Trey Spruance were at the show, and they met Jim Martin and Mike Bordin afterward, handing over a demo tape of their Mr Bungle band that would, less than two years later, lead to the fresh-faced Patton replacing Mosley.

Introduce Yourself was officially released on April 23. The band played a low-key launch party a few days before at the Scream in Hollywood, but it was the follow-up industry launch event on May 16 at Los Angeles's Club Lingerie that showcased the band's fractious and fascinating future.

13

STARTING FROM
SCRATCH

Faith No More had direction and, soon after *Introduce Yourself* was recorded, they acquired career direction. In a sign that they were firmly moving away from the 'friends and family' approach that had marked their early years, the band dispensed with the services of their managers, Olga and Gerry Gerrard. Some of the band felt that they had gotten a bad deal with Slash, though the deal they did sign was typical of most new bands at the time; others felt that the Gerrards were booking them the wrong shows, putting them on the wrong bills.

The ties between the band members and the Gerrards were close. Bill Gould was actually sleeping on their sofa when the professional rupture began in May 1987, and Olga was the sister of the band's kindred spirit, Will Carpmill. Gerry Gerrard would go onto to become one of the leading electronic dance music agents of the 1990s and 2000s, working with Nine Inch Nails, The Prodigy, Chemical Brothers, and Daft Punk.

Mike Bordin: 'It just had run its course, no question. They knew the early electronic scene. And we were not making any headway in that world. We were never going be Depeche Mode. I remember they got us a gig with Cabaret Voltaire. It was interesting, but it definitely wasn't where we were headed.'

Bill Gould was closer to the disintegrating relationship:

> We were in discussions to sign with Slash, and things just went very quickly. We would ask Cliff Burton advice, because he already had a record deal. The deal with the Gerrards was actually a boilerplate management contract—we didn't know that then. And so Cliff would say something like, 'They want a percentage of your publishing on this.' And he said, 'Anybody who'd even ask that is a thief, and you should tell them to go do their business elsewhere.' They were his exact words. And in our naïveté we were like, 'Holy shit, these guys are trying to steal from us.'

The band acted on that advice, and a meeting was held at the Gerrards' to resolve the matter.

> We told them, 'We like Slash and we're going to sign this deal, but we're not going to give you our publishing.' And we were really defensive about it. Looking back, I think they overacted. They said, 'Get the fuck out of my house.' Kirk Hammett's brother was there when it happened. We just went for a regular band meeting, and he was there to take some photos of us afterward, and we all got tossed out of the house.
>
> They had been negotiating the Slash contract, so I went down to LA to try to make sense out of all that shit because we didn't have a manager, so I became the manager. And Slash said that the record deal is stopped; until you get a manager, there is no record offer. Boom, they put the brakes on.

Things escalated quickly. 'The Gerrards then sued us for breach of contract. We did a show at the Mab where we got served with papers. We were getting

RIGHT Sharp Young Men: Mike Bordin, Bill Gould, M. Morris, and a friend of the band, the late Eric Scott, hang out in the kitchen of Wade Worthington's parents' house in late 1981. This is the earliest known photo from the Sharp Young Men days. *Courtesy Wade Worthington.*

ABOVE Bordin, Morris, and Gould prior to the Faith. No Man gig (supporting Red Kross) at the Valencia Tool & Die in February 1983. Bordin had been attacked outside the venue while unloading the van, and the bespectacled Tim, a friend of Gould's, had come to his aid. *Courtesy Wade Worthington.* **RIGHT** Bill Gould in 1983: 'This little scrawny kid from LA, who had a really funny punk rock haircut,' was Mike Bordin's first impression. *Photo by Anna, courtesy Wade Worthington.*

RIGHT Gould and Morris onstage at the On Broadway in February 1983. *Courtesy Wade Worthington.*
BELOW A flyer for the band's first concert as Faith No More, billed as a one-off show. Bottum and Gould made the band's early posters. The quotation from Last Poets reflects Gould and Bordin's tastes at the time. *Courtesy Faith No More.*

FAITH.NO MORE.

SPECIAL ONE-TIME PERFORMANCE

FRIDAY, OCT. 7
at the ON BROADWAY
10pm SHARP!

"... and when it came time for the END,
The men will look like the women,
and the women like the men.
And some will DANCE in hypnotic trance
As if they had no care,
But there are signs of the changing times
That the end is drawing near."

— LAST POETS

RIGHT Wade Worthington at the Valencia Tool & Die, February 1983. *Photo by Anna, courtesy Wade Worthington.* **OPPOSITE** Bill Gould onstage at the Mabuhay Gardens in 1984. The ball gown belonged to Courtney Love, who was also onstage that night. Gould: 'It fit me better than her.' *Photo by Joan Osato, courtesy Bill Gould/Faith No More.*

INDEPENDENT PROJECT RECORDS

POSTBOX 60357 LOS ANGELES CALIFORNIA 90060 USA

9 October 1984.

Bill,

I've finally had a chance to really listen to the two FAITH NO MORE cassettes you sent me and I wanted to drop you a note to let you know my
thoughts. I had listened to part of one of the tapes before I left for
the month of September and had not really been able to formulate an opinion then. I appreciate your patience in hearing back from me.

I'd have to say that of all the material on the two tapes I found the live
at On Broadway stuff the most interesting, in the sense that I would want
to return to it to listen again and again. The instrumental that begins
the side is particularly powerful and you are right -- you have created a
definite SOUND that is quite good. At the point of the recording, however, the one part that needs the most work, and I say this at the risk
of offending one of you, though please realize that it is meant positively,
is the singing. I find myself almost wishing that the songs were instrumental, though perhaps that reflects the fact that that is mostly what I'm
interested in listening to these days -- sound tracks to films, etc. Some
of your material would make very good soundtracks -- the first instrumental, and perhaps you could think of moving in that direction if it interests you. This is not to say that vocals don't fit, as that is not the
case -- I just think that if your vocalist could work on what he does --
and could develop his "singing", that your music would ultimately be more
powerful and satisfying. Your music demands more than a sort of postpunk
shout and if your vocalist could work on experimenting with his voice a
bit he might come up with something quite interesting. An d vocals don't
have to mean lyrics, either. Something we'll be experimenting more with
in SR is using the voice as another instrument rather than a soap box.
There are some real exciting possibilities.

So thanks again for letting me know what you are up to. Best of luck
with the recording, and please let me know when you are playing locally.
I'd like to come see you perform. Take care,

BRUCE LICHER
IPR.

ABOVE Faith No More before a show at the Mabuhay Gardens in 1984: Bottum, Gould, Bordin, Mosley, and Mark Bowen. *Courtesy Bill Gould/Faith No More.*
LEFT Blond ambition: Bowen and Gould onstage at the On Broadway. *Courtesy Bill Gould/Faith No More.* **OPPOSITE** A rejection letter from Bruce Licher's IPR label, including some constructive criticism. *Courtesy Bill Gould/Faith No More.*

ABOVE One of the first promotional shots of the *We Care A Lot/Introduce Yourself* line-up, taken days after Jim Martin joined the band. *Photo by Joan Osato, courtesy Bill Gould/ Faith No More.* **RIGHT** Faith No More play the Hare Krishna Festival in San Francisco, September 1985. *Courtesy Mike Bordin/Faith No More.*

LEFT Bill Gould and Chuck Mosley, as Faith No More kick off their first nationwide tour with a show at the Stardust Ballroom in February 1986. *Courtesy Bill Gould/Faith No More.* **BELOW** Faith No More at the Badlands National Park, during a stop-off on their 1986 tour. *Courtesy Mike Bordin/Faith No More.*

ABOVE AND LEFT Faith No More record their debut album in two weekend sessions in 1985: Jim Martin amuses his bandmates on the piano; Chuck Mosley, three decades ahead of fashion trends, in his ripped T-shirt; the band in the studio with producer Matt Wallace; an angelic Bottum, Gould, and Bordin. *Courtesy Bill Gould/ Faith No More.*

FAITH NO MORE

WE CARE A LOT

sued for $1.2 million. It was probably put there to intimidate us, and it did. We were freaking out.'

Anna Statman came to the rescue, offering Gould office space and a phone at Slash, and a list of managers to cold call. Gould spent three weeks in LA 'calling everyone under the fucking sun', and even made house calls. One such visit took him to Beverly Hills, where he found a middle-aged man sunning himself poolside. Unperturbed, Gould made his pitch, and later that day, the sunbathing man called back. Warren Entner was interested in becoming Faith No More's manager.

Entner had been the dashing frontman and guitarist of the folk-rock group The Grass Roots, who had three US top 10 hit singles between 1967 and 1971. By 1987, he had his own self-titled artist management agency, working with John Vassiliou, and had helped steer Quiet Riot through the Randy Rhoades era and onto the foundation of the hair-metal 80s with their #1 album *Metal Health* in 1983.

'It was a little odd for us,' says Bordin, 'because the bands that he was dealing with at the time were like Quiet Riot and Faster Pussycat. But then again, there weren't a whole lot of options. Warren learned the management game working with Tony Defries, who managed David Bowie for a long time. He'd been around. He knew lots and lots of people in Los Angeles. Nobody seemed to really hate him.'

Entner and Vassiliou had also been recommended to Anna Statman by Slash publicist Grace Ensenat, whose sister Teresa was an A&R rep with Geffen Records. Vassiliou has a slightly different version of how they became Faith No More's managers:

Anna Statman sent over a cassette which sat on Warren's desk forever. She started calling twice a day, and one Friday as I was leaving, Warren asked me to listen to it over the weekend. It took me almost an hour to get home. I cranked it up in my truck, and was struck by Jim's guitar playing and Roddy's keyboard contrast. They painted a pretty picture playing together. I felt the rhythm section was strong, and not all the songs sounded the same, plus they had a song with my wife's name in it. Being Greek, I took that as a sign. Monday driving in, I felt the same way. I listened to a lot of demos that way over the years driving over Coldwater Canyon. I had to like it both times the same way, no ifs, ands, or buts. Warren spoke to Bob Biggs and [Slash executive] Mark Trilling, and they said they were committed to breaking the band, so we got involved.

Billy and Roddy both had a sense of business. We got a call from Billy and met both of them. They were intelligent and passionate about what they were creating, so it was a breath of fresh air. Warren met Chuck first, and I think he scared him. There was a uniqueness about them, and they were musically intriguing. We were concerned about Slash's commitment and how far they would go, but we knew the business was changing again, and we were willing to see it through. Chuck was an artist, Jim and Puffy had musicians' attitudes, but Roddy and Billy both had a sixth sense that we could relate to.

Vassiliou pays tribute to Grace Ensenat as the 'the conduit between success and the band fading into obscurity'. While obviously overplaying the role their astute management played in Faith No More's breakthrough, his words are a reminder that this success was no foregone conclusion. The band had more talent and certainly more drive and sense of purpose than most of their contemporaries, but they still needed to be seen and heard.

Bordin recalls that the band were impressed with Entner's opening gambit to them—'Look, you're going to have to work really hard, if you want to try to make this work'—and that set the tone for what would be a punishing career of road work and recording. By December 1987, Entner had secured Faith No More a slot in *Billboard* magazine, in which he said, 'The strategy is to get them out as much as we can because we want exposure to as many people as possible. Through touring you can really create a ground swell. By the time they come off the road, they will have done about 110 dates.'

Entner also helped categorise Faith No More—'I like to think the aim is a college audience, but they're not solely that type of band. Any kid who likes Metallica or even The Clash will like this band'—and stressed a long-term approach: 'The way to break an act has gotten so sophisticated and so expensive, but this reminds me of how the music industry used to be. If you like something, you stick with it and watch it develop into something. Faith No More is starting from scratch; the band has no reputation or hype to live up to.'

◆

The first of those 110 dates after the release of *Introduce Yourself* was a disastrous industry launch party at Club Lingerie in Los Angeles on May 16 1987. With the great and the good of the West Coast music industry—including representatives from Slash and Warner Bros and leading magazine and newspaper critics—in the audience, the band faced the prospect of playing their Saturday night showcase as an instrumental quartet. Chuck Mosley was in the midst of one of his occasional disappearing acts, having left the venue after the soundcheck. Tension was already high, with the band members' nerves at their most important performance rubbing off on each other. Chuck bolted. The band fretted. The great and the good waited. And waited. Mosley finally reappeared—in body, if not quite in mind—seconds before the band were due onstage. Whether due to nerves and stress, or self-medication to counter the nerves and stress, Chuck was far from his best. He was at his worst. He mumbled through songs. He rambled. He ambled across the stage. He feel asleep.

'It was one of those shows where it just starts out OK, and then just goes from bad to worse,' remembers Mike Bordin. 'Every song, worse and worse. It was a disaster. Especially when there's so much at stake, and you have so little already under your belt.'

Roddy Bottum took a completely different attitude. 'I don't really remember Chuck falling asleep. I remember people talking about it more than I remember it happening. Now that I look back on it, I can't believe how genius it was. What a memorable presence! Someone who actually fell asleep onstage. Amazing.'

The rest of the band, getting it in the ear from management about how they had blown their chance, tore into Mosley backstage afterward, as Gould recalls:

> Slash were totally behind us. We had this great record. We had
> got rid of our old managers. We made it through that, survived

the lawsuit, got the manager, got the booking agent [the band had hooked up with Red Hot Chili Peppers manager Tripp Brown on Anna Statman's recommendation]. And 'We Care A Lot' was already a known song. And this was the fucking show that was going to launch us out of the gate. *Spin* were there. *Rolling Stone* were there. All these people were there to see us. And Chuck got so drunk. This is the pattern that would repeat. The more things counted, the more he would blow it. He actually fell asleep onstage for two songs, and people left. We couldn't get anybody to write about us for about two years after that in America. It was like, 'This band sucks, forget it.'

We'd already been through a lifetime's worth of shit. And then to just blow it like that when you're finally getting what you're working for. I really had a hard time with it. I can be a very focused person. The band was my thing. It was my existence. I couldn't separate myself personality-wise from the band. If Chuck would do something like that, he was doing it to me. So it was like somebody ruining my life on purpose. He is a self-saboteur, like one of the best I've ever seen. And the most consistent I've ever seen. But, unfortunately, I didn't look at it like that, I took it personally. I was just, 'I don't care what he is, he's doing this to me. I want to get him back.'

Antagonising Gould further was Mosley's insouciant reaction afterward. 'It would go nowhere, because he would never even cop to what he did. He probably punished himself, but he always put on a cool front like we were the ones who didn't get it.'

Gould also felt that Slash and Warren Entner could have done more to address the Chuck problem. 'Anna [Statman] liked him. And he does have a natural charm about him. He's very childlike in a way. So she thought we gave him a really hard time. From where I was sitting, we weren't giving him a hard enough time.'

Entner did tell the band that they were blowing it, but they remained hands-off in their first few months with the band. Gould adds, 'I thought that if this is going to get fixed, we've got to fix it. Me and Bordin would take it upon ourselves. He's your singer. He's the guy with the mouthpiece. I mean, he's the only guy anybody cares about, right? So what enforcement was there? You just have to live with it or not.'

The band regrouped for a run of shows nationwide in May, June, and July. The jaunt included a return to the Metroplex in Atlanta, where they had briefly set up camp two years previously. The tour finished with another Steve Blush-arranged show at the Ritz in New York's East Village—a gig that got the band their first, very brief, mention in the *New York Times*.

✢

Slow progress was also being made on the airwaves. The *Gavin Report* music industry weekly noted in early May that *Introduce Yourself* was being played on college radio stations. On May 15, that airplay saw the band score their first national chart placing—a new entry at #30 on the *Gavin Report*'s Alternative Chart. By June 19, they had peaked at #13 on a chart that featured more conventional college rock acts Suzanne Vega, The Replacements, The Cure, Wire, and R.E.M. as its top five.

The band's first video for the 'We Care A Lot' single had also been recorded and released. Looking like the aftermath of simultaneous explosions in a paint factory and a charity clothes shop, the video, directed by Slash president Bob Biggs with Jay Brown, featured regular Faith No More video tropes of effulgent colours and lighting, cross-dressing, and lurid clothing. It also succeeded to some extent in showcasing the band's energy and 'gang of misfits' aesthetic. It was not widely picked up, but it debuted on MTV's weekly alternative music show *120 Minutes* on Sunday May 10, the final song in a four-song block alongside Suicidal Tendencies, Siouxsie & The Banshees, and Fuzzbox.

The band were getting significant local press attention in August and September as they warmed up for their end-of-year nationwide tour with the Red Hot Chili Peppers. Reviewing a show at the Scream club, the *Los Angeles Times* stated, 'Faith No More's snide "We Care A Lot" is as pungent and brilliant an anthem-for-a-generation as 1987 is likely to produce.'

The fractious five set out on their biggest tour to date in October: thirty-nine shows in sixty-seven days supporting the Chilis. Though the bands—or, to be completely accurate, Mr Bungle and the Peppers—later became embroiled in a bitter feud, here they were allies. Mosley felt a special affinity with the main act, and with Anthony Kiedis in particular, so he was on his best behaviour. With the tour finishing just six months before the death of Chilis guitarist Hillel Slovak from a heroin overdose in June 1988, it is unlikely to have been one of temperance and restraint.

While never matching the Chilis' appetite for self-destruction, the two bands partied together with no inkling of future friction. 'I never had an axe to grind,' says Bordin. 'I loved Jack Irons, and Hillel was in the band at that time, and he was a lot of fun. Also Anthony and Flea. I think Flea is one of the nicest people in the world.'

'I was arrested in Florida with Chuck and Joe ['Gandhi' Ventress, band roadie] for smoking pot in our van,' Bottum adds. 'It was out front of a frat house or something. That was the Chili Peppers' base audience at that time. People were being friendly to us, hoping that they'd get to meet Anthony. We had a really different audience and fans—theirs was a little more *dude* and ours were a little freakier. Looking at their success made me think that we'd attract people like that. It scared me. At that time, I hadn't realised there were as many weirdos out there as there were dudes.'

Travelling all over the country in a cramped Ryder truck exacerbated existing band tensions, however, and Martin and Mosley clashed onstage on occasion. The band let loose their frustrations in an interview with Neil Perry from UK magazine *Sounds* which took place in the bowels of the Metroplex—their third show at the Atlanta venue—midway through the tour, though it would not be published until the following year. There was Jim on Mike: 'Mike's a bitter little man.' Jim on Chuck: 'Chuck's pretty riled up all the time but he's like a poodle—highly strung.' Chuck on Roddy: 'Roddy has a high, high, high boiling point. They hold their anger in too much.' Chuck on Mike: 'He is bitter, he wants to bring you down into his doldrums.' Chuck on Bill: 'He wants to construct things, he wants discipline. He's funny and I really love him. He's perpetually tortured by demons.' The same interview also included this philosophical insight on touring life from Chuck: 'These rock stars who do coke for ten years, get shit-faced drunk every night, and still get up and play. They get called assholes but I call them supermen—I couldn't do it.'

'It was summertime in a truck that had no windows, except for the front passenger,' Gould recalls. 'We were all in the dark in the back, sweating in 100-degree heat. It was brutal. I remember coming back from that tour and talking about how musicians didn't have health insurance, and how unhealthy that was.'

The tour gave the band a glimpse of the next step in their evolution: headline status, lavish tour bus, fan adulation, and large venues. By the end of 1987, Faith No More were on the way up. The Chili Peppers support tour had ended triumphantly on home turf at the Fillmore. They were getting some press attention, and their status as college radio regulars was underlined when they featured in the *Gavin Report*'s 'Alternative Top 100' of 1987, with *Introduce Yourself* at #90, just ahead of Sinead O'Connor.

14 FURTHER DOWN THE ROAD

Faith No More were not going to be broken by college radio or by occasional press interest. As Warren Entner warned, the focus in 1988 would continue to be on hard work and heavy touring. A little over three weeks after their tour with Red Hot Chili Peppers ended, Faith No More embarked for London and their first shows outside North America. The tour started at Dingwalls, the former warehouse turned dance club turned rock venue.

Faith No More were in good company on their UK live debut, as Blondie had also made their British bow at the Camden venue in 1979. The band did not disappoint; their freshness, energy, vitality, stage presence, humour, and futuristic melding of genres and styles soon won over the 500 people in the cramped club. *Kerrang!* reported, 'Their rhythms are battered mercilessly before you and me. Chuck Mosley cannot sing. Fact of life. Around him the band look sloppy-tight with the nonchalance of the professional.'

'Joe forgot the key to the keyboard case back in the hotel,' Roddy Bottum remembers, 'and I had to take the Tube back by myself and get it. I'd never taken the Tube before. I was bald and wearing a white paper jump suit.'

The show was an industry showcase for the band. Representatives from London Records, the band's UK label—while Slash/Warners had US rights, in the rest of the world, the band's music was sold on a territory-by-territory basis—were in the audience along with bookers and media. Early momentum in the UK was not completely organic, with San Francisco-based British journalist and friend of the band Steffan Chirizi talking up the group to his UK music press peers at every opportunity.

Faith No More had already laid bare their infighting for media scrutiny in Neil Perry's *Sounds* interview, which was published on the eve of the tour, but they went even further in their first sit-down interview in the UK. Mat Smith from *Melody Maker* met with the whole band in a room in their London hotel, and joined them in the tour van for the trip to Sheffield's Leadmill. The band were in their element, putting all their dysfunction on full display: Mike Bordin's isolation from the rest of the band; the rest of the band's disquieting badgering, baiting, and almost out-and-out bullying of Bordin; Bordin and Jim Martin's mutual loathing (Smith reported that the rest of the band made sure that the pair were forced to room together on tour, so this disaffection could fester even more); Chuck Mosley's increasing anger; Gould's ovophobia; and Chuck and Jim's growing antipathy. Not content for their words to damn them, the interview also erupted into a fistfight.

'It was horrible,' Gould recalls. 'A drunken fight. Chuck had a meltdown.' But he had an epiphany: 'I woke up the next morning with this horrible hangover. But I went to the newsstand and got *Melody Maker*. It was amazing; it was hilarious. That's when I realised that attention could work for us.'

Their touring plans also got a helpful push elsewhere, as John Vassiliou recalls:

Derek Kemp from The Agency Group was a key player in

breaking the band. Without his involvement, I am not sure there would be a band today. When there is no money for rent and shows are sporadic—things can fall apart very quickly. He showed up at the office door one day uninvited. He was an English agent and a real character—a true English gentleman in the old-fashioned sense. He loved the band, and we could tell he was a fan of the music. He was committed to helping us break the band in the UK, Europe, and Scandinavia, and was instrumental in that happening. He got in the trenches and slugged it out for us, and we used our muscle to push it along. He got the band into European cities long before anyone knew of the band, and the saving grace was the band delivering great shows and making friends wherever they went.

Kemp had entrusted Tim Dalton, a young Yorkshire audio engineer, with the responsibility of looking after the band as tour manager and live sound mixer. The poor sound mentioned in the *Kerrang!* review might have been due to the four days' notice he was given. 'It was a crazy day as I drove down from my then home in Hull in an old Citroen, did the gig, and then drove home after the show,' he recalls. 'I'd played the *Introduce Yourself* cassette on the five-hour drive down to try and familiarise myself with the music. The show was much better than the album. By the encores, it was mental; hot, sweaty, and bodies all over the place. I was taken aback by this strange collection of people that shouldn't fit together. The band had a confident swagger, and sounded like nothing I'd previously heard.'

London Records also had more success than Slash and Warners in the USA in getting Faith No More on the airwaves and television screens nationally in the UK. 'We Care A Lot' was released as a single to radio on January 18, just four days before the Dingwalls show. Within a week, it had been added to the playlist of the UK's leading music radio station, BBC Radio 1. It was also picked up by the fledgling MTV Europe—getting regular play alongside Sinead O'Connor's 'Mandinka' and Tiffany's 'I Think We're Alone Now' in February—and the video also appeared on mainstream terrestrial television when it was featured on ITV's flagship music programme, *The Chart Show*, on Saturday February 20.

'There were big, big posters saying "We Care A Lot",' Roddy recalls. 'I was impressed with London's sense of graphics and presentation. They really thought we were odd, and they liked us a lot. We liked them too. Derek was really slow to unfold, and he was super-important to our success there.'

The band even got qualified approval from the doyen of the British music media, BBC radio music presenter and journalist John Peel, who reviewed the sixth show of the tour, at the Baths Hall in Scunthorpe, for the *Observer*. 'Faith No More have wrung such stuff as "iconoclastic", "chaotic power", and "playfulness" from the press department. All of this is apt, although I would not go so far as to claim that their songs "obliterate notions of naivety".' Peel also noted Chuck Mosley's 'studied insolence', 'Furry Freak' Jim Martin's impressive playing, and Mike Bordin steering the band with 'alarming ferocity'.

There was excitement and momentum and attention, but Faith No More played largely the university student-union and small-club circuit on their first tour. The band were travelling in a cramped Mercedes van and lugging their own gear to often-tiny venues. Tim Dalton recalls the band's show at the Stairways club in Birkenhead on the outskirts of Liverpool: 'It was a Friday night with a very drunk audience. Faith No More played late, so the audience was well primed by the time we played. There was probably a capacity crowd of 200 people in a tiny, tiny room, and the gig was amazing. Then, a late night getting gear out and driving through the Mersey Tunnel to a shitty hotel in Sefton Park with three to a room.'

The short tour ended on a high with a two-night residency at London's Marquee Club, just months before that incarnation of the landmark rock club was demolished. Extant audience recordings from the shows just about capture the chaotic energy, the more metallic sound the band then had live—Martin was allowed to cut loose with metal solos on 'Introduce Yourself'—and the band's refusal to give the audience what they want, as shown by their commitment to playing their regular cover of the Nestlé 'Sweet Dreams' commercial that was completely unfamiliar to a British audience. Also evident were some onstage exchanges between Chuck Mosley and Jim Martin, a harbinger of future clashes.

The feeling that the band's first blitz through the UK had been a success was reinforced when 'We Care A Lot' debuted in the official UK Singles

Chart at #71 on the same Sunday night as the Marquee finale. It would peak at #53 the following week.

Earlier in April, 'Anne's Song' had been released as a single, and a video had been produced a few months previously. Chuck Mosley had somehow persuaded the record label and director Tamra Davis that the video should be recorded in the New York apartment of the song's muse, his close friend Anne D'Agnillo, with extra scenes later shot in Los Angeles. The video is quite a faithful interpretation of the song lyrics, starring Anne and Chuck's friends, who were name-checked in the song as themselves. It captures the band's playfulness and youth, and gives a particular focus to Mosley.

Bill Gould: 'We had to do a video with that song. And Chuck says we have to do it in New York. He wanted a free trip to New York on the band. And he had to have Anne in the video. It was like he had a budget, and he blew it on hanging with Anne and buying drinks for everybody that weekend.'

Gould got a modicum of revenge when the rest of the video was filmed in LA. 'Chuck used to really bother me. Chuck and I probably were the most polar opposite of all in as far as he would just drive me nuts. Like anything I tried to do, every step forward, he'd take it a step back. I had an ulcer at twenty-two thanks to him. My dream for that video was that I wanted to get Chuck in a cage, from which he couldn't escape, and I could poke him with a stick. We put that in the video; they gave me my dream.'

As well as being a vivid video illustration of just how strained band relations were at that point—Mike Bordin and Jim Martin were also keen to poke Chuck in the video—the scene also allowed for an uncredited contribution from Metallica's James Hetfield, also poking Chuck in the cage.

Mosley's face might have been adorning the covers of *Sounds* and *Melody Maker*, but he was rapidly running out of chances. His relationships with Martin and, crucially, Gould had broken down completely. Mosley and Gould were now frequently coming to blows. One such altercation had even required police intervention. The previous November, the band were making their way through Kentucky, en route to supporting the Red Hot Chili Peppers in Louisville, when Chuck refused to leave a party.

Gould: 'We waited for like an hour and a half or two hours. When he finally got on the road, I was driving, and he threw a tantrum and got in a really bad mood. Somehow we got in this fight. He was hitting me and kicking at me while I was driving. The whole truck was wobbling and shaking. The police were called and surrounded the vehicle. And he ended up breaking one of his fingers when he hit the steering wheel by accident.'

There were more broken bones and more fights in transit during the band's stint in the UK. In the twenty-four hours between arriving in the UK and their debut show at Dingwalls, the band managed to get kicked out of their hotel, lose a roadie, and almost lose a guitarist through injury. Joe 'Gandhi' Ventress was the band's main instrument technician, and had been in the band Haircuts That Kill with Chuck, with whom he was very close. Gould: 'Something happened the night we got in. They went out for a drink that afternoon. I was a roommate with Joe, and he came in at eleven at night, with big bumps on his head, going, "You're giving me $5,000", drunk and raging. Then Jim comes up and says, "We're firing Gandhi. He's fired."'

Jim had driven Gandhi's head through the wall of the hotel bar after Ventress had become irate while the trio were having drinks with some *Kerrang!* journalists.

Manager John Vassiliou was quickly on the scene. 'Chuck had a big heart and picked the wrong side,' he recalls. 'We had flown in that day, and that night we got thrown out of the hotel at 4am. I gave the night manager my gold Amex card to personally pay for the damage, and he gave us until noon, when I promised we would be gone.'

'Meanwhile, that same night, Roddy and Chuck were roommates,' Gould adds, 'and, like idiots, they had some hash and called the front desk and asked them for some tinfoil. So the hotel called the police. We got kicked out.'

In the process of lodging Ventress's head in the stonework of the hotel, Martin had managed to break some bones in his hand. Gould: 'John [Vassiliou] was getting ready to quit the band, because he was at the hotel with us, and he was really upset. We had to go to a new hotel, the Columbia, late at night, the night we arrived, and Jim had a broken hand. Jim actually taped up his hand and did the shows. I don't know how he did it. It healed wrongly, and he had to have it re-broken. That's the thing I admired most of all the things he did. He did the tour, and he never complained about it, and it was amazing.'

The Columbia Hotel in affluent Bayswater, a former Red Cross Hospital during World War I, then an officers' club for the US Air Force, and the number-one destination in the 1980s for touring bands in London, would become Faith No More's home from home while on tour in the UK. Jim Martin took that literally, arranging for private hairdressing visits, and also running up a £1,500 bill on one occasion when most of his room's fixtures and fittings—including his bed—went out the window. He explained it away to an exasperated Tim Dalton as a chain reaction after he had spilled his curry.

Joe Ventress was sent home by the management, and his friend Chuck Mosley's irritation grew. The band made it through to the end of that first UK run, but matters turned violent once more back in California, in April, as the band were preparing for a show supporting Gould's idols, Public Image Ltd., in Pasadena.

Gould: 'I think the big thing that really did it with Chuck was me and him having an altercation at rehearsal. It was just because he showed up late and really stoned for rehearsal, and he, all of a sudden, wanted us to stop what we're doing to show us this song that he wanted us to learn. It was this really sloppy acoustic song. There's nothing for us to play on it. I was thinking, *This is enough.* I just watched him playing this thing, and I just snapped and attacked him. That was the end.'

It was not the end—yet. Gould—as he had done with Faith. No Man— quit the band, and, as in that instance, the rest of the band resigned in solidarity with him.

'I quit,' says Gould. 'Everybody decided that they were with me. So Chuck was out.'

But Chuck was not out—yet. 'Then we had a meeting at our managers,' Gould continues. 'Warren said, "You just got offered this tour in the UK. Things are really working, you can't quit the shows." So I called up Chuck and apologised, but by that time the damage was done.'

With Chuck in tow, Faith No More were back in Europe in May, making their debut on the continent at Amsterdam's Paradiso, with a show that saw them add T.Rex's 'Life's A Gas' and snippets of 'Norwegian Wood' and 'Stairway To Heaven' to their burgeoning repertoire of covers. Chuck would usually deliver the T.Rex cover solo, adorned with a gold wig, wearing little else, and strumming an acoustic guitar. Three dates in the Netherlands and Germany preceded a return to the UK, and to some of the same universities the band had played earlier in the year, such as Leeds, Glasgow, and Norwich.

Their return to Nottingham's Rock City for a second time (they would go on to play the Midlands venue ten times in total) received a rapturous review in *Sounds*. Neil Perry wrote, 'This gig was a proclamation, a forearm smash reminder that this ten-legged tragic-comedy from America is very possibly live rock's hottest exponent.'

That review is all the more remarkable, given that in the three May days between their final European show in Berlin and that UK opener, the band had again come apart at the seams. Confined spaces, heightened expectations, lingering resentment, and increased drugs consumption finally brought the band's antipathy with Chuck Mosley to a head.

There was a fistfight at a baggage carousel at Zurich airport—between the Dutch and German dates—between Martin and Mosley, the latter still smarting from the former's role in the sacking of his friend Ventress. If Chuck was annoyed that his friend had been kicked off the tour, the rest of the band were livid with Mosley after his disappearing acts, his onstage antics throughout the tour, and his trash-talking in interviews.

The final fights also came in transit, beginning on a cross-channel ferry between Europe and the UK. Again, Quaaludes were a contributory factor. The drug, generically known as methaqualone and colloquially known as 'disco biscuits', entered rock lore in the 1970s, with both David Bowie and Frank Zappa referencing it in song lyrics. The strong sedative produced a pronounced temporary high but, when taken to excess, could render the taker pretty much powerless. By 1984, reckless recreational use had seen it effectively criminalised in both the USA and the UK. When the band and entourage approached British customs on their way back from their European jaunt, the realisation that they had a large amount of the pills stashed in the tour van caused momentary panic, as Gould recalls:

> They were going to search all of the bags. We had to do all the pills. It was like ten in the morning, and we'd been driving all night—but we did them. As our bags were coming out, I was already pretty high. Chuck was, Jim was. I don't think Puffy was doing any. We made it through. They didn't find anything. Then when we were clear in England, one of the crew guys pulled out a bottle of Jack Daniels and started passing it around the van. So we started getting really fucked up.
>
> By the time we got to the hotel, Chuck was on a tirade about something about LA. Then he started going on about how he hates us, and how he hates this band. I said I had already gone through this before, and just wanted to get through the tour. I said, 'Let's make a deal. After this tour you can leave, and we're all going to be happy.' Then he said, 'Fine, no problem,' and I started to feel better about it.

But just as the band had temporarily made up and were ready to sleep off their dose of downers, manager John Vassillou interjected, 'We have a photo session with *Kerrang!* at noon in the lobby,' which garnered a collective gasp of 'Ah, fuck' from the band and crew.

'We all came to the photo session—except Chuck—who wasn't coming down the stairs,' Gould continues. 'It turns out that he was on the phone with his girlfriend for two hours. He spent $200 on a phone call. He was pissed. When he came downstairs, Jim made some smart-ass remark to him.

Chuck just ran at him, and attacked him. Jim was on the floor trying to protect his hand, and Chuck was on top of him trying to get to his hand. I got on top of Chuck, and I was kicking him and holding him with two hands. The whole hotel went crazy; everybody was freaking out.'

'Billy and I pulled them apart,' John Vassiliou recalls, 'but I had to kick Chuck a few times in the ribs so he would let go. Jim had pulled out some of Chuck's dreads, and I hung them from the rear view mirror for the rest of the tour.'

Vassiliou was able to get the band in a fit state to continue the tour. But the last date—a May 24 show at London's Town and Country club—would be Chuck's last show with the band. He went out in appropriate style, opting to do much of the gig while hidden behind the stage curtains.

Rock journalist Mick Wall would remember the show as one that saw Mosley go out on a high. 'They started the way most bands started their encores, with the place already insane, the band already much higher,' he later wrote. 'And they just kept climbing. For the real encores, Chuck came on in a gold tinsel wig, alone, just him and an acoustic guitar—they'd been fighting backstage, didn't want him to do it—to sing "Life's A Gas" by T.Rex. Epiphany. Then blast off as the rest of the band joined him for a version of "War Pigs" that made the original taste like old farts and string vests.'

Epiphany or not, Chuck's fate had already been sealed. Gould: 'I couldn't make myself begin again after the UK tour. I think we already knew. Everyone knew it wasn't going to work. I mean we had already made the decision earlier.'

The band had a meeting in San Francisco to decide what would happen next, and who would break the news to Chuck. Gould jumped at the chance. Calmer minds prevailed. Bottum recalls, 'I called him. He was really close to me on tour, we had a sense of humour together. We found the same things funny. That's a hard thing to lose. Laughing through it was always helpful.'

For Mosley, the dismissal was not a complete surprise. 'I was fired,' he explained in 2013. 'Why? Many reasons, but definitely not drugs or alcohol. Basically, I have a big, opinionated mouth, and am very outspoken, and it was cheaper to fire me after *Introduce Yourself* than it would have been after the third album, which would have been platinum either way, with or without me. That's the way Warner Bros planned it. Put the big-money promo push on the third album after the band does the groundwork that was the first two LPs.'

Given that Chuck was the face of the band, it was surprising that there was not more resistance from Slash and Warners, or from the band's managers.

'The management supported us 100 percent,' says Gould. 'Everybody was fine. It was not just case of them thinking that it was our band and our decision; it was more than that. The general consensus was that he was becoming a liability. It was just a matter of time. The bigger the stakes got, the worse it became.'

'Once we made the decision, everybody questioned it, including our management,' says Bordin. 'Warren and Jon knew that it was unworkable with Chuck. They knew that it was difficult with Chuck, but still and all it was a case of the devil you know versus the unknown or nothing, or worse. But in our mind, we didn't have anything to lose, and we weren't going to settle. We knew it was a massive risk and a big deal, but it was the right thing to do, so we did it.'

Roddy pays tribute to Chuck's contribution. 'He was such an unconventional choice for a singer. Who would choose that voice for a band? I don't know why it was OK with us. We had super-high aspirations, like AM radio, quite honestly, but we had a very twisted sense of style, humour, and ethics, and Chuck just fit the bill. He stuck out in a really defined way, compared to any other band. He was off-key and casual, but intense and thoughtful, and absurdist and intellectual, and ridiculous and really stoned. And so charming. We made a huge splash in the waters of originality—mostly because of Chuck.'

The first public confirmation of the end of Mosley's time in the band came in the July 1 1988 edition of San Francisco's fortnightly music magazine *BAM*: 'Faith No More singer Chuck Mosley, apparently less than thrilled with the band's ever-deepening dive into metal, has left the group.' In August, the *Gavin Report* added, 'Auditions are underway for a new vocalist to replace singer Chuck Mosley in Faith No More, Reportedly Mosley is forming a folk-rock-skate team.'

PART TWO

Like a musical Miracle Mike The Headless Chicken, in the summer of 1988, Faith No More persisted. Despite being reduced once more to a band without a singer, despite the exhaustion of nine months of continuous touring, the singer-less band were back functioning normally. There was no time of readjustment; within weeks of returning to San Francisco, they had decamped to Los Angeles for writing and rehearsals.

Theoretically, being down in Los Angeles would also make it easier for the band to recruit potential replacement singers. But the search for a singer was not an exercise in laser-focused headhunting. They were keen to look after the recruitment themselves, as they had done in the past. Slash Records were involved in the process too, while the band's management were also putting out feelers of their own. The band even went so far as posting an advertisement in LA classified listings magazine *The Recycler*, members of Metallica, Guns N' Roses, and Mötley Crüe having all used the same magazine to help set up their bands in their formative years. Mike Bordin recalls, 'We did one advertisement, and I thought it was very funny and clever and sort of tongue-in-cheek, saying something like, *Band looking for singer, must be able to sing, and must not stuff sausage down his pants.* Something stupid like that, and, of course, it got nothing.'

The band were also calling on old acquaintances, and Joe Pop-O-Pie, the singer from Faith No More's first show, was sounded out. 'In August of 1988, Bill invited me to be the next singer of Faith No More after Chuck left,' he recalls. 'At first I said yes, then I started to have second thoughts about it. The main reason being that I was suffering from severe music business burnout. There was this real soulless vibe that had taken over the music business at some point during 1988. I really didn't want to be a part of what was happening then. Looking in my crystal ball, I saw a future that I might be super-miserable in. I wouldn't want to be tempted to bail on the whole programme, because then I'd be screwing up my pals and their career.'

The band also approached one of their contemporaries, Chris Cornell of Soundgarden. By August 1988, Soundgarden had just released their second EP and signed to SST, but were not yet an established band.

John Vassiliou recalls that the initial push to contact Cornell came from the band. 'Puffy had me call Chris,' he says. 'I didn't know that his girlfriend [Susan Silver] was the manager. Billy and Puffy had a way of getting me to do things without explaining the full picture. Susan answered, and once I explained who I was, she put Chris on the phone. I explained the situation, and he politely passed. He was a kind soul, and very genuine in his concern for the band's situation. I am sure Susan was used to people calling Chris to ask him to join their band. He did have the voice of voices.'

Drummer Mike Bordin became close friends with Cornell, and recalls of the time he first heard Cornell sing when the bands played together in Seattle in 1986, 'I fell in love with that guy the moment he opened his mouth at the Central Tavern. What a voice.' Cornell actually called him after being sounded out, he adds. 'It's funny, because I know there was talk about Chris being the guy. But I loved Soundgarden, and I didn't want to break them up. But having said that, I know that there was some talking. Chris called me once during that time and said, "Look, you know, I got to stick with my band. I love my band, my band is me." And I said, "You're telling me! I know that, and I love your band too." And that was that. It was a bit of a weird clipped conversation in that regard. So there was no fire there. I mean there was a lot of smoke, and I wasn't sure why.'

Bordin, though, may well have been the fire-starter. He even got together with Cornell and Bill Gould in Seattle at this time. 'I went to Seattle, to Chris's house, with Puffy once, for some kind of jam session,' Gould recalls, 'and I didn't realise why I was doing it, and no one ever told me why. And it didn't work. At all. Great, great voice, but not for us.'

The Cornell connection was even picked up by the local press, with *BAM* including this snippet in its July story about Chuck and the band going their separate ways: 'FNM is looking for a replacement and have found one in Chris, the frontman of Seattle's Soundgarden.'

The ad had failed, muddled approaches to singers in other bands had not been successful, and the Los Angeles trip also proved a bust. Bordin: 'We thought being in LA would have made it easier to find singers, but it became pretty obvious pretty quickly that our style wasn't in the menu for singers there. It became pretty obvious that what was out there was exactly the opposite of what we had in mind.'

One promising lead was twenty-three-year-old LA singer Roderick 'Rodcore' Palmer. Palmer was prompted to apply for the role not by an advertisement or approach but by some news from Chuck Mosley's regular pizza deliverer. A friend of a friend of a friend had delivered pizza to Chuck, and had heard from him that he was no longer in the band before it had become public knowledge. And Mosley was the inspiration for Palmer to act. 'I had the same dreadlocked Mohawk that Chuck did,' he says, 'and was a huge fan of the band, with Chuck actually being an influence on me as sort of a lovable loser who put his all into what he was doing when he was onstage. I called Slash Records on the spot, set up a meeting with Matt Wallace, and went down the next day.'

After that meeting, an audition was arranged in San Francisco. Palmer borrowed some money from his grandfather and took the bus. His experience there provides an insight into the somewhat haphazard recruitment process:

> I was greeted by Bill and Roddy, and they walked me around the building and introduced me to a few other folks living there, and explained to me that prior to the place having tenants, it was an abandoned pet hospital. Bill took me to the roof, where there were still cages with various mummified animals in them that had starved to death. They told me their rehearsal spot was in Richmond, and that they liked to take the bus early in the day because the area was a crap hole at night and dangerous to be in. Jim Martin would not be there, as he had just had surgery on his hand and couldn't play, but Mike Bordin would. I could tell they were jazzed meeting me; I'm good with people and I know I made a good impression as a person, and they were also psyched I had a look sort of like Chuck's.
>
> After we got in and I met Mike, who was such a warm,

friendly guy, and everyone tuned up, they asked me what I wanted to sing first. 'Death March' was—and still is—one of my favourite songs, and I wanted to go in with something a little different than 'We Care A Lot', which I figured most would want to start with, so we did that. One thing I took note of was how easily they launched into every song we did that day without Jim Martin, and how it still sounded full and powerful without him. Bill, Roddy, and Mike were a well-oiled machine that clearly had hours of rehearsal after rehearsal under their belts, and I was noting everything.

After 'Death March', we went into 'Chinese Arithmetic', another fave of mine. I sang this song in a higher register than Chuck's low monotone, and put some more melody into it, and they dug it. Then they asked how good I was at creating on the spot; I said I was OK, and then they played the song that would end up on *The Real Thing* as 'Underwater Love'. They played it a couple of times, I came up with rough lyrics, and then we ran through it and they taped it on a crappy old beat-up boom-box they had in the room. After the rehearsal, they were happy, and said they decided to have me back for another rehearsal.

Palmer was under serious consideration. He rehearsed twice more with Bottum, Bordin, and Gould during his San Francisco stay. 'After the last one, they told me I had gotten more time with them than anyone else who tried out for the job, and that they liked me,' he recalls, 'but the main candidate outside of me was a guy Jim was pushing for from another band called Mr Bungle that they'd also had some great rehearsals with.'

'He was a cool guy,' says Gould. 'He was good, but it wasn't the same thing. He just wasn't the right guy.'

❈

The band had the solution right in their hands all the time. In a telling indication of just how far their collective patience with Chuck had already strained to breaking point, both Mike Bordin and Jim Martin had snapped up and absorbed the demo tapes given to them by Mr Bungle's Trey

Spruance in Humboldt College and San Francisco in 1986 and 1987. Martin was impressed with the metal stylings of Bungle's first demo, *The Raging Wrath Of The Easter Bunny*, recorded in 1986. On tracks like 'Spreading The Thighs Of Death' and 'Raping Your Mind', Mike Patton, then aged just eighteen, delivers the most thrillingly pure metal vocals of his career.

According to Bordin, Martin had formed a mental picture of who the singer was. 'Trey came to us after the show in Humboldt College [in October 1986] and said, "We got this band, listen to my band, check it out." He gave us this tape, and it was Mr Bungle in their Slayer phase, *Raging Wrath Of The Easter Bunny*, and we listened to it, and Jim said, "Oh my God, he sounds like he is a three-hundred-pound giant fat guy, we really need that guy, because he has got a big voice, and he is yelling and screaming and growling." So he took the tape and he kept it.'

While it is easy to see the attraction of Patton's guttural vocalisations, death growl, and throat-scream vocals for Martin, Patton's singing on that demo was somewhat one-dimensional and not what the rest of the band were after. Bungle and Faith No More's paths crossed again on December 28 1987, when the Bungle band members travelled to San Francisco to see the Red Hot Chili Peppers/Faith No More show at the Fillmore Theater. Spruance and Patton again met Mike Bordin and handed them their most recent demo, the considerably more nuanced *Bowel Of Chiley*. Bordin was elated at the band's development: 'I told them, "My God, that's fantastic. Good for you for evolving, we love that. We love when people evolve and are not going to be trapped in one stupid thing."'

Independently from Martin and Bordin, Faith No More producer Matt Wallace—seeking a new singer in his new role as Slash's in-house producer—had also picked up a Bungle demo. While Jim Martin had made contact with Patton by phone straight after hearing the first Bungle demo, and would take to leaving messages for Patton—'*The Raging Wrath Of The Easter Bunny* is the way to go, *Bowel Of Chiley* is no go'—Mike Bordin eventually called Patton with the offer to come down to San Francisco and try out for the band.

Bordin was not bowled over by Patton's enthusiasm. 'I don't think that it was something that he was really particularly interested in getting into,' he says. 'I think he was very happy with his friends; he really liked his friends, and they made whatever music they wanted to.'

'I resisted it,' Patton explained in 2013. 'I honestly did. Oddly enough, some of my friends in Mr Bungle were like, *Just do this. It doesn't mean you have to leave our band.* At that time, I was more concerned with completing my degree and finishing school. I didn't see Faith No More as some yellow brick road to success or anything. I just thought I would try it. The music wasn't quite what I was about at the time, but I took it as a challenge.'

Patton was born on January 27 1968 in the coastal town of Eureka, around 300 miles north of San Francisco. His parents were Patrick Patton, a high-school football coach who hailed from Riverside county, not far from Palm Springs, over 700 miles to the south; and Carole Jarvela from nearby Arcata, who had majored in social welfare in Humboldt State College. They married in 1967 and were only twenty-three and twenty when Mike was born.

Patton enjoyed a peaceful childhood behind the so-called Redwood Curtain, the mass of forest separating Eureka and all of Humboldt County from the rest of the state. The area was populated by a mix of rednecks and hippies, and became known as the epicentre of America's illegal cannabis-growing industry. The death of the logging industry in the 1970s hit the town hard, however, as Patton's Bungle and future Faith No More bandmate Trey Spruance recalls:

Eureka used to top the crime rate statistics of California, often above Oakland and South Central LA. Not all of Eureka was a hellhole, of course. I was in the school district that represented the worst side of things. Eureka is certainly a great and unique place in many ways these days, and had its good points back then too. But to give you the picture, back in the late 70s and early 80s, I went to an elementary school that was right across the street from a decommissioned nuclear reactor, a fact which tells you a little bit about the economic profile of the area. If that weren't enough, that particular area was a natural funnel for the toxic plumes coming from the pulp mills, and the high dioxin levels probably had something to do with that valley having the highest cancer rate in the nation at that time. I think the poverty in that area was really compounded by the factor of the lay of the land being something of a toxic cesspool.

Rather than violent and poor, Mike Patton found it dull. 'It's a big, giant fucking graveyard,' he later said, 'and for some reason people live there, and they just fucking dig holes all their lives, and then they jump into them.'

Patton's own hole-digging saw him graduate high school to study English at Humboldt State University, while also working in Eureka's only record store. Writing and music would provide the escape route. Patton's family was not especially musical—he recalls only listening to music, Styx and Kansas, on the radio on trips to the supermarket. But he showed an early musical aptitude nonetheless. 'From a young age I was definitely imitating birds, but I didn't know it at the time. This is what my parents tell me. Once I started making these weird sounds with my voice, they gave me this little flexi-disc of mouth sounds, like guys that could make odd sounds. I don't know why they gave it to me, but that was one of my favourite records.'

Patton was pushed more to sport as a young child, before chasing music more as a way to fit in. 'I only got into music when I couldn't hang around anyone else,' he told *Kerrang!* in 1991. 'At school, I was a hyper geek and I got hassle from the jocks. I wanted to be one of them; that was the thing. So one of the first things I got into was collecting old 45s, beginning with The Partridge Family or something. Then I got into death metal and hardcore: anything that was fast, loud, nasty, and retarded. There wasn't that much to do in a small town in America. You either start up a meth lab or get into music.'

Patton's music lab partners were Spruance and Trevor Dunn. He first sang publicly at Dunn's sixteenth birthday party, and, soon after, he joined Dunn's rock covers band, Gemini. The band and Patton looked the part when they played a series of metal covers at the Eureka High School talent night in March 1984. Existing footage shows sixteen-year-old Patton, in leather vest and gloves, tight jeans with chains, and face makeup, with all the right moves—and high-pitched vocals that sound uncannily like Axl Rose—down pat as he screams through KISS's 'Detroit Rock City', Quiet Riot's 'Metal Health', and Iron Maiden's 'Flight Of The Icarus'.

Spruance: 'I saw him play at Talent Night, singing for a band called Gemini. Trevor was on bass too. My brother thought Patton sucked! I thought he was OK, better than the other local singers.'

Patton: 'My first gig as a singer was because the singer didn't show up. A friend of mine's band, it's not like I thought about it. It just happened.

To me, that's fundamental. Understanding that you don't have to have a plan ... I didn't want to be a singer. I thought I was going to be a fucking poet or something. I was studying English literature.'

Patton was fortunate to find musical kindred spirits in Dunn and Spruance, who shared the singer's voracious musical appetite and curiosity. While Spruance and Dunn joined the school band and received further music education from Eureka High music teacher Dan Horton, Patton was content to keep his music a purely extracurricular pursuit.

'He's one of those people who it would actually slow down if he stopped to thread the needle too much,' says Spruance. 'I personally don't think that anything that would infringe on his spontaneity and artistic perspective, both creatively and as a performer, would really be worth diving into. I think he's felt like he's missing out on some things, but I'd argue against that. Our choices make us who we are, and his choices have been absolutely great.'

After Gemini, Patton graduated to Mr Bungle, formed from a merger of Gemini and Spruance's previous band, Torcher, in 1985. In Bungle, Patton, Dunn, and Spruance—Theo Lengyel and Jed Watts were the other founder members—further explored their early love of various forms of metal, but their tastes and sound soon grew to encompass ska, jazz, and funk. Their 1986 and 1987 demo releases that brought Patton to the attention of Faith No More showcased this evolution in sound, and their third demo, *Goddammit I Love America!!!$t!!*, released earlier in 1988, was described on the cassette cover as 'seven tunes of funkadelic thrashing circus ska'.

✸

Bungle bandmate Trevor Dunn travelled with Patton to San Francisco for the Faith No More audition, though it was Spruance who encouraged Patton to audition, as he had loved *We Care A Lot*. The meeting point was Bill Gould's residence, the abandoned animal hospital. Fresh-faced Patton received a rude introduction to San Francisco life.

According to Gould, 'I was just hanging out and they showed up, and I remember thinking, *Oh my God, they're young!* And I thought, *Holy shit. This guy! This is the guy?!* He was this kid, and he was freaked out. He had never really left his home town, and the pet hospital was basically a squat. We were watching John Waters movies and my room mate threw a bottle of beer at me, and just missed my head. The bottle shattered behind me off the wall just before we left for that first rehearsal with them.'

At the rehearsal space, rather than asking Patton to reprise an earlier track, Faith No More started playing their new music, and Patton responded immediately. 'We just played the songs,' Gould adds, 'and he said, "Ah, I can hear some things here, I can hear song things there," and he just started singing off the top of his head to the music. We recorded on a simple ghetto blaster.'

'The idea of an audition is enough to make anyone want to puke,' Patton later recalled, 'but I did it. And that first rehearsal felt a lot more comfortable than I thought it would. But they didn't give me a thumbs-up or down right away.'

There was no moment of epiphany or eureka; the band were not immediately blown away by Patton's prowess. Soon after, when Gould and Jim Martin left for a weekend trip to the Martin family cabin in the woods, where Martin had previously jammed with Cliff Burton, they took the tape with them. Gould says, 'We went up there and we played the tape. We listened to it a few times, and realised that this was the first guy we had heard who was doing things to the songs that were helping the songs. I wasn't completely convinced, but he was the first person who seemed to have a clue about us.'

Days later, the band discussed Patton's potential with Warren Entner and John Vassiliou. In a move suggestive of where the music industry was going in the late 1980s, the managers did not request a tape, but a photo. The band got together with photographer Mark Leialoha for a quick shoot, and sent a black-and-white group shot—what Gould called 'a great horrible band photo'—to their management. Entner and Vassiliou then flew up from Los Angeles to hear the second audition in person. Vassiliou recalls, 'We flew up to a rehearsal in San Francisco and were impressed with Patton's voice, but Chuck had charisma too. Patton was a contrast to Chuck, but Patton fooled us all. The room was tiny and had another band's gear in it. We could barely fit, and Patton actually sang in Warren's ear. It was so loud you couldn't hear anything. I finally stood out in the hallway.'

Concerns remained that the callow Patton might not fit the band, or that he might be a lamb to the slaughter. 'The managers wanted him because he was this young, good-looking guy,' says Gould. 'But that's what scared me. I was worried we were going to ruin this kid's life. He was like Justin Bieber. He got it musically, but he didn't fit in. And our friends were asking what we were doing with this kid saying that he wasn't one of us. I felt guilty. It felt like we were doing a cash grab. I could see how people could think that. It looked like that. But he actually did get it musically.'

That was the key for the rest of the band. It soon transpired that Patton spoke the same musical language. In October, Patton again came down to San Francisco, this time staying for a weekend at Mike Bordin's place on California Street, and spending some time working on song ideas in the makeshift studio that Gould had in a former surgical room in his pet hospital home. The young singer had worked on ideas for six of the initial songs, which were already at that stage close to the finished versions.

Gould: 'I was like, *Holy shit!* He nailed it. The first song was "From Out Of Nowhere", and I was wondering what he was going to do with this, and he fucking nailed it. That was it. And I thought, *Now we can get back to work.*'

FROM OUT
OF NOWHERE

17

The band had been working. In August 1988, they spent three weeks at Hollywood Rehearsals at the corner of Hollywood Boulevard and Western Avenue, a rundown studio space covered in plastic sheeting and exposed fibreglass. While Bill Gould and Roddy Bottum were staying with their families in the city, Mike Bordin and Jim Martin roomed together in a sketchy accommodation complex called Oakwood Apartments. In keeping with Martin's largely crepuscular existence, the pair would work together on songs from late afternoon until late at night, when Martin would join up with his friends from Metallica until the early hours.

Together, Martin and Bordin had put together parts of what would become 'Surprise! You're Dead!' and 'Zombie Eaters', which both included previously composed parts from the band's earliest days. It wasn't until one week into the trip that the pair went into the studio a little earlier in the day and discovered Bottum and Gould working away. As soon as the quartet were back in harness, music started flowing in earnest, and the absence of a singer was not being felt at all. Bordin remembers, 'We had made the change because we wanted to evolve further. This was proof that we were following through on what we promised each other. We're doing this to get better, we're doing this to write better songs and touch more extremes and directions.'

Within days of that reconnection, the band had significantly developed 'Epic'. Bordin: 'Within a couple of days, very fucking quickly, Bill and I wrote the groove, the rhythm for "Epic", and we knew it was cool and very, very good.' Martin, meanwhile, took some synth parts that Bottum had been working on and put together most of 'Woodpecker From Mars'.

John Vassiliou was also impressed when he heard the fruits of these Hollywood sessions. 'Billy had told me they had written some songs that targeted the sound of popular bands, and musically the songs were strong. He played us songs before Patton showed up that ended up on the record—they were quality band tracks without vocals. We knew that if they found the right singer, they had a great record on their hands.'

By October, that singer had moved down from Eureka to San Francisco, where he took up a more permanent residence in the apartment Bordin shared with his girlfriend. The house also had other guests, as Bordin recalls: 'One of the other roommates had a pet iguana; he was a mean motherfucker and he ended up in Mike's room, and Mike said he was not comfortable. It was an uneasy standoff, to say the least.'

Patton may have been getting to know the wildlife, but Bordin and the rest of the band were mainly interested in a musical connection. 'He stayed in my place for a long time, and that was all fine; I mean, I'm happy to have him, but by that same token, all I was ever about at that time was trying to find ways to make this band work. It was a mania with me. We talked, it wasn't like anything weird. We talked and he was fine, I could relate to him a little bit, and he really liked basketball and I really like baseball.'

The band were speaking the same language musically, and the four demo tracks sent to Slash/Warner—'Falling To Pieces', 'Surprise! You're Dead', 'The Cowboy Song', and 'Underwater Love'—convinced the label that the band had chosen a new singer wisely. John Vassiliou remembers that reaction: 'Patton took the songs into another stratosphere, something at the time I do not think Chuck could have accomplished. The label could not deny the songs were good.'

The singer's vocal prowess and dexterity also impressed his new bandmates. His 'man-of-many-voices' approach was perfect for Faith No More's all-embracing aesthetic. Bottum says, 'I was surprised how instantaneous his takes were, and how effective they were. His vocals were really stylised in a way I hadn't heard with our music before, and it changed everything.'

Bordin was also excited by the new possibilities that Patton brought. 'I never heard anybody that close to my face sound that great. We were looking to continue to get better and then, all of a sudden, here comes a singer who can literally do anything, even beyond probably what he was aware of at that time. You've got no restrictions, you've got no limitations.'

❋

Weeks before going into the studio to record the tracks, the band organised an introductory gig for their new singer at San Francisco's I-Beam in November 1988. The show had been previewed by Steffan Chirazi in *BAM* as, 'Your chance to check out the new version of the SF funk/punk/metal/rap kingpins. New vocalist Mike Patton of Mr Bungle has come on board to replace Chuck Mosley. Early indications are that the group's moving in a more metal direction.'

Chirazi was completely sold on the new singer in his review in December. 'Patton lays waste to the band's previous singer. Patton's advantages: He wasn't drunk, he can sing, he can dance. He has energy and conviction. The band seems recharged, and ready to roar with new material that could break the band big.' That prescient prediction was followed by confirmation that Mosley's ouster was not universally approved. 'By the evening's end, the scene sported a return to real ugliness, broken glasses, a broken camera and a piece of Patton hate mail that read, "You guys were cool, but get this long-haired asshole off the stage."'

Patton revealed his take on that incident about eighteen months later, when he told an Australian magazine, 'The first show I did was in San Francisco about November 1988, and after the gig the bouncer brought this note back and said, "Some girl asked me to give this to you." I'm like, "Oh great, cool, neat—my first groupie!" And silly me, the note read: "You stupid, sexist, macho asshole. What are you doing? Get off the stage. Where's Chuck? He rocks." All this stuff. I just went, "Killer! I'm going home."'

Friends of the band were also letting them know their objections to the new singer, who represented a threat to the band's previously prevailing underground outsider aesthetic. According to Bill Gould, 'Some of our friends wrote us a letter saying, *Why you have this macho asshole in your band? Fuck you, I'm never going to see you again.* Patton was a fish out of water. He didn't fit with us at all. He was this young kid coming from another planet really. Chuck was kind of a dirty guy. We were dirty guys. And then we bring in this squeaky-clean kid, and he's actually singing more like Iron Maiden than Flipper. Some people didn't dig it. I knew what he did with the songs, so it didn't bother us too much. Change happens.'

Undeterred, the band spent around two months perfecting the songs and then demoing them at Dancing Dog Studios in Emeryville with Dave Bryson, later the guitarist with Counting Crows. Then, in December, they returned to Studio D in Sausalito to begin recording. Armed with their versatile vocalist and finished songs, the band also made sure to control the other variables before tracking began. Matt Wallace, fresh from the considerable challenge of producing The Replacements' album *Don't Tell A Soul* in Los Angeles, was back as producer, engineer, and mixer. Gould recalls, 'We were paranoid about bringing outside people in. They didn't understand us. We had our line of protection. Just to protect the quality of our work. And Matt grew up with us; he was our security.'

Wallace's first task was to finally satisfy Jim Martin's thirst for the perfect guitar tone. That involved driving down with Martin to Sound City studios in Van Nuys, Los Angeles, where Rick Rubin was producing Wolfsbane's *Live Fast, Die Fast* album, to watch engineer David Bianco in action. Then, back in Studio D, Wallace and Martin meticulously spent three days to find the best sounds, using twenty-six different mics, and marking off the isolation booth with yellow police tape when the perfect settings had been found. The quest for the right sound was also spiritual, with Wallace and Martin adopting a morning ritual before guitar tracking began each day, as Wallace explains:

> We always played the original version of 'The Good, The Bad, And The Ugly' by Ennio Morricone. We would put that on the cassette deck, and we'd literally turn up the monitors as loud as they could get, which was really loud. And we'd just stand there and listen to it and then we would salute the speakers, and we would salute each other. And then after the song ended, we'd go right to work and start doing guitars.
>
> The energy, and the spirit, and the vibe of that record was really inspired by that song and that music. It was that sense of grandeur. We really wanted something that was big and panoramic and huge.

The pre-publicity for the record—a lot of it generated by friend of the band and close Jim Martin confidant Steffan Chirazi—played up its metal edge. The new way of recording guitar was a factor in that, but Martin was also more involved in the songwriting process than for any other Faith No More release. Speaking to *Kerrang!* just after the album's release, he said, 'The writing certainly isn't any more hard rock than before; at least it wasn't written to be. It might sound like that. If that's the case, it's because you can hear a bit more fucking guitar now.'

Bill Gould also concedes that the guitar was more up front on the record. 'Jim spent a lot of time on that,' he says. 'He spent three days getting his guitar tone with Matt. That was something that I didn't even bother showing up for. But I like the guitar tone they got. We also wrote these songs with Jim more involved in the loop, even though it was difficult. Somehow, he had a way where his parts could fit in better because he was more familiar with the material. The songs are a little bit more straightforward, but he could grab them.'

The grandeur of the record was also aided by the evolution of the band's keyboard sound. Roddy Bottum had upgraded his Oberheim of the first two records to an E-mu Emax, and this and the new MIDI-equipped studio piano helped Bottum deliver such memorable parts, especially on 'Falling To Pieces' and 'Epic'. Bottum's melodies had been key to the band's early sound, and now he had a writing credit on every track. Crucially on *The Real Thing*, Roddy's melodies and outright pop hooks were more melodious and hookier—and they were reflected back and reinforced by Mike Patton's more strident and powerful vocals and, above all, by Patton's own gift for melody. None more so than on album opener 'From Out Of Nowhere', two hundred and one seconds of quintessential pop-metal perfection, and the first of a strident trident of in-your-face, hard-hitting but hook-laden tracks to kick off the album.

For Bottum, the song was a deliberate attempt to forge a hit. Bordin: 'He always fucked around with that, being the MTV fan and being the pop music fan, so he took charge of a lot of the melody—and this one was highly melodic.'

Part of the song had originated from as early as 1983, as 'Mike's Disco', one of the band's long suite of disco-titled songs from that era. When Roddy brought in a melody he had worked on, Bordin suggested it would flow perfectly with the 'Mike's Disco' extract. 'It was about controlling the development of the song,' he says, 'not only just with the actual melodic structure, but you also can use rhythm to break things up, too. And that's obviously different from most bands, where it's the guitar player, and the singer, and *I've got my lyrics and you've got to fit everything to it*. It was the opposite of that, and I'm sure that made it challenging for someone like Mike where it was already written. But that also shows his inspiration and brilliance, and the willingness to just fucking go for it.'

Gould remembers inspiration coming from elsewhere, too. 'That song came from Roddy. That's completely Roddy's melody, so maybe it was deliberately pop. But it was originally called "The Cult Song", because it reminded me of The Cult.'

Gould himself brought in the album's second song, 'Epic', almost fully formed, though he was not a fan of the third prong of the opening album onslaught, 'Falling To Pieces'. 'I didn't care about that song. It also came from Roddy. That's a mean thing to say … I did what I could to try to make it move, but it was never one of the favourites.' Bottum: 'We called it "Madonna" because it seemed to have pop potential. I always like to steer things in that direction.'

Persistent, disciplined bass, metallic guitar crunch, and crushing but also cymbal-crashing drums set the tone, but the song is transformed from rock into pop by positively twinkly keyboards and Mike Patton's versatile vocals and rich imagery.

'That song felt very much like a rock song,' says Bordin, 'but very heavily melodic, keyboard-dominant, the guitar player in the second go-around is playing the upbeats, and the rhythmic guitar appears almost like a dub technique. There's good stuff in there for sure, and the B verse—*A minute here, a minute there*, that part—that's fucking hard to play. It is us getting stronger, getting more effective at what we do.'

The lyrics would appear to refer to Patton's liminal status at the time, as he adapted to his move from Eureka to San Francisco, his transition from student to singer, and to being 'somewhere in between' Mr Bungle and Faith No More. Lines like '*Droplets of yes and no / In an ocean of maybe*' both betray his literary learning, and belie his oft-repeated claim that he merely finds sounds in words to match the sounds in the music. Song lyrics can often appear vapid and vacuous when stripped of music, but when Patton recited the unadorned lyrics in a spoken-word drawl for a film produced to mark the twentieth anniversary of Chilean author Albert Fuguet's *Mala Onda* in 2011, their power and poetic quality was retained.

The first demo version of the song, recorded by Gould on four-track, features slightly different lyrics. Here, Patton is not '*somewhere in between*', as a later discarded line, '*I'm splitting in two, me and you*', precedes the '*my life is falling to pieces*' refrain. That would allow the interpretation that this is a rare Patton love song—or it could be about schizophrenic breakdown. Or, given Patton's denial of meaning in his lyrics, the song might be meaningless. In 2013, he said:

> I really don't enjoy writing lyrics at all. I feel like I'm not very good at it. I think it comes from early band days where we'd have all the music written, and I'd know I had a studio date the

next day, so I'd put on a few pots of coffee, and just try and write everything at that moment.

There's a certain element of panic in writing lyrics that I'm not sure I enjoy. The idea, at least in rock or pop culture, that the singer is on some pedestal in Speaker's Corner—I've just never subscribed to that. I'm not a poet. I'm not up onstage to get something off my chest. I'm making musical statements, or, most of the time, musical questions for people to figure out, and I'm not going to get in the way of that.

Patton later admitted that he, like Gould, did not like the song. 'It bothers me,' he told *Blunt* in 2015. 'I don't know where the hell we were at when we did that.' In the same interview, Gould said, 'We've done it a few times live for the novelty factor. We're literally laughing onstage. It sounds like a cover to us; like "Easy" seems more like one of our songs than "Falling To Pieces" does.'

Patton's spare, stark, and wonderfully sincere lyrics might have provoked some of this retrospective cringing, but more so his insincere and inauthentic vocals. While Chuck Mosley's singing, chanting, and rapping were far from technically perfect, they had punk sneer, Venice Beach brattishness, and one-of-a-kind authenticity. Patton's singing on *The Real Thing* is largely adenoidal, and different from his previous Mr Bungle delivery and any later vocal approach. His voice is different again on the initial demo version of the tracks, notably on 'Falling To Pieces'. Here, he adopts a smooth, pop-soul delivery, especially in the chorus, interspersed by spoken-word passages, which better suit the original slow tempo of the song.

That more soulful singing is mostly absent on *The Real Thing*, despite Matt Wallace's best efforts:

When Patton was singing, he would always sing in that really nasally, almost adolescent voice. And, then, when I stopped recording, he would just break into singing these R&B songs with this big, beautiful resonant voice. And I'd go, 'That's great. That's great. Can we put that on the record?' And he would say, 'No, I'm not going to do that.' And he used to really irritate me, because I felt he was holding back the full sound of his voice. Technically, I was correct, because we didn't get the biggest, best voice from Patton. But, to his credit, it was that adolescent, adenoidal, bratty thing that really spoke to people. I think it was him trying to protect himself, and almost have a separate persona. Like, you're not getting all of Mike Patton. You're getting an aspect or a facet of Mike Patton, but you're not getting the stuff that he would do with Mr Bungle. It was this thing where he could separate himself from the two. I think it was a protective measure for him, but he was absolutely correct.

The pop-rock one-two-three that opens the album is followed by the pure metal of 'Surprise! You're Dead!' The song could not have been more Faith No More: most of the music was written by Jim Martin; the title came from one of the first songs the band wrote back in 1983, which itself was named after a short film directed by Roddy Bottum in film school; the lyrics were written by Patton to fit the pre-existing title. 'I made a short film called *Pets* in college,' Bottum explains. 'Billy and Mike Bordin helped with the soundtrack for the film. It was about a couple with pets in their apartment in compromising situations, and they were trying to adopt a child. It was a story of a dysfunctional family in modern America.'

The title was all that remained, as the main riff of the song was subsumed into 'Zombie Eaters' during the writing session in Hollywood. Patton's prowess as a songwriter was not just, therefore, fitting words and melody to existing rigidly structured pieces, but he was also able to work with other limitations, such as creating a mood and words to fit a pre-existing song and title. That made Bordin sit up and take notice. 'The lyrics of that song came after the music, and even after us calling it "Surprise! You're Dead!" for some reason, and so he went with that, which is amazing. He was willing to take a chance, willing to go with it wherever.'

Bordin was also revelling in the band's diversity. 'It's important to look at "Surprise! You're Dead!" in terms of a song that it just came after. Faith No More isn't just about "Surprise! You're Dead!" It's also about "From Out Of Nowhere" and "Falling To Pieces". The heavier stuff is getting heavier, the aggressive stuff is getting more aggressive, and the melodic stuff was getting more properly melodic. The variety was working well.'

All of the band were contributing, according to Bordin. '"Surprise! You're Dead!" is Jim's. It had been around for him, note-by-note on a demo, a long time before. It's a super-good blast of energy.'

Martin's music was originally known as 'Sailor Song' before taking the title of the earlier track. The band would spend the rest of their careers denying that they were a metal band, but this song facilitated their embrace by metal fans. The riffs were metal, the pulsating rhythm was metal, and the vocals had death growls and screams. But 'Surprise' is also Faith No More, or at least some of Faith No More, playing at being metal. It is these growls and screams that underline the inauthenticity of Patton's vocals as much as his adenoidal rock star pitch, his rapping, or his soulful singing. This was Patton's approximation of thrash metal. 'I pretty much write the words to fit the song,' he later said, 'so with "Surprise! You're Dead!" I ended up writing lyrics that reminded me a bit of Slayer.' And with vocals to match.

18 'WAR PIGS' AND OTHER COVERS

As much as the aggressive marketing to metal fans that greeted *The Real Thing*'s release, it was 'Surprise!' and a cover of Black Sabbath's 'War Pigs' that led to Faith No More's late-1980s categorisation as a metal band.

After establishing their sound in the first months of their existence, Faith No More played their first live cover in late 1984. 'We played "Jump" the first time with Courtney at the Mab,' Bottum recalls. 'It felt very real. I had the same keyboard that Eddie Van Halen used in the recording, and the sound of it, the vibe of it, was spot on. We were really pleased with ourselves.

We were so obnoxious. We really wanted to push people's buttons.'

'"War Pigs" came out of doing stuff like the Nestlé 'Sweet Dreams' jingle or Van Halen's "Jump",' Bordin adds, 'and we'd butcher that and fuck around with that. It wasn't just necessarily us aspiring to be a metal band.'

'War Pigs' was the first cover to feature on a Faith No More album. Several more would follow. The Commodores' 'Easy', added to the live set in place of 'War Pigs' when the band's newfound rock and metal fans embraced it earnestly, was recorded during the *Angel Dust* sessions and added to later releases of the record, which also featured John Barry's 'Midnight Cowboy'. The Bee Gees' 'I Started A Joke' was a bonus track on *King For A Day ... Fool For A Lifetime*. Then there are the many, many more covers released as single B-sides: The Dead Kennedys' 'Let's Lynch The Landlord' in 1993; GG Allin's 'I Wanna Fuck Myself', 'Greenfields' by The Brothers Four, and 'Spanish Eyes', made famous by Al Martino, among others, all released in 1995; and live covers of Deep Purple's 'Highway Star' and Bacharach and David's 'This Guy's In Love With You', both of which appeared on the compilation *Who Cares A Lot?* in 1998.

Faith No More's covers were respectful, somewhere between pastiche and homage. 'Jump' and 'Highway Star' were joined in their early setlists by T.Rex's 'Life's A Gas'—a favourite of Chuck Mosley's—while the band also added pop snippets such as Tears For Fears' 'Everybody Wants To Rule The World' and Terence Trent D'Arby's 'Sign Your Name' to their repertoire. The pop snippets would become a live trademark, as Faith No More became pioneers of the live mash-up. 'Back For Good' by Take That, Technotronic's 'Pump Up The Jam', and 'You Got It (The Right Stuff)' by New Kids On The Block were 1990s favourites, while the reunion tours from 2009 onward saw regular renditions of 'Poker Face' by Lady Gaga, 'Fuck You' by Lily Allen, and 'Niggas In Paris' by Kanye West and Jay-Z. Those snippets served to keep the set contemporary, given that the band had not released any new music for fifteen years. The band regularly used the breakdown in 'Midlife Crisis' for live variations from routine, with mini-covers of such tunes as Stevie Wonder's 'Sir Duke' and the theme tune to the British TV soap opera *Eastenders*. With other common 'Midlife Crisis' grafts—Rick Astley's 'Never Gonna Give You Up' and Eduard Khil's 'Trololo'—Faith No More moved into referential and even meta territory, as both songs had become hugely popular on the internet after being used by trolls to misdirect browsers who, instead of being served up their expected content, were shown videos of the songs.

Trolling fans was fair game, but the songs had to be respected. In this context, 'War Pigs' was treated with the utmost care. Producer Matt Wallace says the band nailed it: 'I think our version of "War Pigs" is devastating. When you put it up against Black Sabbath's, I think it absolutely crushes it, because we went for the jugular in those guitars. We doubled the guitars and got it right.'

The replication is almost perfect. Even without employing trademark Sabbath techniques such as down-tuned guitar and sludgy and stoner droney riffs, Faith No More's imitation of the Sabbath sound, of the song's texture and essence, is such that it permeates the rest of the record. This big, clean sound and feel seemed atmospheric and even organic, but a large part was purely technical.

'When we recorded Jim's guitars, in between the riffs on that track, there was tremendous amounts of noise,' Wallace adds. 'I went, *Oh my God, there's all this noise. What am I going to do?* I didn't know what automation was, so after Jim tracked it, I went back and, not knowing you could spot erase things, I went in and muted everything. On all the guitar tracks, I'd wipe out all the noise. When you put up that master track, it's clean. It was risky for me, because I knew that if I came out too late on erasing, we would lose the guitars.'

The song had been part of the band's repertoire since 1987, and they had it down so well that it seemed a shame to waste it. '"War Pigs" was recorded one night when we weren't getting what we wanted on a track,' Bordin recalls. 'Matt said, "We'll come back and do this tomorrow. Just do a run through 'War Pigs'." It was just one take, and we were all fired up and pissed off, and we played through it.'

The song also did not require a keyboard. Bill Gould says, 'We were waiting around for something to start, and Roddy hadn't shown up yet, so we just started playing "War Pigs". We played it through without having to rehearse it. We didn't think of it as a thing, like it was going to be a hallmark of the band. It was kind of a joke.'

Faith No More's goading and prodding of their fans backfired. As their fan base grew and changed after the 'Epic'-fuelled success of *The Real Thing*, 'War Pigs' became a firm fan favourite. Where once it served to illustrate that Faith No More were different to their peers and audience, now it was the very exemplar of their credentials as a metal act for their new peers and new fans. When the band were joined onstage by Slash and Duff of Guns N' Roses during their album launch party at the Roxy Theater in Hollywood in the summer of 1989, it made perfect sense that the GNR duo jumped onstage to jam during 'War Pigs'. The following November, also in Hollywood—this time at *RIP* magazine's fourth birthday bash at the Palladium—James Hetfield of Metallica joined in the encore during 'War Pigs', with the cover receiving the ultimate imprimatur—Ozzy Osbourne himself replacing Mike Patton on vocals.

'Meatheads started coming just to hear us do that all the time,' Gould recalls, 'and Jim's chest was puffing out. He got to be Mr Black Sabbath.'

The rest of Faith No More had to take back control—and they did. Gould adds, 'We were drunk at a bar, night off, at some hotel. "Easy" was playing on the radio, and I looked at Patton and I said, Here's our next cover.'

THE REAL THING

19

Faith No More's songwriting was always cinematic, and this scene-setting approach reached new peaks on *The Real Thing*. Bill Gould: 'The way we write songs comes not so much from a style, but more like a visual scene that we see in our heads. Then we try to create something that gives us the feeling of that scene. Because so much of our music starts from visuals, every song is different.'

The band's dramatic musical set pieces were perfectly complemented by Mike Patton's gift for character sketches and musical short stories. Patton came straight to Faith No More from studying English literature at Humboldt College and brought a flair for character, scene, and plot. Explaining his approach to lyrics in a 2015 interview, he said, 'I like creating fictional characters and trying to appropriate their psychology. None of the songs have a relation between them: for me, a record is more a succession of scenes in which I will use this or that trick to achieve the desired outcome. They are little films. I do not know exactly myself what some of my lyrics say, because I try before anything else to follow the music. When I discover a new song, I imagine the sounds and the notes on top. Only then do I try to find the words which come the closest as possible to what I have heard in my head.'

These little fictions underscore a tetralogy of tracks on *The Real Thing*: 'Zombie Eaters', 'Underwater Love', 'The Morning After', and 'Edge Of The World'. The primary riff in 'Zombie Eaters' was forged during the band's first sessions in the Vats in 1983. The track has a lightness and freshness, mostly thanks to Jim Martin's counterpoint opening. A connoisseur of classical guitar and a mandolin player, Martins's playing was considerably more nuanced than his largely self- and *Kerrang!*-styled 'rock god' persona. Martin had the song ready to go on his own demo cassette, and he recreated the sound in the studio with his Harmony f-hole acoustic. His delicate E and G chords are matched by Mike Patton's whispered and—a rarity on *The Real Thing*—pure vocals and Roddy Bottum's synthetic violin chords, before the booming riff comes in after 120 sedate seconds.

Matt Wallace remembers that, at this time, the band members were free to bring in their own ideas and go with them. 'One of the things that the band learned early on was that, if somebody had an idea and they were committed to the idea, the band would go with the momentum of the individual. Jim had written that part, and he could play it. And there's some pretty intricate stuff there, but everyone thought, *Let's do it*, as people would support you once you hit that high water mark of showing real intention.'

For Bordin, this song was his first realisation of Patton's prowess as a lyricist. 'It is highly, highly creative; it's maybe the first instance of Mike playing characters. A song from the point of view of an infant—Who does that? Who did that up to that point? It was all "Is This Love?" or Poison and

Bon Jovi, "*I'm an outlaw on a steel horse I ride.*" And here it's "*Hug me and kiss me, then wipe my butt and piss me.*'"

Patton cops to the song's subject matter: '"Zombie Eaters" is about little kids at birth. That's actually one of the titles that has nothing to do with the song itself. It was like, *Ha, you figure it out.*'

While there is an argument that 'Zombie Eaters' is actually a metaphor for a co-dependent relationship—it can be seen as a precursor to 'Separation Anxiety' from *Sol Invictus*—there is no mistaking what 'Edge Of The World' is about.

Gould recalls, 'Before any of the parts of that song were even written, there was the basic, non-musical idea of the song: just imagine a sleazy cocktail lounge, with a fifty-year-old man trying to pick up a fourteen-year-old girl.' The song had real-life origins, according to Bordin: 'It was written about a famous guy in San Francisco—a city supervisor—who got busted for an underage relationship.'

The recording captures the sleaze perfectly, from the finger clicking to the glasses clinking and Bottum's nightclub piano. Gould was not entirely happy, however. 'It didn't come out the way I liked, but it was OK. It's too smooth for me.'

Patton's vocals are remarkably smooth in parts. He ups the creepiness factor a thousand-fold, abandoning his nasal vocals to deliver velvety R&B smoothness on just the seamiest come-hither lines such as '*Hey, little girl*', '*Come sit right down / Lay your head on my shoulder*', and '*I'll do anything for the little girlies*', adding to the overall sense of sleaze and seediness.

'It was more of a mood piece than anything,' says Bottum. 'There were so many different colours or characters on this record. A lounge bluesy one for this song seems crazy now, but we liked the idea of focusing the piano in a spotlight. It seemed audacious.'

For Matt Wallace, this was more evidence that Patton was holding something back on the record. 'I wanted him to sing that way on "Epic". I have to give him credit, retrospectively, as, looking back, it was really the contrast of an R&B crooner singing really sleazy lyrics that really made it work. I think he was smart beyond his years, and he knew, either out of fear or something else, to distance himself and create these characters so he wasn't Mike Patton.'

For the listener, having to inhabit the perspective of a child molester, even for just four minutes and eleven seconds, is disturbing. A casual listen can fool that '*we'll sing and dance and we'll find romance*' is a routine love song, but that little fiction does not survive repeat listens. The words of the writer Juliet Thurman (writing about Balthus in 2013) are also apt here: 'You owe it to the art to examine the nuances of your discomfort. That's where … genius lies.'

Speaking about 'The Morning After', Patton said, 'Fear is a big part of it, a real influence for me. It's probably the most important emotion there is. Why do you walk down a certain side of the street?'

The song began life as 'New Improved Song', which had been released on a cover-mounted seven-inch EP (also featuring The Jesus & Mary Chain, Head Of David, and The Godfathers) given away with the UK music magazine *Sounds* on March 12 1988. That original track was Chuck Mosley's last recording with the band, recorded on eight-track with Matt Wallace some months earlier. This early version of the track lacked any real chorus or obvious structure, so 'New Improved Song' was updated and re-recorded, and thus became 'The Much Improved Song', or 'The Morning After'.

'That was one we had for a while and never figured out how to get it over the top,' says Bordin, 'We also had "New Song" and "The New New Song", which became "New Improved Song", and then we even had "The New New New Song", which I don't remember. But if you have a band that's writing music before the words, you are going to get shit like that.'

Mosley's original lyrics are touching and tinged with regret—'*How can you imagine the day when I'm gone?*' Patton's lyrics for the reworked 'The Morning After' are disturbing and tinged with horror—'*Is this my blood dried upon my face? Or is it the love of someone else?*'—and based on a 1987 Mary Lambert film. 'The song "The Morning After" comes out of that film *Siesta*, where this woman wakes up on an airport runway, only to find out at the end that she's been dead the whole time,' he recalled. The track even references the film's title: '*When I closed my eyes, was it my siesta? Did I encounter a darkness stronger than sleep?*'

On another *The Real Thing* track, 'Underwater Love', Patton's penchant for disturbing imagery and lyrics met record company resistance. He has since given a rather metaphorical interpretation of the song's dark subject matter: 'There's also the whole aspect of fear of relationships. "Underwater Love" comes out of that. It's about drowning. Emotional drowning that is—fears of being exposed, fears of becoming obsessed, fears of being hurt.'

The original version of the track was one of the first Patton recorded on Gould's four-track recorder. It was clearly about the song's narrator murdering his girlfriend, as lines such as '*I hold you under and feel you struggle/ But I can't escape your stare*' starkly showed. By the time the track had been reworked for the album, that line had changed to '*Forever longing to make you mine/ But I can't escape your stare*'. Patton's more murderous lines had themselves been killed off. Why?

The answer lay with Matt Wallace, the album producer, who was also an employee of Slash Records. He spoke to Patton after reviewing the perfectly typewritten lyrics that the singer presented to him prior to recording, and recalls:

> For me, one of the biggest challenges with Patton, and probably that he had with me, is that there's a lot of darkness in the stuff. When he brought 'Underwater Love' to me, I think out of concern, I said, 'Oh, you can't have all these songs about death, and killing people.' He and I used to go to Zim's, a coffee shop on Van Ness and Market, and we would sit down and talk about lyrics. I'd try to impart some wisdom to him, and he probably just nodded his head and said, 'Yeah, whatever,' and did his own thing. I remember trying to say, 'Listen, it's OK to write dark things, but you can couch it in something, or use metaphor. Make it so it's not so blatant.' Again, I'm not sure if he even paid attention to what I said. If it even made a difference.

'I heard Matt was doing that and I got really annoyed,' Gould recalls. 'It's kind of a betrayal actually. Matt did that also with the "Cowboy Song". Matt's a nice guy, but he can be a square guy sometimes.'

There were no lyrics to worry about on 'Woodpeckers From Mars', as Faith No More maintained their tradition of instrumentals on their albums with their most ornate and orchestral effort to date. Gould: 'It started with

Roddy just playing the violin part on keyboard and me and Puffy just coming up with rhythms that went with that. I like that song, it never gets old for me. It's a really cheesy violin sample too, but that's all right. It works.'

'Billy and Mike and I would come up with loops typically, and this was along that vein,' Bottum says. 'It was a melody that I went with. I'd just got the Emax keyboard, and it was a violin sound we all found exciting and live-sounding.'

Bordin: 'We said, Let's do a super-intense thrash song with a violin as the main instrument. Why not? What's the worst that could happen?'

The song actually had two origins. Bottum had that violin synth part that he'd been working on, while Martin appended a guitar instrumental he'd written in one of his many sessions with Cliff Burton many years earlier at a place Jim's parents had in the Coastal Mountain Range. 'We recorded them on the spot as they happened,' he said in 2005. 'A lot of material came out of it that you might be familiar with—"Woodpecker From Mars" has a section in there. A Metallica song would be "For Whom The Bell Tolls".'

Bordin's point that the violin was the main instrument is true, and it is the violin patch that provides the brutality and leads the aural assault. Martin's guitar interlude at two minutes and sixteen seconds in provides relief and lightness. Bordin adds, 'That guitar solo piece is a large chunk from Jim that sort of found its way as an instrumental break within an instrumental.'

The song would also serve as a key element of the band's arsenal, as they found themselves playing to more metal audiences following the release of *The Real Thing*. Bordin: 'That song was a fucking weapon. It's us declaring who we are, and it's definitely not Bon Jovi or Whitesnake, the big bands at the time. It's much more lining up with Metallica and Slayer, although we weren't exactly them either. We're showing what's next. All those things build up, build momentum, and break things loose, and then came Nirvana and they opened it up for good.'

Nirvana may have killed off hair metal and mainstream rock with *Nevermind*, but Faith No More had already inflicted mortal wounds with *The Real Thing*. As Nirvana's Krist Novoselic told oral historian John Hughes for Washington State's The Legacy Project, 'Living on the margins for so long, living in the underground scene, it's like, "Oh this will never catch on." But it did, and it was starting to change where you had bands like

Faith No More and Jane's Addiction. They were these rock bands, but they were more like alternative or edgy. Then they paved the way for Nirvana.'

And tracks such as 'Zombie Eaters', 'Woodpecker From Mars', and 'The Real Thing' foreshadow the expressive range, slower tempo, dynamics, crisper production, and even the lyrical themes of *Metallica*.

'The Real Thing' is a dynamic snapshot of a band at the peak of their powers: confident, ambitious, proficient, together, and self-contained. And it contains some of the best lyrics of Mike Patton's career. He explains, 'A lot of what we're about is a celebration, a real *go out and kill the grizzly bear* primal urge, something to go out and scream your head off about.'

The song brilliantly describes that feeling of pure joy, of happiness, of euphoria. For Buddhists, it is nirvana; for Hindus, it is moksha; for Patton, it is the 'golden moment', 'the pinnacle of happiness', and 'the split second of divinity'. And the track cautions how ephemeral such moments are:

> *Cherish the certainly of no*
> *It kills you a bit at a time*
> *Cradle the inspiration*
> *It will leave you writhing on the floor.*

The song was constructed by Gould singlehandedly, but he deflects praise to Patton's lyrics. 'That's when Mike dropped his character and did something heartfelt,' he says. 'It's very rare.'

Producer Matt Wallace notes, 'What Patton did lyrically was well beyond his years as a nineteen-year-old. There's a tremendous amount of wisdom. It is visceral. Resonant. How he did that, to come from Eureka, which is out in the boonies, and probably with a relatively insular kind of upbringing, and to come up with that stuff? Anybody can feel those things he's sings.' Of the music, he says, 'The song has a lot of movements in it. It is more orchestrated, and it has a lot of air and space in it. It really shows the depth and breadth of a band that allowed space to happen; just emptiness.'

'I got to say two words about that song: Billy Gould,' Bordin says. 'He said, "I wrote a thing around that little thing you have been doing at the soundcheck." I used to play that intro, that little side-stick thing that I do in the very first part of the song. It was nothing, it was just me just farting around with my monitors and the sound. He wrote the song from that. It starts from nothing and goes to everything, and then it goes back to nothing. That's not like a song that we had ever structured before. It's like a bit of a sucker punch, where just you don't see it coming.'

The song would gave the album its name. 'We felt that it really caught the gist of what it was all about for us, and where we were at with it,' Bordin adds. 'Slash president Bob Biggs, being the artist and chaos advocate that he was, he really wanted to call that album *Album Of The Year*, and he made a strong argument for it. Showing how much he liked the album. How would that have been—ballsy right?'

As the band put the finishing touches to the record in mid-January 1989, with final track 'The Morning After' completed, there was an all-too-rare feeling of contentment and camaraderie. Bordin: 'One time, for some reason I was driving to the studio with Jim Martin, and he turned to me and he said, I'm really pleased with how this recording is going. That was nothing he'd ever said before ever. I mean our band was always a band that would dissect something going wrong it and call it out, but if things were going right, it wasn't a backslapping band. So for him to say that was a big deal.'

20   THE MORNING AFTER

Faith No More entered 1989 energised and resolute. The recording of *The Real Thing*, which was mixed and mastered in late January, had been the most seamless and painless in the band's history. But within two months, they had two band members out of action, and still no album on the shelves.

The band and Matt Wallace also had to deal with their reactions to hearing the lush, fully mastered recordings. 'When we mastered *The Real Thing*, I was there with John Golden at K Disc, and I was pretty much at the point where I was going to quit producing, because I thought it sounded so bad,' Wallace recalls. 'I thought my mix had way too much high end and way too much compression. I called my mom the next day asking her how I could get into real estate, because I thought I didn't know what the hell I was doing.'

For Bill Gould, the sound was something of a paradigm shift for the band. 'It made us look more professional than we were. It actually had a big dimension to it. I liked seeing ourselves in that light. I didn't see us like that before. I thought we were just scraggly, filthy people. I was like, *Oh my god, I'm in a rock band.* It was something I never thought I would have been even a year before.'

Leading Faith No More media supporter Steffan Chirazi was raising expectations in his *BAM* 'Raw Power' column in February. 'Let's move on to the new Faith No More album, finished but as yet untitled, though it'll be in stores by March,' he wrote. 'The songs are quite brilliant, singer Mike Patton being an outstanding addition, and the power quota is disgustingly huge all the way, thick and rippling with punch. The guitars ride higher than on previous vinyl and that's a damn fine thing.'

The prediction was somewhat off, as a dispute over the album cover and a succession of injuries derailed the release. Bill Gould and Roddy Bottum, in particular, had always been involved in the band's artwork. Bottum: 'Our covers were problematic. This one was typically hideous. I hate it now, and I wasn't crazy about it then. It was for lack of a better image.'

Being Faith No More, such disputes were aired proudly in public. The following January, the *Chicago Sun-Times* reported:

> Faith No More finished its latest album in two months. The record company spent twice that long working on the album cover. After all that, the group doesn't like the way the cover looks. 'I think it's pretty awful,' vocalist Mike Patton said, describing the cover for *The Real Thing*. The artwork depicts a portion of the Earth being swallowed up in flames. 'Part of the way it turned out was our fault, because when [the record

company] came around and asked us what we wanted, we just said, "We don't know."'

The other reasons for the delays were more serious. Mike Patton and Jim Martin were put on the injured list in late spring/early summer. Martin required surgery after the bones broken in his hand had not set properly. And Patton also went under the knife after picking up a serious arm injury in one of his first gigs with the band, a show at the I-Beam in April that also doubled as a video shoot for the album's lead-off single, 'From Out Of Nowhere'.

After the ill-starred opening show at the same venue in November, the new-look Faith No More had played a series of small shows in and around San Francisco in February and March, as well as headlining shows at Scream and the Whisky A Go-Go in Los Angeles. It was obvious how uncomfortable or just lacking in self-awareness Patton was onstage. At Night Moves in Huntington Beach in March, as the introduction to 'Chinese Arithmetic' plays, Patton initially attempted an Axl Rose-style shuffle before meekly abandoning the mic stand entirely to dad-dance from foot to foot. With his long hair swept back by a backward baseball cap, white T-shirt, long board shorts and white high-top trainers, he looked like a clean-cut American teen from central casting and terribly, terribly out of place.

The 'From Out Of Nowhere' video—directed by Doug Freel, known for videos for hair metal pioneers and acolytes Def Leppard and Poison, not to mention several for Swedish pop-rockers Roxette—captures some of that early gaucheness. It also contains so many hair metal video tropes that many considered it a deliberate parody. Gould was unimpressed. 'He was the director that the label got in,' he recalls. 'He was giving the label what he thought we wanted. I saw it and I didn't dig it. I didn't want to be in that kind of band.'

Patton was the central focus of the video. Where Chuck Mosley had been puppyish in 'Anne's Song', Patton was like a whelp, gambolling and gurning, over-stimulated and eager to please. If Patton, his just-stepped-out-of-the-salon mane flowing, was a whirligig of movement in cycling shorts, Bill Gould looked distinctly uncomfortable. That was not solely due to the video direction. 'I threw my neck out at rehearsal,' he recalls. 'That was back at the Pet Hospital, and at the venue they were giving me massages and

I was taking codeines, just so I could play the show. My neck completely froze when they were filming the video. If you watch it, I'm barely moving. That was a horrible experience.'

Gould's pain paled in comparison to the blood and gore of the final minutes of the show. Patton had been throwing himself with the trademark uncoordinated abandon of his early band years. Having broken a tooth on the microphone stand earlier in the set, during 'War Pigs' he slipped on the stage, stumbled, and gashed his hand on some jagged glass from broken bottles. 'I didn't feel it at first,' he later recalled, 'but all of a sudden there was blood everywhere.'

Luckily for Patton, Mike Bordin's father was at the show. Bordin Jr. recalls, 'My dad was there at that show. He said, "Dude, come on, let's go," and he took him to the hospital, and I think had he not have had somebody advocating for him, it would have been a lot worse.'

Patton required five hours of microsurgery to repair the tendons in his hand. He was told by doctors that he would not recover movement in the hand, but that he would have feeling. The opposite happened, with Patton having full range and movement in the hand and arm but no sensation. The injury necessitated weeks of recovery time and, with Jim Martin also recuperating from his operation, the release of *The Real Thing* was put back until the end of June.

✿

Whereas the launch of *Introduce Yourself* two years earlier had been marked by Chuck Mosley falling asleep onstage and the sense of hard-earned opportunity squandered, *The Real Thing* was Faith No More's coronation as rock royalty. With the album hitting stores on Monday June 20, a launch party was scheduled for that night, at the famed Sunset Strip club the Roxy Theater. Nothing was left to chance, with a full-on industry showcase arranged. Label executives, music media luminaries, MTV and radio station bosses and programmers were all invited, and a selection of bona-fide rock stars were on the guest list.

Bill Gould remembers being taken by surprise. 'Duff and Slash from Guns N' Roses came up and played with us,' he recalls. 'We didn't even know they were there. It was another one of these things that were arranged behind our backs. All of a sudden, the Def Leppard guys loved us. I had no idea. But I only found out onstage. Duff was like, Give me the bass, give me the bass. And I was like, Sure. After the *Introduce Yourself* Club Lingerie disaster, this got us back on the radar. Kim Kaiman was our press person, so she probably arranged those guys to come and play with us.'

The *Los Angeles Times*' review echoed Gould's comments:

> You once might have expected Faith No More to jam with the likes of the Red Hot Chili Peppers, but the San Francisco band's show at the Roxy concluded with Guns N' Roses' Duff and Slash joining in for an old Black Sabbath stomp. Is Faith No More, which four years ago set the standard for post-punk cynicism with its rap-metal anthem 'We Care A Lot', now a bandwagon-jumper deserving that cynicism itself?

Also in attendance at the launch was former band member Courtney Love. Roddy recalls, 'Courtney and I were laughing and laughing about the Gunners onstage. It felt absolutely surreal and ridiculous.'

The band's induction into LA rock circles was complete as the party spilled over to the next-door Rainbow Room. Rather than being wowed by rubbing shoulders with rock's great and good, Faith No More were bowled over by meeting the fakest pop outfit in history.

'Bill and Mike were screaming like teenagers because this new group that they'd seen on MTV was walking into the Rainbow—it was Milli Vanilli,' Bordin recalls. 'They were freaking out and chasing them down like Beatlemania or something. Def Leppard comes around, and Guns N' Roses is playing with us, but the guys were going crazy over Milli Vanilli. I'd never heard of them.'

'Milli Vanilli were getting out of their limo, and we went up and shook their hands and told them what big fans we were,' says Gould, 'They didn't know who the fuck we were. We ended up dancing with Milli Vanilli, and we were doing chest bumps, and we got them out on the dance floor. The guys couldn't actually dance to their own song. The moves in the video, they didn't know them. The whole surrealist aspect of being in the industry was a lot of fun, and we always had an affection and revulsion for pop culture.'

❀

In the album press release, the band's press department were still trying to paint Faith No More as some dysfunctional infamous five, while also boasting that the fans would be 'treated to a more metal edge'. If that's what the label wanted the media to think—and the choreographed appearance of Guns N' Roses and Def Leppard at the launch laid this bare—then it was no surprise that Faith No More soon became regarded as a metal band.

The buzz continued with a series of positive reviews. Greg Kot in the *Chicago Tribune* awarded the album two-and-a-half stars out of three, noting that 'Mike Patton is better suited to this San Francisco band's chameleonic music' and that the album 'stomps more forcefully into Metallica territory than the debut'. Kot praised the band, and especially Bordin and Bottum's 'ferocious virtuosity'.

The less august *Reno Star-Gazette* was positively effusive: 'Faith No More's second LP for Slash roars straight out of the gate like a three-alarm fire and never stops burning,' reviewer Eric McClary wrote, adding that the band 'proceed to cut a swath through the turgid heavy-metal music scene'. He too made a Metallica comparison: 'Faith No More is the most innovative force in heavy metal since Metallica.'

They may have been regarded as the future of metal in Reno, but the big-hitters of the US music press, such as *Spin*, did not consider *The Real Thing* worthy of a review, and *Rolling Stone* waited until November to offer its own bandwagon-jumping assessment.

The band embraced the question of metal in an interview in *Kerrang!* in June; they—or rather Jim Martin, taking over from Chuck as the face of the band—would score their first *Kerrang!* cover a month later. Martin said, 'The writing certainly isn't any more hard rock than before; at least it wasn't written to be.'

❀

A five-date run in July was the first of an unprecedented five British tours to promote the album. For booking agent Derek Kemp, the hype and buzz of the band's 1988 shows and attendant media exposure counted for little this time around. 'Nobody knew what Mike Patton would be like,' he recalls. 'For a band to change lead singer that early in their career is quite a big thing and so, effectively, we were starting the band from scratch. Hence the reason why we were playing smaller venues on that first run in the summer of 1989.'

The run again included two shows, on July 6 and 7, at the Marquee. Neil Perry, who had introduced the band to the UK the previous year in *Sounds*, reviewed the first show for the same publication. 'Mike Patton's vinyl performance may have hinted at a certain something lacking,' he wrote, 'but, onstage, there are no worries. Faith No More are now realising the multi-pronged vision you knew was always there, but had never achieved before.'

That UK trip was met by another splash in *Sounds*, with Paul Elliott's piece entitled 'Chucking It All Away'. It showed that, without the 20/20 vision of hindsight, the replacement of Chuck Mosley with Mike Patton was not a pre-ordained success. 'Maybe all it needs is time and space for Patton to grow, but Chuck Mosley will not be forgotten easily,' Elliott wrote. 'Faith No More's attempts to shrug his memory off their backs are rather unreasoned and, occasionally, smack of bullshit.'

Within days of the brief UK jaunt, the quintet was back on home turf, playing six tracks from the album during a radio session for New York's WNYU FM. A low-profile headlining tour followed in August. The one-month national jaunt was a precursor to Faith No More's biggest tour to date, supporting Metallica during September. The band barely had time to take a breath, with less than a week between the tours.

Metallica drummer and founder Lars Ulrich explained to *Kerrang!* why they had chosen Faith No More as support act:

> We had The Cult supporting us for almost four months in America, then they basically backed out of playing the West Coast dates with us for reasons I don't want to get into. We thought, *Let's give some people that we know really well, who have an album that everyone in the band loves, our management loves, everyone in the business loves and who don't seem to be getting as much exposure as they maybe could or should, the chance to come tour with us for three or four weeks*. The vibe was great—it was like family.

For co-manager John Vassiliou, it was a no-brainer. 'Jim's relationship with

James [Hetfield] was the key. And, from a marketing perspective, the band would play in front of larger crowds.'

The support was appreciated, says Gould. 'That was a friendship thing. I mean James always really supported the band by wearing our shirts. They were very cool. They were great to us.'

Faith No More were playing with brio and belief, with Mike Patton quickly metamorphosing from over-energetic eager-beaver to focused, forceful, and flamboyant frontman. The band revelled in goading their audience. In Salt Lake City, on only their fourth show on the tour, agitator-in-chief Bill Gould asked the crowd, 'Are there any Mormons here tonight?' When the inevitable and desired chorus of boos arrived in response, he launched into his well-practised tactic for winding up crowds: a ten-minute one-note bass solo. Mike Bordin recalls, 'Bill's bass solo was well known. They're the guys in the zoo that are going to poke the fucking animal just to get a reaction. If everybody's happy and cheerful, I think some of the guys don't feel they've really done their job.'

'Us playing for their fans was a stretch,' says Bottum. 'They weren't that open-minded. I remember trying to go to a Metallica show in San Francisco, and I was wearing a full red long-johns union suit and big white puffy tennis shoes and a yellow rain slicker, and it was not cool for the Metallica people. I got laughed at and called names, which I was OK with. But it was like, *Wow, you people like live in caves.*'

The bands themselves got on famously. Kirk Hammett joined Faith No More during 'Epic', turning the song's solo into a scorching but still subtle dual lead with Jim Martin, while James Hetfield joined in during 'War Pigs' and 'Surprise! You're Dead!' Bordin even joined in a Jimi Hendrix tribute section during Metallica's set, and Martin played a cameo on Metallica's Misfits 'Last Caress' cover. While there was some booing of the Faith No More set, especially when the tour got to Los Angeles, the reception was largely positive. Jason Newsted said at the time, 'We haven't had a vibe like this since we went out with Danzig. The first show kicked the shit out of the previous nine months. We watch them and they watch us, it's like a family thing, and I think Metallica fans are way more apt to appreciate sideways stuff like FNM than any other fan base. I'm seeing lots and lots of fans being won over show by show.'

This exposure was not yet translating into sales or any other commercial success, though according to Gould, 'I think actually they really helped us a lot. I think if those guys had not have done that, people wouldn't take us seriously because we were at a point before the Metallica tour where we only had 25,000 records sold. After the tour we were like, *Where are sales now? We've just played for all these people.* It was, like, 25,000. We didn't sell anything. How the fuck does that work?'

While Gould's observations question whether exposure should have been the goal for Faith No More at this time, there is no denying that they were part of an era-defining tour, as Metallica inched ever closer to their mainstream breakthrough. Their show—Metallica's show—at the Irvine Meadows on September 21 quickly sold out, and was extended to a three-night run. If sales of their own were not yet happening, Faith No More were getting media exposure. In a perfectly prescient profile piece in the *Los Angeles Times* on September 29, Mike Boehm speculated that Metallica may achieve greater success by embracing lyricism, grandeur, and harmony, and also forecast a Faith No More breakthrough: 'If Metallica doesn't leap into the metal future, Faith No More may get there first. Singer Mike Patton spent too much time fretting aloud about the less than rapturous reception the band was getting. He ought to relax: An adventurous approach always takes some time to sink in.'

And there was work going on to raise the band's profile. Kim Kaiman, who did press and PR for the band with Concrete Marketing, had secured Faith No More top slot at the Foundations Forum 89 in late September at the Sheraton Universal Hotel in Los Angeles. The forum was a sort of metal festival/convention hybrid for industry bigwigs, organised by Concrete Marketing and mostly by Kaiman herself, and had raised the profile of Winger and Warrant the previous year.

In between presentations and panel discussions on such subjects as 'Video: $$$ Well Spent or Spend It Elsewhere?' and 'Understanding Music Publishing' (one that FNM might have benefited from some years previously), and a keynote address from Gene Simmons, there were performances by King Diamond, Suicidal Tendencies, and Soundgarden. Faith No More were the final act to play on the final night, and had to race over from their final Metallica show. They almost did not make it. As industry magazine the *Gavin Report* noted, 'Faith No More members were held up at the door even though they were next to perform.'

The Forum underlined that heavy metal was a growing force in the music industry. A *Los Angeles Times* feature on the event reported that 'hard rock and heavy metal account for a sizable percentage of the record industry's $6.5-billion-a-year gross—as much as fifteen to twenty per cent, according to some estimates', while at the time of the convention, three metal albums (by Skid Row, Mötley Crüe, and Warrant) were in the *Billboard* top 10. And Faith No More were being unashamedly associated with the rise of metal. The same *Times* report stated, 'This year, performances by Excel, Babylon A.D., and Faith No More, among others, may speed the plough for those bands.'

In particular, the band were benefitting from their association with the biggest band on the planet, Guns N' Roses. Axl Rose and Duff McKagan were at the Faith No More Forum show, and they even got into the mosh pit, with Axl also stage-diving during the band's set, losing his wallet in the process. It was a time of rising excitement for the band, according to Bill Gould: 'We were playing really well, and we were into the music. We were getting a lot of validation. We were taking what we could get.'

THESE WALLS WON'T KEEP THEM OUT

21

'From Out Of Nowhere', the lead-off single from *The Real Thing*, was finally released on October 30 1989. The video was released to MTV and other outlets in August, but had actually debuted on MTV's alternative and indie music show *120 Minutes* in June. It was then played on the channel's

Headbangers Ball on August 5, wedged between Skid Row's 'Youth Gone Wild' and Onslaught's 'Let There Be Rock'. Strangely, although the show featured two short Faith No More interviews in September and October, it did not play the video again until November. The single had died in the water; one minute here, one minute there, and that was it.

The band were back in the UK, for the second time since the album release, within three weeks of the end of the Metallica tour. Derek Kemp was aware that he was breaking new ground with the band: 'We did six tours in a year. Nobody had ever done that, and I was breaking every rule by doing that, and people were looking at me going, *Is this the right thing to do?* The demand was there. That's all I can say.'

The introduction to Mike Patton was going better this time than it had on the first tour. In his review of their October show at the Leadmill in Sheffield for *RAW*, Phil Alexander—future editor of *Kerrang!* and *Mojo*, and then presenter of the UK's only heavy metal terrestrial television show, *Raw Power*—reported, 'If the last UK tour back in July saw new boy vocalist Mike Patton busy introducing himself with a fair degree of nervousness to the Faith crowd, this time around he runs the joint. The dirt and grime is still part of the FNM sound, but they've found a new sense of professionalism.'

Mike Bordin agrees. 'All the shows were sold out,' he recalls. 'It was mayhem. Everybody wanted free tickets. Everybody wanted something. We were signing shit for people, which was very, very strange. It was exciting. You're still playing the same clubs that you'd played three or four times previously. First time, there's twenty people. Second time, there's 150 people. Third time, there's 300 people. The fourth time, it's sold out in advance.'

The band's UK run meant that they were out of the country when a 6.9-magnitude earthquake rocked their home city on October 17, killing sixty-three people. They had just finished a show in Newcastle's Riverside when the news broke. Bordin remembers it vividly:

> I'm a big San Francisco Giants fan, and my team was in the World Series. It was the [cross-town rivals, the Oakland] A's and the Giants. We had season tickets. When I got a little bit of money, that's the first thing I bought. I split them with my sister.

My wife was there. My brother-in-law was there. My sister was there. All my people were at the fucking ball game. After the show, I was listening on a transistor radio, an AM radio, to *Voice Of America*, the military channel, because I knew they would have the World Series. It was around probably two or three in the morning. I turn on the radio, and the announcer says, 'This is *Voice Of America* radio. Please stay tuned because we will give you more details about the massive earthquake that has just hit San Francisco.' I just went, 'Oh my God' and, 'Well, I guess the World Series isn't going to happen.' But everybody I knew was at the ball park, at Candlestick, so I knew that they were probably OK.

✦

In contrast, three weeks later, the band were, for perhaps the only time in their career, in the right place at the right time. It was November 9, and they were in Berlin. It was another show at the Loft Club, run by the charismatic Monika Döring in the roof space of the Metropol Theatre, and their fourth German concert in a week. East Germans had begun escaping the Communist regime through Hungary for Austria in June of that year, and in mid-October, the long-time ruler, Erich Honecker, was forced to resign as his party tried desperately to cling on to power in the face of demands for reform and a continued exodus to the West. In the first nine days of November, 30,000 people had fled to Czechoslovakia, so on the ninth—the day of the Faith No More concert—East German authorities decided that they would enact new travel laws that would allow free travel between East and West Germany, and even between the east and west of Berlin, a city that had been divided by the Berlin Wall since 1961. The new law was not due to come into effect straight away, and had not yet been fully approved by Communist party ministers, but that afternoon, the East German press spokesman in Berlin, Günter Schabowski, said, 'We have decided today to implement a regulation that allows every citizen of the German Democratic Republic [East Germany] to leave the GDR through any of the border crossings.'

By the time Faith No More arrived at the Loft, hundreds of people had began congregating elsewhere in the city, at the Bornholmer Street, Checkpoint Charlie, and Sonnenallee checkpoints; by ten past eight in the evening, the Bornholmer Street crossing started to allow a trickle of people into West Berlin. A trickle that turned into a tide during the rest of the night. Back at the Loft, Faith No More tour manager Tim Dalton was manning the mixing console as the band neared the end of their performance. 'The show was a super one,' he recalls. 'I remember Monika, bright purple Mohican, leather trousers and body piercings, leaning over the mixing console and asking me to turn it up! Just as the main set was coming to a close, the club manager told me that he had heard the Wall was coming down and it was happening now. He rushed backstage to tell the band before they took to the stage for the encore.'

'It was our third time in Berlin,' Bordin adds, 'and we could tell something was up. The first two times we went, it was fucking scary. We had guns pointed at us. There were dogs under the fucking vehicles. This time, we roll in, and it seemed like the guard was drunk first of all. We had a dude in our crew, his name was Steve Gosbee. He was a full-on fucking English lad. So the guard was checking our passports, and he said, Ah, Bing Crosby. We're like, *What?* Checkpoint Charlie was life and death. It was fucking serious.'

Gould recalls, 'We were in the club, and somebody said to me, "The Wall is falling down. Say something on the stage." So I say to Mike Patton, "Mike, the Wall has opened up, say something about it. Say the Wall is gone." That's what he said. Nobody in the club thought it was real. They thought, *Why is he saying that?* It wasn't until after the show we walked outside, and we were like, *Holy, shit. It actually happened.*'

So a thousand Berliners first heard the news from Mike Patton. During the first song of the encore—appropriately their regular encore opener of 'War Pigs'—he shouted, *'Der Mauer ist weg! Der Mauer ist weg!'* Even in his finely mimicked German, it elicited no reaction, so at the end of song—shrewdly recorded for posterity by Dalton and released as the B-side to 'Epic' the following year—Patton addressed the crowd in English: 'Thank you, Berlin, fucking night, see you later, man. And guess what? The Wall is gone!'

The band were not able to join in the celebrations straight away, as they had to deal with a dispute over a trashed room before leaving their hotel.

But they did take in the scene as they embarked on their 1,036-kilometre overnight drive to Oslo. Bordin was fascinated. 'I saw a guy dressed up in a waiter's tuxedo, with a fucking cart, handing out champagne to people,' he remembers. 'Strangers were kissing each other. At the KaDeWe store, people were looking in the windows like they'd never seen anything like it in their life. It was insane.'

✱

For many, the fall of the Berlin Wall signalled the premature start of the 1990s—but, in music, *The Real Thing* had kick-started the decade a few months early. So it made sense for the standout track from that album not to be released until the 1980s had breathed their last. 'Epic' was finally unleashed as a single on January 29 1990. 'From Out Of Nowhere' had disappeared somewhere, elsewhere, nowhere, and *The Real Thing*'s album sales had stalled at a stubborn 30,000, so the band needed a boost.

If the Metallica tour had not brought the desired results in terms of increased sales, a slot at the bottom of the bill with Voivod and Soundgarden in the early months of 1990 was unlikely to do so either. But as with the Metallica tour, Faith No More were again on one of the most talked-about tours in rock, a triple bill that showed that as much as hair metal was becoming old hat, 'alternative' metal was the coming force for the new decade. Quebec's progressive metallers Voivod had received wide critical acclaim for their fifth album, *Nothingface*, upon its release in 1989, and their distinct version of Pink Floyd's 'Astronomy Domine' was enjoying heavy rotation on MTV. Soundgarden had made quick progress since Chris Cornell was being considered for a spot in Faith No More eighteen months previously, and their second album, *Louder Than Love*, also their major label debut on A&M, would enter the *Billboard* 200 chart days after the first leg of the tour finished.

Both Soundgarden and Faith No More were handpicked by Voivod. 'In the States, nobody still knew who we were,' Gould recalls, 'so we got the Voivod/Soundgarden tour and tried to make something work there, but we were the opening band.'

It was one of the most enthralling tours to rock the USA in years. All three bands—and especially the younger pretenders, Soundgarden and Faith No

More—were at the peak of their powers, and the tour was a riot of vitality, urgency, and exuberance. The run kicked off to over a thousand people on Voivod's home turf in Montreal, with Faith No More's thirty-minute set composed mostly of *The Real Thing* cuts, except for 'Introduce Yourself' and 'We Care A Lot'. Patton's transformation to the band's agitator-in-chief was now complete; as the band started 'Zombie Eaters' midway through their sixth date at Chicago's Old Vic Theatre on January 14, he could be heard berating Jim Martin: 'You know why it takes him so long to start a song? Because he's sixty-five years old.'

Another highlight was a show on January 19 at the Ritz—the former Studio 54—in New York, when Faith No More played to a crowd of nearly 3,000 in the 2,400-capacity venue. The audience included a 300-strong guest list of industry insiders keen to get a glimpse of music's future. The following night, the tour made its way to Long Island, and Faith No More kicked off their set with a brief cover of 'Fever'—Patton's voice silky, smooth, and soulful—before brutally segueing into 'From Out Of Nowhere' as a succession of audience members took turns to stage-dive.

Faith No More's last show of the tour was at the Trocadero in Philadelphia. To celebrate, Soundgarden attacked the stage with silly string, and joined in on guitar during Faith No More's final song, 'War Pigs'. Later, during Soundgarden's set, Chris Cornell paid tribute, as the *Rocket* reported:

> 'We got a surprise for you,' announces Chris. 'We've been on tour with Faith No More a couple of weeks now, but tonight's our last show with them. We really love those guys, and we're going to miss them.' Bringing out Patton and Voivod guitarist Piggy for a house-wrecking rendition of 'I Awake', Chris turns over the mic to Patton, and dives head first into the audience. The stage security pushes him back into the crowd during the song, thinking he's a fan trying to get onstage.

Audiences, reviewers, and bands all agreed that they were witnessing and participating in something significant and era-defining. Voivod drummer Michel 'Away' Langevin later reflected, 'By the time we hit the US West Coast, they were huge; both of them had exploded in popularity. We were still headlining, because they had full-on respect for Voivod, but they were getting really popular. So we had a sort of a taste of the explosion of college rock right there; right before it really happened with Nirvana. We could feel it.'

The Faith No More explosion did not come until the second part of the tour. In the two months in between, Faith No More released 'Epic', received a Grammy nomination, and took in a third UK tour in less than six months. The first leg of the Voivod tour was certainly perfectly timed. On the morning of the second date in Porter Hall in Ottawa, January 11, both Faith No More and Soundgarden were nominated for Grammy awards in the 'Best Metal Vocal or Instrumental' category for their albums *The Real Thing* and *Ultramega OK*, alongside Dokken, Queensrÿche, and Metallica. In an interview with the *Boston Globe*, Soundgarden's Kim Thayil revealed Jim Martin's reaction: 'It was pretty weird. We're sitting here eating lasagne, and I said something about the Grammys, and he goes, "Yeah, who … cares, that's all I got to say!" adding an expletive.'

Bill Gould: 'It was great, because we were recognised, but nobody at the Grammys knew who we were. It was just a bizarre experience we happened to find ourselves in.'

WHAT IS IT?
THE MAKING OF 'EPIC'

22

The bizarre experience was only just beginning. Released in January, 'Epic' was initially received as coldly as 'From Out Of Nowhere'. The track was a breakout on MTV in the first two weeks of January. The band also featured on MTV's *Headbangers Ball* on January 28, with Mike Patton and Roddy Bottum undergoing an awkward interview with Riki Rachtman.

'Epic' was picked up by a number of radio stations in January and February, notably Los Angeles's KROQ, WXVX in Pittsburgh, and XTRA in San Diego, but it was far from a hit. Industry tip sheet the *Gavin Report*'s observation—'"Epic" is a mix of rap and metal. I know what you're thinking. Radio poison'—was looking spot on.

'Epic' started life when the trio of Bordin, Gould, and Bottum were working together in Los Angeles in the immediate post-Mosley interregnum. The rhythm section quickly worked up the groove of the song, and Bottum was also involved in the genesis, playing around with a horns patch on his keyboard. 'I remember us wanting it to sound like *2001: A Space Odyssey*,' he recalls. 'The horns were a reference to that. The song was all about space and not playing, as opposed to playing.'

'Quickly, Bill and I wrote the groove, the rhythm for "Epic",' Bordin remembers. 'We knew it was cool, and it was good, and it was fun, and it was natural. We'd played it and said, wow, that's just so massive—it's just this huge broad, wide, open powerful thing, it's epic.'

The name was one of the band's few working titles that survived to become an actual title. Gould: 'The name has to do with how it felt to play. It was epic because of the horns. The parting of the Red Sea. That was the visual imagery.'

Building on that groove, Gould wrote the rest of the song almost singlehandedly. Matt Wallace remembers Gould's demo as 'a terrific piece of music. Before I even heard Patton sing on it. We probably spent two or three days on it. Tracking the drums, getting Bill's bass, and then getting guitars even before the vocals.'

Gould was keen to spread the credit. 'Jim put some of his guitar the way he would play it,' he adds, 'and actually Roddy had a little bit to do with that, too. We all did it together, though I wrote the piano part at the end and the middle part.'

Jim Martin picked up on Gould's demo and refined and expanded the guitar part. He later told *Guitar* magazine, 'I was just noodling around on the demo, and there was one little part at the beginning of the solo that grabbed me. Sometimes, that's all it takes.'

Gould, rather than Bottum, was primarily responsible for the keyboard coda. 'It actually didn't even come off the way I wanted it to come out,' he says. 'It took me a long time to listen to it and let it go, because I would have done it differently. I am probably the only person who would notice the difference.'

The outro was played by both Bottum and Gould: Roddy playing the new studio piano for the more melodic parts, and Gould playing the chords on the Emax keyboard. 'The piano was all about the drama,' Bottum adds. 'That's all we cared about. It was real moody.'

Matt Wallace also worked to make the track as tight as possible, making the unusual move of adding a click track for the metronomic Bordin. 'The song has twenty-seven razor blade edits. I wanted to get that one just right. Mike was thinking too much about that song and he, like most of us, once we get into our heads too much, it's hard for us to do our best work. I had the idea to do a striptease for him, taking my shirt off behind the desk, and then I'd I hit record. Just to get him thinking, *Oh my God, there's Matt acting like an idiot, taking his clothes off.* It worked just enough where he got out of his head and just played it.'

Vocally, the song is the peak of Patton's Mosley-aping rapping. 'Chuck did it first, obviously,' says Gould, 'because "We Care A Lot" was a rap vocal. But the rap on "Epic" was Patton's idea. He was listening to a lot of R&B, and we already set a little precedent for doing it. It wasn't that much of a departure.' Not everyone was impressed. 'It felt a little bit shouty-boy rap-rock to me,' says Bottum. 'But, whatever. The shoe fit.'

The '*It's it*' refrain was sung by all of the band, as well as by the various friends and associates who happened to be around the studio at the time, including Les Claypool from Primus.

Lyrically, Patton provides one of the most perplexing vistas in the Faith No More canon. Like 'The Real Thing', the song is not a character study but something more metaphysical. Normally loathe to interpret his lyrics, Patton has indulged in some 'Epic' exegesis over the years. In an interview with *Circus* magazine, he said, 'It was about sexual frustration. Sex and lack of sex.'

With Patton suggesting elsewhere that he had based the rhyme structure on Blondie's 'Rapture', the lyrics are either an ode to self-love, a homage to the first white rap song, or, more likely, another evocation, like 'The Real Thing', of the fleeting nature of pure pleasure. Or not knowing what you want until you get it, and then not being able to get it again. Or, as music writer Robert Barry put it in the *Quietus* in 2010, in typical *Quietus* style:

> The lyrics present a near-perfect diagnosis of Freud's *Das Ding*, what [French philosopher Jacques] Lacan calls the 'true secret' of the unconscious. This Freudian Thing is the lost object, the obscure object of desire, that impossible, intractable element in the thing you desire which makes it irresistible. 'What is it?' begs Patton. 'It's It,' the band yell in response, summoning the failure of language and logos to banish the feverish mystery of the Thing.

It is possible to extend this line of thought further and take a deep dive into superficial erudition, but it is nonetheless worth noting that it is possible to interpret 'Epic', 'The Real Thing', and even 'Zombie Eaters' in Freudian or Lacanian psychoanalytic terms. So, in 'Epic', we see there is a limit to pleasure, and when the limit is contravened, pain is the result: '*And it feels so good, it's like walking on glass ... It's dark, it's moist, it's a bitter pain.*' Similarly, 'The Real Thing' posits life as a continual search for the 'golden moment'; this 'pinnacle of happiness' like Lacan's *objet petit a*, the unattainable object of desire, the lost object that is continually craved. For Lacan and Patton, 'The Real Thing' is the impossible thing. To finish with the psychoanalytical, 'Zombie Eaters' is, of course, the perfect sketch of the mother-baby relationship and such Lacanian concepts as the devouring mother ('*I melt in your mouth*') and the symbolic mother ('*You're everything that's why I cling to you / When I emerge my thoughts converge to you*' and '*I begin to see through your eyes / All the former mysteries are no surprise*').

If 'Epic''s explanations get ever more esoteric, the song's video was no less confusing. After 'From Out Of Nowhere' had flopped its last, the band were given one more shot at a video to salvage the album. 'Warner Bros told us that they'd pay for one more video,' Gould recalls. 'But that was pretty much it. It was the end of the record. It was dead after that. We could pick whatever song we wanted to. We just picked "Epic" because that was the song we liked the best. The record company never would have picked it. They probably would have done "Edge Of The World" or something.'

The video was filmed quickly when the band had a free day in London in mid-November between their Oslo show and a date at west London club Subterrania. Warners video executive Randy Skinner chose twenty-six-year-old South African Ralph Ziman, who had directed 'The Wanderer' for Dave Edmunds, the US *Billboard* top 10 hit 'Let Me Be The One' for Exposé, and the LA Guns song 'Sex Action', to direct.

'I got a call from Randy Skinner,' Ziman recalls, 'and she said that Faith No More were going to be in town in three days and, "Could you shoot a video with them?" It was like some ridiculous time frame. That video was an oddity, because even in all my years of working with American record companies, and I did lots and lots and lots of videos—it was the only cut where we didn't have an executive from the record company on set.'

Both Ziman and Bill Gould lay claim to the original idea of the famous fish flopping out of water in the video. Gould: 'The floundering goldfish was my idea. It was a John Waters thing, where you try to get maximum attention for minimum money!' For Ziman, the inspiration came from elsewhere: 'I threw a bunch of ideas together. But I had the idea of doing the imagery that came from the song. I thought about a fish flopping. I thought about that beautiful piano at the beginning and the end. And floating hands and eyes. For the fish, I'm sure I'd seen it on some *National Geographic* video or something.'

The song was filmed on a cold London day—and the video necessitated the band getting very wet on the sound stage in a fake thunderstorm. 'Every time you'd point the camera at Patton, it would look really amazing,' Ziman says. 'Everybody was supportive—you'd ask someone to chuck a bucket of water on their head, they'd do it, and there was no complaining, no attitude.'

The band largely brought their own clothes—Martin in a Cliff Burton tribute T-shirt, Bottum in a plain white tee with 'Master' on the front and, later, in a white shirt with red stars—and, of course, Mike Patton in a 'There's A Tractor In My Balls Again' T-shirt from his other band, Mr Bungle. 'I asked Mike, What's Mr Bungle?' Ziman continues. 'He said that it was his other band. I picked up fairly quickly that it was a bone of contention, and that the other guys didn't like Mr Bungle.'

It was another brightly coloured Faith No More video, after 'We Care A Lot' and 'Anne's Song'. 'I like bright colours—that's my thing,' Ziman reflects. 'But I think they liked it as well. I just wanted something that would talk more than the black and white. The song and the band had so much energy.'

And what about the fate of the famous fish? Faith No More folklore and the band's penchant for tall tales in interviews had it that the fish died, or that the fish had belonged to Icelandic singer Björk, only to be kidnapped by the band at a party. But the fish was a koi carp rather than a goldfish, and according to Ziman, 'The fish is definitely not Björk's. We had an animal handler on set. He brought some bugs. He brought some snakes. He brought the fish in the bucket. We took the fish out, it flopped around for thirty or forty seconds in slow motion, and we put it back in the bucket.'

After a sixteen-hour shoot, no dead fish, one exploding piano, and a $60,000 budget spent, the video was wrapped and delivered to Warner Bros in Burbank. Some in the band were underwhelmed, especially Gould. 'The video is horrible,' he says. 'I'm embarrassed about it. I never liked it. The ending is Las Vegas shit.'

The video was played once by MTV before 1989 ended, premiering on the December 2 episode of *Headbangers Ball*. The music of the 1990s would have to wait.

23 THE UNSEEN GLITTER OF LIFE

The 'Epic' video got its proper debut across the MTV network on January 6 but, as with radio play, it never came close to medium, never mind heavy rotation, in early 1990. So the first ripples of the Faith No More explosion would be heard in the UK and not the USA.

The group returned to the UK for the third time in six months in late January 1990. The tour kicked off at Sheffield's Octagon, and *Kerrang!* was again loud in its praise of the tour opener, declaring, 'Faith No More have dragged metal kicking and screaming into the '90s.' Mike Patton attracted particular praise: 'Wandering onstage like the bastard son of Alex in *Clockwork Orange*, Patton soon dispenses with his stripy pullover and pork-pie hat to unleash a vocal performance of pure magnitude. Patton is the difference between Faith No More and most rock acts.'

'Epic' was still being ignored by radio stations and the early cable music channels in January and February, but the band were on fire on the road through Newcastle, Edinburgh, and Birmingham in the week 'Epic' was released as a single. A party after the Newcastle show saw the band lumbered with a £110 bill after Bill Gould's hotel bed crashed under the weight of fans, while Patton had earlier ripped the stage curtain apart after several stage dives.

It was in the second week of February that things started getting really crazy. Critical were a pair of shows at London's Astoria. Some high-level executives from Warner Bros, including Randy Skinner, were in the UK to work with the London shoe-gazing outfit Lush, and they decided to attend the first Astoria show on the Thursday night, February 7. The show was manic, and several fans were injured when a crash barrier gave way during 'Falling To Pieces', prompting the rest of the crowd to shout 'You Fat Bastards' at the security staff trying to help. That would become a Faith No More fans' rallying call for years to come, and also the name of their live video release later in the year.

The mayhem worked—*Kerrang!* breathlessly declared, 'hyped-up, hypermarket rock'n'roll, a salivating, ambitious beast'—and Skinner promptly got on the phone, Marvin Berry from *Back To The Future* style, and told her higher-ups in Warners, 'Something is happening here and I feel like we're missing it.'

'The barrier at the stage broke,' Bottum recalls, 'and we had to stop playing. It was insanity, and couldn't have played better for our record company, who were really slow to allow us any tour support. We were like, *See! People like us!*'

John Vassiliou also credits Warren Entner and two other Warners executives—Roberta Peterson, vice-president of A&R, and Michael Linehan, vice-president of rock promotion at Reprise—with pushing the band, and says the wheels were in motion even before that Astoria show:

> London Records got it, but, of course, they had a battle on their hands. The live shows and the press response kept growing on every trip over. After the Astoria, Warren set up a meeting with [Warner Bros president] Lenny Waronker and pleaded his case. I am sure Lenny's kids were in his ear. He is a music guy, but he also has a company to run. Warren and Lenny visited all the departments at Warners to get an assessment on where we were with the band. It was a positive response. Faith No More were at their best when selling themselves, because they were real, and the label responded to that. Warren got Roberta and Michael to come to London to see the Astoria shows and see what London was doing. They went back to LA and got Lenny to spend money on marketing, and it slowly worked.

The last of the old-school major label bosses, Waronker already liked the band, and his daughter Anna (who would later front the indie group That Dog, co-produce an album for Roddy Bottum's post-Faith No More band Imperial Teen, and inspire their song 'Birthday Girl') was a big fan. According to Gould, 'Lenny Waronker called MTV and said, "We're 100 percent behind this. Get behind this."'

Complicating the Slash/Warner relationship, the band were put on another Warners imprint. 'Lenny liked us,' Bordin explains, 'and he looked us in the eye and said, "You're unique and unusual. And you guys are the future." They put us on Reprise. Reprise was the label that Warner Bros started to woo Frank Sinatra away from Capitol Records. They thought we could do business for them there.'

Later the same week of the Astoria shows, 'Epic' entered the UK singles chart at #38. It was quite a coup for the band, and testament to their live shows, as the song had not been play-listed by any major British radio station. London Records' ongoing promotion campaign for *The Real Thing* might also have been a factor. The press and poster campaign saw well-known, and mostly metal, musicians proclaiming their wild enthusiasm for Faith No More and their album. Axl Rose said that Faith No More were 'by far the best band I've ever seen. I'm jealous'; Kirk Hammett of Metallica said that *The Real Thing* was 'the best album of the year'. His Metallica bandmate James Hetfield added, 'The press has trouble categorising the band Faith No More; so it must be something original, and that's what we need in the world of same sounding shit new bands'. Slash added, 'The new Faith No More album is fucking brilliant. The new lead singer is amazing, and the band itself is the most soulful and original rock and roll band to come along in a long while.' The Def Leppard duo Rick Savage and Joe Elliott, meanwhile, opined that the album was the best in two and five years, respectively.

John Vassiliou recalls, 'Warren took a lot of heat for that campaign, but a lot of our business associates thought it was genius. Warren asked every manager whose artist gave a quote for permission. That was a monumental task in itself.'

Patton admitted in an interview with the late-night UK TV show *Raw Power* that he was 'embarrassed' by such quotes, while Bordin said, 'The first question in interviews would always be, "How does it feel that Axl Rose thinks you're the greatest?" Or, "How does it feel to know that Def Leppard thinks you're the greatest?"'

✿

Faith No More's initial chart impact in the UK was short-lived, as 'Epic' climbed one place to #37, and then down to #45, and then all the way down to #72 by the time the European leg of the tour ended in early March. After initially charting at #56 on February 17, its subsequent numbers were like the average ages on a modern rock tour: 60, 55, 55, 62, 64, 75, 74, 70, and 71. In the USA, meanwhile, MTV had yet to heed Warners' efforts, but *The Real Thing* finally entered the *Billboard* 200 album chart at #188, also on February 17, fully eight months after its release. It then rose to #184, and then ran up a chart run of difficult darts finishes: 164, 158, 151, 150, 154, 146, 158, 145, 126, 120, 134, and 108.

In March, the band played a further handful of dates with Voivod and Soundgarden, and squeezed a total of twenty-five shows into five weeks in the USA in March and April. A highlight was Soundgarden's final night on the Voivod tour on St Patrick's Day at the L'Amour in Brooklyn, known as the CBGBs of metal. Bottom of the bill, Faith No More, led by a completely integrated and at-ease Patton in a Mr Bungle T-shirt, played an insanely energetic eight-song set. One break, though, saw Patton throw out packets of Nestlé chocolate to the audience, while delivering a particularly soulful rendition of the company's 'Sweet Dreams' jingle, segueing into the faux-death-metal of 'Surprise! You're Dead!' without a pause. Soundgarden joined Faith No More onstage for a chaotic and charged 'War Pigs', with Patton taking the opportunity for a series of stage dives and a passionate smooch with Chris Cornell.

In an interview the same month with the *Toronto Star*, Roddy Bottum laid bare the band's eight-month touring struggle to break *The Real Thing*. 'The past year has been brutal as far as getting things off the ground again … this album has taken a long time to sink in. I don't blame people for being sceptical, because if a band I really liked changed singers, I'd probably wonder about it too. But I think, more than most bands, Faith No More is the sum of many different, distinct parts, not just a band for a singer.'

A review of the band's Mississippi Nights show on March 28 in the *St Louis Post-Dispatch* noted the huge increase in attendance since the band's last visit to the city, and the *Los Angeles Times* dubbed them 'the biggest band to come out of the US punk circuit since the Misfits' in a review of the penultimate date of their spring US tour at the Palace in LA on April 10.

Their breakthrough would eventually come back across the Atlantic, where, on April 14, 'From Out Of Nowhere' entered the UK singles chart, like 'Epic', at #38. That earned the band a slot on the landmark weekly BBC chart programme *Top Of The Pops*. The latest European tour kicked off with a recording of 'From Out Of Nowhere' for the show at the BBC Television Centre in White City, west London. The programme dictated that artists mime to backing tracks, and, typically, Faith No More showed their contempt for the directive, with Patton, clad in trademark Mr Bungle shirt, 'singing' while sticking his tongue out of the side of his mouth.

This increased exposure was leading to a different type of fan base. Bottum told *Kerrang!*, 'There's no common ground at all, apart from loud, heavy, and loud. No common philosophy about life in general, none whatsoever. But this is a high-profile time—ten million people for *Top Of*

The Pops, insane! People that never knew anything about us. And I like the idea of fooling ten million people that I'm playing and having a great time, that's funny.'

After recording on the Wednesday for transmission on Thursday, the band had to depart quickly for a show the same night at the Top Hat in Dún Laoghaire, south of Dublin. Though a significant portion of the crowd missed the end of show as they raced for the last train back into Dublin city centre, Faith No More, with Prong in support, delivered another high-octane, sweaty masterclass in mutated metal on their Irish debut. On the same night that *Top Of The Pops* aired on BBC1, the band played Belfast's Ulster Hall in Northern Ireland, just a few hours up the road, but over the then heavily fortified border. They stayed in the Europa Hotel, revelling in its reputation as the most bombed hotel in Europe.

The band were excited to be playing in Ireland for different reasons. Bordin: 'I was really happy about going there, because some of my childhood heroes were Rory Gallagher and then Thin Lizzy. I loved Rory Gallagher, I saw him play three or four times. Phil Lynott was the greatest Irish rock star for me, not Bono. And I almost equate our band with them; people know them for one big hit. Then, there were The Undertones and Horslips, who I saw with Cliff supporting Be-Bop Deluxe.'

Gould: 'The American ambassador had us over for dinner and cocktails at his house, The Chieftains were there. We thought it was because we were high-profile, because we were on *Top Of The Pops*—but it turns out that the ambassador's daughter was fifteen years old and liked us. He had a bulletproof car, and his daughter wanted to steal the car with Patton and go out. And Mike was saying, She's a fifteen-year-old kid, keep her away from me.'

The day after the concert, Patton and Gould did get a car together: one of the traditional city black cabs (introduced on both sides of the city's Catholic/Protestant divide, but initially and mostly in Catholic/nationalist areas as unofficial public transport when official transport was being targeted by paramilitary groups) for a tour of the city's nationalist area.

'Before we left, Mike Patton and I got in a black cab and went up the Falls Road to get away from everything and see what's really going on here,' Gould remembers. 'We were told by everyone, *Don't go out, don't go there, don't do that.* The cabbie was really a cool guy. He was an older guy; he had family that lived on the Falls Road. So we went to [IRA hunger striker] Bobby Sands's grave. He took us to the [nationalist party] Sinn Féin bookstore. That was just a stupid thing. I bought some books. We also got pulled over by the military patrols. They had their fingers on the triggers too. It was for real.'

Gould's new acquisitions later almost landed him in trouble. 'I bought books and got a T-shirt, like a republican shirt. We flew back, and one of the next shows was in Birmingham. I was drunk and I forgot to pack that in my suitcase and left it behind in the hotel room. I was like, *Holy Shit. I'm on a list for sure.*'

The band's star continued to rise in the UK. Boosted by their *Top Of The Pops* performance, 'From Out Of Nowhere' rose from #30 to a peak of #23 in the singles chart. At Newcastle's Mayfair on April 23, one fan dived from the balcony into the crowd below, and the venue was dangerously overcrowded, with a crush developing at the back (not the front) of the hall. At yet another show at Nottingham's Rock City, a favourite stop as the venue paid higher fees owing to a business model focused more on drink sales than ticket revenue, the band debuted their 'Easy' cover.

To London on April 27 and 28, where Faith No More's rise saw them playing bigger venues, the Hammersmith Odeon and the Brixton Academy, which would be preserved for posterity on the *You Fat Bastards* live video and album. 'Brixton was an afterthought in lots of ways,' Derek Kemp explains. 'We had sold out the Astoria on the previous tour, so the next logical step was to play Hammersmith Odeon. I put the Odeon on sale, and it sold very quickly. I tried to get a second night there, couldn't get the dates, so found out Brixton Academy was available, so put the band into there. At that time, the capacity for Hammersmith Odeon, because it was all seated then, was about 3,500, maybe just a little bit less, and the capacity of Brixton Academy was around about 5,000. In two nights, the band played to over 8,000 people in London alone.'

On the day Faith No More played Brixton, *The Real Thing* leapt to #44 in the UK albums chart. The decision to record the show and release it (as what is still the band's only live release) was down to this increased appetite for the band; the show would be packaged and repackaged as video and audio products four and ten months later, and would still pack the same gut punch of future shock.

The rest of the band felt their new singer was not able to contextualise Faith No More's success, as Gould told *Melody Maker* in May. 'He's getting his perspective, while we've all had eight years. Like last night, he's saying a top 40 single doesn't mean shit, he has no scale, no perspective. He's going through shocks every day.'

Patton, of course, had been thrown in at the deep end. 'Sometimes I feel pretty distant,' he admitted in that same article. 'I don't really know the others. Playing is comfortable, but personality-wise … the age has something to do with it, they give me shit for what I'm into, and me them.'

MTV PLUGGED

24

The shocks kept coming. In May, the band blazed through Europe (*The Real Thing* having entered the European albums chart at 98 in the first week of May), but despite such highlights as eight shows in nine nights in Germany, new covers of the Haribo commercial and Heino's 'Carnaval In Rio', and Bill Gould and Tim Dalton waking up hungover in a high-security US Air Force base after one post-gig party, the continent would prove unfruitful ground.

It was a different story in the USA. MTV had finally picked up on 'Epic' in earnest, with the song back on *Headbangers Ball* on May 12, and then played every week on the show. The push from Warners was paying off. Rick Krim was MTV's head of programming at the time and could make or break bands. Skid Row's Sebastian Bach once said of him, 'Here I am today, standing in my huge house with platinum records all over the wall, and I owe that to two things: Rick Krim and my cheekbones.'

By 1990, Krim liked Faith No More. Of MTV's role in breaking a band, he says:

> MTV often led the way, and radio followed. I think from the hair band era to the grunge era to the early hip-hop era, there's many cases of videos that we put on just a handful of times a week, labels saying, 'Try this.' Even in the pre-Soundscan days, you could see the reaction. They saw it in sales. Radio started getting requests. Some were seminal artists, but in other cases, you had these great songs with an amazing video, like Living Colour and 'Cult Of Personality'. And you had Faith No More, and you had Blind Melon's 'No Rain'. With those, you just had a funny feeling that if people get to see this, on America's radio station, then people are going to react just because they just stand out. In the case of Faith No More, you had a really great song, but the video took it to another level.

'The video really got a *What the hell is that?* reaction,' says Gould. 'The song got accepted through the visual.'

Krim thought so too, and he wanted everyone else at MTV to know it.

> I just remember beating the crap out of the powers-that-be there, whether it was Abby [Konowitch, MTV's vice-president of programming and, then, senior vice-president for music and talent] or Tom Hunter, who was the head of music programming at the time, we got to give this a shot. I'm feeling this one. I only did that a handful of times. I felt like I went out of my way, feeling like this is really something that could become a big thing.
>
> I just think that the video spoke for itself. I think it was a great piece of television—a really cool song that didn't sound like anything else. It's one of those iconic videos from that era that everybody remembers as much as the band or the song.

While Lenny Waronker had contacted MTV in February, it was not until May that 'Epic' began getting regular MTV airplay. Krim also nails the myth that the flopping fish posed any problems for the music network: 'It's an iconic image from that video, but I dealt with Standards & Practices, and that was never an issue.'

Faith No More were equal parts repulsed and attracted by the mainstream. MTV and pop culture held special interest, for Roddy Bottum and Bill Gould especially. Gould was fascinated by conditioned behaviour, and intrigued that MTV showed that the human psyche's feedback loop could be hijacked to reinforce certain types of behaviour. Bottum was a pop-culture and television junkie from the time he first lived in San Francisco. A television set was virtually the only piece of furniture in the first apartment the pair shared, and the just-launched MTV was their channel of choice.

'It was another universe—something we never thought we'd connect to,' Gould recalls. 'At the same time, it was something that was like a little code you could crack. We looked at it like we were hackers: *Imagine if we could actually get through that. How would you crack that?* It was like robbing a bank.'

Faith No More finally cracked the code in 1990, but it wasn't a simple hack. Press and promotion work, an outstanding video allied to an outstanding song, and high-level executive interactions had all played their part, but mostly it came down to inspiration and perspiration; talent and touring. Abby Konowitch reflected on MTV's power in an interview with the *Chicago Tribune* in 1991: 'The breakthrough of Faith No More wasn't because we put the video in heavy rotation—it was a few plays and a record company doing its job, and more plays, and a little more action in the press and a tour, and few more plays after. You build.'

❖

Faith No More and MTV kept building. MTV had put 'Epic' on stress rotation, heavier than heavy, in the final week of May, on air every hour of every day. Radio stations from KXYQ to KUBE, Q104 to X106, and KSAQ to KZZU had added 'Epic' to their playlists. In radio industry parlance, the song was getting 'significant action'. The following week, it was added to the playlists of sixteen US radio stations, including KPLZ in Seattle and

WHYT in Detroit. Hindsight can often suggest that 'Epic''s breakthrough was a *fait accompli*, when, in actual fact, even at this stage in early June 1990, songs that never made any sales or chart impact, such as Energy Orchard's 'Belfast' and Alias's 'Haunted Heart', were getting much more national radio airplay.

Buoyed by what was by far the greatest success of their seven-year career, Faith No More returned for a short North American tour in early June, playing out-of-the-way venues such as the Ranch Bowl Entertainment Center and the Iguana's club in Tijuana, Mexico. Their stop at the Ventura Theater in Ventura on June 9 was notable in that, on the same day, *The Real Thing* finally entered the top half of the *Billboard* 200. Weeks later, they had a bona-fide chart hit. In what was becoming a pattern for album and single releases and chart entries, though, Faith No More had already left the USA for another European tour when 'Epic' entered the *Billboard* Hot 100 at #71 on June 23—exactly one year and three days on from *The Real Thing*'s release.

Either side of that breakthrough day, Faith No More played their first two European festivals, Finland's Nummirock and the Netherlands' Parkpop. The collective attendance over the whole week at Parkpop that year was 450,000, and Patton, wearing a poncho picked up and also worn in Tijuana days before, seemed to commune individually with each audience member. Playing before by far their largest crowd at that point, goofy Patton was slowly metamorphosing into Patton 2.0—but not quickly enough that he didn't spend much of 'The Real Thing' mummifying himself in toilet roll. By playing an afternoon set on a blazing hot day, Faith No More managed to avoid the experience of later headliner Gary Moore, who played to a rapidly decreasing crowd heading for home to watch the Netherlands succumb 2-1 to West Germany in a World Cup knockout match.

Six days later, on June 30, Faith No More's 'Epic' was at #69 on the US singles chart and 59 in the US national airplay chart, while *The Real Thing* was #87 on the *Billboard* album chart. The album was now selling 75,000 copies a week in the USA alone, having taken a year to reach its first 75,000 sales. Six days later, Faith No More played Roskilde in Denmark, another huge festival. Also on the bill were the Red Hot Chili Peppers, Nick Cave, and The Cure. And Lenny Kravitz. And Sinead O'Connor. Cue Mike Patton telling the huge crowd, 'You're a special crowd, so I'm going to tell you a secret. Right now, the Jesus of hippies, Lenny Kravitz, is fucking the Virgin Mary, Sinead O'Connor, in the hospitality tent.' Needless to say, Kravitz, looking on from the side of the stage, was not impressed.

By the end of that three-week US tour, on July 21—almost three years since Chuck Mosley had been replaced—Faith No More's 'Epic' jumped to #27 on the US singles chart; it was also #36 on the national airplay chart, and *The Real Thing* was #19 on the *Billboard* album chart. After years of barely breaking even, Faith No More were breaking big.

THE SPLIT SECOND
OF DIVINITY

25

Faith No More missed the peak of Faith No More in the United States, because they were busy being Faith No More in Australia. And New Zealand. And Germany. And Belgium. And Italy. During the band's three weeks in New Zealand and Australia, 'Epic' and *The Real Thing* rose still further, with both single and album reaching the top 20 in the US charts. Their rise was not confined to the United States. Within a month of jetting in for their first-ever show in the country, in Brisbane, Faith No More had their first #1 single in Australia (or anywhere else).

After a show in Auckland and that Brisbane gig, the band were introduced to the Australian population with a session on the popular Triple J radio station on July 30. They played pretty much a full set at the studio in Sydney, with Mike Patton aiming digs at Sebastian Bach, Mike Bordin's back, and Jim Martin's love of the seventies. He tested the permissiveness of the Australian broadcasting regulators by repeatedly shouting 'fuck' at the start of 'Chinese Arithmetic', while also singing snippets of 'Vogue', 'The Right Stuff', and '911 Is A Joke', before finally taking over on drums. Bordin gave up the ghost halfway through the penultimate song, 'War Pigs', due to his back injury—and the insults that the band, and Patton in particular, were adding to injury. The session finished with Patton on drums, with Gould and Martin taking turns to occasionally bark vocals.

The first two days on tour had seen bungee jumping and football injuries almost incapacitate Bordin. Such was the band's new profile that the bungee jump in Auckland harbour was filmed by MTV.

Bordin doesn't have happy memories of the jump. 'Everybody dived head first, like you're supposed to. I couldn't bring myself to dive head first, so I stepped off the platform and fell, fifty, seventy-five, whatever feet it was, with my feet first. At the bottom I turned; I fell and I flipped at the bottom. You want to talk about a violent torque!'

Or the football. 'After the show we were playing football indoors in the Auckland Town Hall. I'd never played before. I'm all of a sudden getting what it's all about, and I'm hitting the ball with my head, or twisting this and that. I twisted something during that game. With the pain, I couldn't breathe. I couldn't breathe at all. But I still did a couple of shows.'

The Triple J session was the last straw. 'That's where it got bad, and I had to stop playing. Patton took over, I couldn't do it.'

There was more pain in store for Bordin to relieve the problem. 'The next day, one of the tour guys took me to a physio, and the guy said, Your two free floating ribs on the bottom of your ribcage have folded up underneath your ribcage. He reached in under my ribs and pulled them out. It was so painful I almost passed out, but immediately after I felt better.'

Bordin was back behind the kit the following day in Paramatta, as Faith No More played the first of twelve shows in thirteen days.

'Epic' had been re-released in Australia in mid-July, with 'The Morning After' as the B-side, and entered the chart on July 22 at a creditable #31—the highest new entry of the week. On August 5, it hit the top 10, reaching #2 the week after. But 'Epic' was held at bay for two weeks by the band's Bay Area peer MC Hammer with 'U Can't Touch This'. Hammer was wrong. One week later, on August 26, Faith No More touched #1—their first chart-topping single anywhere in the world. It would stay there for three weeks.

The Real Thing narrowly missed out on the #1 spot in the album charts, peaking at #2—pipped by Van Morrison's *Greatest Hits*—on August 8.

Well-timed touring, strong promotion from Mushroom Records, and a killer song and video all combined to earn Faith No More their first #1. Local record store Utopia also claimed some of the glory. In September, the *Sydney Morning Herald* featured an interview with Dave Defig from the Sydney store, who said, 'We basically discovered Faith No More here years ago; somebody woke up to them finally, and they've now had a #1.'

The band's schedule was as relentless as their rise was irresistible. The end of that Australia jaunt epitomised everything for the band. En route from Australia to Germany, the band stopped over at LAX, and had time between flights to be presented with their gold disc by Slash Records for sales in the United States for *The Real Thing*. Gould recalls, 'We were getting faxes: "Oh my God, you're selling 20,000, 50,000 a week. Holy shit." We were over in Britain or Europe or Australia, but it was blowing up in the States. Then we flew from Australia to LA, stopped off and had that record company photograph, and then kept going.'

They kept going, into two festival dates in Germany, playing before Die Toten Hosen and Status Quo. The same week, on August 20, the *You Fat Bastards* video was released. That same day, the band received a fax in their hotel from Warren Entner, which started, 'To FNM: The good news. Album 5-day 123,001.' The record was selling so fast that the figure on the fax for total album sales of 858,327 was scribbled out and replaced with, 'It's over 900,000 now!' The message concluded, 'Single: 5 Day: 26,829 Total: 512,007 Congratulations on a GOLD SINGLE!, Warren. PS Stay healthy—I know you!'

Faith No More had now sold more records in five days than they had sold in their previous seven years as a band. That week, 'Epic' was the sixth best-selling single in the United States and the twenty-sixth most played song on radio (the singles chart was based on both sales and airplay, so 'Epic' was #13 on the *Billboard* Hot 100). And *The Real Thing*, thanks to well over 120,000 sales, was at #14 on the *Billboard* 200.

Among the very few people who were not hearing 'Epic' blasting out from television screens and radios were the band members themselves. 'By the time we got back to the States, it had peaked,' says Gould. 'We actually

ITH NO MORE

BELOW The new-look Faith No More, pictured before Mike Patton's first show, at San Francisco's I-Beam in November 1988. *Photo by Ron Delany.*

ABOVE As soon as Mike Patton was recruited, management requested a photo, and the group quickly organised this 'great horrible band photo'. *Courtesy Mike Bordin/Faith No More.* **LEFT** Mike Patton in a Mr Bungle shirt. *Courtesy Bill Gould/ Faith No More.*

RIGHT A band portrait from 1991. *Courtesy Bill Gould/Faith No More.* **BELOW** Faith No More play the I-Beam in San Francisco in April 1989—a show that also served as a video shoot for 'From Out Of Nowhere'. *Photo by Jay Blakesberg.*

ABOVE Mike Patton and Jim Martin and Faith No More are joined onstage by Metallica's Kirk Hammett in 1989. *Photo by Mark Leialoha.* **BELOW** A fax from Warren Entner in August 1990, when the band were struggling to keep up with rocketing record sales. *Courtesy Bill Gould/Faith No More.*

AUG-20-90 MON 17:09 WEM   P.02

To: FNM

THE GOOD NEWS:

ALBUM: 5 DAY - 123,001

Total to date 858,327
ITS OVER 900,000
NOW

Single:
5 DAY: 26,829

TOTAL: 512,007

Congratulations on a
GOLD SINGLE!

Warren

P.S- stay healthy - I know you

RIGHT Bill Gould and Mike Patton onstage in 1990. *Courtesy Bill Gould/Faith No More.*
BELOW RIGHT Mike Patton, topless and intense at the Hammersmith Odeon, April 1990. *Photo by Mark Leialoha.*

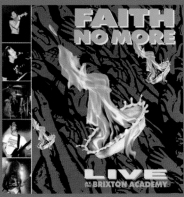

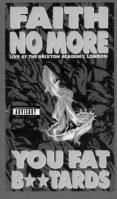

ABOVE Manager Warren Entner with Mike Bordin at the Palace, Los Angeles, April 1990. **RIGHT** Mike Patton, September 1989. Photographer Mark Leialoha explains, 'We were in Las Vegas, and at one point during the show I see Patton looking to take a leap off the back line of speakers. As I'm making my way over to that side of the stage, he launches himself off the stack, and a brilliant shot is missed.

Later that night, I asked him, if he ever does that again and I'm heading his way, if he wouldn't mind hanging out till I get there. The very next night in Reno, he did it again, but this time I'm on the move sooner as he rises up on the speakers, ready to launch. He hesitates just long enough to for me to get into place, and he goes for it.' *Both photos by Mark Leialoha.*

missed the boom. We were up there on top, but we were never actually physically here when it was happening. It was a little bit afterward, we still had a high profile, but we missed the rush.'

❀

The rush continued in Europe, as Faith No More tackled a week of festivals. In the UK, where they played the rock mecca of the Reading Festival on August 24, Faith No More fever had seemingly already crested. After 'Epic' scraped into the top 40, a *Top Of The Pops*-propelled 'From Out Of Nowhere' peaked at #23 in May, and 'Falling To Pieces' had surprisingly just failed to reach the top 40, stalling at #41.

Next, Faith No More lined up with the Monsters Of Rock in Italy and France. In 1990, the Monsters Of Rock line-up included Vixen. And Whitesnake. And Poison. At the first of the festival shows in Bologna, where Patton would later live, Faith No More took aim. With 'Faith No More, Faith No More' chants ringing out, and the opening beats of 'Edge Of The World' playing, a topless Patton addressed the crowd, initially in Italian, before continuing in English, 'I have a question for you—out of all the members of Poison, which one can suck his own dick? Is it the singer? Is it the guitar player? Is it the bass player? Well, you're right, because it is the drummer!'

That should have been that, but the band that had served up such humorous titles as *Swallow This*, 'Shut Up, Make Love', and Talk Dirty To Me' failed to see the funny side, as Mike Bordin recalls:

> We had heard for years that one of the members of the band used to suck his own dick at parties for entertainment value. We thought it was great, but there's two members of the band onstage with their big security guards who didn't hear exactly what was being said. And they thought he was saying, 'Poison sucks dick.' So they started freaking out. They're jumping over the top of the security guards, 'Let me at him, let me at him.' By the time we got offstage, we were going to get our asses kicked, and we were told were going to get arrested. We were told. 'You have to leave now.' So we had to sneak out.

Faith No More failed to make a dent in continental Europe during the peak of their popularity elsewhere. *The Real Thing* spent sixteen weeks in the German charts, but peaked at #37. It reached #53 in the combined European album charts, #38 in Sweden, and #56 in the Netherlands. 'Epic' reached #14 in Sweden, #27 in Ireland, and #51 in the Netherlands.

The band's rise in the UK and the USA continued. 'Epic' was re-released in the UK in the first week of September, and shot to #25 within weeks, driving *The Real Thing* to its peak position of #30 by September 22. In the USA, peak Faith No More day was September 6 1990. That week's single sales and airplay propelled 'Epic' to #9 on the *Billboard* 100. That day, Faith No More were featured on the cover of *Rolling Stone*—relegated to text with MC Hammer having the cover image—under the strapline, 'Faith No More: Most Unlikely To Succeed'. That night, Faith No More performed at the MTV Video Music Awards at the Gibson Amphitheater in Los Angeles.

The *Rolling Stone* feature interview traced the band's story: a seven-year overnight success. The band would not quite play along with the rags-to-riches narrative, however:

> When they are asked about the changes wrought by their new-found celebrity status, it's clear that there is something this gang of pranksters doesn't find very funny—namely, that they have yet to see any spoils. 'Our time isn't that much our own anymore,' said Bordin.
>
> 'It's like living in jail, only they take us out to eat lunch at the Ritz. And then people come up to you and say, Hey, Axl Rose likes your record,' says Patton.
>
> 'Yeah,' says Bordin. 'It's like, *Can Axl loan me twenty bucks?*'

A few months later, Bill Gould told *BAM*, 'Axl Rose sent us a letter with a note and a twenty saying, *Sorry you feel this way. Here's twenty bucks.* And he should have sent it to the Puff. I'm embarrassed. Me and Jim are going to write a letter back to him saying we didn't say that.' Almost three decades on, Bordin admits, 'It came off a little undignified. But the point was that everything was changing. But nothing had changed.'

That was particularly true for Gould, whose royalty payments were being sent to a different William Gould, due to a record label mix-up. 'Wherever you go, people give you free drinks,' he recalls. 'It's just weird. You don't know how long it's going to last. It's almost like time stops. You died and went to heaven. But we still didn't have any money then. It was still a hassle, because I hadn't gotten a cheque yet with all this success. You start to wonder if all the things they say about the music industry are true. So I wasn't going out without telling everybody, It's fucking bullshit.'

That did not stop the band performing at the MTV Video Music Awards show, where 'Epic' was nominated in the 'Best Metal/Hard Rock Video' category alongside 'Janie's Got A Gun' by Aerosmith, 'Kickstart My Heart' from Mötley Crüe, and 'Up All Night' by Slaughter. Gould recalls, 'All these famous people knew who I was, and were calling me by my first name. Where were they a couple weeks before? It's a drug rush, like everyone says. All of a sudden, everyone in the world knows you, and you can do whatever you want.'

The band even caught the attention of the *Los Angeles Daily News*'s fashion correspondent:

> The hard rock group Faith No More's fashion choices are as uncategorisable as their music. Their mix of rock, rap, and cabaret sounds is reflected in their attire. An example: singer Michael Patton's green satin tuxedo from Paris, pants tucked into high silver lace-up boots, worn with a quilted silver satin vest. Or his performance outfit: woolly vinyl vest under a spotted blazer with a plastic hand flapping off his sash belt. Of course, it's all set off by his rhinestoned cat-eye sunglasses and crayon-red streaked hair.

And Jim Martin wore a *Forbidden Planet* T-shirt and a leather waistcoat with a sheriff's badge. 'I remember all of us getting kinda wiggy on what we were going to wear,' Bottum recalls. 'It was a circus. I remember meeting RuPaul. I think Madonna might have played. Maybe C+C Music Factory. It was a real moment.'

The band performed 'Epic', but Aerosmith won the award for their David Fincher-directed video. 'That was intense for me, playing on live

TV,' Bordin recalls. 'Counting off a song cold on live TV. I think we might have soundchecked, but you're still playing live. I remember breaking a few sticks during that one song. That's real.'

There was no escaping the feeling that the band had just wrestled a pig. 'Any time we went to an awards show and played the game, I think we felt like idiots,' he adds. 'There's just a difference between being in it, and being of it.'

❖

The band had now been on the road for fourteen months. Thoughts were turning to going home. And to getting back in the studio. But the band had to play on. With 'Epic' and *The Real Thing* both having broken, Warren Entner and John Vassiliou pushed the band back on the road for two high-profile support tours—first with Billy Idol, starting three days after the MTV Awards and seven days after returning from Europe, and then with Robert Plant, starting ten days after the Idol tour ended.

Gould: 'Billy Idol was a management call; a fun tour for us, but I'm not sure it was the right choice for our career. We were actually drawing crowds then, and he was on the wane, and on top of it all, it wasn't much of a pay cheque. That was our successful period—that we squandered.'

Newsday's review of the show at Jones Beach, Long Island, echoed that point. '[Idol's] worst break, though, was landing Faith No More as his support act. Charismatic without working at it, powerful, enigmatic, and reasonably unaffected, they made Idol seem bottled. If Faith No More isn't yet a great band, it is at least a real interesting one with a great singer.'

The rivalry implicit in such reviews played itself out in a series of pranks between the two acts on the final night of the tour, Halloween night at the Seattle Center Coliseum. Idol's dumping of dead fish on Faith No More as they opened the show made headline news, but Bordin recalls, 'He dumped 100 pounds of smelt on my drums. Ruined my drum set. Literally ruined it. Dumped all that fish on us.' Worse was to follow as Faith No More sought sanctuary and showers back in their dressing room. 'He took all of our stuff out of our dressing room and put farm animals in. Goats, sheep, chickens, and whatever.'

The band would have their revenge, and they ran onstage naked except for bags over their heads during Idol's encore, dancing a conga line around the stage. Someone took offence at the nudity, and the police were called. 'We sneaked out of the venue hiding in a truck,' says Bordin, 'and the next morning, we're driving to the airport. The guy who's driving us has got the radio on, and they're talking about it. They're saying the Seattle Sheriff was still looking for those guys to arrest them.'

During the tour, Faith No More reached peak popularity and critical acclaim. On October 13, while they were toiling in Texas, *The Real Thing* reached its peak of #11 on the *Billboard* 200. The following day, the *Los Angeles Times* anointed the band as the kings of the neo-metal movement. 'If the "movement" had a leader (which it doesn't), a Metallica or a Sex Pistols against which all the other bands could be measured, at this point it would have to be Faith No More—the only neo-metal band to have played arena tours, placed a single in the top 10, or sold a million copies of an album.'

26 BUNGLE GRIND

Just as all seemed rosy in the Faith No More camp, rumblings started to appear that Mike Patton was not happy with the band, and that the band was not happy with Mike Patton. On October 27, an article in the *Orange County Register* revealed that Patton had been banned from all media engagements and from speaking to the press.

Gould: 'He put his foot in his mouth, and he's in trouble. It's part of the growing process in a way, because, without the friction, the changes wouldn't have been made to keep growing.'

Patton, like his band colleagues, had no filter when it came to interviews. In August, he told *Kerrang!*, 'I think the rumours are really, really healthy. They keep me on my toes. My favourite one is that they kicked me out of the band because I'm such a brat. The other rumour that's great is that they're going to kick me out because I wear the Mr Bungle shirt all the time.'

Patton's 'other band', Mr Bungle, was always going to be a bone of contention. And Patton did wear his Mr Bungle tee at the most opportune moments: the 'Epic' video, the *Top Of The Pops* recording, the showcase gigs in New York.

Throughout the year, various band members had themselves fuelled rumours of Patton leaving the band in interviews, and in June, at the end of a show at the Élysée Montmartre in Paris, they announced from the stage that they would be recruiting a new singer for their next tour. Asked about rumours that Patton was leaving, Gould told *Raw* magazine:

> We heard that. We're neither confirming nor denying it. At our last show in Paris, we told everybody that it was Mike's last show! The rumour came from somewhere in San Francisco apparently. The London magazines heard it, and said, 'Well, we heard it from a source in the States.' We managed to trace it to a source back in San Francisco. And then some girl in Texas showed up at a radio station, and told the DJ that she was Mike Patton's girlfriend, and that he was leaving soon.

Rumours of Patton's departure were certainly exaggerated, but Mr Bungle signed for Warner Bros later in early 1991, and the deal definitely caused tensions within Faith No More. Gould recalls, 'This was a parallel thing happening while we were doing our stuff. Jim had real problems with Mike doing anything outside of the band. He was super, super hard on that one. Mike had real problems with that. It got worse.'

For Slash and Warner Bros, and for the band management, it made sense to have both Patton projects under the same label. Bob Biggs told the *Los Angeles Times*, 'Mike is going to be one really tired guy. But the two bands are very different, so I think it could be a healthy outlet for him in the long run.' Warren Entner said in the same article, 'It is an unusual situation, and

Mike is biting off a lot by doing two separate projects at the same time. But if Mr Bungle can establish its identity while Mike stays committed to Faith No More, we're hopeful it will all work out.'

While Faith No More were signed to Slash, Patton's deal was with Warner Bros itself. There was surprisingly little coordination and communication between the departments managing each band, making planning and logistics difficult at times for Faith No More, and leading to such situations as when both Patton bands released albums in 1995.

One major source of irritation for Patton's FNM colleagues was the sheer size of the advance that Mr Bungle had received, believed to be in the region of $100,000. Gould: 'I'm not sure what deal he ended up getting, but it was not connected to ours, and he didn't do a very good job of keeping us informed about it, or even discussing it. It was a problem at the time.'

In hindsight, Patton was the victim of a musical industry in which, unlike now, the concept of a musician having multiple acts was anathema. 'They tried to squash the idea of me being in two bands,' he recalled. 'Well, I said two or none. It sucks, because my back was really against the wall. To make threats like that and act like a spoiled brat, well, I was sort of forced to. And it did not endear me to the rest of the band members. But they gradually figured out what it was about. The band thing is really an uptight, incestuous, creepy thing. When you step outside of the cocoon, a lot of people look at that like, *You adulterer.*'

Roddy Bottum gave some perspective in a 1990 interview, noting, 'It was difficult for him. He had never flown on a plane, never lived outside of his parents' home in Northern California, never left the small town in the woods, where he lived a very sheltered life. Then, all of a sudden, he joined our band, made a record, and he's onstage with Metallica, frontman for a band, in front of 10,000 people. It was hard for him to deal with. And if sometimes he has to be a brat to deal with that, then it's not that big a deal.'

❀

Despite the rumbling discontent, Faith No More's ascent continued when they played the Hollywood Palladium for *RIP* magazine's fourth anniversary party on Friday November 9. It was a true celebration of the band's successful hybrid of rap or hip-hop and rock or metal. As they were joined by Young MC, the rapper who had scored a US top 10 album and single the previous year, Gould said of 'Epic', 'This next song is an interesting fusion of metal and rap.' Patton added, 'That seems to be the thing these days, so let's call it that.' For the encore rendition of 'War Pigs', they were accompanied by twin monarchs of metal, Ozzy Osborne and James Hetfield. The audience went berserk, and some in the large crowd were injured when barriers collapsed.

Sharing a stage with Ozzy for the first time was an emotional moment for Mike Bordin.

> Ozzy sat in the corner on his own, drinking a Diet Pepsi and shaking with the DTs. I went over to him—I was the only one to approach him. And we got talking, and he asked, 'Why do you guys do "War Pigs"? Are you guys taking the piss?' I said, 'No, you have to understand that when I was ten years old, my mom died and my family was devastated and destroyed. That's 1973, and you've got *Vol. 4* out and you're speaking to me, and you're telling me things are dark, fucked up, and you're telling me the truth. I can't tell you what you've given to me. I can't tell you how important you've been to me in my life, keeping me in a positive direction. If it wasn't for that and you, I wouldn't have made it, no way.' And he's crying. He's blown away.

❁

Two days later, Faith No More were in Albuquerque, supporting Robert Plant. The former Led Zeppelin singer was a fan of the band, going so far as to list *Introduce Yourself* among his favourite records in a May 1990 feature for *Q* magazine.

The affection was mutual. 'Robert Plant was an amazing guy, super-sweet, really supportive,' Bottum recalls. 'He was a fan of ours, and a legend. It was flattering that he wanted to take us on tour. He had an idea about playing shit holes in America that was interesting to us. There wasn't a lot of pomp in his presentation, he was straight up a good guy. One day, we rode with him in the back of a pick-up truck in some weird city, and stopped and had drinks at a gay bar. That blew my mind. At the time, it was a big deal.'

Bottum's description might have been more colourful, but the tour did get Faith No More visiting new cities, such as Sioux City and Saginaw, and Mississauga and Muskogee. 'That was a great tour,' Gould reflects. 'Different crowd, but it was great, and he was amazing. He was a great guy. He hung out with us. He was a legitimate friend and fan.'

While Faith No More's follow-up single, 'Falling To Pieces', complete with another Ralph Ziman video, only just scraped into the *Billboard* Hot 100 in November, and *The Real Thing* slipping to #83 by year's end, Faith No More were all over the 1990 end-of-year charts and award lists. In the USA, *The Real Thing* was #41 on the *Billboard* 1990 album chart, and the band were #47 in its 'Top Pop Artists' ranking, with three charted records in the year, while 'Epic' was ranked #75 in the *Billboard* singles chart of the year. 'Epic' also went platinum in Australia, and was #22 in the ARIA End Of Year Singles Charts and #5 in New Zealand's annual chart, with *The Real Thing* #37 in Australia's album chart for the year. (Going against the myth that Faith No More were always bigger in the UK and Europe, neither song nor album registered in the best sellers of the year in Britain.)

In the *Village Voice*'s annual Pazz & Jop Critics Poll, calculated from the year-end lists of hundreds of American music critics, *The Real Thing* was ranked at #27, while 'Epic' was #4 in the *Rolling Stone* Critics' Poll (beaten out by Deee-Lite and Sinéad O'Connor, plus Jane's Addiction), and #3 in its Readers' Poll.

Newspapers were queuing up to lavish praise on the band, and *Spin* chose Faith No More as its Artists of the Year. The magazine's music editor, Frank Owen, wrote, 'Faith No More is the band of the year, no contest. It's metal without the male fantasies of omnipotence and invulnerability, metal without the LA glam sleaze, metal without the sword n' sorcery imagery.'

Faith No More would deny that they were metal at all, and their desire to shed the funk metal tag as they prepared to record *Angel Dust* in 1992 was in keeping with a battle against categorisation, labelling, and genre throughout their career. Faith No More had no mimetic desire. They did not want to have what others had: imitation was not a form of creation for them. Neither indie nor mainstream in terms of distribution, ethos, and popular appeal, they were genre fluid. They first fell between the cracks of Californian underground music in the 1980s; then they pioneered popular alternative music two years too early in late 1989; and they were then miscast as mainstream metallers, thus missing out on Lollapalooza labelling and lucre in the 1990s.

Faith No More had a dazzling array of genre titles applied to their music. Reviews of their early demos and *We Care A Lot* labelled them death rock, post-punk, and punk-metal. By the time of *Introduce Yourself*, they were variously labelled heavy rap, punk rap, and punk-funk. They were hard rock, punk-funkers, heavy-metal punk, and post-punk. They were heavy metal dance, dance floor heavy metal, funk-punk-metal-rap.

Come *The Real Thing*, press reports called them funk-metal, rap-metal and, rock-funk-pop. They were nihilistic rock, metallic punk-funk, and metal-funk punk. By the time 'Epic' hit, they were labelled neo-metal, rap-thrash, metal-funk, and hard rock. Metal-rap, alternative metal, and dance-rock. Intelligent metal and speed-metal. Reconstituted punk. They were rock'n'roll, speedball metal, rap-metal, and metallic funk. Heavy metal funk, metal art, funk-metal-punk. Funk rock and thrash-funk. Punk-metal-progressive rock. And there's more. They were also labelled art-rock, metal rock, gloom rock, doom rock, regressive rock, aggressive rock, avant-punk, funk'n'roll, alterna-metal, punk-funk-rap-metal-jazz, and—almost a decade before nu-metal—new metal.

Not many were reaching for the funk appellation when *Angel Dust* was released. Instead, they were thrash-and-mash, art-grunge, *sturm und drone*, and thrash-punk. Groovy thrash, lyrical metal, metal-sonic. Punk'n'metal, and jazz-metal. Hybrid rock.

By *King For A Day ... Fool For A Lifetime*, the media were still coming up with new labels and new genres to categorise the band. They were art-metal, anti-pop, eclectic rock, alterna-rock. Punk-progressive, hip-hop/thrash, heavy metal fusion. Alternative/funk/metal/disco/punk.

By *Album Of The Year*, the descriptions were drying up, but the band were still described as art-rock, choppy metal, 70s progressive rock, sci-fi funk. Eclectic metal, skeletal metal, alt-rock. Progressive-rock fusion, punk-funk-rock, indie-college-metal. Organ-led elaborations on rock'n'roll.

Right from the start, the band detested categorisation. In a 1985 interview, Bill Gould stated, 'Alternatives to major labels have now taken on the point of view of major labels, especially in LA. They want a certain genre of music that they can package and find a market for, even in college radio. We're not even talking about selling a million records anymore, we're talking about selling maybe 10,000, but they still want to have a predictable package. We're not heavy metal enough, we're not disco enough, we're not psychedelic enough.'

Later, Gould's pronouncements on genre echoed the cultural industry criticisms famously made by Frankfurt School philosopher Theodore Adorno in *On Popular Music* in 1941.

This is Adorno: 'The whole structure of popular music is standardised, even where the attempt is made to circumvent standardisation. Listening to popular music is manipulated not only by its promoters, but by the inherent nature of this music itself, into a system of response mechanisms wholly antagonistic to the ideal of individuality in a free, liberal society.'

This is Gould: 'In the US, cultural responses are so programmed. Everything is conditioned, everything is categorised. It's a certain type of conditioned behaviour that creates more conditioned behaviour. It's a fast-food-mentality.'

From the start, Gould took an anti-rockist stance: 'Public Image Ltd. put rock music in its grave, and paved the way to new discoveries. There has always been a band philosophy, but it was always more intuitive than spoken about. We knew what we were, and what we weren't. And we always tried to be ourselves, for better or worse.'

'Being ourselves' meant five driven musicians bent on pursuing their own differing and sometimes divergent dreams of music-making. Faith No More operated like some sort of plasmodium—a giant, many-headed slime pushing simultaneously in many different directions, capable of pulling itself into pieces, able to fuse back together, its forward momentum determined as much by what repulsed as what was attractive. *Angel Dust* was, in part, a reaction to their funk-metal labelling.

'It just so happens that while it's cool to play around with funk and metal influences, being part of a genre with this title sounded absolutely horrific and limiting,' says Gould. 'We continued to write songs, but didn't shy away from things like atonality, or going in whatever direction we felt the need to. It's always been about following gut feelings without judgement, or discovering new structures.'

Jim Martin sounded like Gould—and Adorno, for that matter—when he complained to *Metal Hammer* in June 1992, 'For some reason, all music has to be segregated and labelled, the only reason can I think of for that is to give the marketing departments in record companies, and the press, a black-and white substance to work with. God, without labels, there'd be no business, apparently."

Faith No More were also complicit in this. After all, they were largely griping in niche heavy metal magazines. Their big promotional tour after the release of *Angel Dust* was with hard-rock and heavy-metal heavyweights Guns N' Roses and Metallica. Lead single 'Midlife Crisis' premiered on MTV's heavy metal show, *Headbangers Ball*, and the band were guest hosts when *Angel Dust* was released. They may have dropped the funk, but they were still being marketed as metal.

Faith No More's managers, Warren Entner and John Vassiliou, had made their big breakthrough managing one of the original hair metal bands, Quiet Riot, so a certain predilection for metal categorisation had to be expected. Vassiliou maintains that they tried as much as possible to push back against the label. They turned down a support slot on AC/DC's mammoth arena tour at the end of 1990 and start of 1991, Vassiliou explains: 'Once the band started blowing up, there were a lot of offers. I remember AC/DC but, as management, we would have passed. If it was some sort of stadium-type date, we might have considered it. I think we got a Megadeth offer too. We wanted to stay away from the established metal bands. We might have taken a one-off date, but not a whole tour.'

The Real Thing has also been pivotal in creating a whole new genre of alternative rock, a label that was appended to Faith No More *ex posto facto* in the wake of the breakthrough of Nirvana. During the *Angel Dust* era, they succeeded in alienating the Guns N' Roses/Metallica demographic by not being metal enough, even as they were considered too metal for Lollapalooza. And afterward, despite soul covers, sharp suits, and short hair, they would continue to be troubled by categorisation, even as they continued to seamlessly surf genres.

28

THE CHILE
CONNECTION

'Huge in Chile' has not permeated the vernacular like 'big in Japan', or even 'world famous in New Zealand'—but the phrase could have been coined for Faith No More.

The tale of Faith No More's popularity in Chile starts in 1991 with a mayor, a radio presenter, a novelist, a song contest, and a teenage fan.

The radio presenter was Iván Valenzuela, host of the Sunday late-night music and talk show *IPC* (*Interferencia Por Concierto*) on Radio Concierto. The novelist, his fellow presenter, and the *enfant terrible* of new Chilean literature, Alberto Fuguet, was turned on to Faith No More in December

1990, when he started reading band's *Spin* 'Artist of the Year' article while on air. 'My mind was absolutely blown,' he recalls, 'and I began to read, to translate, on the air. I said, wow, this guy, Mike Patton, this is the most intelligent onanist in the world. I felt like he was a character of mine, and we squeezed that orange for the whole show, reading and translating bits of this fascinating interview.'

The fascination heightened a month later, when Valenzuela returned from seeing Faith No More at Rock In Rio in Brazil, and could speak of little else. Fuguet recalls, 'He said, "I don't remember who was at Rock In Rio. The Rolling Stones were there, but who cares. The only thing important is Mike Patton and Faith No More—the famous onanist Mike Patton was there."'

Valenzuela continued the theme when he penned the next of his regular music columns for Chile's leading newspaper, *El Mercurio*. 'Seeing the show, one realises that Chile is so fucked up,' he wrote. 'Viña del Mar is so cheesy. When will the Viña del Mar festival and Chile as a country decide to grow up? They should get Faith No More to play.'

The seed had been sown, and when the allotted headliners, Level 42, pulled out, Valenzuela was contacted by a festival representative—an advisor to the city's mayor, Juan Carlos Trejo—to help choose a replacement. He demurred, but he later learned that Faith More had been approached.

Valenzuela's article had piqued the mayor's interest, prompting him to make enquiries with his sixteen-year-old son, Juan Luis Trejo Piazza. 'My brother David and I were skateboarders,' Juan recalls, 'and, at a time when it was still difficult to find foreign music, we had *The Real Thing* on cassette after a friend had brought it back from the US. When my dad asked us what teenagers were listening to and about Faith No More, we told him that they were an excellent band, and were the revelation of Rock In Rio.'

Finances were a factor, Juan notes, to which Gould adds, 'They wanted to get the cheapest band that played Rock In Rio, so they didn't have to stretch their budget, and that was us, as it turns out.'

The fact of Faith No More playing Chile was, in itself, not that inconceivable, but playing Viña del Mar was something altogether different. The festival, founded in 1960, was based around an international song contest and designed to promote the best of Chilean music, and to attract tourism to the seaside town. After the right-wing military coup of Augustin

Pinochet on September 11 1973, it had other uses. Fuguet states, 'Pinochet used it to show that Chile was a country connected to the stars and, in a way, that ordinary people had fun. It was camp; it was our Eurovision, actually.'

It was also a target for dissidents. As the opposition Committee of Chilean Musicians put it, 'The Festival of Viña del Mar is scandalous. In the city of Viña itself and in Valparaiso, there is a high level of unemployment and lack of housing. And yet, they pay Sheena Easton $70,000. Scandalous.' The Police, John Denver, KC & The Sunshine Band, and REO Speedwagon disagreed, and they all played the festival in the 1980s. One visiting act did take a stand. In 1988, Mr Mister bass player Richard Page pulled a scrap of paper from his pocket and read out a message of support for dissidents, in Spanish. Later, he was persuaded to apologise onstage alongside presenter Antonio Vodanovic.

The festival was not a music festival per se, more a made-for-television music programme. Acts played short sets of around forty minutes, with competitions, contests, and comedy interspersed throughout the evening. The festival also prided itself on its audience, and the legend of *El Monstruo*. Audiences were portrayed as so boisterous that they would devour the acts, often booing and jeering acts off the stage.

Two days before their two shows, Faith No More arrived in Chile for the first time. Gould says, 'It is the same distance from the equator as Santa Barbara, so, getting off the plane, what struck me was that the landscape looks like California. We did press conferences where we were just talking shit. When we'd do it in Brazil, people would laugh. In Chile, they didn't laugh. They were offended. The connection was born at Viña. Most of the people there hated us, but the young people watching on television loved us.'

'It felt a little bit oppressive,' Bottum recalls. 'I remember there was a man in our party who wanted to take a guy up to his room in the hotel, and they wouldn't let him.'

Faith No More topped the bill ahead of festival veterans and Latin American favourites Myriam Hernández and Chayanne. A significant segment of the audience had already departed when Faith No More took to the overly lit, game-show-style stage. Apart from a brief interlude when festival presenter Vodanovic handed over the commemorative trophy of the festival symbol of a dove of peace—traditionally given to festival participants before they perform the final two songs of their set—to Gould, it was a typical Faith No More performance from the *Real Thing* era. But there was more enough in the aggressive on-form show to provoke the ire of the conservative Chilean press the following morning.

La Segunda, previously the mouthpiece of the Pinochet regime, railed, 'When they started their performance, they had 12,000 people; after seven minutes, there were only a few thousand. Where were the others? They fled in terror, covering their ears.'

The morning after, the band were guests on the TVN show *Aqui Vina*, filmed in the lobby of the ornate Hotel O'Higgins. When Gould was asked about their first night, he pointed at the camera and said, 'The right people left, and the right people stayed.'

Faith No More's second appearance at the festival the following night forged their Chilean connection. Not content with antagonising the easily antagonised through aggression alone, the band upped the ante to deliberate provocation. Their cultural adviser was none other than Fuguet. The writer was based in the same hotel as Faith No More during the festival, writing diary pieces for *El Mercurio*. Assigned with bringing the festival to life for the paper's readers, he instead aimed to puncture its pomposity.

He had met Patton at the hotel breakfast buffet, where the pair bonded over Fuguet's copy of *The Catcher In The Rye*. 'He asked me, What's the deal with Chile?' Fuguet recalls, 'and then he said, How can I fuck this thing up? I began to give him a crash course.'

The pair then conspired to 'fuck this thing up'. The most striking aspect of the start of the second night was Patton's attire. He was dressed like a slightly too-old rebellious schoolboy: light blue shirt not tucked in, striped yellow-and-red tie, and short trousers. The shirt, tie, and inspiration all belonged to Fuguet: 'I suggested that he should dress like a private schoolboy in Chile. I gave him my shirt because he did not have one, and I gave him this yellow-and-red tie, which looked very *Dead Poets Society*, which was a huge movie in Chile, because of its anti-authoritarianism theme. The thesis was that Mike Patton was the misunderstood Chilean schoolboy.'

Fifteen minutes into the show, Patton cut across Bottum's 'Buenos nachos' greeting with 'Esta canción está dedicada a Myriam Hernández, mi amor' ('This song is dedicated to Myriam Hernández, my love'). Hernández was the previous performer, a popular Chilean singer who served up romantic ballads, and whose most recent album, *Dos*, had just spent eighteen weeks at #1 on the US *Billboard* Latin Pop Albums chart. 'I explained to Mike who she was,' Fuguet continues, 'and he said that she didn't look like a star. I said, Why don't you say that you're in love with her? He agreed, so I wrote him down some lines and said, Why don't you play the worst song you have, the loudest, and dedicate it to Myriam Hernández?'

Patton's dedication was greeted with loud cheers, and he and the band launched into 'Edge Of The World'—not the band's loudest song, but a controversial one. Fuguet adds, 'Immediately, there were reports and rumours that they were together. The press is very tabloid. Some felt that he was disrespecting our media, our culture, and a star, a nice, proper, Chilean girl.'

Hernández was a star, but Antonio Vodanovic was an icon. The presenter of the Viña festival since 1976, he was also one of the most familiar faces on television. His 'Viña has a festival' remark to kick off each evening of the festival was his trademark, and one of the most recognisable phrases in contemporary Chile. He was also considered as the television face of the Pinochet regime, a charge he denied.

He was also the perfect prank victim. Vodanovic was first called into action as a set prop during 'War Pigs'. Spotting him, Patton raced, all the time singing, to the other side of the stage. As Patton placed his arm around Vodanovic's shoulder, the presenter performed some awkward dad-dancing before being assailed by Patton's screams. Patton then spat and threw water onto the seats, as well as onto the expensive Epsom computers of the contest judges below.

Vodanovic returned to the stage for his customary chat with the band before their final song. He called to Patton to join him with forced amiability—'Mike, Mike'—for the presentation of the dove of peace, only for Patton, as he received the trinket from presenter Paulina Nin de Cardona, to lean in and kiss Vodanovic on the cheek, and, then, while the audience was still whistling and cheering, to carefully pat the presenter several times on his backside.

'Patton said to me, What would happen if I kissed the presenter?' Fuguet recalls, 'and I said, Pinochet will come back to power.'

Ivan Valenzuela recalled, 'He kissed Antonio Vodanovic, which is a totally trivial gesture, but at that moment it acquired a very powerful symbolic connotation, because Antonio had been, and still was, an icon. Chile had just returned to democracy. We are talking about an incredible level of control, a very important level of respect for authority, and Patton somehow symbolises a first scratch of the paint of that order.'

The festival organisers blamed Valenzuela, and the local *La Estrella* paper captured the tone with its headline, 'Please, No More'. Another newspaper reportedly lamented, 'If this is democracy, then we don't want democracy.' Juan Luis Trejo Piazza remembers, 'My father was the first democratic mayor, and that festival was marked by a series of messages. Not only FNM, but it was also the first time that Los Prisioneros, a rock band that opposed the Pinochet dictatorship, played at the festival. Many people criticised my father for being so progressive and having Faith No More. Now they say it was the important milestone of the festival.'

Patton spent the following day with Fuguet, who wrote an extensive feature on him for *Wikén*, the weekend culture supplement of *El Mercurio*. The piece was entitled 'Isolated among all these people', but it was bumped from its pre-agreed front-page slot by Fuguet's reactionary editor.

Fuguet was unperturbed, and he had a second piece, entitled 'Kicking Groupies', published in the main section of *El Mercurio* later, detailing his night out with Patton at the festival after-party. 'If they just would have come to a venue in October, this wouldn't have been so big,' he says. 'And if they came to Viña without my support and *El Mercurio* and all we did, the biggest paper going against the grain, supporting them, it would have been more an anecdote. Instead, it turned into a phenomenon.'

Patton also helped Fuguet out of his own crisis of creative confidence as he struggled to deal with the acclaim and criticism for this debut short story collection, *Sobredosis*: 'I realised watching him onstage that I knew how to continue with *Mala Onda*. I had to not be afraid of being a rock star or a literary star. I realised when watching that the book had to be much more like a rock prose. It had to be more visceral, that I had to put more music in the book, not only literally and not just kids listening to records, but musical prose. I felt saved—liberated—after that show.'

Fuguet's debut novel, *Mala Onda*, which was published later in 1991 and saw him anointed the 'principal spokesman for his generation', repaid that debt. Lyrics from 'Falling To Pieces' serve as the novel's epigraph, and one small but significant character, an American rock star named Josh Remsen, is modelled on Patton.

'Patton looked like a kid, but also like a mass murderer,' he notes. 'He's like one of my best characters. He's part of my literary universe. Josh Remsen is totally inspired by Mike. He plays a pivotal role in the psyche of Matías, the main character. He reads about him in *Rolling Stone*, like I read about Mike in *Spin*, and Remsen turns into his saviour, his *doppelganger*, and also his Jedi, someone who guides him through the last part of the book; he feels that somebody understands him and somebody is giving him advice.'

❦

Sales figures in Chile are hard to quantify, but the Viña visit did lead to a major uptick in sales of *The Real Thing*. Later that year, band manager Warren Entner told *Billboard*, 'It went from 7,500 to where it now is approaching 200,000 in Brazil alone. We went back down to Viña Del Mar in Chile, and had the same type of explosive effect. The opportunity to play Rock In Rio II broke the whole area wide open, and Chile and Argentina have since broken wide open.'

In that same *Billboard* industry guide, Entner said that Faith No More would make Argentina and Brazil part of a 'continuing tour pattern', but Chile would have to wait four years until the band returned. At the Monsters Of Rock Festival in September 1995, Faith No More again pushed limits and ruptured conventions. The spitting started straight away. By the third song, 'Midlife Crisis', Patton's T-shirt was damp with saliva. Ten songs in—a cover of Portishead's 'Glory Box'—and the singer was showered in spittle, his face and shaved head dripping with saliva.

Was this a more extreme version of the Viña del Mar opprobrium? It was merely tradition. Since the early 80s, performers at hard rock shows had been spat at, in a regional variation of the gobbing at 70s punk shows. It usually did not go down well. Axl Rose stormed offstage when spat on in Santiago in 1992, and then Iron Maiden singer Blaze Bailey cut a song short after he was spat at in 1996. Patton embraced it. During 'Midlife', he opened his mouth wide and pointed inside, directing the spitters to their target. During 'Glory Box', he picked a spit globule from his temple and tasted it.

'It was such a disgusting display of honour,' Bottum notes, 'but I remember all of us were really into the spit.' Gould adds, 'That was a high energy show we gave them. It was September 11, so it was the anniversary of the coup. People were really jacked up, and we fed off of that. People liked to spit. We were totally fine with that. He had no problem with that. He did what he had to do.'

During his 1991 visit, Gould had befriended teenage brothers Fernando and Francisco Mujica, who featured the band in their fanzine, *Extravaganza*. In 1994, he returned to Chile on his own. 'When I was so sick of the band that I just wanted to get as far away as possible, the farthest place I could think of was Chile. I just showed up with a suitcase, and I stayed there for two months. I stayed mostly in Santiago, and I hung out with the guys that I met when we played Viña del Mar. I hung out with them, and became a *Chileno*. I lived anonymously and learned Spanish.'

After 1995, the band did not return to Chile together until they reunited in 2009. Now, Chile was their home from home. Their return was scheduled for October 30, at the Estadio Bicentenario de la Florida, and 22,000 tickets sold out in days. Another show was arranged for Teatro Caupolican the day before, and its 6,000 tickets were also snapped up straight away. The bond between band and audience was palpable at both shows, most notably the stunning crowd rendition of 'Midlife Crisis' on the first night.

Even more so than elsewhere, Faith No More had become more popular in their absence. They benefitted from an amplified reminiscence bump. The kids who had watched them in 1991 and 1995 were now adults, and Faith No More's performance at Viña was part of the foundation myth of Chile's transition to democracy. In an article in *Paniko*, writer Daniel Hidalgo stated, 'Just like the Stones or Ramones for Argentina, Faith No More is part of a secret story for a generation that was told that democracy was just around the corner. It only knew limits through the things that Patton professed as religion: the absolute rupture of all the conventions and norms.'

'The transition had been very polite, trying not to break any glass,' Alberto Fuguet adds. 'People were very afraid, afraid that if they misbehaved, democracy would be taken off them. But freedom also means not being afraid of what freedom could bring. For my generation, and especially for the even younger generation, the kids watching Viña on TV, when TV was the main source of information, the Faith No More performance was a big expression of freedom. Of creativity, of wildness, and that things could be different. The dictatorship did not end on March 11 1990, but on February 5 1991, when Faith No More played Viña.'

Faith No More embraced the myth, and added to it. They returned in December 2010 to play 'Ashes To Ashes' and 'Midlife Crisis' at the televised charity event Teletón. There, Patton declared, 'Chile is a very special country. A very important country for us.' Thanked by the event's presenter, Don Francisco, Chile's leading television presenter since 1962, Patton replied, 'Thank you, Don Corleone,' and kissed his hand. The band played to 25,000 people the following night at the Estadio Bicentenario de La Florida, billing it as their last-ever show. It wasn't, but the band's Chile connection was further strengthened when they played 'Qué He Sacado Con Quererte', as a tribute to the song's composer, the late Nueva Canción pioneer and social activist Violeta Parra.

For their 2011 return, they played the whole of *King For A Day … Fool For A Lifetime*, complete with Trey Spruance in his only live performance with the band. There were other bonds: Bill Gould signed and mentored Chilean group Como Asesinar A Felipes; Mike Patton appeared in a TV ad for the Sonar 105.3 radio station; and Roddy Bottum made his acting bow in *Tyrel*, a film by the Chilean director Sebastián Silva.

In 2015, Faith No More played the Santiago Gets Louder Festival for the penultimate show of the *Sol Invictus* tour. 'The best thing that could happen was to finish here,' Mike Bordin said at the time. 'Playing in Chile is like dessert after dinner.'

After the accolades and awards of 1990 and the culture shock of Chile, Faith No More would experience real adulation as they concentrated their 1991 touring on South America, and Brazil in particular. On January 20, two years after they finished recording *The Real Thing*, Faith No More played in front of their biggest-ever crowd—180,000 people at the Rock In Rio II festival at Rio de Janiero's Maracana stadium. The festival, a follow-up to the 1985 original, attracted a million fans over nine nights. It was broadcast throughout Latin America by TV Globo and elsewhere by MTV, and featured as headliners Guns N' Roses, Prince, New Kids On The Block, George Michael, INXS, and Norwegian electro-pop act A-ha, who attracted the largest-ever attendance for a paid concert of 198,000 for their Saturday show.

The band's Brazilian record label marked their arrival by hiring a small plane to repeatedly fly over the Copacabana beach, trailing a banner reading 'PolyGram welcomes Faith No More'. Playing third on the third night before Billy Idol and Guns N' Roses, they did not look out of place. Looking back at the band's composed, controlled, and confident show, it seems remarkable that they did not go onto to join those acts in rock and pop's inner circle. Patton, sporting a shorter haircut and the plaid shirts he first adopted as stage wear the previous year, looked like a grunge harbinger, and won over the crowd with a dedication to Pelé. He could command their attention and acclaim just by lying prostrate on the stage at the end of 'Epic' or by hanging from the stage during 'War Pigs'. 'It was the biggest show we've ever done,' he said at the time. 'It was really scary. I couldn't tell how many people were actually in the audience until later when I watched Guns N' Roses, because they lit up the crowd. I thought it was just people in front of me, but there were people here, here, here.'

Faith No More were the lowest-paid international act at the festival, pocketing $20,000 when the festival generated $5.2 million in ticket and concession sales alone. But according to a report in the magazine *Veja*, 'The presentation at Rock In Rio II reverberated abroad, consolidated the group among fans of heavy rock and had a side effect: turning the singer and leader of the band Mike Patton into an idol in Brazil, mainly among the girls aged fourteen to eighteen.'

Late 1990 and 1991 looks like a misstep in the band's commercial if not artistic evolution, however. Rather than continuing to slog on tour after *The Real Thing* broke through, a fresh and fired-up Faith No More could, and should, have been back in the studio, ready to return with new material in 1991 for a public clamouring for more. Instead, there was an attempt at repackaging existing material. The album version of *Live At The Brixton Academy* was released in February, featuring eight songs from the Brixton show and two extra tracks from the *Real Thing* sessions, the instrumental 'The Grade' and 'The Cowboy Song'. Underlining the fact that the public were hungry for new Faith No More material, it rocketed into the UK album chart at #20, ten places higher than *The Real Thing* had reached.

Faith No More received their second successive Grammy nomination in January 1991, this time for 'Epic' in the 'Best Hard Rock Performance' category, alongside Mötley Crüe's 'Kickstart My Heart', AC/DC's *The Razors Edge*, *Ritual de lo Habitual* by Jane's Addiction, and Living Colour's *Time's Up*. That meant another glitzy ceremony for the band at the Radio City Music Hall in New York in February. Faith No More again emerged empty-handed, with Living Colour winning. Bordin says, 'I remember going the second time to the Grammys and not winning. You feel like a fool. The next day, the bass player for Living Colour, during all the radio interviews, he walked by and he said, "You guys should have won. You guys are great. We've won two, but you guys should have won one."'

The band had a more successful night the following month at the annual Bammies, the *BAM* magazine awards for Bay Area artists. They won outstanding song ('Epic'), outstanding group, outstanding male vocalist, outstanding drummer, and outstanding keyboardist, but lost out to MC Hammer for artist and album of the year. The magazine later noted that 'the group plans to begin recording the follow-up to its breakthrough LP, *The*

Real Thing, at least by the end of 1991'. The awards ceremony and party provided plenty of opportunity for more mischief, including Patton taunting Gould for not winning an award—'Billy didn't win a Bammie! Billy didn't win a Bammie!'—and referring to the award as the 'magnificent golden dildo' after picking it up from En Vogue, while during one acceptance speech, Gould pronounced, 'I'd like to thank Satan.'

✸

Faith No More spent the rest of the year between their early and late South American dates either working on new material or left to their own devices. Mike Patton attracted the greatest amount of attention for Mr Bungle's eponymous debut album, released in August, but he was not the only Faith No More member learning and playing in other projects in this brief downtime. Mike Bordin played drums on some tracks on the Primus album *Sailing The Seas Of Cheese*, recorded and released in 1991, while that same year, Roddy Bottum played organ on *Hearts & Minds*, the major label debut, on Reprise, by another San Francisco band, Sister Double Happiness. Even Bill Gould, despite feeling record label pressure, found time to record with Brujera (the supposedly anonymous Mexican extreme metal outfit that comprised members of Napalm Death and Fear Factory, as well as Jello Biafra, friend and early champion of Faith No More Pat Hoed, and Gould himself), playing bass on their first two singles, '¡Demoniaco!' and 'Machetazos', in 1990 and 1992.

The band also managed to parlay their growing fame into an appearance on the soundtrack to the Keanu Reeves science-fiction comedy, *Bill & Ted's Bogus Journey*, released in July 1991. 'Sweet Emotion'—a track culled from *The Real Thing* that was first released in September 1989 on a cover-mounted *Kerrang!* disc called *Flexible Fiend*—was re-recorded with new lyrics as 'The Perfect Crime' for the film, which also featured a cameo by Jim Martin as a guest speaker at a lecture at the Bill & Ted University in its opening scene.

✸

After Patton returned from touring with John Zorn's Naked City during the summer, Faith No More went back to South America for one final haul in their mammoth *The Real Thing* campaign. After two dates in Argentina, the band played thirteen shows in three weeks in Brazil in September that were 'really like Beatlemania', says Gould.

> That was a crazy trip. It was early days for touring in Brazil, so a lot of the local promoters were gangsters basically. I was going out every night and not sleeping, and just trying to get the full experience of Brazil. Kids were climbing up the side of the hotel. There were ten-year-old kids on the third storey on the outside of the hotel. I was getting tackled by twelve-year-old girls, like really tackled. It hurt, like you're trying to run away and they bring you down.
>
> We were supposed to hunker down in the hotel and stay safe, but we went out—even Patton went out. We spent a lot of time with the Cavalera brothers [Max and Igor from Brazilian thrash giants Sepultura]. We had a friendship with them. So they took us around. Just to get us away from all the bullshit.

'I was told not to wear jewellery and wear dark clothes in the streets of Brazil, so we wouldn't get mugged or whatever,' Bottum adds. 'I took that as a challenge, and put on all the jewellery I had, as well as an all-white outfit, and hit the streets looking for drugs.'

The first show of the September tour was right in the Amazon rain forest, as Faith No More became one of the first American bands to play Manaus. Local paper *Veja* noted that they had sold 120,000 copies of the *The Real Thing* in Brazil, and that they were earning $55,000 per show on the tour. In an interview with the same publication, Patton reflected on his celebrity status in the country: 'It feels like being an animal at the zoo. I am not used to this, since I am only admired like this in Brazil. I feel like I'm a Disneyland attraction.'

The tour also included four shows at the Olympia in Sao Paulo, and consecutive nights at the Ginásio Maracanãzinho in Rio. Such was the band's popularity in Brazil and back in the USA that MTV sent a film crew to shoot them hang-gliding off Pedra Bonita, with Bordin saying, 'That was probably the greatest thing that ever happened to me in my life.' These

South American shows also allowed the band to showcase new material. 'RV' and 'The World Is Yours' were played for the first time at the Estadio Obras Sanitarias in Buenos Aires, while an early version of 'Caffeine' was unveiled in Recife. All three were also played on a two-date stopover in Tokyo.

Faith No More's final date of 1991, and the final date of *The Real Thing* tour, which had kicked off twenty-six months previously, was back on home turf. They played the A Day On The Green festival at the Oakland Coliseum on October 12, along with old friends Metallica and Soundgarden, as well as Queensrÿche. Clad in a red Texaco mechanic's shirt with floppy hair, Patton was only an eyebrow-ring and some self-harming stage flips away from *Angel Dust* Patton.

The band had reached their limit. 'We had no time to ourselves,' Gould says. 'Vassiliou did a great job in some ways. He let us be who we were, but our general quality of life wasn't as much a priority to him as keeping the band productive. After Day On The Green, it was, *How soon can you get a new record?*'

PART THREE

If Faith No More had birthed alternative rock and metal with *The Real Thing*, it was now a monster. The original crossover kings had paved the way for Metallica to soften their thrash metal into fifteen-million-selling bites, as well as Nirvana's own MTV-fuelled rise in 1991. Fittingly, just a week before Faith No More entered Coast Recorders in San Francisco in January 1992, *Nevermind* went to #1 on the *Billboard* 200.

Both Nirvana and Metallica benefitted from the new way the album charts were calculated. In March 1991, *Billboard* started using Soundscan data to much more accurately show what music people were actually buying in record stores, not what stores and labels said that people were buying. The new data immediately showed that people were purchasing more hip-hop and country albums, but also much more metal and alternative rock albums than the previous system had shown. The labels, after initially resisting the new charts and the new reality, then did what they did best to regain control. As *Ultimate Classic Rock* reported, 'Popularity begets popularity. If an album's doing well, people will check it out and see what the fuss is about. The major record companies began to throw tons of promotion money into acts that they recently discovered could compete in the mainstream.'

Faith No More had already shown that they could compete in the mainstream in the pre-Soundscan era, and they would be expected to match and exceed the success of Metallica, Queensrÿche, Jane's Addiction, and Extreme, who were all among the 100 best-selling albums in 1991, not to mention Nirvana, Pearl Jam, and former tourmates the Red Hot Chili Peppers, who all had top 10 albums in the first half of 1992. And contemporaries and cultural commentators alike were quick to note Faith No More's role as gatekeepers to this alternative revolution: 'Like Faith

No More last year, Nirvana is the buzz band of the moment,' claimed the *Detroit Free Press*. All of which meant that when the band regrouped at the Coast Recorders studio in San Francisco's Mission district, the stakes had been raised.

'We were told that *Angel Dust* would go gold right out of the box,' Gould notes, 'but that Warner Bros did not see this as enough sales to keep their interest and make it a priority.' Not that the band felt the pressure too much: 'We have always insisted on 100 percent freedom on our musical content, and always got it. There were no guns to our heads, no leverage being made. However, we were strongly advised not to open up too many extracurricular avenues before we could properly establish ourselves.

'I don't think Warners exactly understood us,' Gould continues. 'They knew that we had something, but left it to us to say what that was. It was clear that they needed some type of vehicle to cut though the noise, where their machinery could be put to use. That could mean a successful video, radio track, or anything else.'

The whole experience of *The Real Thing*—recording, release, promotion, and touring—certainly influenced the band's approach to *Angel Dust*. In both positive and negative ways. 'There's no doubt that touring *The Real Thing* made us better musicians,' says Gould. 'Playing to hostile crowds was never an issue for us—we'd done that since the beginning—but being physically and mentally exhausted did contribute to the darkness on that album.'

And, rather than embracing the new market possibilities, they were again keen to break free from the constraints of rock. 'We're all different people, but as a main songwriter, and checking in with Mike Patton, we felt *in general* that we had become a bit pigeonholed in the rock world through the success of *The Real Thing*. With the success of that album, we saw an opportunity to challenge that perception, though we all had different ways of doing it. The album took a couple of months to make, partially because we did have different views on what could sound good that we needed to work out. And which we eventually did, aside from Jim.'

That became evident to the wider world later in January. An MTV film crew took up temporary residence at Coast Recorders studios to bear witness to Faith No More recording the next big 1990s rock record. But when MTV edited its four hours of in-studio filming into a three-minute snippet for

In The Studio '92, broadcast at the end of January 1992, it became clear that Faith No More would not be producing *The Real Thing* redux. Patton referenced British industrial metal pioneers Godflesh as he thrashed out the riff to what would become 'Malpractice' on Gould's borrowed bass, while Bottum recited the piano melody from 'RV', calling it 'one of the country & western songs we are doing for our new record'.

●

Work on the new album had already begun in the summer of 1991 and during the South America and Japan tours, when—with management's exhortations ringing in their ears—Bottum, Gould, Patton, and Bordin started writing, rehearsing, and recording on the latest Sony DAT recorders that producer Matt Wallace had gifted each member after the success of *The Real Thing*. They also worked at Gould's home studio (all four had all purchased property in San Francisco in the preceding months), which had a Tascam Portastudio multi-cassette recorder, and a half-inch eight-track machine, which allowed Gould to work out song arrangements on his own.

Some things stayed the same for *Angel Dust*—it was one of only three Faith No More albums where the band composition was the same as the preceding album, and Wallace was again on board—but there were significant changes in having a new studio, more money and time, and a new way of writing and recording. Bottum told MTV, 'I don't think we have evolved. We have devolved to a certain process. Before, when he wrote songs, the core of it was the keyboard, drums, and bass, and normally we would start from there. But we had other songs where the guitar player would come in with a riff and add a couple of ideas. This time, it didn't work out like that, and we stuck to the core.'

The band had played 'Caffeine', 'RV', and 'The World Is Yours' in South America in Japan in late 1991. Album opener 'Land Of Sunshine' was already completed in 1991, and most other songs were pretty much written and arranged by the time the band entered the studio. 'Smaller And Smaller', 'Jizzlobbler', and 'Crack Hitler' were initiated outside of the recording studio, but fleshed out substantially during the recording process. Gould, in particular, wanted as much done as possible before the band actually went into the studio. 'Pre-production is considered a later stage of writing, really. I don't like to waste money and time in the studio, I have always been a believer of band control in the process, and I also believe it's important that the material feels natural to the players before it is recorded.'

Hence why the bass player was so put out that Jim Martin and Mike Patton were dragging their feet at this stage. Martin had been completely absent from the early writing, rehearsing, and recording following the death of his father at the end of 1990. The band had tried to meet the guitar player halfway by moving their rehearsal space closer to him.

'The band is situated in San Francisco,' Wallace recalls. 'All of them, except for Jim Martin. Jim was still staying at home, in Hayward. As a compromise, they decided, *Well, OK. We'll rehearse in Oakland*, so that Jim could get there. We were all coming to Oakland [Jackson Street Rehearsals] to rehearse, but Jim wasn't showing up. His dad died a month before we started that record. I said to Jim, and I'm sure all the guys said, *Listen. Let's just stop. We don't need to make the record right now. Let's wait a few months*. But he also had to pick up his dad's business, and so Jim was, to some extent, sidelined.'

Patton also took his time getting involved. 'Pretty much the whole time off consisted of just making excuses and putting things off and patting each other on the back and saying, "Everything's going to be great," and then not answering our phones for a while. A couple of guys in the band got worried. I took some pleasure in that, but I kept really busy doing a bunch of other things. I got that out of my system and then it's time to go back to work. Songs were being written, but certain people like our guitar player were really, really hard to find. Now everyone wants to work, and everything's great now, but we almost broke up it was so bad.'

When the band first stepped into Coast Recorders in early January, they did so surreptitiously. 'We weren't telling anybody what we were doing at this stage,' Gould recalls. 'We weren't playing anybody our music. We were combative about it, because of things like that "From Out Of Nowhere" video. There were little things that were happening beyond our control so we decided, we're not going to tell them what we're doing. We have our deal with them. They were obligated to release it, so we were going to do it our way and make our record. Matt was probably the guy who was trying to toe the line on both sides. I don't know what he was telling them. I'm sure he had conversations, but we didn't. We were very militant about it.'

Wallace had got a deal on a new studio for the band, and they were happy with the change of scene. 'It was a different approach,' Gould adds, 'a cool place because we were used to always recording in these big drum rooms, and here we wanted somewhere a little tighter and punchier.'

The Coast studio building had been opened as Mercury Recording in 1969, before being renovated as Coast Recorders by Bill Putnam—the studio designer and audio engineer considered by many to be the father of modern music recording—in 1971. Putnam had previously used the Coast Recorders name for several studios in the Bay Area in the 1950s and 60s, and it became known for a mix of jingle and jazz recordings.

For Wallace, Coast was also more convenient. 'The band all had homes now, in San Francisco, and we didn't want to go to Sausalito anymore. This was a more acoustically, less ambient room. We wanted to go for a classic, thicker, more present sound.'

There was also a bigger budget, of around $150,000, and the opportunities that came with such resources. Mike Bordin was excited: 'We were confident, creative, and fearless, and had the tools and the resources to do what our wildest dreams could conceive. That's a fucking miracle. That's the most pure sense of creativity you could ever have, and it's not ever to be repeated.'

The band were looking for a different sound from the start. Part of this was a reaction to the funk-metal label they had acquired during the *Real Thing* era, and part was their usual desire to change and evolve. As Mike Patton said at the time, 'The only way to keep Faith No More together is to motivate ourselves. And you can only do that by experimenting.' He went even further when he told MTV, 'The only way to really progress is to be ashamed of what you've just done. It may be a strong word, but you got to do something completely different. This album is going to be different lyrically, musically, everything.'

31

Angel Dust marked the emergence of Mike Patton as a composer, as well as a lyricist. Though he may have missed out on some early writing and rehearsal sessions, he was still involved in the writing process much earlier, telling MTV, 'Last time they wrote all the songs, and I just came in and wrote the words. This time, arrangement-wise, I was more involved, and definitely spent more time on writing.'

Matt Wallace concurs:

> You can argue that *Angel Dust* was the first real Mike Patton album, because he could actually get in there, do things, make suggestions, and bring in things like 'Malpractice'. Patton came in with multiple background vocal ideas. And we had the space, the audio space, the storage space to be able to capture what he was trying to do.
>
> He came in with these amazing melodies. He'd would walk in, and he'd go, 'OK, I'm going to do this harmony. OK, here's another harmony.' Sometimes he'd do the main vocal and then the harmony, and I was like, 'I don't know if that's in tune.' That's dissonant. Are they right notes? Not so sure. I heard that same story about Brian Wilson doing harmonies with The Beach Boys, I looked at Patton and said, 'I don't think that's the right thing.' But then he'd add the final part, and it was like, *Oh. OK.* He could hear in four dimensions. He knew what it was going to sound like. It was really gorgeous.

Gorgeous is not an appellation anyone could use to describe 'Malpractice', a song about surgical violation. The track, which Patton had previewed in that MTV footage, was so much his work that it had the working title of 'The Patton Song'. Influenced heavily by English industrial metal pioneers Godflesh, it was Patton merging his industrial influences with his band's unique rhythmic approach, while re-injecting some of their gothic DNA. It was also the sound of Patton learning to compose.

Patton wore his ardour for Godflesh on his sleeve, wearing a band T-shirt the previous year when the band performed 'Epic' at the International Rock Awards in London, where Faith No More were introduced by Leslie Nielsen as the 'future of rock music'. On the MTV studio footage, while strumming the song chords on Bill Gould's unplugged bass, he tells Jim Martin, 'That last thing is like a machine, Godflesh thing.' Patton may well have had his Godflesh interest piqued by Gould, who had long been a fan of the band's Earache label, and of Napalm Death and Carcass in particular, and who had arranged for the band to visit the label's Nottingham offices before one of their many shows at Rock City during the tours for *The Real Thing*.

Patton's metamorphosis from shiny pinup to malcontent misanthrope maverick from *The Real Thing* to *Angel Dust* can be overstated—after all, his lyrics on his first album referenced murder and child molestation—but as *The Real Thing* Anakin firmly embraces the dark side on *Angel Dust*, 'Malpractice' is his maiming Mace Wandu moment. The subject is dark, the lyrics are dark, the mood is dark, the music is dark, and the vocals are positively demonic. While 'Surprise! You're Dead!' was fake horror, 'Malpractice' chills, no more so than when, at one minute and twenty seconds in, Patton screeches his fourth 'applause' from the song's chorus. The alternating, industrial-style chromatic riff, the unorthodox song structure, the odd and changing time signatures, and the harsh synths add to the unsettling effect, which reaches its peak with the perfectly apposite sample of four seconds of Dmitri Shostakovich's *String Quartet No. 8* (as performed by the Kronos Quartet on their album *Black Angels*), providing gothic peril three-quarters of the way in and thereafter.

The song began with some drum parts that Mike Bordin had recorded onto his DAT machine. Patton borrowed the tape while on tour in Auckland in July 1990, and built the song around them.

As well as a new way of composing, 'Malpractice' represented a lesson for the rest of the band in Patton's songwriting style. 'I don't know how to write a song in the sense that it has a form like ABAB, 1-2-3-4,' he told MTV. 'I don't really know how to make things sound catchy and in order in a little package that you can call a song. That's why it sounds like a collection of sounds. It won't sound like Faith No More at all, which I think is a pretty good thing. It sounds like death metal movie music. I hadn't written anything with them before, so no one really knew what the intention was, so we made a little chart, a list of parts since it's nothing you can really remember, and, out of repetition and rote memorisation, we learned the thing.'

For Wallace, 'This was him teaching the band what he wanted. It was also obviously an outlier, it's a weird song. It's closer to Bungle than anything else.'

❋

Seán Clancy, senior lecturer in composition at the Royal Birmingham Conservatoire, composed a piece of classical music based on Faith No More music. He says:

> Patton's personality, eclectic taste, and willingness to engage with a multiplicity of different projects contribute to what could be described as a magpie, or a schizophrenic approach to songwriting and composition. Patton's gift is being able to collate such a disparate source of methods and approaches, and present them in a form that is utterly unique, with no single influence being more prevalent than another. On 'Malpractice', we hear Patton channelling influences from contemporary classical music, highlighted by abrupt tempo, time signature, and textural changes. These techniques are juxtaposed with Pierre Schaeffer and Pierre Henry's *musique concrète* techniques, in addition to rock tropes and moulded into something that, in the early 1990s was incredibly innovative.
>
> Patton's virtuosity and technical ability mark him out as one of the most talented vocalists working today. Often critics note

that his range of six-and-a-half octaves is the most impressive thing about his voice, but it is the timbre and quality of his voice that makes it absolutely singular. It is this technical ability, tonal range, and clarity—coupled with an eclectic but focused approach to composition and a phenomenal work ethic—that make Mike Patton one of the most exciting and unique figures in music of any genre today.

William Winant, who teaches at Mills College and the University of California at Berkeley, has worked with Patton on various John Zorn projects, and as a percussionist with Mr Bungle and Mondo Cane. 'The difference between Patton and most great rock musicians is that most people stick to one thing, they don't move out of their safety zone,' he says. 'Patton is able to bring his interests and ability to play so many styles of music into whatever project he's working on at the moment. He also has an exceptional ear for melody, a great sense of rhythm, and he has a keen musical memory, and is able to learn complex tunes and compositions really fast.'

✦

'Malpractice' was Patton's sole solo composition, but he had musical contributions on another five tracks on *Angel Dust*. He also wrote the lyrics for everything, bar the covers and 'Be Aggressive'. This was not all entirely new to Patton, but he was embracing his new role. Brash, edgy, awkward, he was a lively presence at Coast. He was not a constant presence, preferring to hang out with his Mr Bungle bandmates, but he was in a rich vein of creative form. As he explained to MTV, 'It's inevitable that some of the stuff that I did with Zorn will creep in. Song structure and arrangement-wise probably not, but really distorting my voice, disguising it, and making it sound like a machine and taking it as far away from the sound of a voice.'

He achieved that in 'Smaller And Smaller', where it is never entirely clear whether the chants, grunts, and rumbles are Patton or sound effects samples bought pre-packaged from Sound Ideas, the Canadian royalty-free sample company, which received an album credit. Certainly, the sniggering heard two minutes and thirty-three seconds into the track sounds uncannily like MTV and Mike Judge's *Beavis & Butt-Head*, but according to Matt Wallace, this too is all Patton. The song is largely a Bordin-Bottum-Gould production, and is a rather unloved song in the Faith No More canon, never performed live. Patton's Stakhanovite lyrical theme of unremitting and unrewarding toil could easily be applied to the song's own construction; as Gould puts it, 'There's a bass line and drums that we had at rehearsal, but we couldn't get anything out of it. It was overworked and overworked and overworked. I had a really Russian/Eastern Europe fascination, not knowing much about it still.'

Patton had no input into the musical compositional of 'Crack Hitler', but he brought his vocal production input to a Faith No More track for the first time. He strenuously beat down Wallace's objections to using distortion on the track, with the producer aghast that the new microphones he had purchased at $20,000 apiece to remove all trace of distortion were being put to such use.

'Caffeine' was a completely Patton/Gould composition, with Patton writing the lyrics. The song was the result of the singer experimenting with a combination of sleep deprivation and high caffeine intake to engender a transcendent creative state. He told MTV:

> I stayed up for about three or four days straight. I basically wrote the entire song in delirium. You get weird dizzy spells for ten or fifteen minutes, and I felt really weak, and then I'd feel great again, and the great thing about that is after you go through a spell of feeling really weak, no matter what time it is, you can convince your body that it's morning, and time to start over again. What I would do is at three in the morning or something, I'd fix eggs, take a shower, and act like that was morning, and it totally works. You can really fool your body. It's just a pretty delirious song, a dirge, a droney funereal thing, and it's not really conscious.

'He'd stay up for three or four days at a time,' says Wallace. 'He'd come in and say, OK, I'm ready to sing the vocals, I've been up for three days and drinking all this coffee. I told him to just go get some sleep and come back in, but he goes, No, I want to do it while I'm in this state.'

Patton also brought an interesting lyrical approach to the album, and 'Land Of Sunshine' is his example of using the cut-up technique of re-arranging existing text into new lyrics. The inspirations were fortune cookie messages and the Oxford Capacity Analysis personality test offered by the Church of Scientology, with questions 27, 69, and 196 repeated in the lyrics. Patton's inspiration was not Scientology itself, but the whole self-help, self-improvement culture of the time. The result, he later remarked, was 'just a grotesquely positive song, so I watched a lot of late-night TV to get in that frame of mind.'

SEX, DRUGS, AND RODDY BOTTUM

32

Most of the grotesque in 'Land Of Sunshine' came from Roddy Bottum, and his creepy, carnival-esque chord forty seconds into the track sets the tone for the remainder of the album. Bottum chose the album title *Angel Dust*, as it was 'a really beautiful name for a really hideous drug'. The beauty was buried deep in *Angel Dust*, and just like the synthetic drug that inspired its name, the album came with agitation, disorientation, and addiction as side effects.

And Bottum, perceived as and portrayed by the band's own publicity as the pop sensibility and melodic touchstone of Faith No More, provided much of that agitation and disorientation with his frankly disturbing keyboard riffs—and the inventive use of sampling and *musique concrète*.

The re-purposing of new or pre-existing sounds in music and in other art forms was pioneered in the 1940s, primarily by Pierre Schaeffer. Innovation moved into popular music itself in the 1970s in Jamaican dub, along with the use of tape loops and voice sampling on The Beatles' 'Revolution #9' and the plunderphonic restructuring of Elvis Presley's 'Blue Suede Shoes' that was James Tenney's 'Collage No. 1'. When new technology made sampling easier and cheaper in the early 80s, it became the building block for hip-hop. And Faith No More were themselves sampled, with the main beat of 'We Care A Lot' subtly used in MC Hammer's 1990 hit 'Pray', while a guitar part from the same song was more obviously sampled by Pop Will Eat Itself on their UK chart hit 'Can U Dig It?' one year earlier.

Sampling was treated with suspicion, if not outright disdain, by most rock bands. Rage Against The Machine, another band managed by Warren Entner, boasted in the sleeve notes of their eponymous debut album, released later in 1992, that there were 'no samples, keyboards, or synthesizers used in the making of this record'. But jarring again with any notions of rock authenticity, Faith No More enjoyed working with emerging technologies, and in Bottum they had a deft weaver of keyboard, synthesizers, and sampling into their overall sound. Speaking to *Kerrang!* in 1993, Bottum said, 'I get really turned on by current influences that I'm listening to. Recently that meant a lot of the techno stuff that's going on, that whole basis of taking a sound and looping it, using that as a sound source and getting the accidents that occur, those strange arbitrary noises.'

Sampling was not entirely new for Faith No More, as Bottum had used the in-built samples on his E-mu Emax II on *The Real Thing*, including cello on 'Woodpecker From Mars', strings on 'From Out Of Nowhere', and horns on 'Epic'. Matt Wallace helped broaden the sampling possibilities by gifting each band member a Sony DAT recorder. 'Each of those things was 700 bucks,' he recalls. 'But I wanted to give them something, because now we're into the digital era and everyone had their own DAT recorders. And, because we were travelling so much, I wanted them to be able to record stuff. It was *musique concrète* or *audio vérité*, really an attempt to get them to pull in some of their experience and use it on the record.'

A large part of the hours of raw footage that MTV gathered while they spent two days in the studio on January 9 and 10 shows the band getting to grips with splicing the right sounds together. 'In those days, making samples was a big deal,' Bill Gould recalls. 'Some days, you'd be working on it, and Matt would take half a day and get a couple of samples in. I liked to be in the studio every day, but at times like that I was like, *Tell me when it's done, and I'll listen.*'

The process got a whole lot harder when most of the samples went missing on the first day of recording. Chris Gott, Bordin's drum technician, known by the band as 'Feelie', was loading all the band equipment, including a cardboard box containing a hard disc and several discs of samples, from a van at the back of the parking lot backing onto the studio's main tracking room, all while leaving the back door of the van open to make unloading easier. Job done, Gott settled down in the studio, only to be confronted by an irate Roddy Bottum, swearing and losing his usual cool: 'Where is my box of fucking samples!'

'With the somewhat sizable amount of gear the band had, I wasn't totally sure what cardboard box he was talking about,' Gott recalls. 'I didn't really understand the scope of the situation, until Roddy, who normally was a very mellow and calm guy, made me aware that this was serious, and that he was pissed. Roddy was pacing around the studio, screaming obscenities and looking like he was going to punch something. He actually had to take a walk out of the studio for a breather. Looking at him, I had the growing feeling that my days working for the band may be coming to an end.'

The record itself was in peril. 'That was going to stop the entire process,' Bordin remembers, 'because we couldn't do it without all the samples that Roddy had spent months preparing.'

But as the fretful Gott retraced his tracks, a man—one of the area's many homeless—knocked on the back door of the studio and stuttered, 'I think I have something, but I don't know what it is.' Gott dashed out the door and shouted, 'Yes, if you have what I think you do, it does belong to us—and I need it back!' Inching closer, Gott added, 'And I'll pay you for it.' The mysterious man didn't reply to the inducement, saying simply, 'I'll take you to them.'

Desperation trumping discretion, Gott followed the man across the road to an eight-storey building, and up the stairs before barging past him into his apartment. 'Before I realised what I had done, I heard the door slam behind me, and that was when the feeling that I may have just made the last mistake of my life hit me like a ton of bricks. The instant feeling that I could turn around to the end of a gun barrel or a cloth filled with chloroform shook my nerves hard. I had no idea who this guy was, or what he may be capable of, or what freaky shit he may be into.'

But when the man fell into a religious reverie of mumbling and pacing, Gott spotted his own holy grail, grabbed the cardboard box from the corner of the room, and bolted.

Disaster averted, Bottum's samples proceeded to provide much of the album's misanthropic soundscape. As well as composing all of the unsettling 'Land Of Sunshine' and the lyrics for 'Be Aggressive', Bottum injected much of the record's jittery skittishness: the howling monkeys on 'Caffeine', the samples as melody and texture in the breakdown of 'A Small Victory', and the menacing melange in 'Smaller And Smaller'.

The *musique concrète* approach was another reflection of the band's touring in the record. 'Sampling was suddenly a thing,' Bottum explains, 'and we were exploring it for sure. We always wanted guitars to be part of the mix, but there was new technology going on, and we liked the idea of incorporating where we'd been in the last years into what we were doing in the studio. Like the sample of the woman announcer from Brazil in the airport for "Crack Hitler". It felt like we could make a sort of audio diary.'

The woman in question was Iris Lettieri, whose soothing flight announcements had made her something of a celebrity in Brazil, and later internationally. She became the country's first female radio announcer and newsreader in the late 1950s, in her teens, and she then became the flight announcer at Rio de Janeiro–Galeão International Airport in 1976. For Roddy, her seductive tones soundtracked their tour of Brazil in 1991 and now, duly recorded on a DAT machine, her announcement—'Flight 8-1-0 to Miami. Now boarding, gate 12'—served as the opener to 'Crack Hitler''s evocation of a 1970s crime film aesthetic.

When Lettieri read in a Brazilian newspaper that her voice had been used on the album, she immediately went out to buy the record, 'to make sure it was my voice'. She was not a fan of the music—'I confess that it is not my genre, I am, and I have always been a jazz fan'—but she recognised her voice, and eventually started legal proceedings against the band's Brazilian label. In the end, a financial settlement was agreed to compensate her. She says, 'I had two reactions: one of indignation, because I thought it was disrespectful to a professional announcer, and also that this only happened because it was Brazil. Today, I can see a silver lining.'

The most intriguing use of *musique concrète* was in the songs 'Smaller And Smaller' and 'A Small Victory'. Samples here are central to the song dynamics, and the chanting and sniggering provide a perfect example of what the French composer Philippe Leroux has called the 'moment of madness' that every piece of music needs. 'A Small Victory' owes more to Bottum's straightforward, delicate but insistent piano riff than anything else, but the procession of bells, sirens, and pulses two-thirds of the way in sets the song up for Patton's spoken-word finish. Composer Seán Clancy says of this sampling, 'These sound-worlds fulfil a number of functions; on a track like "Smaller And Smaller" they add a structural interest, giving the song its "moment of madness". On something like "A Small Victory", they add timbreal interest, keeping the ear engaged as the song pushes forward, and in many ways, they are offering an alternative to a guitar solo.'

❋

Bottum's lyrical contribution to the album was the outstanding, one-of-a-kind 'Be Aggressive', the greatest celebration of man-on-man oral sex ever put to music. The song was mostly written by Bill Gould, starting out life as a bass and drum track, with Jim Martin adding the solo and Bottum the lyrics. The song featured a cheerleader-chanted 'Be Aggressive' as the chorus. According to Gould, 'The "cheerleaders" were Mike Patton's friends from high school who moved down here. He recorded them on Matt Wallace's DAT player in his living room.'

While not a pure sample, the 'Be Aggressive' chorus was a direct lift from rap pioneers Sugarhill Gang's 1983 track 'Winner Is', though the refrain had been used as a cheerleading cheer for decades in high school sports. Completely original are lines such as '*Malnutrition, my submission / You're the master / And I take it on my knees / Ejaculation / Tribulation*'. The successive organ and guitar solos at the track's midpoint are the finest musical representation of sexual release since Frankie Goes To Hollywood's 'Relax' in 1985.

Roddy clarified his sexuality in two landmark interviews in 1993, but he had never really hidden his homosexuality. Though Bill Gould and Jim Martin had discovered Bottum *in flagrante delicto* on the band's first national tour in 1986, Roddy's first confidant in the band was Patton, and the pair would subsequently share tales of their sexual exploits. Getting Patton to deliver the 'Be Aggressive' vocals was therefore a natural step. Bottum explains, 'I saw it as a challenge to Mike to sort of embrace this character. It was super-obnoxious of me in retrospect, but what can I say?'

Patton sounded positively buzzed about the song when he spoke to Canadian magazine *Music Express* in an interview published in August 1992. 'Pretty fucking extreme, isn't it?' he said. 'As long as we make a few people squirm—our job is done.'

In the early 1990s, long before the concepts of gender fluidity and sliding scales of sexuality went mainstream, famous public figures who were homosexual were still expected to endure a public coming-out. While almost every interview with Bottum since 1993 has included some questioning on his sexuality, interviewers rarely delve into his bandmates' personal lives. Bottum had attempted to take ownership of his coming-out by arranging an interview in late 1992 with *NME* journalist Gina Morris, a friend of his friends in the group L7. When the interview was published in January 1993, Bottum was not impressed. Months later, in June, he told LGBT-interest magazine the *Advocate*, 'I thought my coming-out was an important angle, and I don't mean that in an egocentric way. Kids who are into hard rock and who may be dealing with the possibility of being gay themselves don't see a lot of positive role models. But, as it turned out, that was only a small part of the final article. The writer had a thing for our singer, and that's who she ultimately focused on.'

Mike Patton graced the cover under the strap-line 'Patton: Lust For Glory', while inside, Bottum's big coming-out revelation sat under the headline 'Faecal Attraction', and alongside a full-page photo of Patton. Bottum's explanation was also buried deep in the article:

Throughout our career, the representation of the band and the way I've been portrayed—everything has been so homosexual. Every video we've ever done, I've portrayed some absolute blatant, stereotyped homosexual. I've been the boy in bondage, the sado-masochistic cop, the homo-cowboy. I've been so blatant about it—it just blows me away that people don't pick up on something like that. What am I supposed to do? Hit people over the head with this? That hurts, right? It hurts your head, and it's an insult to people's intelligence.

In the *Advocate* interview, Bottum also spoke about telling his family that he was gay. 'My parents are very Catholic, and it had always been a very touchy subject,' he said. 'In the end, though, when I did finally tell them the news, they were really good about it. Well, my mom took it a little hard. She cried. But my dad was very good, and he helped Mom get through it.'

Bill Gould, Roddy's childhood friend, only found out by reading the *NME* article. 'I found out by reading it in a music paper,' he told *Q* in 1995. 'I really hadn't known he was gay. It was never discussed. So it pissed me off. It's not that him being gay is an issue, but hearing about it that way.'

Even if the circumstances of his coming-out were not to his liking, Roddy succeeded in breaking down barriers. The writer of the *Advocate* article repurposed his piece for *Kerrang!*, then reflective of the macho and misogynistic metal culture, and which had featured Jim Martin with scantily clad dancers in a photo feature just three years previously. The metal bible even published its version of the article and a front-page splash reading 'Faith No More Gay Star's Sensation!' in May 1993, one month before the *Advocate*'s publication date.

Twenty-five years on, Roddy reflects, 'I had no option but to treat it as a big deal. It was a very big deal. We were surrounded by a world of very hetero fan base at this point in history. Gay in that world didn't really exist. At all. [Judas Priest singer] Rob Halford was not out. Even Bob Mould [Hüsker Dü singer and guitarist] wasn't. There were no role models, and it was a scary place. It's hard to imagine in this day and age why that would be problematic or scary, but it was. I don't think I 'owned' it as much as I could have.'

When 'Be Aggressive' was recorded, Bottum's homosexuality was not public knowledge. Neither was the heroin addiction he was struggling to hide at the time. Heroin usage was so common in 1990s music circles that music journalist Everett True would declare, in *Nirvana: The True Story*, that 'at least one person in pretty much every American band I knew was doing smack'.

Even before that, various members of Faith No More had dabbled in drugs. Weed and alcohol fuelled many of their early rehearsal sessions in the Vats, while they would often smoke opium before shows in the mid-80s. Chuck Mosley, of course, developed a penchant for Quaaludes, an indulgence frequently shared by the rest of the band. When Gould had to forgo alcohol when he developed a stomach ulcer around 1988, he cultivated an interest in alternative means to get high, building up an encyclopaedic knowledge of legal stimulants and smart drugs, and where to find them. Even Patton, despite myriad press pieces stressing that caffeine was his only drug, tried acid and smoked cannabis on occasion in this period.

Bottum had started using heroin in 1991. Remarkably, it did not impede his creativity during the writing and recording for *Angel Dust*, and he contributed music or lyrics to eight tracks, but it did put a strain on his relationship with Gould in particular. 'We suspected while we were mixing the record that he was doing drugs,' Gould says. 'We went through a long period with Roddy, knowing that he was doing it, but not tackling it. It sucked.'

In November 1993, in the wake of the death of actor River Phoenix, *Entertainment Weekly* published an exposé on drug usage among celebrities in the bars and clubs of LA's Sunset Strip. The piece featured a contribution from Roddy on the allure of heroin: 'It's romantic. That's why I did drugs. Famous people do drugs.'

But Roddy's real reasons were a little less romantic, and more reflective of the theme he had suggested for *Angel Dust*. 'It was basically friends, and a lifestyle that I was immersed in at the time,' he says. 'It was a beautiful time in our lives, and I think we all, not just me, had the impulse to shit on the beauty of what we were doing.'

On an album of unconventional, inaccessible, and experimental tracks, the most unconventional, inaccessible, and experimental is the album's climax, the penultimate track, 'Jizzlobber'. As remarkable as the track is in itself, the most surprising thing about it is that it was not composed by precocious polymath Patton, production genius Gould, or sampling savant Bottum. It was almost all the work of the band's self-styled guitar hero, Jim Martin.

Amazon River sound samples, odd and lurching time signatures, and a completely unorthodox and evolving song structure, allied to Patton's guttural but clean singing and the Gould-conceived organ coda, makes it near nausea-inducing and mind-bending. Over twenty years later, the track would inspire a piece of classical music by Irish composer Seán Clancy entitled 'Changing Rates Of Change', who explains:

> If you look at other heavy music released in 1992, for example Kyuss's *Blues For The Red Sun*, Napalm Death's *Utopia Banished*, or Pantera's *Vulgar Display Of Power*, I don't think any of them touch the real heaviness of the choruses of 'Jizzlobber'. The most interesting thing about this song is the structure, the first part (starting with the concrete sounds, semitonal clashing keyboard line and drums) just has material added to it—firstly guitar and bass, secondly vocals. This is a similar technique to Ravel's *Boléro*. Without warning, this gives way to the chorus, which for me is quite unrelated (guitars become more riff-based, drums moving away from hats to toms, vocals becoming more aggressive, etc). This AB structure repeats itself before being extended and bridged into a C section, which quickly moves

into a riff-based D section with a complex drum pattern added. Before outstaying its welcome, it moves back into a variation of the C section. We then get the most unbelievable cross-fade into that organ/midi voice section.

Martin, the band's reactionary, had produced a track as revolutionary as any on the record. But for him, the track was intended as his attempt at reproducing the song of rock guitar instrumentalists such as Steve Vai and Joe Satriani. 'I just wanted to have a song of mine on the album,' he said at the time, 'and I wanted to write something really horrible and ugly. The title is my idea of a joke, because I'm not really a fan of true guitar-jizz music. Of course, I can't play like Satriani or Vai anyhow. I feel like those guys are playing another instrument altogether.'

Martin had even recorded the samples himself on a band boat trip up the Amazon during their second visit to Brazil in 1991, with the chirping crickets and river sounds slowed down with an Eventide Harmonizer pitch-shifting device. All of this belies both his and his bandmates' verdict that guitarist and band were completely out of sync. Martin's 'Jizzlobber' was *Angel Dust* in microcosm. But it was effectively Martin's only contribution to the album as a writer, save for some parts of 'Kindergarten', and the solos on 'Land Of Sunshine', 'Everything's Ruined', and 'Be Aggressive'.

Describing his solo on the latter track—actually three separate takes edited together—to *Guitar* magazine later in 1992, Martin got to the heart of his creative input: 'The band doesn't really like guitar solos that much. It was a part of the song where it really belonged, but that hasn't stopped the band from chopping a guitar solo apart in the past. Very little of what I write is actually appropriate for Faith No More. When I write a song for the band, I write most, if not all, the parts. When it works out, it's great, but they don't really know how to write songs from a guitar point of view; they're used to writing songs from a bass, drums, and keyboard point of view.'

That had always been the case. Faith No More were never a guitar band and, as their rapid cycling through guitarists in their early days testified, they did not really want a guitarist. They wanted a guitar sound, and a particular guitar sound at that: the chunka-chunka sound that Roddy Bottum later referred to in the liner notes for the *We Care A Lot* reissue.

In 1997, Mike Patton told the German magazine *Visions*, 'The guitar player has an easy job. I could play those parts if I wanted to, and sometimes I even do it. A baby could do that. Guitar parts that you can play with one finger. The problem is that most guitar players don't know that kind of playing. We have certain things we want from a guitarist. His role is more like a DJ. A specific sound, rather boring. Nothing that a guitarist really wants to do. And we all know what guitar players want to do. Play fucking solos. They are nearly as weird as vocalists.'

Martin had always found a way to contribute prior to *Angel Dust*. But after the death of his father months before recording was due to begin, he missed the writing and rehearsal sessions, specifically arranged to be nearer his East Bay base.

After weeks of waiting, in late 1991, the band adopted a new tactic to get Martin back on board: diplomacy. 'He was kind of not in the band,' says Gould. 'We decided that we were going to do something different. We took him out for dinner. We had Jim meet us in a Mexican restaurant. We said to him, "Dude, is everything OK? I know your dad died. You don't seem like yourself. We're worried about you." Jim replied, "No. Everything is fine. As a matter of fact, I'm offended that you would call me here to say this." We actually did have the best intentions, but this is the way the interaction has always been with Jim. Reaching out, you get your hand bit even harder.'

'I said, "Jim, do you need some time? Do you need some help?"' Bordin adds. 'And he was, "Don't ever ask me anything, ever." That's our relationship right there. That's why it doesn't work. That's why it can't work.'

Gould was moving on without Martin. He recorded the demos to release the band's recording budget, and wrote guitar parts for the album without Martin's input. When Martin received the tapes to add guitar at this stage, he baulked. '*Angel Dust* was more contrived musically than I thought was necessary,' he told the Faith No More blog. 'I wanted more of the record to happen in the studio, and Bill wanted every last tack nailed down before we went in.'

'We're trying to take this to new places,' Gould retorts. 'Puffy gets scared. Puffy likes security. If we start going in a direction where he's not getting validation from other people, he doesn't want to go there. He was on the fence, but he was on our side. He would go there with us. Roddy was down. Roddy had his own things going on, but in theory he was good. Patton was like, *Fuck yeah, let's go for it*. Jim was like, *This sucks. I hate it*. He had no problem telling anybody in our vicinity that it sucks. He's not coming to the rehearsals. I'm writing some of the parts and telling him what to do. Our tones sucked. We weren't getting good tones, and I found myself scrambling to think of guitar parts. I was like, *Fuck this guy*.'

❁

Things went from bad to worse when Jim reported to Coast Recorders in January 1992. He insisted on working separately from the rest of the band, with Bordin, Bottum, Gould, and Patton recording tracks during the day, and Martin arriving to work alone with Matt Wallace late in the evening.

Martin: 'Everyone wanted to be in the studio with me while I recorded, endlessly tinkering and fucking with me and fucking with Matt, and Matt is a really fucking wound-up guy already. I had to kick everyone out, and, even though it was not a new concept, it really pissed everyone off.'

Gould: 'He didn't want to come if we were there. He was really difficult. It was killing morale, because he was really negative. We'd come in the next day, and I'd ask Matt, "OK, what did you work on last night?" And we'd listen to it, and it wasn't working for us at all.'

Wallace was stuck in the middle:

> The band would work on the tracks and then Jim would come in, and that's actually where a lot of the friction began, because Jim, literally, just called that record 'gay disco'. I used to say to him, 'Listen, if you bring in your big nasty guitar, it won't be gay disco. You're the one who can tip the scales, and make it not gay disco.' It was a constant fight. The band would do their stuff, and then they would leave. He'd come in, and play this more melodic, twiddley stuff, and it would make me really upset and I'd say, 'We need the chords.'
>
> We wanted him to bring in his sound. To me, intuitively and instinctively, Faith No More was like a five-trajectory spiderweb. Each guy was pulling in these opposite directions, but because there was no *de facto* leader, if Jim wanted to go too far metal,

you'd have Roddy pulling in this direction, so there was always this tension there. It was essential that Jim brought his bit in, because then it was Faith No More. But he was not inspired by the music to bring in those chords.

Eventually, Gould and Wallace took a more direct approach. They spent two days in Gould's home eight-track studio and put up the already-recorded rhythm tracks while Gould added his ideas for the guitar parts. 'I'd give the tape to Jim,' Wallace adds, 'and he's just be like, *No, fuck you.*'

Gould, as was his wont, was not going to just let this slide. 'I would then get on the phone with him,' he says. 'Everybody else would disappear, so I had to go and confront him. It sucked. I'd go home and I'd get my four-track, and I'd be all pissed off. I would be recording bass, and I'd have to write guitar parts because he wasn't coming up with anything. I'd have to go get his tone. And I have to sit there and have to listen to this fucking guitar tone. Using the only free time I had. It sucked.'

The phone calls between the pair would descend into shouting and swearing matches. On one occasion, Gould screamed down the phone, 'What the fuck are you doing on this record?'

'I don't know if I've ever seen a band at that level of animosity in all the years I've worked on records,' says Wallace. 'I think the feeling was, with Bill and the guys, that Jim was intentionally subverting the record. I think Jim was honestly trying to do his best, but he didn't know his way, or didn't know what to do with it. And both sides were taking it so personally.'

With the benefit of hindsight, Bottum is more understanding of Martin's position during *Angel Dust*. 'Our ideas of esoteric and Jim's notion of esoteric were very different,' he says. 'Looking back on it, I wish we'd entertained his whims more. At the time, though, we took his ideas as passé and old-school Frank Zappa weird, when we felt like the rest of us were a lot more progressive and forward in where we were going with the sounds.'

Eventually, Gould called a band meeting, and a majority decision was made that Gould would be present when Martin tracked his guitar parts, much to the guitarist's displeasure. It was hardly a recipe for creative harmony, but Martin delivered the guitar parts, even if it was not what he or the band really wanted.

Gould: 'He had become this persona of Big Jim that he wasn't in the early days. He became this guy who bossed everybody around. He was really hard on Puffy—really, really, hard. Puffy sometimes deserved it, but not always. And then Patton has another energy that's equally difficult. Him and Jim had it with each other. Patton also had guys he'd go after. It was hard—it was a stressful time.'

34 'COMMERCIAL SUICIDE'

Gould felt challenged to marshal the album to completion. After a few days laying drums and bass tracks, a challenging week on keyboard and samples, a troubling ten days on guitars, and a final few days on Patton's vocals, the main recording was completed by the end of January 1992. Gould had taken charge of the demos; written music on nine tracks; written guitar parts for 'Land Of Sunshine', 'Caffeine', 'A Small Victory', 'Kindergarten', 'Everything's Ruined', and 'Smaller And Smaller'; all while fighting and babysitting the band's guitar player, and watching his oldest friend begin to retreat into addiction. 'There were periods where I felt I was completely on my own,' he says. 'We just had to get this fucking thing done.'

Gould worked with Bottum on the country waltz 'RV', which started with a verse from Bottum. The pair arranged it together at Bottum's house in San Francisco in the summer of 1991. Martin plays a Fender Stratocaster with a harmonizer to get a rich country twang, while Patton inhabits the role of disillusioned and dissolute white trash with relish. He has described the song as a profile of the average redneck mentality, but, with a twenty-first century perspective, it is hard to avoid thinking of the lyrics as Donald

Trump, evolved to trailer trash in an alternative reality, tweeting, 'Someone taps me on the shoulder every five minutes. No one speaks English anymore. Newscasters, cockroaches, and dessert. Sad!'

Gould brought in 'Kindergarten', a groovy, bass-heavy track that provides respite from the rest of the album's intensity, though Mike Patton's preschool-as-purgatory lyrics are disturbing enough. Gould's compositions provide much of the groove and lightness on the album. Future single 'Everything's Ruined', as its working title of 'The Carpenters Song' suggests, started out as a high-tempo, major-chord blast of cheeriness, but the addition of some discordant F-sharp minor chords, Patton's financial disaster lyrics, and Martin's solo tip it over back into the disturbing category. Without those facets, the song sounds like a track from *The Real Thing*—a point not lost on Patton, who told *Hit Parader* upon the album's release, 'There are some very strange songs on this record. A lot of them have a lot of despair in them, they're very disturbing. "Everything's Ruined" is a good example of that. It's one of the more straight-forward rockers we have on this album. Compare it to something like "Surprise! You're Dead!" from the last album. You'll see how we've changed.'

Patton's lyrics are among the best of his Faith No More tenure. Precise enough to invite pause but unresolved enough to demand reflection, they apparently take aim at parenthood, ownership, unfettered speculation, and capitalism in general. Certainly, phrases like '*Everyone knew the thing that was best / Of course, he must invest*' and '*He made us proud / He made us rich*' can be read as presaging any bubble or crash, from dot.com to Celtic Tiger to Lehman brothers to Bitcoin. Or, closer to home, the words could also be a reflection on record label demands on Faith No More, and Patton in particular: '*Working overtime / Completed what was assigned / We had to multiply ourselves.*'

Gould also played a key role in the two lead singles, 'Midlife Crisis' and 'A Small Victory', which were the most purely group compositions on the album. He also first had the idea to cover 'Easy', the Commodores song and album bonus track recorded during the *Angel Dust* sessions; and the album closer, 'Midnight Cowboy', a cover of John Barry's instrumental theme tune from the 1969 Academy Award-winning film of the same name. The inspiration to cover that song echoed the inspiration for the album as a whole. 'After *The Real Thing*, and us getting labelled alongside all these really horrible bands, I was getting all these funk metal demos all the time,' says Gould. 'I just tuned out and started listening to other songs; a local radio station, Magic 61, which played easy-listening songs like Rosemary Clooney and Frank Sinatra. A station here for old people. I discovered so much.'

The Faith No More bassist had steered *Angel Dust* to completion, and his importance to the band was appreciated by most of his colleagues. 'Bill Gould is an idiot genius; he's an idiot savant in so many ways,' says Bordin. 'Bill was always the guy that would end up with seven sets of keys and none of them were his. He's not going to be the guy that's going to keep track of every single detail of meaningless things, but he remembers the important things. He can tell you what time it is to the minute without a watch. Bill's got music in his head that none of us could even conceive of. He was the one who would figure out how to get there. How to put all the ingredients together, and get it on the plate.'

✦

The band had successfully kept the record label representatives from Slash and Warner Bros at arm's length while recording at Coast. But Slash president Bob Biggs was allowed to breach their sanctum, as the band and Matt Wallace were mixing tracks at Scream Studios in Sound City in Los Angeles in the first week of February. Hovering over Wallace and Gould at the mixing console, Biggs could not hide his unease. He told the band straight: 'This is a hard run to take. I don't know if I can do it, but I'll do my best.' On his way out of the studio, he was more direct to Wallace, who recalls, 'I'm sure he said, Can you make it more like *The Real Thing*?' As Wallace walked him out to his car, Biggs turned and said, 'Is there any way you can rein this in?'

That was never going to happen. 'Even if I wanted to, I couldn't have,' says Wallace.

'The record company president came into the studio,' Jim Martin recalled in 2012, 'and said, I hope nobody bought houses. All the air got sucked out of the room. That was one of those great moments when reality slaps you in the face. Some of my associates had bought houses.'

In actual fact, it was band manager Warren Entner, who had sat in during some recording sessions, who had uttered the 'I hope nobody bought houses' line during an album playback with the band and management in San Francisco. For Gould, Martin's version of events served a purpose: 'Jim really enjoyed that phrase because he thought we were going in the completely wrong direction, and that validated that for him.'

Bob Biggs did tell the band that he could not hear a single, however, and suggested that the album could be called 'Commercial Suicide'. On the former, the Slash president might have had a point. While 'Midlife Crisis', 'A Small Victory', and 'Everything's Ruined' were in their own ways catchy standout tracks, none of them was 'Epic'. And as 'Epic' and later 'Smells Like Teen Spirit', 'Enter Sandman', 'More Than Words', and 'Under The Bridge' showed, big singles drove alternative rock and metal albums more than anything else in the early 1990s.

The band were not going to let label and management concerns change their focus. 'We made the record we wanted to make, and we fought for it,' says Bordin. 'Houses, cars, whatever. All that, you can return them. We were making the record we wanted to make. We were making the record we had to make.'

According to Patton, 'The record company wanted another version of *The Real Thing* with a new cover basically, so we gave them something totally different. If they'd liked it, it would have been wrong—it's better to have them nervous and twitching.'

Patton's use of 'twitching' was apt. *Angel Dust*, at first listen, brings on twitching and tremors, and the convulsions and confusion of over-stimulation and hypnogogia. This unsettling and confounding otherness persists with each fresh listen. But the record was not an act of self-sabotage, though that did not stop the band from pushing that narrative in the many, many interviews they did to mark the album's release.

Gould told *Billboard*, 'There's nothing totally like [Lou Reed's noise album] *Metal Machine Music*, but there's some really ugly stuff on this record.'

Bottum told *Raw*, 'This new stuff is a little weirder than our last record, just to confuse our fans and alienate our public.'

Patton told the *Washington Post*, 'We were getting a little flak from the record label concerning the commercial suicide potential for this record. We were a little put off, so we said, "All right, we're gonna call the record 'Crack Hitler', how do you like that?" It was a childish tactic, but it worked.'

Gould told *Melody Maker*, 'Lots of kids bought the last album on the strength of "Epic" and didn't like it. They're not going to like this one much either.'

Despite pointing out the non-commercial nature of the record in almost every one of the interviews around the record release in June 1992, the band were nonetheless peeved by Jim Martin talking down the record at every opportunity. As the album was being mixed in February, Martin told *Kerrang!*, 'It's been very unpleasant, but not really much different to my experiences in making records with Faith No More before. It's always been a very unpleasant experience—a lot of people scrambling to get henchmen on their side to play silly games, to blow smoke on a situation.'

'He had no problem telling anybody in our vicinity that it sucks,' Gould reflects. 'We're taking a big fucking leap here, and he's undercutting us. It was doomed from the beginning.'

35 THE MAKING OF 'MIDLIFE CRISIS'

Despite the warnings and the pre-emptive strikes in press interviews, mixing and mastering of *Angel Dust* was completed in February.

The record was completed, but the acrimony continued. For the third album in a row, choosing the artwork posed problems. Matching the vision that produced the album title, Roddy Bottum wanted a beautiful bird on the front cover and something much darker on the back. 'The idea was for the artwork to be a lot more beautiful and Hallmark than it ended up being,' he says. 'I wanted a beautiful swan taking off from a lake with fuzzy focus, dripping in clichéd picturesque narrative. We let Jim get his way on the photo we used, but the visual presentation was way darker than I'd intended it to be.'

Jim Martin took ownership and contacted photographer and friend Mark Leialoha, who put him in contact with Werner Krutein, who ran a stock photo agency and found a wonderful but stark shot of a snowy egret. On the back of the album was an unsettling photo of a meat locker and hanging chickens and a cow's head by Mark Burstein. The album's inlay was initially supposed to be a rather artistic series of shots of the band member's heads on a black background, but that eventually became the band's heads superimposed on the bodies of some Russian soldiers. Martin explained, 'I had the idea of the Russian army in the sleeve, inspired by The Pogues' album *Rum, Sodomy, And The Lash*, which I was really into at the time. I rode hard on that, and made sure it happened the way we wanted it to happen.'

Band control also included the choice of singles. The album's third track—the track with most all-round band input, 'Midlife Crisis'—was the obvious choice. The band were agreed on that and recommended it to Slash through a quick call from Warren Entner. Its four minutes and twenty seconds—released to the world on May 26, and debuted on MTV on June 6 as an exclusive alongside Guns N' Roses' 'November Rain'—was the sound of modern rock forming. It was certainly a huge jolt to the majority of fans that had flocked to Faith No More in the wake of 'Epic'. It sounded nothing like *The Real Thing*. It sounded nothing like funk metal. It sounded nothing like heavy metal. It sounded nothing like grunge.

It starts with a looped drumbeat, apparently borrowed from Simon & Garfunkel. Then, a sampled shriek followed by Patton's '*Go on and ring my neck*', with every fricative emphasised. It is syncopated and percussive, with Roddy's samples, synths, and string chords weaving all the disparate threads into a rich tapestry. Gould recalls, 'I remember telling Matt, when we played in song rehearsal, "I'm just going to play one note in the whole song." Matt came over, and I remember him just shaking his head laughing, "Why are you doing this?" I was just laughing, like, "Fucking you up. I did it to piss you off, I'm going to do a song that only plays one note."'

Bottum's use of samples and Emax effects to drive the song is among his high points as a composer. The breakdown after the second chorus incorporates a slightly warped sample from the start of the Beastie Boys' 1989 track 'Car Thief' (itself purloined from Trouble Funk's 'Drop The Bomb'), split into two, some stock crowd chants, and a record scratch delay effect, all meshed together. It's *musique concrète* as melody, and twenty seconds of glorious suspense and delayed gratification. It is the twenty seconds that emoting, turntable-troubling Linkin Bizkits and Crazy Chambers chased like a holy grail as the old millennium gave way to the new.

Equally, Mike Patton's sibilant, almost spat, verses became the sound of every cargo-shorts, chain-wallet, mask-wearing band in the years either side of the new millennium. For Patton, the rhythm-chasing chants were only one string to his bow, and, in May 1992, the song also highlighted his new pure vocals, on the soaring chorus, and also a greater confidence and ambiguity as a lyricist. The song had the working title of 'Madonna'—'Falling To Pieces' off the previous album also had mononymous Queen of Pop's moniker as a working title for a time—suggesting a tribute of sorts. Patton explained, 'The song is based on a lot of observation, and a lot of speculation. But, in sort of a pointed way, it's about Madonna. It was a particular time where I was being bombarded with her image on TV and in magazines, and her whole shtick speaks to me in that way. It seems she's getting a bit desperate.'

The lyrics do not seem very Madonna-specific, though lines such as '*morbid self-attention*' and '*rent an opinion*' could be applied to her, or to most contemporary pop stars. More intriguing is Patton again returning to the theme of co-dependency in relationships in the sublime chorus stanza:

> *You're perfect yes, it's true*
> *But without me, you're only you (You're only you)*
> *Your menstruating heart*
> *It ain't bleeding enough for two.*

More prosaically, the track saw the band again confronted by the legal implication of sampling. The band bit the bullet and paid up for their pilfered several seconds from 'Car Thief', a Beasties track largely made up of samples itself. 'We cleared that one through the Beastie Boys,' Gould says. 'They stole it from somebody else. We didn't have to clear samples back then. We weren't sure what to do: *Should we do this? It would be the right thing to do. OK, let's call the Beastie Boys.* That's the only one. Then they said, OK, $5,000 and you can use it.'

*

In April, the band recorded a video for the track in Los Angeles and San Francisco. The director was a childhood friend of Bill and Roddy's, Kevin Kerslake. He earned the commission on merit, as he was then the hottest music video director in alternative rock. He had directed three Sonic Youth videos in the late 1980s, and videos for Soundgarden, Hole, and even Mr Bungle's 'Travolta' (later known as 'Quote/Unquote') in the early 1990s. In 1992, he started working with Nirvana, and his video for 'Come As You Are', one of four videos he would shoot for the band in little over a year at the height of their fame, had just been released.

'Our parents went to school together,' he recalls, 'and we had been family friends since birth. We are all products of the Jesuits.'

While he occasionally ran into Bill in various underground clubs in Los Angeles in the 1980s, it was only when he moved to San Francisco in the late 1980s that he reconnected with the Faith No More duo. He was asked by Warner Bros, rather than Bottum and Gould, to submit an idea for the 'Midlife Crisis' video. It was, he says, 'our first dance. I had never done any videos or even written any treatments for consideration for Faith No More.'

The video was duly selected, with Kerslake's vision for the video resonating. '"Midlife Crisis" was based more on an experimental film process than any elaborate narrative. The scene ideas obviously tugged on some tortured strain of our Catholic roots.'

That overexposure and time lapse, plus the use of the colour palette that references the album artwork—the matching pastel white of the egret and the video's horses, the darker-than-midnight blues of both—produces an aesthetic unlike any previous Faith No More video. 'Going with a darker colour palette in "Midlife Crisis" than what the band was known for wasn't necessarily a reaction to that aesthetic but more a natural inclination on my part,' he adds. 'I just tend toward that end of the scale.'

The video was also figuratively darker, and the shots of a man being quartered or pulled apart by horses caused controversy and near calamity. Historical reports show that quarterings were often botched, and staged versions were also problematic, as Kerslake recalls:

> With all the stories we have read throughout the years about people getting quartered by horses, none of us, including the trainers, stopped to consider the one instinctive trait of horses that might pose a problem in a re-enactment of this type of punishment—horses are by nature pack animals, and they all want to move in the same direction. That's going to be a problem when you face four horses in opposite directions, with a man in the middle. After struggling to keep the horses faced toward the four corners of the universe, the trainers gave us the thumbs-up to shoot. Right at that moment, one of the horses reared up on its hind quarters just as the horse opposite charged forward, pulling the horse on its hind legs backward, narrowly missing the stunt man in the middle as it rolled on its back. Luckily, the stunt man had lightning-quick reactions, and scooted out of the impact zone just in the nick of time. Nobody, including the horse, was hurt, but I was mortified that I had put any creature, human or animal, in danger. Thankfully, everyone came out unscathed.

That scene—referred to as 'human vivisection to a beat' by *Billboard*— managed to upset the MTV Networks' Standards & Practices Department, and the video was re-cut with additional shots included of the altar boys running, and some of the more suggestive quartering footage removed.

Most of the video was shot in two days on a stage in Los Angeles, with the band performance and the horses' scenes shot on separate days. The shooting finished with the shots of the altar boys filmed in San Francisco. Kerslake: 'Other than that censorship issue, the edit went smoothly. The only other concern that I can recall involved making sure there was equal representation of all the band members, but I usually try to be democratic anyway, so that was fairly standard. The band was always on when the cameras rolled, and completely drama-free. Totally professional, with just the right amount of darkness and goofball.'

After the video's debut on June 6, it aired every week on *Headbangers Ball* in June, and was then added to the channel's 'Buzz Bin'—its small selection of videos guaranteed at least three plays a day, seven days a week—for seven or eight weeks. The music industry was behind the track. UK industry magazine *Music & Media* told its readership of radio station programmers, '"Midlife Crisis" is the band's most ingenious and commercial song to date. Repeated airplay will have lasting effects in your playlist, and leave your listeners wanting more'. In the USA, *Billboard* said, 'A few spins are required in order to absorb the intricacies of the track, watch alternative programmers devour this one in no time flat. Ultimately, a highly pleasing listening experience.'

Both predictions were right. On June 6, 'Midlife Crisis' entered the official UK singles chart at #10. One week later, it entered the *Billboard* Modern Rock chart at #29. Faith No More were back with a bang.

THE WORLD IS YOURS

36

As they kicked off the European leg of their tour supporting Guns N' Roses at an atypically sun-drenched Slane Castle in Ireland on Saturday, May 16, Mike Patton personified the new Faith No More. Hair cut short, eyebrow pierced, bearded, he looked different and acted differently. The band made no concessions to the fact that *Angel Dust*'s release was still two weeks away as, without introduction, they abruptly launched into a particularly searing rendition of 'Caffeine' to open their set.

As well as new music, the Slane concert showcased Patton the stage demon. His self-destructive stage behaviour veered close to deliberate self-harm during 'Jizzlobber' when, seemingly out of control, he crashed into microphone stands and monitors. His acrobatic flips, which regularly saw him land flat on his back during *Angel Dust* tours, seemed design to hurt. He came close to rationalising this behaviour in a 2010 interview with *Revolver*: 'To me, the stage is like the free zone. That's what makes it exhilarating. For whatever reason, there's this weird little square where it's a romper room for adults.'

Slane had been preceded by another return to Rock City in Nottingham, and the official *Angel Dust* album launch at London's Marquee on May 13. The band were billed as Haircuts That Kill—a tongue-in-cheek reference to Chuck Mosley's pre-Faith No More band—for the Marquee show. The show was preceded by a play-out of the new album to the media and industry figures in the Marquee Cafe. With Bottum, Gould, and Patton clad in Carcass T-shirts (the Liverpool extreme metal act were on the same Earache label as Napalm Death and Godflesh), the band launched into 'Caffeine'. They played mostly songs from the album, but old favourites 'We Care A Lot', 'Introduce Yourself', 'The Real Thing', and 'Surprise! You're Dead!' were squeezed in before the band encored with 'Epic' and 'From Out Of Nowhere'. The band also spoke to the audience about their upcoming Guns N' Roses shows. 'We're playing Wembley in June,' Gould said. 'Don't come.' Patton added, 'Stay at home and phone in some bomb threats.'

Whatever one thought about the responsibility of such behaviour weeks after an IRA bomb had killed three people in the city, the barbs revealed unease at being part of the Guns N' Roses tour. Bottum recalls, 'They were bombastic and abusive and gross, but kind of fascinating as well. To be part of that was a real conflict. We were not that. We were not those people, but we were lending our name and our art and our creativity to their presentation. That felt wrong, and a betrayal to what our vision was. We had an awful lot of laughs, and got through it together, but it was difficult.'

The band found the initial jaunt through the UK and Europe more bearable than the later US leg. And the logistical demands of such huge shows meant that Faith No More had a less hectic schedule. Their second show took them to Prague four days later, and the band took the opportunity to explore the nightlife in the Czech capital, and get to know the local music scene. Foreshadowing his support of Eastern European bands later on his Koolarrow label, Gould took to the stage in a T-shirt of local band Michael's Uncle.

The band were keen to explore the real Czechoslovakia, as it still was for a few more months, and they did so in the company of local music publisher and promoter, David Berdych, who recalls, 'They were really curious, so they scattered almost immediately to find out what was going on here. During the three days they spent here, I spent a lot of time with Billy, while Patton and Roddy borrowed bikes and went to explore Kunratice, where they talked to some grandmothers. Faith No More were simply not guys who would come and just chase dealers and women.' Excerpts of the concert were shown on MTV in the USA and throughout Europe, with Patton introducing 'Midlife Crisis' to the 70,000 crowd at the Strahov stadium with the words, 'This is a new song, hate it for us.'

The Guns N' Roses support tour—Soundgarden joined as the third act from Prague on—rumbled into eastern and central Europe, taking in Budapest and Vienna before hitting Germany. In Berlin, Bill Gould seized the opportunity to escape from the Guns N' Roses circus and tour bus torment. 'I did the whole German tour in a Trabant,' he says. 'With no insurance and no licence. I did a radio station interview, where I asked to buy one, and someone showed up and gave theirs to me. The first trip was after the Berlin show. Mike P. and I took off around 6pm, and drove twelve hours to Stuttgart at a steady fifty miles per hour. We got in at 6am to the hotel; the bus had arrived hours before us.'

The band again chose alternative transport when they returned to London for the June 13 show at Wembley stadium, to which they took the tube. Wembley was a validation for some in the band; just two years after appearing at the bottom of the bill on the Voivod tour, Faith No More and Soundgarden were now playing one of the most famous stadiums in the world, on the biggest rock tour in years. Again belying their support status, Faith No More almost incited a riot during 'Epic'. A *Spin* article stated, 'Patton is rampaging through the crowd. Wembley personnel are running round in circles like stunned cockroaches when the lights go on. The stage crew is intent on Patton's pit-activities: From stage left, a riot seems inevitable. But Patton, with a bleeding forehead, scrambles back up onstage and the show continues.'

Patton's head wound was not his only injury, as he again hurt his back after again crashing down hard on it during a forward flip. Despite the incendiary show, the mood was sombre backstage, as captured by William Shaw for *Details* magazine: 'Afterward, the group sit backstage in painful silence. They thought they performed abysmally. Mike Patton looks destroyed. Billy's face is a mask of depression. They no longer have any perspective on how good a show FNM put on. I follow Jim Martin out of the room. He's the only one who doesn't look bummed. "It was a sluggish, ponderous, sloppy show, but I had fun," he says.'

Gould: 'There was a lot of this frustration that definitely came out in our playing. We were young, we had a lot of days off, so we'd play to get rid of that. They weren't our shows. The whole time we were playing this really weird music. We weren't sure if the people were getting it or not, and we did it for five months.'

One source of frustration was Guns N' Roses' tendency to cancel shows. Six were cancelled on the European leg alone, among them Manchester and Madrid. According to Gould, 'It was a city that started with *M*, and every *M* was cancelled, including Montreal later, because Axl had a fortune teller who told him not to do any shows with the letter *M*.'

The European leg of the *Use Your Illusion* tour continued through June and July in the UK, Germany, Switzerland, the Netherlands, Denmark, Italy, Spain Portugal, and Sweden. The band again let off steam with a stand-alone show at an even more febrile than usual Paradiso club in Amsterdam. Once more, Faith No More were playing on the same day of an important Netherlands football match, and Patton rubbed salt into the wounds of any audience members mourning a penalty shootout defeat to Denmark by disingenuously asking, 'So did you lose or win?'

Angel Dust was released on June 8, not long before the Wembley show. Faith No More folklore—and the band members' own memories—have it that album reviews were lukewarm, especially in the USA. In actual fact, most leading American critics embraced the album, and understood Faith No More's motivation in making the record. *Rolling Stone*, for one, stated that *Angel Dust* was 'a roiling, musically adventurous record that represents yet another leap forward'. According to the *St. Louis Post-Dispatch*, 'Faith No More broke through with the single "Epic", but in fact it's *Angel Dust* that sounds like the group's true music epic,' while the *Dallas Morning News* declared, '*Angel Dust* would be a commendable experiment even if it didn't break so much ground. It's rare for any album this intricate and dark to be this good.'

There were some negative reviews. The *Chicago Tribune* said, 'While it's easy to respect *Angel Dust* it's difficult to enjoy.' *Entertainment Weekly*, meanwhile, caught the essence, noting that the band had created 'probably the most uncommercial follow-up to a hit record ever.'

The UK music weeklies were more receptive, with Simon Reynolds, who had interviewed the band for the *Guardian* in May, declaring, in *Melody Maker*, 'This is tightly constructed noise on the grand scale that belies its simple metal calling. It's loud, it's aggressive and, like any rock record worth its salt, it excites at the most instinctive level. Their time has surely come.'

Despite such panegyrics, the band found the reviews part of their self-fulfilling prophecy of an alienating album. 'This was the best thing that we could do,' Bordin says. 'When that went sideways, with *Rolling Stone* and other magazines saying what they said, we knew it wasn't going to happen.'

USE YOUR
DISILLUSION

37

It was happening. *Angel Dust* entered the *Billboard* 200 at #10 on July 4 1993. In the UK, it entered the album charts on June 20 at #2, kept off the top spot by Lionel Richie, whose compilation album *Back To Front* included the original Commodores version of 'Easy'. Faith No More's own version was appended to later editions of their album.

For good measure, in June and July, *Angel Dust* also hit the top 10 in Ireland (#3) Australia (#4), Austria (#4), New Zealand (#6), Norway (#7), Germany (#8), and Switzerland (#9). And within three months of the record's release, it had sold 500,000 copies in the USA alone. But there was little escaping the perception that the record was not the success that Slash, Warners, or the music media had expected. By the end of the year, Mike Patton was telling *Sky* magazine, 'Our manager sent us a fax the other day saying that since our record isn't doing so well, we better start hanging out with groupies to boost sales.'

The perception of a flop was created by how quickly the album tumbled down the charts after peaking almost everywhere in its first week. Within eight weeks, *Angel Dust* had fallen out of *Billboard*'s top 50, and after thirteen weeks it had exited the top 100, never to return.

This illustrated what little effect the July-to-September tour supporting both Guns N' Roses and Metallica had on sales. The rock juggernaut tour was not the only tour in town that July, and Faith No More also had an offer to play Lollapalooza. The festival—created by Jane's Addiction singer Perry Farrell in 1991, with the aim of establishing an American touring version of European festivals such as Glastonbury and Reading—kicked off near to Faith No More's San Francisco home base, at the Shoreline Amphitheater in Mountain View. The second edition of the thirty-six-date tour featured former Faith No More tour partners the Red Hot Chili Peppers, Ministry, and Soundgarden, as well as Pearl Jam and Lush. While Faith No More chafed as much against the term 'alternative' as they did against 'metal', and might have rhymed in with Jello Biafra's assessment of the tour as 'Vegas with a flannel face', Lollapalooza seemed such a natural habitat for the band that the *Globe & Mail* used an *Angel Dust* song title in the headline for its festival preview feature: 'A small victory for a gathering of tribes'. But as John Vassiliou puts it, 'The stadium tour had bigger crowds and more money. On Lollapalooza, you got lost with all the other acts, and we would have needed tour support to do it. The band was involved with the choice.'

Bill Gould disagreed. 'From what people have told me, Perry Farrell has never liked us, being an LA band. But Vassiliou told me three or four years

later about Lollapalooza. I asked him, Why did we do that fucking Guns
N' Roses and Metallica tour when Lollapalooza was happening? He goes,
Well, actually, we were offered that, and I passed. That really took me by
surprise, because had we known, we would have taken that in a second.
That really pissed me off.'

Roddy Bottum had a more philosophical reaction. 'As a meta art
statement, it was a little bit confrontational of a gesture, to go on tour with
Guns N' Roses. Maybe our public would have expected us to do something
more like Lollapalooza, but it was a teensy bit cool that we were doing
something so radically disgusting.'

Faith No More were in no doubt about their status on the tour, with Kirk
Hammett telling the launch press conference, 'We'll be co-headlining. Faith
No More will be the opening act. We wanted to get Nirvana, but Kurt's
expecting a baby, or his wife is.' For Mike Bordin, 'Trading Soundgarden
in for Metallica, touring the *Black Album*, and us moving down the bill and
playing in America was a terrible dynamic. It didn't work.'

The dynamic was that Faith No More played in the afternoon, as early as
3 or 4pm, and often left for the next stop before the other acts had started.
Guns N' Roses had their own Boeing 727, leased from MGM Grand Air,
with private bedrooms, a fully stocked bar, and a cinema. Metallica travelled
on their own customised Grumman Gulfstream One executive jet, complete
with Metallica livery inside and out. Faith No More travelled on a tour bus,
in which no one was allowed to use the toilet. The co-headliners had also
agreed to equal playing time onstage to split the tour receipts, believed to
be around $1.5 million per night, 50-50. Faith No More were given between
thirty-five and forty-five minutes and no soundcheck, and were paid a set
fee, albeit one of the larger tour fees they would ever earn.

The band were discouraged from interacting with Guns N' Roses
backstage, with band members sometimes slammed against walls and out
of the way by security when Axl or other Gunners passed by. Faith No
More reacted as they usually did, by griping and gossiping to any journalist
who would listen. Gould told *Select*, 'I hate the whole circus thing. At the
moment, we don't have the power to do what we want to do, so we still have

to eat a little bit of shit. Every band in the world might think they want to open for Guns N' Roses, but let me tell you, it's been a real ugly personal experience.'

Roddy Bottum, meanwhile, came up with the best comment ever uttered about Guns N' Roses when he told *Select*, 'I'm getting more and more confused about who's who in Guns N' Roses, and it's blowing my mind. There's Dizzy and Iggy and Lizzy and Tizzy and Gilby and Giddy. Onstage now there's a horn section, two backup singers, two keyboard players, an airline pilot, a basketball coach, a couple of car mechanics.'

Small wonder, then, that the band were summoned by Axl Rose to explain their comments—which also included threats to urinate on Rose's stage monitors and to defecate in the singer's drinks. At Orlando's Citrus Bowl stadium on September 2, Axl and Guns N' Roses manager Doug Goldstein came to the Faith No More dressing room area at the stadium to discuss the band's ongoing media comments with FNM managers Warren Entner and John Vassiliou. Gould recalls that when he then arrived at the dressing rooms to start getting ready, Axl immediately turned on him, saying, 'Where do you get off! You're the guy who has been talking shit about me in the press.' Before Gould could answer, Goldstein addressed him and the managers: 'We want you to be honest here. Do you really want to be on this tour? Think about whether you really want to be on this. Let us know after the show.'

After their own show, Faith No More held a crisis meeting to decide whether to continue and who would speak to Guns N' Roses. Gould recalls, 'My first reaction was to come clean and tell them it wasn't working, but not everyone in the band agreed with it.' The band opted to play on, and Gould, after being singled out as the chief provocateur, was chosen to break the news to GNR.

Patton and Bottum volunteered to accompany him, and the trio hung around until Guns N' Roses had finished their set, which only started at 11:20pm. They waited and waited, and even went along to the show after-party for the first time on tour. The downside was that, while they were there, they were served free and unlimited drinks, and by the time they were finally summoned to Axl Rose's trailer at 2am, they were all quite drunk.

The tipsy trio were met by Axl and Slash. Gould recalls that an upset but not irate Rose started by saying, 'I only like you guys, Nirvana, Jane's Addiction, and two other bands, and all of you hate me. Why do you hate me? It's like I went away and came back home to find you guys fucked my wife.' For almost an hour, the Gun N' Roses main men took the Faith No More trio to task. Slash was direct: 'If you don't like it here, just fucking leave. It can't be like this. Either let's do this thing and make it great, or forget it, go home.' The sheepish Bottum, Gould, and Patton duly apologised, and gave their excuses, with Gould saying, 'We just try to stir up as much shit as we can. We feel like that's our job.' Rose laughed, and, after some further discussion, an uneasy detente was reached.

'They were quite cool with us,' says Gould, 'much more than we probably deserved. They earned some respect from me for the way they handled it.'

The Orlando show was the fifth show since the tour had resumed following a pyrotechnic explosion that injured James Hetfield in Montreal in August, where there was also a subsequent riot after Guns N' Roses had cut their set short. The band were on their tour bus leaving the venue when the riot kicked off, and, when news filtered through, Gould wryly noted that Montreal was another city beginning with *M*. Hetfield's injuries were serious enough that seven concerts were cancelled, and a hometown sideshow at the Warfield—a show punctuated by near incessant screaming from female fans—was Faith No More's only gig in that three weeks. The band had to leave the GNR/Metallica tour early, as a new headlining tour had been booked to start on September 16. There was very little rest for the band; their final GNR date took place just one day before, when, on a Tuesday evening at 5:30pm, they played to 5,000 people in the 50,000-capacity Metrodome in Minneapolis.

There was a sense of relief that the Guns N' Roses circus was over. Mike Patton summed it up to *Kerrang!*: 'I'm looking forward to playing the smaller venues on our own tour after this. I just can't imagine this band becoming as big as Metallica. I don't think I'd enjoy it.'

38

There was no respite. The band's US headlining tour with Helmet—the post-metal act breaking through after the June 1992 release of their second album *Meantime*—squeezed thirty-four shows into five weeks.

The band hit the headlines in Buffalo on October 1. They started the night with a show at the Alumni Arena at The State University of New York at Buffalo, before 'playing' a late-night WGRF-FM/97 Rock radio event. After the University show, they were invited to attend the 97 Rock party in the Impaxx Night Club across town. As Gould recalls, 'Our promoter said to us, "This guy owns all the radio stations from Buffalo all the way down to New York City. The whole northeast, we need to go to this thing."

The band, who had a show in Connecticut the following day, agreed that they would stop by in their tour bus, stay for an hour, and then continue on their overnight journey. The guest list at the party included Buffalo's own hard-rock legend, Billy Sheehan, then of Mr Big, as well as Foreigner's Lou Gramm. The band, fresh from the Guns N' Roses tour and even fresher from a show earlier that night, were not impressed with what they saw when they arrived: a Black Crowes cover band onstage, and scantily clad hostesses walking around posing for pictures and distributing free shots, as Gould recalls:

> It wasn't our scene at all, and, after having been so long on the road, we didn't have a lot of patience. But it was OK, and we were taking pictures with people, and signing stuff, and it was all going good. And they were giving us booze; I had like three, four shots of vodka. I looked around and saw that Patton was having a lot of fun—he was getting pictures taken with the

strippers with his mouth open, and really starting to have fun with it. It was actually getting a little dangerous. Then, this guy came up from one of the organisers, and said, 'Hey man, you sure you guys don't want to just go up onstage and play a song?'

Gould and Patton exchanged glances and conferred, telling each other, 'Fuck it, we're going to do it, but we're only going to play one note, right?' The band duly got up onstage. The cover band happily yielded the stage and handed over their instruments. Faith No More started playing the same repetitive riff—dah, dah, dah—over and over and over again. Then Patton started singing along: '*We're not going to stop, ha, ha, ha / We're not going to stop, ha, ha, ha.*'

The effect was akin to a skipping record. The club fell silent, all eyes on the stage; the party buzz was killed stone dead. Unperturbed, the band continued repeating the riff. Then, Patton decided to up the ante, singing, '*97 Rock, suck my ass/ 97 Rock, suck my ass.*'

'We were in deep, we were just getting deeper and deeper—no turning back,' remembers Gould.

Patton upped the ante again. He dropped his trousers and underwear, and started rubbing the microphone around his crotch and backside. Then Jim Martin moved in and rubbed his guitar neck between Patton's legs. That was the last straw. The guitar player from the first band screamed, 'That's my '67 Les Paul, you assholes!' with his friends struggling to restrain him as he ran for the stage, trying to get to Patton and Martin.

'The next thing I know, there's this bang,' adds Gould, 'and blood gets on my shirt, and I look over and Patton's bleeding from his head. Then, these two guys in the front are high-fiving each other. One had thrown a bottle at him, hit him in the head, and the two guys are high-fiving each other.'

Bloodied but unbowed, Patton gripped the microphone like a baseball, adopted a pitcher's stance, and, from five feet away, sent a full-on pitch toward his assailant. It hit him smack in the face, sending him into the air and across the bar. Then another bottle hit Patton, who was now bleeding heavily from the head, and the band threw down their instruments and ran for the fire escape. They jumped straight onto the waiting bus and sped away. Jim Martin, the last to make it to the sanctuary of the bus, turned to his bandmates and said, 'You guys! That was one of the best shows I've done with you in a long, long time.'

'We'd bonded with Jim!' Gould recalls. 'After all that fighting, we were back again! We drove all night, and then we stopped to get a coffee from Waffle House, and picked up a *USA Today* to read on the bus, and we were on the front page!'

The story was also big news in Buffalo. The *Buffalo News* quoted one concert-goer, who said, 'I was shocked, I've never seen anything like this in my life. I'm not a prude, I've been to a lot of rock shows, but Faith No More did things that were absolutely sick.'

Inevitably, there were calls for the band to apologise, but instead a label representative told local media, 'Mike said he had a great time in Buffalo and the band did, too. They view the performance as a total rock'n'roll assault. No malice was intended. They'd love to do it again if 97 Rock would let them.'

Behind the bravado, the band knew that the incident had seriously dented their chances of getting radio airplay. 'That's the way it goes with our career,' says Gould. 'It probably explains little bit of the vibe at Warner Bros afterward with *King For A Day*. Basically, if you looked at a map of the United States, and you looked at where we were popular, you could just scratch anything from Detroit to New York City, just take that part of the map out. We were done—that was it, goodbye, rest in peace. Never to be played on rock radio again.'

❈

Despite the Buffalo rapprochement, another feature of these headline shows was the onstage friction between Mike Patton and Jim Martin. Patton revelled in poking fun at the guitarist, laughing at his Marshall stack or, at Roseland, swinging a microphone at him, or, in Columbus, tackling him to the ground. Martin had complained to *Kerrang!* in September, 'It feels like there's the four of them against the one of me. Whatever opinion I take, I end up as the minority. Sometimes I hate those fuckers.'

Faith No More had three days, transatlantic travel included, between finishing that US tour in October and commencing a European headline tour with L7 in Helsinki on October 28. The band's every step in the Finnish capital was filmed and packaged for later transmission on MTV Europe. But even this was another opportunity to publicly pillory Martin. An *MTV Post-Modern* competition offered a prize of a trip to see Faith No More in Milan in December. The next scene showed Patton putting the competition questions: 'We're all pretty much grown-ups in this band, we're all real independent except for one of us, who is a bit of a baby. He still lives with his mom. If you can guess who that is, you win the contest. You come to Milan, we take care of you, spank you, and treat you well.'

The European tour was another marathon trek, with forty-six shows scheduled in just over two months. The tour took in Scandinavia, Germany, Austria, the Netherlands, and Prague again, before the band pitched up for another lengthy stop in the UK, along with a date at Dublin's Point Theatre, in November and December. The band still had to slum it in taking the ferry from Holyhead to Dublin for their brief visit to Ireland. But they played some huge arenas on that UK leg, including capacity 13,000 crowds at the Sheffield Arena and Birmingham's NEC. The Sheffield show was recorded by BBC Radio 1 for later broadcast, and the band also recorded an in-studio session for the *Jakki Brambles Radio 1 Lunchtime Show*, playing 'Everything's Ruined', 'Epic', 'Midlife Crisis', and 'RV'.

There was some antipathy in the band to playing such larger arenas. 'The rest of the band were not comfortable in these venues,' says Bordin. 'I'm accepting of that. They weren't comfortable doing it. Then, when I was playing with Ozzy later, it was really clear to me the difference. That was his element. But it wasn't ours.'

Building on the success of that sold-out European run, a fifth single from the album was released on December 23: a double A-side of 'Be Aggressive' and 'Easy', which had been recorded during the *Angel Dust* sessions. Prior to that, 'Land Of Sunshine' had been given a promo-only release in June 1992, while 'A Small Victory' was released on August 3. It was accompanied by the most ambitious video of the band's career, a beautifully shot baroque film directed by Marcus Nispel—who had also helmed Mariah Carey's 'Make It Happen' and three C+C Music Factory videos—and featuring expensive World War I battle scenes shot in Empire Studios in New York.

The single reached #29 on the UK singles chart and #11 on the *Billboard* Alternative Songs chart in September—the same chart that 'Midlife Crisis' had hit #1 on in August. Roddy Bottum dolefully noted, 'It's the most radio-friendly song we've ever done, although it doesn't get much friendly airplay.'

Fourth single 'Everything's Ruined' featured a cheap and deliberately cheap-looking video, again directed by Kevin Kerslake, about which Bill Gould told the *Faith No More Blog*, 'Warners spent the video budget on "Small Victory" and "Midlife", so that when it came time for "Everything's Ruined", there wasn't much left. It was our idea to take this further, and make a video as cheap as humanly possible.'

The song was released on November 9 to coincide with the band's European tour, and it hit #29 on the UK singles chart, with the band performed a blistering version of it on Channel 4's *The Word*, which aired on November 15.

❖

'Easy' was a surprising and confusing choice as the final *Angel Dust*-era single. 'It was added to the album in Europe without us knowing,' Gould recalls, 'and it became a hit in Europe. We were like, *That song? Really?* So our management told us that Warner wanted to make it a single in the States. And we were like, *Fuck yeah. Absolutely. Just go for the R&B people*. But then the label came back and said, 'You can't, because it's not a rock song. That can't come from a rock band.' They half-assed it.'

'Easy' hit #3 in the UK on January 23, becoming the band's highest-charting single there. It also became the band's second #1 in Australia—more than AC/DC, INXS, and Nick Cave combined—on May 16, while it charted at #2 in Norway, #3 in Belgium and Finland, #5 in Ireland, #6 in New Zealand, and #9 in Switzerland. Despite the abortive R&B campaign, the track was also a minor hit in the USA, reaching #58 on the *Billboard* Hot 100.

While Faith No More had scored another chart hit, one year on from recording *Angel Dust*, the band had still not directly addressed the tension with Jim Martin that had almost derailed that album, and the friction had been allowed to fester.

Friend of the band and Martin confidant Steffan Chirazi interviewed them for *Hot Metal* in January. He asked Gould and Bordin whether the friction with Martin could be resolved amicably. The responses were not exactly emphatic. Bordin: 'Sure, anything's possible.' Gould: 'Stranger things have happened.'

The impression given is that the rest of Faith No More were going through the motions with Martin, fulfilling promotional and touring obligations while waiting for the right time to resolve the issue definitively. Back in 1988, the band had taken Chuck Mosley back briefly to fulfil touring obligations before dismissing him definitively. Dissolving the band partnership when Mosley left had opened up a vista of legal complications and consequences, some lasting decades. The band didn't want to go through that again.

Faith No More kicked off 1993 playing 'Midlife Crisis' and 'Easy' on *The Tonight Show With Jay Leno* on NBC, Patton giving Martin a withering side-eye look as he played the song's solo.

March saw the US release of 'Easy' on the easy-listening *Songs To Make Love To* EP—described at the time by Patton as 'muzak' and also containing 'Das Schutzenfest', 'Midnight Cowboy', and a version of the Dead Kennedys' 'Let's Lynch The Landlord'. The band also released a video compilation, *Video Croissant*, on February 2 in the UK and February 23 in the USA. That month, the band also picked up another Grammy nomination for *Angel Dust* in the 'Best Hard Rock Performance' category.

Just as in 1990, Faith No More's second Australian #1 came just after they toured the country. The band's eleven shows in two weeks—during which they added snippets of the *Twin Peaks* theme and songs by The Happy Mondays and The Birthday Party to their set—saw them play bigger venues to sold-out crowds. After nine weeks on the chart, 'Easy' hit #1 on the ARIA singles chart on 16 May.

In the UK, the music press was putting two and two together and coming up with five. When Faith No More returned to Europe in May and June, the perceptive Mary Anne Hobbs went behind the scenes with the band for a *Select* feature. 'Mike Patton is quitting Faith No More,' she wrote. 'That's it.' She got close to the truth: 'Apparently, FNM are drawing up a legal charter, protecting the actual band unit, in case of serious internal conflict between members. Well, you have prenuptial agreements—why not something similar for bands? It's just the timing that seems unusual. After all, the last man in, Mike Patton replaced original singer Chuck Mosely in January '89.'

By the time the band hit the European festival treadmill in June, July, and August, the band-versus-Jim chasm was plain to see. They almost came to blows at the Rock Werchter festival in Belgium on July 2. Steffan Chirazi witnessed the scene for *Kerrang!*: 'There is an obvious polarisation onstage between Patton/Gould/Bottum and Jim Martin. At one point, Patton, with his back to the crowd, picks up a bottle of water and hurls it over his head in the direction of Martin. It misses by only a couple of feet.'

The same article quoted Gould: 'I don't think Jim has any idea what we're doing; I don't think he understands our music at all.'

Faith No More played their last show of 1993, headlining the middle Saturday night of the three-day Phoenix Festival (Sonic Youth and The Black Crowes were the other headliners) on July 17. Patton abruptly ordered Martin to stop playing the introduction to 'The Crab Song', ostensibly to have a silent tribute to GG Allin, who had died two weeks previously. In introducing 'A Small Victory', Roddy teased, 'Jim is gay,' while Patton shrieked, 'Everybody's quitting, it's all over. It feels great, I admit it.'

Paul Rees noted in his *Raw* magazine review, 'Everyone is tired of hearing their back-biting, self-loathing, antihero tales of personal conflict and post-fame sickness. It could have been a big, bad joke, except Jim Martin is standing miles away from the others, playing his ugly heavy metal guitar to himself. Mike Patton takes the piss out of Jim whenever there's a lull.'

✦

Once back in the United States, the issue needed to be resolved. But the resolution was long and painful. The Faith No More Four and their management took convoluted steps to avoid legal wrangling. In particular, the band had learned that a band member who was part of a legally binding band partnership, could not simply be sacked. After several months, during which time the band were unable to contact Jim by phone or in person, they finally informed him that he was out of the band by fax. The decision was announced through a band statement on November 30 1993.

'In reality, he was done for a year before that,' Gould recalls. 'It has to be said that, during the time he was in the band, there had been times when we felt we were on the same side, and we had a lot of great times together. But when things began to break down, in my opinion, he overestimated his value, he acted like we couldn't do anything without him.'

'We loved Jim in our own ways,' Bottum adds. 'We all did, Mike Patton included. How could we not? We'd been through so much together. It was not easy or fulfilling to let him go. I think the fax was an example of us dealing with it in a way where we didn't have to get personally involved. It was nothing but sad and scary.'

The fallout from the split was bitter and public. Jim's friend Steffan Chirazi gave the guitar player's version of events in *Kerrang!* in January 1994. Martin said, 'Faith No More, as you know it, is no longer. I believe the fact that we went in different ways musically was actually an integral part of the band.'

✦

After dealing with Jim, Faith No More had one more issue to address: Roddy's increasingly obvious drug habit. Bordin, Gould, and Patton took the opportunity to stage an intervention at the video shoot for 'Another Body Murdered'—the band's collaboration with Boo-Yaa T.R.I.B.E for the *Judgement Night* soundtrack—in early September.

'The closest people in my life were concerned about me,' Roddy remembers, 'and that forced me to sit up and take note. I went through a rehab right after that video shoot, and quit doing drugs. At the end of the day, I was super-grateful to have the band and my family to help. It was certainly an option to kick me out of the band at that point. I'm grateful we pushed through it, and worked it out.'

40 — EXILE IN BEARSVILLE

'Hey Butt-Head, you know who these guys are?'

'No, and I don't care either.'

'This is Faith No More.'

'Yeah, right. *Faith No More.*'

'No, I'm serious, Butt-Head, it is. You see they have a new sound, and a new look.'

'They just look and sound like everything else.'

'I don't know, it kind of rocks.'

In August 1995, Beavis, the sage of 1990s alternative culture, was speaking for many when Faith No More unleashed the video for 'Digging The Grave', an early taster from their *King For A Day ... Fool For A Lifetime* album. Shorn of Jim Martin, shorn of their hair (Mike Bordin excepted), and shorn of synths and samples, Faith No More had a new sound and a new look.

Rewinding to the end of 1993, and Faith No More were, for the ninth time as a band, looking for a new guitarist. Justin Broadrick from Godflesh was sounded out. 'He never came out,' says Gould. 'Someone told me that he was afraid of flying. But he's cool—he's a great guitar player, too.'

So in early 1994, the band listened to demo tapes and tried guitarists. Gould: 'They were all terrible.'

Later, Gould and Bordin contacted Kevin 'Geordie' Walker, guitarist for Killing Joke, another British group that the band hugely admired. Walker came out to San Francisco and stayed with both Gould and Bordin, and spent some time playing with both. 'We liked how we played,' says Bordin. 'We liked his texture within the music. We liked the fact that he was incredibly aggressive with his tone, but wasn't a soloist. He was cool, he talked about jamming with Jimmy Page, smoked a lot of cigarettes. We knew there would be some stuff that would be right up his alley, and some stuff that probably wouldn't be. It was probably a bit of a long shot, even to get him to do it. But it was fucking fun.'

'He's a great guitar player,' Gould adds. 'One of the best I've ever seen. He would have been amazing, but he is so distinctive. I think he would have rendered us into a Killing Joke cover band.'

As in 1988, when the band was replacing Mosley, they had the answer within easy reach. And the answer was again to be found in Mr Bungle. Born in 1969, Trey Spruance grew up, like Patton, in Eureka, and was a founder member of Mr Bungle. He was as prodigiously gifted as Patton, but he was also schooled in music, having studied music at Humboldt State University.

By spring 1994, when Faith No More were seeking a guitarist to put the finishing touches to around twenty freshly constructed songs, Spruance was in the right place at the right time. But as Gould recalls, there was an issue: 'I just wanted somebody to play the guitar better than me. That could play the shit that was already written. Patton discouraged it as much as possible. He wasn't looking forward to taking on another project with Trey.'

Spruance recalls that his recruitment was far from a sure thing:

> I don't exactly remember who spoke to me initially about it. Maybe Patton mentioned when they were trying out Geordie or something. I remember talking to Mike Bordin about it before making the audition demo. The audition demo was how it went

from what I saw. There were a bunch of people in the running. Good musicians. Ralph [Spight] from Victim's Family was one of them. So, it was pretty much like, *Here are some songs with just drums and bass. Add some guitar parts and we'll see.* They liked what I did, so that was cool. A bit unexpected. I added keyboard parts to some of those demos, because I always naturally thought of the role of Faith No More guitar parts as being kind of minimal pieces of a puzzle working in conjunction with everything. As an example, I thought the best way to write a guitar part for the ideas they were developing into 'Cuckoo For Caca' was to have the guitar serve what I considered to be a 'Roddy-esque' keyboard part. So I just wrote a few keyboard ideas and put them on there. It ended up that a lot of those ideas survived into the final drafts of the tunes.

'We kept on trying to find people,' says Bordin, 'all the while thinking of Trey Spruance. He's got the musical language. He speaks that language, and he can go between metal and not metal. We want a certain part of that metal-ness, but not some of the other things that go along with that metal-ness. He not only speaks the same language as us, but, in my opinion, he speaks even more languages than we do. Why wouldn't we want to have a guy like that in our band? And Patton was saying that there's personal stuff, and that they don't get along or whatever, or it might be weird. That's all fine and dandy, but the actual music, oh my God.'

Bottum agreed. 'He has a really good ear for writing stuff, he has a really good ear for what sounds great, he understands keyboards really well, the bonds between keyboards and guitars, and he's really diverse. We've never wanted to limit ourselves to one particular kind of music or one particular anything. And it was clear from the start that Trey was the same way.'

The feeling was indeed mutual, as Spruance says:

They really do have their own unique musical universe, especially Mike Bordin's approach to drumming is totally singular. He has his own terminology as well. It all goes along with some unique physical differences in the way he plays and even thinks about drums, which really sets him apart from other set drummers. As a fan, I was intrigued by all that from the beginning. And the way Billy sank into the pocket with the drums. It's a really special chemistry there. I actually think the biggest 'musical language adjustment' for me was to resist the temptation to interpret everything in a way that, to those guys, would just be the 'old' Faith No More sound. I showed up ready and excited to do just that, to fulfil that role, and found out they had much more adventurous intentions for the guitar.

There were some harbingers of future friction, however. 'From the start, Patton made sure to inform me it was *not an ideal situation*,' Spruance recalls. 'I didn't sign a contract. I do remember their accountant tried to corner me off-guard at one point during rehearsals and have me sign a salary deal. I hadn't put any thought into the matter at all at that point, nor had any idea what I was looking at, so I wasn't going to sign right then and there. I figured there'd be a more natural arc to things than that, and I assumed, somewhat naively, that everything would pan out.'

The band announced Trey's arrival in a feature with *Kerrang!* in July 1994, which included the news in a special pull-out that showed 'Trey' masked in a reference to Slipknot and the new wave of masked nu-metal bands (many of whom had taken the masks concept from Mr Bungle in the first place).

❖

With Spruance on board, the band were ready to record. Twenty songs had already been written during 1994. The band again had a clear vision for the record. 'On *Angel Dust*, there was rich, dark, convoluted music,' Gould recalls. 'Getting rid of Jim was like this explosion. It was this collective sigh of the band. So with this music, we wanted more power.'

Patton told *MEAT Magazine*, 'We all knew that we wanted to make a record with short, concise statements—three-minute songs.'

The idea of a more stripped-down and direct record did not include getting Matt Wallace, who had produced all of the previous Faith No More records, back on board. 'After *Angel Dust*, I felt like I had taken the band as far as I could,' he says. 'Maybe with a different producer, maybe they could go further. It was an act of love, for lack of a better phrase, where I just thought I wanted to let them run free.'

'We just needed just some fresh ears,' says Gould. 'We could be ourselves, begin again in a different way.'

One Wallace was out, but another was in. The band approached Andy Wallace, best known for mixing Nirvana's *Nevermind*, who had also produced Slayer's *Seasons In The Abyss*, Sepultura's *Chaos A.D.*, and, in 1994, Jeff Buckley's *Grace*. 'Andy had been involved with Slayer and Run-DMC,' says Bordin, 'so you got two good extremes there. We felt Andy had an expertise for bringing guitar out, and really making it in your face.'

Gould concurs. 'Andy Wallace was a really down-to-earth guy. We met him at a breakfast lunch. He was expensive, but what the fuck?'

❧

One of the provisos of working with Andy Wallace was that the new album would have to recorded in his favoured Bearsville studio, an isolated live-in facility near Woodstock in upstate New York, so the band flew up there in September 1994 and settled in to living in their appointed wooden cabins.

'We got out of our comfort zones,' says Gould. 'We thought we'd see what would happen. It was very isolated. He always recorded in Bearsville, and he always mixed in the same studios. That's where his sound came from. Our sound is kind of an Andy Wallace sound on that record.'

'I loved the big room there,' Bordin adds. 'It was a big bare room, where they track the drums, and the sounds were big and loud. There was a little bit of chaos with car wrecks, people being bored, Roddy coming in and out.'

The least serious of the car accidents had seen the band repeatedly burst tyres on the narrow dirt roads leading to the remote studio. After the third such incident, the rental company provided the band with a sturdier and nicer car. But days later, the two Mikes—Patton, who was driving, and Bordin—were involved in a serious smash in which their car flipped over. The driver of the other car was seriously injured. 'I know it freaked Mike out a lot,' says Bordin. 'I feel bad for the guy who was in the car, and I feel bad for Mike for being behind the wheel.'

The band were subsequently banned from hiring cars from the only car hire company around. Gould: 'It was very isolated and weird. I just had internet. It was a weird time. The studio was going out of business around then, too. I caught pneumonia. It was different, but that was what we wanted.'

For Trey Spruance, that sense of weirdness came not just from the isolated environment:

> Bearsville is an incredible studio. I felt it was an honour to get to work there, and the live-in situation was super great. To me, it seemed like a tumultuous and uncertain time for Faith No More, both as a collective entity and for individual band members. There were multiple tensions happening simultaneously. I knew so little of the history of any of it from not knowing anyone too well—except Patton—and, even here, he was in a totally different circumstance than the one I was familiar being in with him. I think I was feeling like I should try to be a positive force in everything in some way, so in classic wide-eyed West Coast idiot fashion, I sort of stumbled through the surface of the various issues.
>
> If I think back from my admittedly immature perspective back then, yes, there was a tense background of dark and bitter feelings going on during a lot that recording. Not animosity so much as anxiety, and it went all the way around the table, and there were plenty of reasons for it. I picked up on bits and pieces of it, whether I liked it or not. I fully appreciate that it was a really tough and uncertain period for Faith No More. What's incredible is that none of that adversely affected the final musical outcome. Faith No More are spectacularly good at rising above and delivering the bottom line when it really counts.

Clif Norrel, the recording engineer for the album who had worked with Wallace on *Grace* the previous year, has a different take. 'There were probably a lot of band dynamics that I was not made aware of that Trey might be recalling. It was all pretty easy going, and the band seemed to get along fine.

And the band did find some distractions, playing golf and table tennis, going to see *Pulp Fiction* at the local cinema, and hanging out with Fear Factory, who were recording their *Demanufacture* album in another one of the complex's studios in November and December 1994.

❀

One of the issues that the band was again presented with was the absence of Roddy Bottum, who was only an occasional visitor to Bearsville. Roddy's father had died in November 1993, and he was still recovering from his heroin addiction.

'After rehab I went through a lot of loss,' he recalls. 'A good friend, my dad, Kurt Cobain, I was surrounded by a lot of very real and dark issues. Also, being out recently in that point of history was challenging, especially with the kind of band we were. I felt like prioritising my goals. I wish I'd had the wherewithal to seek solace amongst the band and push through it in that way, but I felt alone and solitary in where my life was going. I was in no way prepared to make another record, that's for sure, and as I withdrew, the record became more what I was not. That made me pull back even more. I was able to be there physically for the process—but barely, honestly. It was a really difficult time.'

Roddy's absence heaped more creative burden on his oldest friend, Bill Gould. 'Roddy was more checked out,' he recalls. 'His dad died and some of his friends died. His musical heart was heading toward indie pop. He decided that's who he was now. Our kind of rock music was for dinosaurs and indie-rock was where things were at. It's like, *Well, how the fuck do we write with this?* That was a real tough one to bridge. It was really hard to reconcile that record. There were a couple of things he got into, like "Take This Bottle", which was good, but he was not very active in the writing of that record. Then, when we got the reviews, they said, Where's the keyboards? Tell me about it. I wish I knew where they were too.'

The writing credits on the album tell the story of Roddy's absence: two partial music credits on 'Just A Man' and 'King For A Day'. Bottum acknowledges that he got off lighter than Chuck Mosley and Jim Martin had. 'The band were absolutely sympathetic,' he says. 'Fed up at the same time, but sympathetic. We'd been through a lot with Jim. *Firing Roddy* was not an affordable loss for anyone. Continuing without me would have been weird, internally and in the public eye. That said, there wasn't a whole lot I had to offer in that record cycle. I learned the songs, and toured and tried to have input as we moved forward, but it was a dark and difficult time. I got more involved in visual presentations, the T-shirts, housekeeping tasks. It was a time of repair.'

✤

The band stayed at Bearsville from September until November, and got used to the different working styles of Wallace and Norrell. Of Wallace, Gould says, 'He's got a more technical way of looking at things, which I liked. He got less involved in the aesthetic. He didn't get in the way. Andy was really about being a technician. How much time is this part? Does it need to be there? Also, with tones, he was super into that.'

Norell adds, 'We didn't really discuss a particular sound or vision, but being familiar with Andy and the band's previous work, I went for an aggressive and punchy sound overall, and then made adjustments once I heard the band running through the songs, according to how I thought it should sound. Occasionally, Andy and the band would have some input on the sound as we went along, but mostly they liked what I was doing, and went with it.'

'I learned so much from working with Andy Wallace and Clif, and watching how they ran an expensive production like that,' says Trey Spruance.

> If anything was frustrating, it was having that huge, killer tracking room at Bearsville to work with, having Mike Bordin's drums all miked up with C24s at the back of the room, hearing Andy capture the majesty of Bordin's sound for once on a recording, only to have the band themselves decide to go for a more stripped-down sound on *King For A Day* … aaargh! That for me, as a long-time fan, was hard to stand by and watch happen. Ultimately, everyone liked the sound of that record, including me, despite the missed opportunity to have the most crushing drum sound of all time. It's just a personal

lamentation—I should be able to get over the fact that the record didn't milk every ounce of that killer drum tone achieved by the combination of Bordin, Bearsville, and Andy Wallace. Holy Hell, that was on another level ... so it's not easy to let go.

Lead single 'Digging The Grave' showcased an aggressive, guitar-driven approach. Spruance's guitar and Patton's rock vocals start straight away, and the chorus crashes in just thirty-three seconds into the track. 'The Real Thing' or 'Midlife Crisis' this is not. 'I wanted to get that sound we had on our first records,' Bordin notes, 'but tighter, faster, and harder.'

'Digging The Grave' is one of five in-your-face rock tracks on the album, none of them coming in at more than three minutes, thirty seconds. Album opener 'Get Out', completely composed by Patton, is an even more emphatic statement of intent than the first single. You can almost feel and taste the dryness of the production, as he asks:

What if there's no more fun to have?
And all I've got is what I had
What if I have forgotten how?
Cut my losses and get out now.

Patton was also heavily involved in the music for the even more going-for-the-jugular 'The Gentle Art Of Making Enemies'. Gould recalls, 'I had some riffs that I couldn't do anything with, and Mike just took them and went home and arranged the whole song. He came back the next day, and was like, *Look what I did with those riffs you had.*'

At not much more than two minutes, 'Get Out' and 'What A Day' were the shortest songs since the band's first two releases, indicative of a desire to shed the layered complications of their previous album. In the last of this propulsive pentad, 'Ugly In The Morning', Patton's chorus vocals are again biting and aggressive, developing into a demoniacal rap by the song's conclusion. The song's lyrical content typified a sea change away from the general misanthropy of *Angel Dust* into a more specific, if still character-driven, self-loathing.

That sentiment is also evident in the epic 'King For A Day' and its payoff, '*Don't let me die with that silly look in my eyes.*' Gould had written much of the track on computer at his home studio, but the more dramatic middle sequence was the result of a studio jam, a true rarity in the Faith No More songbook. All five band members receive writing credits, and the song is also an exemplar of the easy flexibility of Spruance, as he grounds that section with restrained Les Paul chords, while providing the song's ambiance with delicate acoustic work, giving the song its 'Acoustic Groove' working title. 'It gets really dense in the middle,' says Bottum, 'which is a part of the whole journey of that song, but my favourite parts of the song are going into it and coming out of it. It's very Roxy Music to me, almost David Bowie.'

The band described the country ballad, 'Take This Bottle', as Guns N' Roses music with Hank Williams lyrics. Gould, who wrote the music, says, 'It had a weird vibe, but we were, *Let's do it, it's fine. Don't be ashamed of it.* That's how cocky we were at that stage. We had our insecurities with each other, but we all made compromises really. Anyone who says we didn't make compromises is ridiculous.'

'Take This Bottle' was also one of three clear genre pieces on the record, with 'Caralho Voador' an attempt at *bossa nova*, complete with Portuguese lyrics. After the lounge jazz of 'Edge Of The World' on *The Real Thing*, 'Star AD' is more pure jazz—and, in parts, the closest the band came to real funk in their career. Gould had again written most of the song, and wrote the horns section with a patch on his own Kurzweil keyboard. For Bordin, that song went back to a visual way of conceiving music: 'It felt like Las Vegas, ripped vinyl seats, and dirty shag carpet, $1.99 buffets. It felt shabby and glam, glam and shabby at the same time.'

'Cuckoo For Caca' was another song that illustrated Spruance's contribution. 'Bill was a bit stumped, keyboard-wise, what to do on that,' Bordin recalls. 'Trey came with a big, dark keyboard, that Hammond-organ melody, that descending thing that was really doomy and heavy. I was stoked that someone outside of this trio of musicians could come and contribute something like that. It was like starving, and someone coming along and throwing you food. It showed that we weren't being unreasonable. People *can* do stuff like that.'

The band whittled their twenty songs down to fourteen for the album.

'The World Is Yours', 'I Won't Forget You', and 'Hippie Jam Song' later appeared as B-sides or on bonus releases. 'Ricochet', the last song finished at Bearsville, almost joined the off-cuts but was rescued by Bordin's insistence that it be included. The song contains a luscious opening couplet—'*All of that thick time without you / Has made me so thick and drunk*'—and the memorable line, '*It's always funny until someone gets hurt / And then it's just hilarious!*'

Bottum memorably describes 'Last To Know' as 'Pearl Jam on mushrooms', and the song has a sludgy, grungy vibe unlike anything else Faith No More ever recorded. It had the apt working title of 'Dirge'. It also features two Spruance guitar solos, both unlike anything from the Martin era. This first is molasses thick, almost oozing forth. Bill Gould recalls, 'I wanted it to be a big pile-driver song. It sounded a little more in the direction of Stone Temple Pilots than where we were actually shooting for, and we didn't quite get there.'

While all Faith No More members were highly impressed by Spruance's ear, versatility, and ability, Gould had one reservation: 'He could do whatever we wanted and do it better, but he didn't have the animal thing that Geordie [Walker] had. There was a certain violence about Geordie. Trey doesn't have a violent bone in his body.'

In contrast to the rest of the album's striking simplicity, the band threw everything but the kitchen sink at closing track 'Just A Man'. The song featured real orchestral strings and a choir. Gould credits Loris Holland— who had worked with Andy Wallace on Jeff Buckley's *Grace* and would later work with Mariah Carey, Whitney Houston, and Aretha Franklin— for his role in getting that strings and choir just right. 'He wrote the arrangement at the end of "Just A Man",' he recalls. 'It was brilliant. He did it in like an hour.'

But newcomer Spruance also played a key role here:

I somehow didn't realise that the job of scoring the string and horn parts for the record had fallen exclusively to me until the day of the recording. The choir didn't need anything, they were fine—the director was totally familiar with and able to adapt to a rock band who want a gospel choir to do their thing over their music. They made it happen. But it's another thing when you have classical violinists, violists, cellists, trumpet and trombone players staring at you wondering what the hell you want them to do, and charging their time by the hour. I scrambled everything together.

For the string section, I remember listening to the keyboard parts in the control room, and just going off to the bathroom to blind score a bunch of things I thought would make for appropriate complementary parts. All the voicing and orchestration decisions, plus rests and repeats, were done in shitty, scrawled notation in something like twenty minutes. It was a miracle it worked out. The horns were easier because, after transposing for Bb—I can't remember if there was Eb alto sax—it was just a matter of voicing a few chords and stabs, notating some riffs and crescendos that were pretty much in the music already. It was a really good learning experience, working under that kind of real 'showbiz' stress in what was probably my first taste of scoring for serious professional musicians. They were nicer about the whole thing than they should've been. I think they went easy, because they saw there was so little time to cobble their parts together.

Recording was completed by the end of October 1994, and the record was mixed by Wallace at New York's Soundtrack Studios by the end of November. The band brought in New York artist Eric Drooker to provide all the album artwork. Patton, in particular, had greatly admired Drooker's graphic novel *Flood! A Novel In Pictures*, and portions from the book were used in the album artwork, including the policeman and snarling dog of the cover.

Preceded by the 'Digging The Grave' single, *King For A Day ... Fool For A Lifetime* was released on March 13 1995 (the album had a slightly earlier release date outside the USA, which also had a limited-edition vinyl release two weeks before the regular release). By that time, Faith No More had already shed another band member.

Within weeks of finishing recording *King For A Day ... Fool For A Lifetime*, Trey Spruance decided to leave Faith No More. Mike Patton told *Raw*, 'Trey simply didn't want to make the commitment to tour with us. It's like getting married—some people panic at the eleventh hour, and Trey fucking threw the ring back!'

The tour schedule was admittedly daunting—six weeks in Europe from March, then five weeks in the USA, a week in Australia for the Alternative Nation festival shows, then back to the States and Canada in April and May, European festivals in June and July, then back to Australia and Japan, and finally a tour of South America—but scheduling was not why Spruance chose to leave the band:

> Once I fully understood the situation they were placing the new 'band member' in (me or anyone else), which I admit wasn't readily apparent to me as I naively went along, I made haste to walk. Long story short, I'd been asking to set a date for a renegotiation of the salary deal I was on. Just at some future point. A year from then, whatever. But it was after recording the record when management levelled with me that the organisation wouldn't even agree to set a date for a renegotiation. Then, it became crystal clear to me that this was going to be a salary deal, pure and simple. The way management put it was, 'You'll just have to trust us.' Ha! Yeah, right!

The split, initially at least, was acrimonious, with Spruance taking umbrage with an article in *NME* in February 1995 that stated, 'Patton advised against having his childhood chum join the band. The guy might be a good musician, reasoned Patton, but he was a spoilt rich kid (an heir to the DuPont industrial empire) who wouldn't last the course, who would prove to be an even bigger pain in the arse than Martin ever was.' Spruance recalls:

> Some time after I'd quit Faith No More, I got a call from Gregg Turkington [then a San Francisco-based musician and owner of Amarillo Records, and later the stand-up comedy character Neil Hamburger]. He asked me if I'd seen the new issue of *NME*. I replied that I hadn't, and he advised me I should see it, though he wouldn't say why. Once out the door and on my bike, I reasoned I could take a detour to Tower Records and have a look at the magazine Gregg had mentioned. I rode over the hill, locked up my bike, went upstairs into the Tower in the Castro (a record store long since gone), and stood there at the magazine rack reading the article about Faith No More, wherein it was claimed that I was a snotty rich kid heir to the DuPont fortune who couldn't be bothered to tour.
>
> I savoured the moment. Not having enough money for both the magazine and a burrito forced to choose between them. I opted for the latter. Pulling up on my bike to the taqueria among the junkies and crackheads, ordering the same pretty good vegetarian burrito I ate every day at El Castilito, I distinctly felt that this was one of the big Phil-Dick-ian (or Herzog-ian) moments of my life. Biting into that burrito made me feel like a real DuPont billionaire. I can tell you, thinking about this again, these various little humorous public attempts at whitewashing my after-all not-so-damning reasons for quitting the band by pre-emptively smearing my character to the rock press (a world I hate anyway) have always had the net effect of cementing my initial convictions: the departure from the Faith No More scene had definitely been the right move!

As for not wanting to tour, Spruance adds, 'Jesus, I'd rather be guilty of the charge at this point. Just talking about the last ten years, Secret Chiefs 3 has done something like seven hundred shows in over fifty countries (on a below-shoestring budget). But who's fucking counting?' Nonetheless, he looks back fondly on his time in the band:

> Then, as now, and before, I have the hugest respect for Faith No More and their music. More importantly, as people I love them. That's why, of course, some of those shenanigans after I quit surprised me a little bit—feelings got hurt, you know, nothing too bad. And it's never been hard to bear in mind that this was a very difficult time for the FNM guys. For all of them. It's not like as a band they had the full confidence of their record company. Adding to that, a lot of anxieties within the band. It's hard to feel good about where things are when the vocalist is increasingly uncertain about his future commitment in the band; the keyboardist with the crucial pop sensibility is on the outskirts of the band during the process, dealing with very real hardships; the iconic metalhead is gone; and, now, there's this new weirdo on guitar—who knows what the fuck is up with him? And it's all going down while rock is dying an unglorious 90s death, boring pop punk is taking over 'grunge', the record company is on your ass because they have this bug up their ass that your last record was too 'experimental' to be marketable— absolute patent bullshit, Warner Bros really messed up there— and here you are, with new songs that you think have lots of potential to make everything work for everyone, trying to maintain musical and personal dignity in a world of all this shit … and then the band comes through that period with a good record! It says a lot.
>
> In the end (and I say this with the perspective of someone who for decades now has been working very closely with some of the most extraordinarily genius musician/savants of our times), my time with Faith No More was a massively good experience for me, and they are really some of the best humans I've ever had the pleasure of working with.

Of Spruance's departure, Bill Gould recalls:

> I was in Chile when I got a call from Puffy and Patton, with Patton saying, 'Trey's quit the band.' I asked Patton what happened and he said, 'He doesn't want to tour.' And Puffy goes, 'It's OK, we got Dean. I called Dean up and I asked him, and he joined that same day.' So then I went, *click*. It was a beautiful day, so I hung out with my friends and thought, *I'm not going back there for another month. Whatever. It's their problem.*
>
> By the time I got back from South America, it was done and dusted. Dean had already been rehearsing with them. I never saw Trey again, except when we had to settle with him anyway. I read what he wrote. I was really surprised to read it. The way he talked, that wasn't my experience at all.

The Dean in question was Dean Menta, who had been Roddy Bottum's keyboard technician from 1992. Dean had been making music since his early teens, and played on Duh!'s second album, which also featured Greg Werckman, who managed Jello Biafra's label, Alternative Tentacles, and would later establish Ipecac Recordings with Mike Patton.

Menta first met Bottum in 1991. 'I was working at an art gallery in San Francisco and running a digital recording studio there,' he recalls. 'Roddy came in one day inquiring about classes I was teaching. He eventually hired me to tutor him on the new computer-based digital audio technology that was developing at the time. Soon after, we became friends, and then he needed a keyboard tech for the big Guns N' Roses/Metallica tour, so he asked me to do that.'

By 1994, he was sharing an apartment with Gould, so again the band did not have to look far for a new band member. He fitted right in with the band's philosophy. 'All the guys loved Dean,' says Bordin. 'They all got along well. They saw eye to eye about music, especially, and about the folly of being self-serious.'

✤

The band played out their new album to Warners publicist Barb Deegan in

January 1995 and received an enthusiastic response, so they were in good spirits when they played one of their regular pre-album visits to Warner Bros' headquarters in Burbank soon after.

'I remember mixing the record and the big thought among everyone was, *How is Warner Bros even going to understand what we're doing*?' Gould recalls. 'The last record really wasn't a good seller for them. It only went gold. How are we even going to get them to care? But Barb loved the music. It made a difference that she was genuinely into it. I remember it left an impression on me, because if someone at Warners actually cared about what we were doing, maybe there's hope for it.'

Faith No More did have some executives at Warners in their corner over the years, including future label president Steve Baker, label vice-president Roberta Petersen, and head of alternative promotion Jo Lenardi. Anne Marie Foley and Bruce Maguire worked tirelessly on their behalf in regional sales, but they still relied on their original advocates, Slash president Bob Biggs, and Anna Statman—even when she moved to Geffen and, later, Interscope Records.

'Biggs would go beat up the people at Warners when we needed it,' says Gould. 'Anna Statman would too. Anna would go there and kick some ass. She was like our godmother—she still looked out for us.'

The band travelled en masse to Burbank:

> We go up to meet the guy who's running the whole thing and he's cool, he's happy to see us in. We're all sitting at the desk. He's getting us some water. He's got our poster on the wall. We're like, 'Fuck yeah! We've got his attention at least. Maybe something's going to happen.' We're feeling real positive. He's like, 'We're just finishing the artwork for the album right now. Come down and we can meet the guy who's doing your art.' We're like, 'Yeah, this is great.'
>
> So we go down to the art department downstairs, and the guy is working on our stuff, and he's got our poster on the wall! 'Boy, him too!' We talk to him for a while, and he says, 'Why don't you come down and meet some of the sales guys working on it.' So we walk down there, and he's got our poster on the

wall too, but it's a little shabby. It doesn't look too good, like it hadn't been very well taken care of. Dean went and looked behind his door, and there's a box with a bunch of different band posters in there. He figured it out: we were in the building that day, so everybody put our poster up on the wall …

RUNNING TWICE AS FAST TO STAY IN THE SAME PLACE

42

Ahead of the release of the album in March, Bob Biggs told *Billboard*, 'Some people will get it, and some won't. But if you accept this band for what it is—complex, anti-authoritarian, very much of its own making—you'll come to the conclusion that this is a great record.'

It wasn't an opinion shared by a lot of major critics. *Rolling Stone* stated, 'The album is almost desperately eclectic. *The Real Thing*'s genre hopping was effortless.' Critics were falling over themselves to point out how much music had moved on in Faith No More's three-year absence. *Spin*'s six-out-of-ten review began, 'What seems like several thousand years ago, before Lollapalooza, in the days when Kurt Cobain was probably still working out KISS songs on his guitar, Faith No More was the king of "alternative" rock.' *Entertainment Weekly* called it 'archaic progressive-rock fusion, oddly out of step with the times'.

The previous year had seen a new wave of punk acts such as Green Day and Offspring emerge in the USA, the post-Cobain implosion of grunge, and the birth of Britpop (Oasis's Liam Gallagher told Belgium's *Ka2* later in the year, 'Faith No More are not my cup of tea') and trip-hop in the UK. Faith No More were suddenly written off as anachronistic and uncool.

King For A Day ... Fool For A Lifetime limped in as a new entry at #31 on the *Billboard* 200 on April 15. In February, Warners' Peter Rauh told *Billboard*, 'We'd like to reintroduce the band market by market, starting with a small theatre tour through selected major cities. The band has absolutely exploded overseas, so that will be the focus immediately thereafter.' But according to 'overseas' tour promoter Derek Kemp, 'There was definitely a degree of reluctance to put the band into shows of the same level that they played on the previous UK tour. Promoters felt that there might be a backlash. It was a difficult time, and I think that it's about that point in time we parted company.'

Demand was down Stateside, too. Lead single 'Digging The Grave'—the video was shot in San Francisco by Marcus Raboy—was on medium rotation on MTV Europe, but it barely got played on MTV in the USA, *Beavis & Butt-Head* appearances aside. While 'Midlife Crisis' and 'A Small Victory' had charted highly in the *Billboard* Modern Rock charts, 'Digging The Grave', like all singles from *King For A Day ... Fool For A Lifetime*, did not register. By mid-May, *King For A Day* had plummeted to #110 on the US album charts, and a month later it had disappeared off the chart radar completely.

There was chart success 'overseas'. 'Digging The Grave' went straight in at #16 on the UK Singles chart. It was also #5 in Finland, #11 in Norway, and #12 in Australia and Ireland. The album fared even better, reaching #2 in Australia—where it was kept off the top spot by Silverchair—and Finland. It peaked in the top 5 in New Zealand, Sweden, and the UK, and in the top 10 in Austria, Belgium, Germany, Ireland, the Netherlands, Norway, and Switzerland.

The band began touring the album in March in the UK. Their first date, a 'secret' gig at a pub in Windsor called the Old Trout, served as an introduction to Dean Menta, and was accordingly billed as 'Introducing Another Fat Bastard'. *Kerrang!* reported, 'The band's first Brit dates since the 1993 Phoenix Festival will be the ultimate in "intimate", with nearly all shows to take place at venues with less than 1,000 capacity!' They quoted a band spokesman as saying, 'Faith No More wanted to kick off their tour with some small UK shows as a special thank you to their fans.'

The UK music press, which had previously featured Chuck Mosley and Jim Martin as faces of the band, seized on a new angle in 1995, with seemingly every interviewer obsessing about Mike Patton's overstated scatological antics. *NME*'s cover feature in February laboured under such puns as 'Bowel Wow Wow' and 'Mike Patton gets on the throne', while a *Kerrang!* piece in March was headlined 'Royal Flush' and featured a cover photo of Patton on a toilet.

The short UK trek also included some notable television appearances, as the band returned to *Top Of The Pops* to play 'Digging The Grave' for episodes aired on March 2 and 9. 'I used to like to take a bath at the *Top Of The Pops* studio,' Bottum recalls. 'There was a bathtub in the dressing room, and I would get all spread out and spa-like. I remember asking one of the Radioheads if they all hated each other in the same way we did. No answer.'

The band's latest appearance on Channel 4's *The Word* was broadcast on March 3. After performing 'What A Day', Patton and Gould made their way to the studio sofa to sit beside the then MTV *Alternative Nation* presenter Kennedy and behind a table adorned with a framed photo of Jim Martin, to be interviewed by presenter Terry Christian. His opening question began, 'I'm sure you're sick of being asked about this, but Bill Martin has now left …' As Bill Gould queried 'Bill Martin?' and Christian mumbled an apology, Patton threw the contents of glass of water in the presenter's face. Gould and Patton then laid into him with playful punches and pushes. Gould recalls, 'We were told by the record company guys and our friends, "This guy is a fucking wanker. It's a really popular show, but feel free to abuse him." We said OK. But he was actually a good guy in private.' Later, Christian introduced the band to play 'Easy', but after playing the first few notes, the band segued into their cover of The Bee Gees' 'I Started A Joke'.

The band's March 5 show in Norwich was filmed by MTV Europe, and later broadcast, along with an interview with Davina McCall, during which Gould said, 'In small shows you can have a good time and it's a lot more personal.' Their next bizarre television appearance was on MTV Europe's *Most Wanted* show on March 14, where, live throughout the programme, Gould painted an impressive portrait of Larry from The Three Stooges. The band also played 'Digging The Grave', 'What A Day', and 'Midlife Crisis'. They were appearing so often on MTV in Europe in 1995 that Patton and Bottum were even asked to appear in a public safety clip, promoting the safe use of sex toys, for the channel.

ABOVE Calm before the storm: Jim Martin and producer Matt Wallace relax during the recording of *Angel Dust*, January 17 1992. **LEFT** Mike Patton, suited and booted in 1991. *Both photos by Mark Leialoha.*

FAITH NO MORE
Angel Dust

ABOVE Rock pool: Mike Patton and Rob Halford of Judas Priest catch up poolside while in Brazil for the Rock In Rio II festival, January 1991. **LEFT** Kirk Hammett watches Mike Bordin in action as Faith No More and Metallica play with Guns N' Roses in Dallas, September 1992. *Both photos by Mark Leialoha.*

RIGHT Bill Gould and Matt Cameron of Soundgarden try to figure out how to start Gould's recently acquired Trabant on the German leg of the Guns N' Roses/Faith No More/Soundgarden tour, May 1992. *Courtesy Bill Gould/Faith No More.*
BELOW RIGHT Mike Patton and Mike Bordin prepare and relax backstage at the Paramount Theatre, Seattle, January 1993. *Photo by Dustin Rabin.*

ABOVE New guitarist Jon Hudson poses with the band in 1997. *Courtesy Bill Gould/Faith No More.* **LEFT** Dean Menta, pictured soon after joining the band in 1995. *Photo by Mark Leialoha.*

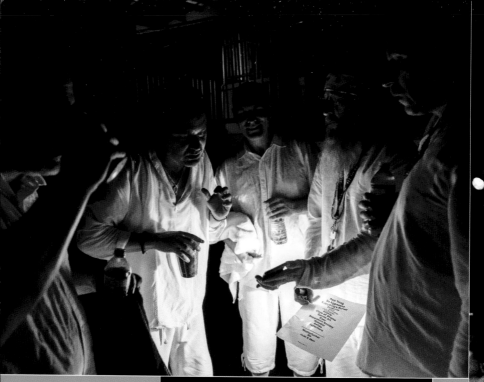

ABOVE Faith No More manager Tim Moss shows Mike Patton a message as the band prepare to take to the stage at the Ricoh Coliseum, Toronto, August 2015. *Photo by Dustin Rabin.* **RIGHT** Trey Spruance returned to play his only live show with Faith No More at the Maquinaria Festival in Chile, November 2011. *Photo by Gonzalo Cancino/@gonzata.* **OPPOSITE** Mike Patton's onstage antics and stage diving were not diminished on Faith No More's reunion tour. He is pictured here in the crowd at the Warfield, San Francisco, April 2010. *Photo by Dustin Rabin.*

ABOVE The late Chuck Mosley, pictured with Mike Patton at the Troubadour, August 2016. **LEFT** Mike Bordin and Bill Gould in the studio in 2014. *Both photos by Tim Moss, courtesy Tim Moss/Faith No More.*

On April 5, Faith No More recorded the video, directed by Alex Hemming, for their second single, 'Ricochet', before and during their show at Paris's Élysée Montmartre. The single again failed to pick up much traction, reaching #27 in the UK charts, but making little impression elsewhere. It only reached #57 in Australia, the band unable to make it a hat-trick of #1s on Australian soil on their Easter weekend trip for the Alternative Nation festival in Brisbane, Sydney, and Melbourne in mid-April.

Four days later, they were back onstage in Vancouver, and thirty-three US and Canada dates followed in the next five weeks. 'They just worked us like horses,' says Gould, 'I think that they might have had good intentions, but the message I was getting from the managers was, *You need to go back to work, otherwise it's done. You're going to be as broke as you were when we met you.* I took it to heart. I didn't want to go back. It didn't change what we did musically, but it ratcheted up the anxiety—for me, anyway.'

The American press had also noticed the band's declining popularity. In May, the Dallas Morning News reported, 'In the post-punk light of Green Day, the rap-funk favoured by San Francisco quintet Faith No More is basically over. The proof is all around you: the band's new release, *King For A Day ... Fool For A Lifetime*, seems to be DOA at record stores, and the band's performance Monday night at the Bomb Factory attracted "half a house", maybe 700 fans, many of whom seemed to be there for opening trio Steel Pole Bath Tub.'

Whatever about their punishing schedule and diminishing returns, Faith No More were having fun onstage. 'You had Mike onstage, looking over and seeing people he liked, Bill onstage, like looking over and seeing people,' says Bordin. 'They liked being there. There's value in that in itself, they liked playing with Dean. Dean did a fine job.'

The band's final show of their summer North American tour came as part of the New Rock Fest at Milwaukee's Marcus Amphitheater on May 29. Faith No More were on the same bill as Bush and Duran Duran, but their headlining slot outside in the 23,000-capacity venue clashed with the Ramones playing on a small stage, leaving Faith No More playing to swathes of empty seats. That tour had opened the band's eyes to their reduced status in the USA. Mike Bordin recalls, 'We realised then that in the US, while it wasn't going to be a mega audience, there was an audience. It was important for us to come to terms with the fact that there was an audience listening to what you're doing. The crowds were definitely small, and the press, at that point, genuinely didn't care.'

Appreciating that audience was made easier by Gould and Menta being early adopters of the internet. Gould and Bottum took part in an AOL Cybertalk chat session, organised by Warner Bros, in November 1994, and Gould also regularly frequented the Caca Volante mailing list and website, created by Andy Couch, which brought together fans of the band. Long before David Bowie's BowieNet ISP and long before Audiogalaxy, never mind Napster, Faith No More were internet innovators, becoming the first artists to publicise their website on MTV in 1995. Attired in a mustard suit and buttoned-up shirt, Gould looked every inch the dot.com businessman as he explained the internet and the site on the *Super Rock* programme. Presenter Jackie Perry asked, 'Tell me about this world wide web for Faith No More?' and Bill replied, 'There's a website, and if you have Mosaic or this thing called Netscape, you can do a search and write *Faith No More*, it takes you to the spot and it shows all of our tour dates, and you can download screensavers.'

In April 1995, in an interview with *Consumable* magazine, Gould said, 'It's a good way to get information out and a good way to write information. If you want to know something, ask the source. Better than hearing it from some other asshole!'

✦

The final attempt to break *King For A Day ... Fool For A Lifetime* was the album's third single, 'Evidence', released on May 8 in the USA and on July 17 in the UK. The song and the video, helmed by the English director Walter Stern, known for his work with The Prodigy, and filmed in a club on Eddy Street in San Francisco, showcased the band's 'new look and new sound' much more than the 'Digging The Grave' cut so enamoured of MTV's Beavis. The song is smooth 70s soul, delicate funky bass, and seamlessly spliced strings, played live in the studio by a string quartet with their parts arranged on the spot by Trey Spruance.

Bill Gould again brought the song to the band, but admits he was reluctant to do so. 'I was almost ashamed,' he recalls. 'They were like, *Let's do it.*

Patton said, Why not? We had the confidence to do it. If it was up to me, I probably would not have done it.'

'We've always wanted to write a great pop song,' Patton said. '"Evidence" is just that. I think we needed to lose a guitarist to achieve the end result.'

Pop song or not, 'Evidence' failed to achieve any significant MTV or radio airplay. It peaked at #32 on the UK singles chart and hit #5 in Finland and #27 in Australia, but it made no impact elsewhere.

In August, Faith No More were back in Australia, and a long overdue return to South America—Argentina, Brazil, and Chile for the Monsters Of Rock festival—in September was again rapturously received. The band played three more shows back in the States in October, and then abruptly stopped. Further dates in the USA and an autumn tour of the UK were summarily cancelled. And a *Kerrang!* headline in October screamed, 'Faith No More "We're Not Splitting!"'

43 ROCK, HUDSON, ROCK

Faith No More were once more teetering on the brink. The official version of events—that they had cut short touring to concentrate on writing songs for a new album—was, at best, only partially true. The reality was that the band members' other commitments were increasingly taking priority.

It would have been very difficult to play shows in October, November, and December, given that Mr Bungle released their second album, *Disco Volante*, on October 10 1995, and then played a twenty-one-date American tour in November and December. Similarly, Roddy Bottum finished recording his debut album with Star 69, by then renamed Imperial Teen, in late 1995. He wrote, sang, played guitar, and played drums on various tracks on *Seasick*, released in 1996, and, at the time, considered side projects as a healthy development for Faith No More. Asked in June 1995 in Canadian music zine *VAJ*, if such projects interfered with Faith No More, he said, 'Hopefully, in the future, they will. I would love to see a band fucking things up. It's like a lot of diversity—you start getting into the pattern of Faith No More, and you need something else. I'd like to see other things become important.'

He got his wish. In 1996, Imperial Teen were, for a time, a more acclaimed band than Faith No More. *Seasick*'s brand of Breeders-like three-chord jangly indie pop and the album's killer melodies and *ad rem* lyrics made them critical darlings (the album was #24 in the *Village Voice*'s 1996 Pazz & Jop Critics Poll). The album was released through Slash, and label president Bob Biggs told *Billboard* in March 1996 that the band was Bottum's 'release valve'. In the same article, Bottum said, 'This is emphatically not a side project. They're a really important band.'

Looking back, more than two decades on, Bottum is more philosophical. 'Everyone started side projects, and it was rewarding for everyone to get their creative kicks, but, at the same time, it all felt mildly disrespectful of what we were doing as a band. Me included. We tended to take the Faith No More project for granted, and once one or two of us started doing that, it was contagious. I wish we'd respected the process more at this time.'

Mike Bordin was also getting his creative kicks. In 1996, he was approached by his idol, Ozzy Osbourne, to work with him. 'It started on the *King For A Day* tour, when we opened for Ozzy at Monsters Of Rock in South America,' he recalls. 'Ozzy saw us and said, I want that guy to play in my band. I know Ozzy wasn't super-stoked on all of the people in his band, because he told me that. He told everybody that. A couple of months later [in February 1996], he played in Oakland, with Deftones and Korn. I saw him then, too. At that point, I was hanging out a bit, we knew each other, we're comfortable, we're friends. After that, he said, You know, I'm making the change, you want to come on? I said, I'm in, 100 percent.'

Bordin's recruitment was announced in the *San Francisco Chronicle* in May 1996, with the former Black Sabbath singer saying, 'I've always thought he was a great drummer, and, having done a few shows with him, he's just a total pro.'

Bordin, who had been sounded out to play on the abortive Led Zeppelin reunion in 1992—a perhaps apocryphal story had Jimmy Page asking, 'We're getting a reggae drummer?' when shown a photo of the potential new recruit—adds, 'At the age of thirty-one, thirty-two, it's perfect timing. I wanted to keep going. I felt that the experience that I had with Faith No More, big and little and everything else, was going to serve me well with them. Everybody was doing something. Roddy's got his band, Billy's doing things, Mike's doing things. That's how it was.'

Gould had been busy, too. In 1995, he again toured Europe in a Trabant, taking in Albania, the Czech Republic, and the former Yugoslavia, including Bosnia during the end of the conflict. 'I grew up in a sheltered environment,' he says, 'and America is a sheltered country. When you got to places like this, you see how places really work, without the varnish. This is what appealed to me, because I wanted to know the truth. Sometimes, I feel like I've been lied to all my life. I wanted to understand the people, and I wanted to know how the system worked. The war in Kosovo that wasn't declared— we drove right through that. We, me and my friend Eric, were in Bosnia, and we got to Sarajevo the day the war ended.'

Gould was fascinated by Eastern Europe, and the former Yugoslavia in particular. In 1993, he had arranged for Faith No More to play in Moscow, St Petersburg, and Ljubljana, the capital of a newly independent Slovenia. They were one of the first American bands to play in the former Yugoslavia, and while conflict in Bosnia and Croatia was still ongoing.

'The show attracted young people (i.e. soldiers) from all the warring countries,' he continues. 'Someone who worked at the venue remarked how they were all drinking, partying, and singing together, but, when they were leaving, they split off in groups, and were saying things like, *See you on the front* and, *Next time you'll have a bullet*. We had three days off on the Istrian coast, and my tech Jim and I rented motorcycles and went exploring into the Rijeka area of neighbouring Croatia. It was my first taste on the first of many trips.'

❦

When Bordin and Bottum appeared on MTV's *Headbangers Ball*, interviewed by Vanessa Warwick at Bordin's San Francisco home in early

1996, they maintained the little fiction that *King For A Day* touring had been cut short due to an eagerness to start working on music on a new album. But Roddy also outlined the work that had commenced on the new record:

> The three of us, Mike and Billy and I, had been writing stuff since we stopped touring, and we've written a whole bunch of songs. Mike is away doing his Mr Bungle thing for a while, and we came to a point last month where we decided that we've done all we can do with the writing right now, so let's just go in and record this rather than sit on it any longer than we had to.
>
> It's a little bit of a simpler approach than on *King For A Day*. It just sort of dawned on us all collectively that we didn't really need to spend as much time as we did on the last record. This time, we went in very casually and just laid stuff down.

The elephant in the room was the contribution of guitarist Dean Menta, and, when asked what Dean would bring to the new record, Roddy answered diplomatically, 'We're realising at this point that most of the writing that we've done going into this record has just been the three of us, Mike and Billy and myself, and that's the three that started the band, and started the writing process of Faith No More.'

In actual fact, the trio were struggling to connect creatively with their latest recruit. In a 2016 interview, Menta explained, 'Certain members of the band wanted to immediately start writing songs for another record. I think at that point in time we were all burnt out, at least I was.'

'Dean was cool, but the writing wasn't there,' Gould adds. 'The worst thing about it was, we had parts and we'd write stuff and we sent it to Dean to work on it. He would just not return my calls.'

In the summer of 1996, Faith No More and Dean Menta parted company. 'I got pushed off the boat before it totally sank,' the guitarist added. 'I was disappointed yet relieved that it was all over. I was mostly baffled and confused by the entire experience. I did have bad feelings afterward, but they've faded away a long time ago. I still love and admire those guys a lot.'

❖

With an album half-written and recorded, by March 1996, the search was on for Faith No More's twelfth guitarist.

The auditioning process was straightforward, as Bordin recalls. 'We sounded out people who we personally felt musically spoke the same language. Then we would give them a tape and say, What would you do with this? That was the weeding-out process, and there were a few of them.'

One of the players the band tried out was well known in the Bay Area music scene. 'My good friend Bryan Kehoe is a local legend,' Bordin says of the guitarist who featured on local band MIRV's 1993 release *Cosmodrome*, a record that makes Primus sound restrained and low in funk. 'Incredible guitar player. He was one of the guys we spoke to. Think about how different that would have been!'

An even more intriguing prospect was a twenty-three-year-old guitar player then between projects. His band Kyuss had supported Faith No More on their 1993 US tour, and Faith No More—Bordin in particular—were huge fans of their 1994 release *Welcome To Sky Valley*. The Californian guitarist and singer told MTV in 1995 that Faith No More were one of his five favourite artists. Josh Homme seemed, then, the perfect solution. And, in between leaving Kyuss and starting Queens Of The Stone Age, he came to San Francisco, staying with both Bordin and Gould.

'He came over to my house for three days,' Gould recalls. 'He stayed at Puffy's house for a bit. A great guitar player. Kyuss was finished at the time. His approach was entirely different, and, to my ears, it didn't quite work. But he was a great guy. We came to a conclusion that we were both doing the same thing, but we were both approaching it from completely opposite directions.'

❋

As with Patton, Spruance, and Menta, the solution was right under the band's noses. Jon Hudson was a mutual friend of Bill Gould and Will Carpmill, and had worked on some musical projects with Gould some years previously. Born on April 13 1968 in the East Bay of San Francisco, Hudson picked up his love of music from his older siblings. His brother, a highly proficient pianist—who played everything by ear—took classical lessons and played piano in the family home when Hudson was a child. 'It was always Chopin,

Beethoven, and what have you,' he remembers. 'We would all just sit back and listen to him practice, and it seemed like he was glued to the piano—you couldn't pry him away from the thing.'

Classical American musicals, Elton John, and The Beatles played on the living room turntable also fuelled this early interest. 'The first record I got was Elton John's *Madman Across The Water*, when I was in the first grade, probably because I was scratching up everyone else's albums. Right around 1980, my sister was majoring in music, and my brother had joined this punk band in San Francisco called GRR. He played either a Farfisa or a Vox Continental, depending on whichever one happened to be functioning at the time. He'd play me their rehearsal tapes. I'm not sure how long he was in the band, but it definitely piqued my interest right when I started to pick up the guitar.'

Aged eleven, Hudson became a huge KISS fan, and he started playing guitar around the same time. 'I bought *Love Gun* and worked my way back to the early records,' he says. 'I hadn't yet had any exposure to hard rock, and I had never heard a guitar sound like that—when I heard Ace Frehley, it completely blew my mind.'

Hudson picked up a starter guitar from a record store in Berkeley and took lessons, but he soon grew frustrated at being taught old jazz standards such as 'Autumn Leaves' and 'Pennies From Heaven'.

My new teacher had the most beautiful Gibson L-5 hollow-body you have ever seen, and he was extremely charitable. He'd say, 'Ugh, that sounds like shit, I'm going to go out for a smoke while you work on that.' This was the store's in-house guitar teacher for all ages including beginners, mind you, and my mom had just purchased this student guitar in the shop probably like a week or two prior. Needless to say, I was sold and knew that I was in the right place. After several months and a few more cigarette breaks, I had about three scales and some barre and jazz chords under my belt, and also a handful of lead sheets for the songs I was working on.

Things finally started to develop when my friends and I got together to jam one afternoon in the eighth grade. It wasn't

official unless we had a name, of course, so we decided upon
The Dry Heaves, and it felt exhilarating to be in a band.

In the summer of 1983, a friend of the family who was doing live sound
for local bands got in touch to suggest more appropriate lessons. He told
Hudson, 'I'm doing shows for this band called the Squares. There's this guy,
Joe, I'll give you his number. He teaches out in Berkeley.'

The Joe was Joe Satriani. He had not yet embarked on his stellar solo
career, but had been a teacher to Kirk Hammett and Steve Vai, among others.

> I went around ten times to this guitar shop in North Berkeley for
> lessons that summer, but after getting into *Led Zeppelin II*, I was
> so floored with it, I just thought, I want to learn this stuff myself.
> I might've been playing half of it incorrectly anyway, but there's
> a lot of value in trial and error, finding your own way through
> it. I wanted to learn string bending, vibrato, and whatnot—that's
> something I had to do on my own.
>
> So, I went through this metal phase, then progressive rock,
> briefly into hardcore punk or whatever, back into Led Zeppelin
> or Queen or Hendrix, followed by early Prince records and back
> around again, but I struggled to retain interest after sitting with
> any of it for too long. I loved all of it, and yet I always considered
> that to be a major liability; in terms of where I wanted to place
> my efforts in some musical endeavour, I was lost. I also took
> a music theory class in high school, and it was probably the
> first time that I felt inspired in school, like there really was a
> foundation which you could build upon.

Though he played with his friends and in high school bands, Hudson
was unable to find a regular band. In his late teens and twenties, work
commitments took over. Eventually, in 1989, after not playing seriously for
several years, he met Will Carpmill after replying to the ad he had posted
in a record store. He met Carpmill and his band at their rehearsal space—
the same abandoned pet hospital that served as Carpmill and Gould's
living quarters, though Gould had left on tour, and would never return to

live there. Within two weeks, Hudson had moved in, too. The band were Systems Collapse, a vital and ahead-of-their-time combo fusing industrial synths and guitars. They played approximately twenty-seven shows in the next two years in the Bay Area, and Hudson took on the role of singer as well as guitarist. 'We were on this never-ending search for a good vocalist, and as appealing as it might have been to keep playing instrumentals, it was next to impossible to book shows without a singer. Also we knew that we were never going to find a singer without any exposure. I told Will and our drummer Dave that I'd handle the vocals so we could at least get some shows, but I didn't particularly relish the idea of being in that role.'

In 1992, Carpmill managed to get a demo of their music into the hands of Anna Statman, who had signed Faith No More for Slash back in 1987. She liked what she heard, and gave the duo a $2,000 contract to make a demo for Interscope Records. 'It was great to have that chance, but the timing was completely off. Bill was around, and I think he had already made up his mind that he wanted to get into producing at some point, so he helped us out in the studio, and he connected us up with a drummer that he knew. But I'm not a singer, and I'm not a lyricist, and we're trying to come up with some ideas, enough for a demo to send to this record company, so it didn't pan out. But that's when I got to know Bill a little bit more.'

Systems Collapse collapsed definitively in 1994, and that same year, Jon and Bill worked together again. Hudson was one of the guitarists in the frame to replace Jim Martin. He worked on some music with Gould to tease out his suitability at the time. 'I wasn't surprised when they picked Trey,' he reflects. 'He and Patton had played together since they were kids, so he was a known quantity, and he was obviously very talented. It seemed like the perfect match to me.'

Not long after that, Hudson moved back to the East Bay. He set up his own home studio, and had not long returned to college for further study when he received a call from Gould in late April 1996. Gould told him, 'I know we've talked about this before, but we're in another situation where we need a guitar player, and I'm wondering if you might consider giving it another shot? We're really not considering other people at this point. If you want to put the time in, we could make this work.'

'I knew that was my one chance,' Hudson remembers, 'so I had to go all in. I dropped everything and started working on their existing demos.' His work over the previous few months also proved fruitful, as he gave Gould a cassette of some of the songs he'd been working on. 'It turned out that he took to a couple of the ideas for songs, and then some of the other band members liked them as well.'

'I knew technically he could do it,' Gould recalls. 'I said, "Here's a couple of things. Try it out." And he did well. Then he had "Stripsearch" in as an idea. I said to the rest of the band, "Guys, I've known John forever, he's a solid dude."'

'Jon was friends of our good friends,' Bottum adds, 'and they had music projects together. He was energetic and talented and cooperative, and super willing to step in and help. It was a really strong decision.'

44

With Hudson on board, Faith No More could get back down to the business of recording their sixth album. That meant going right back to the start. Twelve of the songs initially tracked by Mike Bordin, Roddy Bottum, and Bill Gould in Brilliant Studios in San Francisco at the start of the year were shelved. Mike Patton, who had not been involved in the tracking due to tour commitments with Mr Bungle in early 1996, told German magazine *Zillo* in May 1997, 'We did about seven or eight songs for a long time that won't appear on the album. I don't know if they will ever appear somewhere. Its like making coffee, you have to throw it away when it's bitter.'

Bottum told the *Herald-Sun*, 'He only liked about half of the songs, and only felt he could sing on about half of the songs. It sort of turned me off, I was really pissed off about it. But, at the same time, if it isn't effortless for him, then I would really rather he didn't anyway.'

Patton, who was also living in Italy for much of this time with his new wife, was not the only one with competing commitments. Bottum was busy promoting Imperial Teen's debut release and touring with the band in the USA in the autumn, while Bordin's commitment to Ozzy Osbourne saw him touring for six months straight until October 1996.

That left Gould working in tandem with Jon Hudson, who recalls, 'He was spread out pretty thin. The rest of the band were gone, and the band was still obligated for a couple of records. They did have some material, and the writing often comes in stages, so they had that first batch, and it was all on Bill to manage everything.'

Gould adds, 'Jon and me probably worked on that record the most. But everyone wanted me to work. Puffy would call me up and tell me things like, *Get Patton on board. We got to do this. We got to do this.* Everybody was getting me to fight everybody else's battles. They don't tell you when they don't like something. They just don't respond.'

Meanwhile, Hudson was learning the ropes:

> I would take their demo tapes, and then bring them home onto my little four-track, and work on them. And then compare notes. Initially, there was sort of an adjustment period. I would think that I had just come up with the best idea ever. It's not like it was disheartening or anything, but it would some times be like, *Oh yeah, that could be better, or maybe we'll try this or that.*
>
> I went back to the drawing board quite a few times. Instead of being frustrated, I figured, this is just part of the process—deal with it, you know? I'm joining this band—they're obviously well into their career and don't need direction from anybody else, and they tend to have very specific ideas in mind for the guitar parts. My job is not to jump in and fix what isn't broken. You collaborate, and you pick whatever works or sounds or feels best, and that's it.

For Bordin, whose duties with Ozzy took him to the Monsters Of Rock festival at Donington in August and the three-date inaugural Ozzfest in October, his new gig brought a fresh outlook. 'I understood the band, not what it should be, but what it actually was. The functioning, somewhat healthy entity that it was—and not needing to bust a gut going after the biggest of the big tours, the biggest of the big exposure, but being comfortable with the place where it was naturally.'

Bordin was able to contribute to the new writing process, both on tour and in breaks from the road. In the autumn of 1996, Hudson and Gould were joined by Bordin, Bottum, and Patton to lay down basic tracks back at Brilliant, but the five were never in the studio at the same time. The tracking took two weeks, with some additional work and overdubs done at a rehearsal space on Divisadero Street in the city, and, at the end of that time, the band had twenty songs near completion.

Hudson recalls, 'Initially, we figured that we'd be tweaking things here and there, but then Patton showed up while we were wrapping up at Brilliant. He wanted to make even more changes to some of the guitars, so we re-tracked some stuff, but mostly on his songs.'

'Patton was in Italy all the time,' says Gould. 'He wouldn't come home. He'd say he's coming home on June 2, and we could start working. Then June 2 comes by, and he doesn't return your calls. Then, all of a sudden, it's August 2, and now he's back. He had your tape, and he wrote something, but he only has an hour to record it. He just got off the plane. He went straight from the airport, straight to the studio, and he's going to give you one hour. It was like that.'

Finally, Gould snapped in the studio. 'This is it,' he raged at Patton. 'It isn't working. I'm out. I'm done!'

When he had calmed down, the pair reached a rapprochement. 'We worked it out, kind of,' Gould recalls. 'He was really bratty about it.'

According to Hudson, 'After the blowout, Mike and I headed down the street to the M&M Bar for lunch, where all of the old newspaper guys hung out. He said he wanted to redo the intro to "Naked In Front Of The Computer" with a different amp. It was "too big" or something to that effect, referring to the existing track. He told me he wanted that part to be like a fourteen-year-old kid with a tiny practice amp. I took a few moments with that, and then it clicked, it made complete sense. It was like, at this point, these guys don't need an outside producer in there; they just need to give each other some space. So, I think, *We've got the fourteen-year-old, now let's go borrow a practice amp.*'

Patton was also frustrated. 'He struggled with us, too,' Gould admits. 'He got a little worn-down, because we had the guitar player thing again. Again. Roddy was out. Again. Roddy would not come to rehearsal. You'd get a music magazine, and he'd be on the cover with his band, talking about this being his main thing.'

Patton's frustrations were such that they even occasionally slipped out in album promotional interviews. 'We have another guitarist. I really wish I could say that "this is the man!" and that everything is beautiful, but we've said that three fucking times already,' he told *Beat*.

✿

Despite his other commitments and his new life with his Italian wife in Bologna, Patton remained a crucial component of the band's creativity and composing. But his way of working had changed. Now, he was more inclined to bring in songs fully formed. The most fully realised of these was 'Got That Feeling', two minutes and twenty seconds of musical adrenaline inhabiting the mind of a compulsive gambler. 'Those songs he brought in like "Got That Feeling" and "Home Sick Home"—he did great work there,' Gould says. 'I liked those songs a lot.'

Hudson had adapted to his role, too. 'Patton's songs for that record were pretty fleshed out,' he says. 'It was one of those things, where if it sounds like it's working, there's no point in trying to reinvent it.'

Another song that needed little embellishment was the presciently titled 'Naked In Front Of The Computer'. Despite being a completely guitar-driven track, it was again a Patton solo effort. Hudson: 'Those were pretty much his guitar parts verbatim. The only idea that I added to that track was this little descending line that runs counter to the main riff in the outro, and that was it. It didn't need anything else.'

The title—ahead of its time for 1996, when it was written—came from Gould. Patton explained in 1997, 'Billy is completely hooked, and he found this sex chat room with that name. As I understand it, anyway.'

Hudson initially conceived the first two songs on the album. 'Collision' kicks off *Album Of The Year* in typical Faith No More 'don't bore us, get to the chorus' album-opener style. Hudson provided the skeleton of the song, but some of the other sounds are actually keyboard strings played through a tube amplifier simulator. 'We used a SansAmp and ran this low synth drone and like a high-pitched sound into it,' he recalls. 'The synth module sounded fine on its own for the demo, but in the studio, the verses seemed to lack urgency. Just the addition of another variable seemed to make all the difference, and those sections were then able to keep up the pace.' Adding to the song's twitchy feel are fluctuating and unusual time signatures in the verses, and other sonic effects such as a shortwave radio, which was Patton's idea.

Hudson's other main contribution was the album's second track and the third single to be released from it. 'Stripsearch', Faith No More's taste of trip-hop, was also the song that effectively sealed Hudson's place in the band. 'The most amazing thing was that he wrote a song which worked with us, and we didn't have to teach him to do it,' Gould states. 'Musically, we connected. I think he was the first guitar player we had where that happened.'

Hudson adds, 'It benefited from everyone else's input. Bill added an arpeggio which became this central motif to push the song along. He felt like it was falling a little bit flat without that.'

Elsewhere, the Ottoman feel of 'Mouth To Mouth' was inspired by Gould's trip through Eastern Europe the previous year. 'I was in Albania,' he says. 'I heard the street music. I heard some guy on the street playing this Ottoman-inspired music.' To recapture the sound, he bought an Arabic version of a cheap portable keyboard.

Both songs benefitted from the post-production work Gould did with the help of former Swans percussionist and long-time Young Gods producer, the Swiss-born Roli Mosimann. Gould sent a tape to Mosimann, who liked what he heard and was happy to help. But rather than doing so remotely, he came to San Francisco and stayed with Gould for several weeks. In the home studio in a shed in the bottom of Gould's garden, they were able to transfer the tracks recorded in Brilliant from analogue tape to Pro Tools, allowing the tracks to be edited digitally—a first for a Faith No More album. The tape transfer was painstaking, involving two fifteen-hour sessions, but perhaps the most onerous part of the process was having to wheel the unwieldy, borrowed two-inch tape recorder into the shed studio, dodging dog droppings along the way.

'Once Roli came in, we got a real shot in the arm,' Gould recalls. Mosimann spent several weeks editing and mixing (at Plant Studios in San Francisco) the tracks with Gould. For 'Stripsearch', he cut up some of Mike Bordin's original drumbeat, making a total of thirty thousand individual edits. The other percussion at the start of the track is actually some mouth noises from Patton, an outtake from a vocal track, edited into the song by Mosimann.

The lyrical introspection and self-loathing of *King For A Day* ... *Fool For A Lifetime* continued on some tracks on the new record, notably 'Helpless', where the plaintive narrator, voiced by Patton, sings, '*I even tried / To get arrested today / But everyone looked the other way.*' It was also one of many lyrics that could be seen as referencing Faith No More's diminishing commercial appeal. Similarly, 'Mouth To Mouth''s '*I can dress up the dead man / but I can't bring him back to life*' and almost every line in 'Last Cup Of Sorrow' seem to foreshadow the end of the band.

Part a by-product of new production technology, part a reaction to the crisp production of their previous record, but mostly a reflection of where Faith No More imagined themselves to be in late 1996, there is no disguising that *Album Of The Year* is an extended elegy.

Gould and Mosimann began mixing the album on January 3 1997. On Sunday February 16, Joel Selvin reported in the *San Francisco Chronicle*, 'Amid rumours of a breakup, Faith No More is celebrating its fifteenth year of togetherness with the June 3 release of its seventh album. The band just delivered the yet-untitled album to Reprise Records and is concentrating on getting everyone in one spot to begin discussing a summer tour.'

Fans were given a first taste of the new record when Warners' Reprise imprint posted a thirty-second clip of 'Last Cup Of Sorrow' on its website on 18 March. Within days, fans were already commenting on internet news groups on the mournful lyrics. Some of those lyrics found Patton and the band almost daring themselves into a sort of suicide pact: '*It won't begin / Until you make it end*', and the chorus, '*Finish it today / It's your last cup of sorrow.*' The pre-chorus ('*So raise it up and lets propose a toast / To the thing that hurts you most*') was borrowed from an early Mr Bungle demo track, their paean to menstruation, 'Bloody Mary'. While more upbeat than other tracks on the record, the toy piano sounds (actually a Kurzweil K2000 preset), the rich guitar, and Patton's compressed verse vocals lend it a foreboding sensation.

With 'Paths Of Glory' more a mood than a song, this funereal feeling permeates the album. 'Pristina', another product of Gould's trip to the Balkans, is effectively the band's epitaph. The words are mournful in isolation—'*You shall weep no more / It's your last breath of air*'—but huge open distorted chords, space, and Patton's breathy vocals instil an exequial air. 'I'd been to Pristina before the war,' Gould explains. 'It was a collapse in a place that nobody knew about, including myself. Meanwhile, in the band, I knew we were dying. We all knew we were dying. I figured that the best control you can have is to at least write your own funeral.'

The album's artwork was another product of that mournful mood and Gould's eastern European trip. The front cover image shows the first president of the independent Czechoslovakia he spent much of his life fighting for, Tomáš Masaryk, who died, aged eighty-seven, in 1937, just two years after leaving office due to poor health. The inside artwork features photographs from his funeral and his personal motto, '*Pravda vítězí*' (truth prevails), which became the motto of the newly independent Czechoslovakia in 1993, and subsequently of the Czech Republic.

The idea again came from Gould, who stumbled upon the photo in a Prague thrift store.

> The whole thing about Masaryk on the cover was that he had the brilliant idea of merging different places together into one thing, like we tried to do with music. He brought people together, as the funeral images showed, and we tried to bring people together. He had to leave the free Czechoslovakia he created in 1937, and, at that time, the band was dying too.
>
> We tried to make the record an honest record. It's atmospheric, it's depressed; it's a very sad record. I was sad as hell. I mean, you have to be honest.

The band were still in a robust enough state to embark on a promotional tour in April and May 1997. A tour of the UK and Europe, that is. The Buffalo incident, the poor chart performance of *King For A Day*, and another shift in tastes toward nu-metal, R&B, and hip-hop had killed the American market for Faith No More, and no American dates were scheduled until September.

In early 1997, Jon Hudson had only a few months to learn to play the whole Faith No More oeuvre. 'I wasn't given a list of songs, and I didn't have *Introduce Yourself* or the first album,' he recalls. 'I went to the local record store to see if I could find them ... they didn't have *We Care A Lot*. It seems ridiculous to me now, but I remember in soundcheck on the first leg of the tour, someone could call out one of the tracks on the first album and I'd have to tell them, I don't know that one.'

Press and promotional commitments, extracurricular activities, and the shooting of the first two videos didn't leave much time for rehearsal before the tour. Still not fully conversant with all of Faith No More's material, Hudson's baptism of fire was to play live at Maida Vale studios in London on April 22 on the UK's most popular music radio station, BBC Radio 1. The band were booked in to play a live session for the *Late Show* with Mary Anne Hobbs. Hudson and Co played 'Ashes To Ashes', 'Midlife Crisis', 'Last Cup Of Sorrow', and 'The Gentle Art Of Making Enemies'. 'It was my first thing with the band,' he says, 'and I remember that one of the managers John [Vassiliou] just walked up to me afterward and said, laughing, Well, you're fired. I enjoyed it.'

Hudson's first show proper was at the Electric Garden in Stockholm six days later, while in the UK, the band returned to such familiar haunts as London's Astoria and Rock City in Nottingham. The Astoria show concluded with Patton covered in his own blood. Climaxing a maniacally energetic performance, during the first notes of set closer 'Caffeine', he jerked his head against the drum riser and fell flat on his face on the stage floor. He carried on without missing a note, still thrashing wildly across and against the stage despite blood streaming down the right side of his face. Two days later, on May 16, he sported butterfly stitches on his forehead as the group played 'Ashes To Ashes' on Channel 4's *TFI Friday*. When the band returned to the show later in the year, presenter Chris Evans declared them the loudest band ever to appear on the programme.

Faith No More also appeared on French TV, on Canal Plus' *Nulle part ailleurs*, live on the beach at Cannes. As the band were preparing, they were swarmed by a team of security guards and corralled into a tiny corner of their dressing room. They were ordered to stay away from the windows, not allowed to leave even to get water or visit the bathroom, and kept there for over an hour. All because Bruce Willis, promoting his new film *The Fifth Element* at the Cannes Film Festival, had just arrived on his yacht along with Jean-Paul Gaultier, and his entourage had ordered the area to be cleared. As the five members struggled to find space to even move, Willis sat all alone in the rest of the huge room, not speaking to anyone. Never sticklers for protocol, posturing, or being told what to do, Faith No More baulked. Mike Patton jumped up, shouted 'Fuck this', and made his way into the larger area and onto the rest room.

Then, while soundchecking, the band spotted Michael Jackson waving at adoring fans from a nearby hotel balcony, and immediately tore into a reworked, expletive-laden cover of 'Bad'. When they did get to play live on the waterfront for French TV, Patton introduced 'Ashes To Ashes' with, 'This one's going out to Bruce!'

In May 1997, Faith No More returned to *Top Of The Pops*, as 'Ashes To Ashes' had crashed into the UK singles chart at #15—the band's third-highest UK chart placing. The song was the album's opening single outside the USA, where 'Last Cup Of Sorrow' got the nod. It was one of the few tracks to survive from the abortive recording sessions in February 1996, and it was also the only song on which all band members received a writing credit. It stands as one of Faith No More's finest singles, the opening riff commanding attention while Patton delivers one of his most accomplished vocal performances. It remains in step with the rest of the record, conveying a brooding intensity in its huge chords before Jon Hudson inserts some relief and dynamic with the late restrained solo. Gould, who initially conceived the song, notes, 'That one was old school. It was "We Care A Lot" revisited. It was a big grand chord with a solid rhythm. And Patton got it straight away. We sent a tape to Patton and got vocals straight off.'

'They're loud, they're proud, but they look very posh,' was *TOTP* presenter Victoria Beckham's verdict. Faith No More had adopted a new look for the *Album Of The Year* tour, resplendent in smart, well-cut black suits, crisp white shirts, and shiny black shoes. Dressed for a funeral, in other words.

Mike Bordin was absent from the show, due to a combination of needing to be back in the States for the birth of his first daughter and commitments with Ozzy Osbourne at Ozzfest. Faith No More needed a replacement, and they found one in session drummer and later Rachel Stamp band member Robin Guy. The band, who would be miming as was the norm on *Top Of The Pops*, instructed the stand-in drummer to wear a specially made cardboard Puffy mask on the show:

> They had this mask with the two eyes pushed in and pushed up against my nose. I couldn't see anything. I said, 'But I can't see, I can't play properly,' and they're like, 'We don't care, we just want some idiot at the back to wave their sticks.'
>
> The opening riff starts and I put the mask on thinking, *OK, here we go, see you at the end.* The second riff kicks in and the mask just fell on my snare drum, the little elastic knot had just popped. By the third riff and the drums are kicking in, I had this war inside me—*Fix it real quick or they'll kill you*—but the other half was going, *Screw them, get it off.* So I just whisked the mask off, and carried on rocking, thinking it'll all be fine. Then, Mike Patton turns around, and he sees me, and he threw me the middle finger.

✸

With 'Ashes To Ashes' a minor hit in Europe and Australia, where it reached #8 in the charts, Faith No More released *Album Of The Year* on June 3.

Rolling Stone's stinker of a review—'Faith No More are floundering around desperately, groping for a sense of identity and direction in a decade that clearly finds them irrelevant'—suggested that the album, already with no airplay, no hit single, and no immediate tour, would bomb on home turf, and created the impression that the record was widely panned. But many publications celebrated the album as a return to form, with some even saying it lived up to its name.

Old *BAM* and *Kerrang!* supporter Steffan Chirazi turned up in the *San Francisco Chronicle* to declare, in a four-star review, 'In naming its seventh release *Album Of The Year*, Faith No More might be attempting both self-congratulation and humour. Actually, the group may simply be telling the truth.' *NME* agreed and, in a review otherwise comprised of painful scatological puns, said, 'For once, the tongue-in-cheek title is a review in itself.'

Justin Seremet in the *Hartford-Courant* saw the bigger picture, arguing, 'Forget the radio stations too dumb to play it, Faith No More has returned with a vengeance.'

With no radio play, the album peaked at #41 on the *Billboard 200* on June 21, and exited the chart in the second week of August. Again, the chart performance was markedly different 'overseas'. The record was a #1 in Australia (again), the Czech Republic, and New Zealand. It went straight in at #7 in the UK, the second-highest new entry behind #1 Hanson. It was also top 5 in Australia, Belgium, and Norway, and top 20 in France, Sweden, and Switzerland. Thus it made sense for the band to tour in those territories in July and August of 1997.

Jon Hudson was finding his feet. His last show before 1997 had been with a friend's band two years previously in front of four people at the Berkeley Square. On July 20, he played in front of 40,000 at the Phoenix Festival in Stratford, before the headlining David Bowie.

In the summer, the band experienced a modicum of success back in the States when 'Last Cup Of Sorrow' spent several weeks hovering around the #14 spot on the *Billboard* Mainstream Rock chart, which ranked the most-played songs on 'mainstream rock radio stations'. That small sliver of success was helped by a high-concept video, based on Alfred Hitchcock's *Vertigo*. The video starred Jennifer Jason Leigh, fresh from a career-defining performance in *Georgia*, reprising Kim Novak's character, Madeleine. Mike Patton, meanwhile, put his leading-man looks to good use in taking the Jimmy Stewart/Scottie Ferguson role.

The director was twenty-four-year-old Joseph Kahn, who would go on to have a hugely successful music video career. He told *Billboard* at the time, 'The idea of Mike Patton playing Jimmy Stewart seemed funny to me. You're taking this really subversive person and putting him in this clean, sterile, Technicolor 50s world, yet pieces of the subversiveness of his persona keep coming through this world. It's like blending an old film with this totally weird 90s type of guy.'

The video was shot in San Francisco in March, and used some of the same locations as the original film. In the same article, Bill Gould explained, 'We usually pick the video treatment that's the least bad, but in this case, the idea sounded pretty good.'

PART FOUR

If 1997 was an extended funeral for Faith No More, in September they got to be witnesses at the birth of the monster they had spawned. Nu-metal.

Limp Bizkit were recruited as the band's support act for the American tour. The Fred Durst-led crew had just released their debut album, *Three Dollar Bill, Y'all*, two months previously. And, years before Durst and his backward red baseball cap became ubiquitous; years before their second album, *Significant Other*, sold a million copies in a week in the USA; and years before Rapestock, 'Nookie', and 'Break Stuff', Faith No More had already seen enough of Limp Bizkit to chafe at the idea of sharing a bill with them.

The band were approached by their management, Warren Entner and John Vassiliou, in the summer of 1997, who said, 'The promoters want you to tour with this band Limp Bizkit. There's a buzz on them.'

After discussing it among themselves, Bill Gould answered for the band: 'We'd like to research other bands.' But management quickly got to the nub of the matter, responding, 'The promoters really want Limp Bizkit. They are not so hot about taking on the band alone.' It was Limp Bizkit or nothing, so the band relented.

Prior to the tour, Faith No More played the Rockstock festival in Illinois, the last act of a fifteen-hour, twenty-band marathon alongside Limp Bizkit, Megadeth, Silverchair, and Helmet. It was another radio promotion, sponsored by WRCX Rock 103.5, and again the band bit the hand that feeds. After Dave Mustaine had spent most of the Megadeth set offering gratuitous shout-outs to the radio network, pushing back Faith No More's stage time, Gould immediately shouted to the crowd, 'How many people here listen to the radio?' prompting an immediate reply of 'The radio sucks!' from

Bottum. That was not an attitude shared by their new touring partners, with Bizkit's label infamously paying an Oregon radio station $5,000 to play their breakthrough single fifty times as a paid advertisement four months later.

Out on tour, Bizkit were not well received by Faith No More fans, but there were few issues between the bands. 'We didn't really connect as people, though they were friendly enough,' Gould remembers. 'The first night, Patton and I went into the pit to watch the band, and both of us had to concede, at least they did what they did well.'

Later on the tour, Fred Durst snapped at the audience and called them 'fags'. 'We heard it in the dressing room and were like, *Oops!*' says Gould. 'Someone from the management must have told him about Roddy right after they played, because he came backstage to apologise.'

In 2003, an advertisement for *This Is It: The Best Of Faith No More*—the second of six compilation albums that Warners and affiliates would put out in the space of eleven years—proclaimed, 'Before nu-metal was new, it was Faith No More.' That same year, *Angel Dust* was #1 in *Kerrang!*'s list of the '50 Most Influential Albums Of All Time'. The magazine was clear what influential meant: it meant they had influenced the music of the late 1990s and early 2000s, and the bands were helpfully listed out: Korn, Limp Bizkit, Glassjaw, Finch, Hundred Reasons, Incubus, System Of A Down, American Head Charge …

It is certainly clear that elements of Faith No More's various sounds were picked up on by these bands: the brief merging of rap and metal on 'Epic'; the rhythmic vocal style of 'Midlife Crisis'; the counterpointing of delicate keyboard chords to chugging riffs throughout. But equally, many of the distinctive elements of nu-metal sounded nothing like Faith No More. Faith No More never employed turntabling: never used detuned guitars; and never wrote deeply personal, emotional lyrics.

Lyrically and emotionally, Faith No More had no effect on nu-metal. Nu-metal lyrics were powered by anger, resentment, and misogyny; Faith No More's lyrics by mordancy, misery, and misanthropy. Nu-metal punched down; Faith No More punched up. Nu-metal lashed out at the world; Faith No More poked it in the eye. But nu-metal musicians fell over themselves in the genre's heyday to lay bare their debt to Faith No More.

Slipknot's Corey Taylor, who made a pilgrimage to meet Faith No

More backstage at the Download Festival in 2009, testified that Faith No More had snapped him out of a severe depression and changed the way he looked at music. Jonathan Davis, Serj Tankian, and Jacoby Shaddix have acknowledged Faith No More as an influence. But they all did so in very general terms. Davis said, 'Faith No More made it so that you could play metal and not be a hair metal or glam band. They truly started to change things.' For Davis and Durst *et al*, Faith No More did not influence their sound but their outlook. They were gatekeepers, breaking down genres. They were an affirmation that it was OK for white rock fans to listen to rap; they were a gateway for others to melding metal and hip-hop.

And what ultimately appealed to nu-metal bands from merging metal and hip-hop? As Mike Patton said in 1990, 'They can both be really aggressive. They can both be really stupid too.' And, as Australian writer Craig Schuftan argues in *Entertain Us: The Rise And Fall Of Alternative Rock In The Nineties*, 'Patton suggested that the aspects of metal and hip-hop least loved by indie intellectuals might be brought together in a form of music that combined the worst of both worlds—the mindless aggression of Megadeth with the casual misogyny of NWA, the morbid preoccupations of metal with the materialism of gangsta.'

Mike Bordin played with Korn in 2000 for a spell, and Bill Gould joined Korn's James 'Munky' Shaffer's project Fear & The Nervous System in 2008, but Patton presciently told *Metal Hammer* in 2002, 'Nu-metal makes my stomach turn. Don't blame that poo-poo on us, blame it on their mothers. Believe me, we'll all be laughing about nu-metal in a couple of years. Heck, I'm actually laughing at it now!'

Gould takes a more considered view. 'All of these bands were Faith No More fans, and really, in the late 90s, they seemed to be the only musicians cheering us. I was happy that at least our music was being appreciated by someone. On the other hand, I didn't hear much of ourselves in those bands; maybe in some instrumentation, but not so much in the humour and perspective.'

❧

Back in 1997, Faith No More's last headlining show with Limp Bizkit was at Seattle's Moore Theater on October 11. At 10:23pm, the band finished their second encore, Burt Bacharach's 'This Guy's In Love With You'. They would not play again in the United States for another twelve years, six months, and one day.

47 — IT WON'T BEGIN UNTIL YOU MAKE IT END

The band limped on for another six months, with another tour in New Zealand and Australia and further trips to Japan, Europe, and the UK to round out 1997.

Jon Hudson remembers, 'It was apparent that everyone else was ready to check out, and I was the new guy who was just getting into the situation. I knew it was all the more important for me to enjoy it as much as I could. I wasn't making any plans.'

Bill Gould adds, 'The shows were good, and the band stuck together. But, psychologically, the damage was done. I kind of gave up after that because of what they put me through to make that record. I didn't want to do it anymore. People in my band smell that, and then it was done.'

Rumours circulated online, and in San Francisco, in late January that the band would be splitting up after one final European tour. News from Portugal in the first week of February that tickets would go on sale the following week for two shows in Porto and Lisbon in April did not squash the speculation.

The band met up in late December, not long after their final 1997 tour date in Lille, to discuss whether they should continue, and whether they should take up the offers from promoters that were on the table. Mike Bordin recalls, 'I remember saying, "Yeah, I'll do a couple of things here and there but not much," and everybody said, "You know, I understand that. I agree with that. I can see that. It makes sense." It wasn't a big sort of bang, boom thing. It wasn't even a whimper. I think we were fairly on the same page.'

The band returned to action in Granada, Spain on April 4, and played Porto on April 6. Their final show came at the Coliseu dos Recreios in Lisbon the following night. The band did not know that at the time, as they crashed through their standard *Album Of The Year*-era set, adorned with covers of Deep Purple's 'Highway Star' and Vanilla Ice's 'Ice, Ice, Baby'. Sometime before midnight, at the end of their second encore, they played 'As The Worm Turns', a song from their first album—the last they would play for eleven years.

'It was a great show,' says Gould. 'We really kept it good live right up until the end.'

✻

The end came two weeks later. The exact timeline is a little murky. What is clear is that the band were mulling over the prospect of a co-headlining tour with Aerosmith in June and July. The financial offer was in the region of $500,000, which would have made it the most lucrative of their career. On April 16, details of the tour's first German show—on July 9 in Cologne— were even posted on Faith No More's website.

On July 3, when Faith No More would be playing in Denmark if they accepted the offer, the third edition of Ozzfest was due to start in New Jersey. Mike Bordin could not be in two places at once. '[Aerosmith] wasn't a lot of shows,' he recalls. 'We were asking each other whether we were going to do those or not. Maybe I had a feeling, deep down, that it might be the end, because I was already with somebody, in Ozzy, whose demands were 100 percent. If you're going to work with him, you have got to be available.'

Just one week prior to Faith No More 1.0's final shows, Roddy Bottum was in Austin at the South by Southwest Music and Media Conference for an Imperial Teen industry showcase, and he would continue working on second album *What Is Not To Love* up until June, ahead of its September release.

In April, Mike Patton was also focusing on a new project. He had composed an album's worth of new music, a structured but spasmic avant-garde-metal and hardcore hybrid—'like constant data being thrown in your face'—and had sent tapes out to Trevor Dunn from Mr Bungle, Buzz Osborne from the Melvins, and Slayer's Dave Lombardo. The band were initially named Diabolik, but by April, the new moniker of Fantômas was put in place. On April 4, Faith No More fan site *Caca Volante* and then *Metal Hammer* reported details of the project, and that the new band would be playing shows in July.

On April 12 the *San Francisco Chronicle*'s 'Datebook' section featured a small item headlined 'Faith No More's Patton has new band':

> Faith No More's idiosyncratic frontman Mike Patton is close to unveiling his own supergroup. So where does that leave Faith No More? Insiders say Aerosmith asked the veteran band to open for it on upcoming US dates, but the offer was declined—because most of the members are ready to give up the ghost. In addition, Patton has confided to friends that after FNM returns on Friday from a string of festivals in Portugal and Spain, his commitment to the band is over. No matter what Faith No More's future is, Patton is making plans to debut his band in San Francisco in July. After that, look for the hometown group to play showcases in Los Angeles and New York to generate label interest.

With the Aerosmith offer—for Europe, rather than the US—on the table, Patton seemingly on the cusp of moving on, and Bordin mulling over his Ozzy Osbourne future, Gould called Bordin, Bottum, and Patton to a band meeting at his house in the city for later in the week. Last man in Jon Hudson was not invited.

The meeting turned into a wake. Patton arrived at Gould's with a bottle of champagne. He dramatically popped the cork and offered his bandmates a glass, declaring, 'Guys, it's been a beautiful experience.' Bordin refused to accept the glass. Bottum took a glass, and so did Gould, joining in the toast. But the Faith No More bassist counselled Patton to manage the situation collectively, telling him, 'Tell you what. Be smart about this, OK? Don't quit the band. Let's do this properly. We've worked together. We've been through all this shit. We do it as a unit.'

The following day, Gould awoke to a stream of calls from journalists, asking, 'Is it true? Do you have any statements?' Patton had released a press release firming up his Fantômas plans, and announcing a debut concert at Slim's in San Francisco for June 18.

Days later, on 20 April, Bordin called the rest of the band to confirm that he would not be able to take up the Aerosmith tour offer, preferring instead to play at Ozzfest. Gould says, 'Puffy got this thing with Ozzy, and it was a case of which one are you going to pick? And he picked Ozzy. He called me up and said, "It's not my fault, but we're cancelling the tour. It's over." I said, "Well, if you do that, that's the end of the band."'

Gould's bluntness stemmed from the knowledge that the band, especially with other members more interested in other projects, could not continue with the loss of another member, especially not a founding member. Gould's reaction was to call Patton, to call manager Warren Entner, and to ask his girlfriend to put on a strong cup of coffee. He scrambled together a statement.

> After fifteen long and fruitful years, Faith No More have decided to put an end to speculation regarding their imminent breakup … by breaking up. The decision among the members is mutual, and there will be no pointing of fingers, no naming of names, other than stating, for the record, that 'Puffy started it.' Furthermore, the split will now enable each member to pursue his individual projects unhindered. Lastly, and most importantly, the band would like to thank all of those fans and associates that have stuck with and supported the band throughout its history.

❧

The split garnered Faith No More the sort of worldwide media coverage that had eluded them since *The Real Thing*. The *New York Times* provided some light relief in its explanation of the statement: 'Puffy did not refer to the ubiquitous rapper and executive Puffy Combs but to the band's drummer, Mike (Puffy) Bordin, who decided to play drums behind Ozzy Osbourne on the Ozzfest this summer.'

'For the Aerosmith dates, it just didn't work out timing-wise that I could do them,' Bordin says. 'It was certainly nothing like a fuck-you or anything like that. I was super-grateful and proud that I was able to go and play with

Ozzy. It came down to the fact that I could either work for the big boss [Osbourne] for this block of time, or take these dates with my guys, and then nothing after that was guaranteed anyway. It wasn't much of a choice at that time.' (In a curious twist of fate, the Aerosmith concerts that brought issues to a head were cancelled when Steven Tyler injured his knee on April 29.)

Roddy Bottum finished recording his second album with Imperial Teen within two weeks of the announcement of the end of Faith No More:

> I think we were all looking for an out, and were a little bit spent and fed up. Initially, it was a relief when we broke up. I was trying to do Imperial Teen, and I was only able to give it half of what I should have, and it was the same with Faith No More. I was going back and forth and not committing either way. The vibe was that way with most of us in the band. It's a long and difficult haul to do what we did.
>
> Billy and I had been friends since we were ten years old. To follow the course of what it takes to get success with a band: the touring, the business, the artistic decisions, the proximity factor, the growing up, it's an awful lot to ask of young men. It was fifteen years of really hard work. Really, really hard work. I mean, great times and super amazing achievements, but it was a huge chunk of our lives that was very trying.

Mike Patton had barely time to take stock, as he prepared for a series of summer shows with a new band that had never all been in the same place, never mind played music together. 'The band had to break up, otherwise there would've been all that anger garbage,' he said. 'It was very civilised: we decided together in one room. The thing that was amazing was that we all turned that page together. I was afraid that there would be people disagreeing that it was time to end. It was almost a let-down.'

Jon Hudson's reaction was philosophical: 'I didn't want to stop. But I knew if I continued, it had to be something else, so I bought some more equipment, and started working on some ideas on my own.'

Bill Gould concludes, 'It was really hard for me, because I had nowhere to go. This was my thing. This was who I was.'

For Faith No More fans, after the group's disbandment—with apologies to Douglas Adams—for years, nothing happened. Then, after a day or so, nothing continued to happen.

It was, of course, different for the individual members of Faith No More themselves. They moved on. Mike Patton was busy with Fantômas for the remainder of 1998. In 1999, after initial major label interest in releasing their debut album turned lukewarm, he set up his own label, Ipecac Recordings, with Greg Werckman. Over the years, Ipecac has released records by the Melvins, Queens Of The Stone Age, The Young Gods, and Omar Rodríguez-López, among many more, plus several Patton projects including Fantômas, Tomahawk, and Peeping Tom.

Patton told the *CMJ New Music Report* at the time, 'I was nervous starting this label. I didn't think it was the right time for me. I was too busy making music, why should I want to run a label now?' He admitted that support from Werckman and John Zorn and especially Buzz Osborne (whose band, the Melvins, put out two albums on Ipecac in 1999, and would go on to release another twelve on the label) convinced him that Ipecac was the right move. Later in 1999, he said, 'Ipecac is not just about artistic freedom, it is also a business opportunity. It's a way to put out records we like, and hope others do too. We go in with modest expectations and with no one else to blame. Greg and I have been in this industry a long time. Why not do it ourselves?'

Also doing it himself was Bill Gould, who set up his own label, Koolarrow Records, in 2000. While Ipecac has been 'making people sick since 1999', Koolarrow sought to bring 'light and ears to a diverse range of music'. It was a learning experience, as Gould explains:

I was doing Koolarrow Records, which was working with bands that are pretty obscure. I was their label, so I had to learn how distribution worked, had to learn how PR worked, had to learn how accounting worked. I had to meet the guy who was doing my media in the UK, had to learn who my salespeople were in France and go meet them. The fact that I was in Faith No More meant nothing to most of these people.

There were bands that didn't have the experience that I had, so they needed my help. I took on the role of being their manager, as well as their label. We got involved in all of their plans, all of their touring, all of their PR, all their artwork. I'd try to do it as cheaply as possible, so I would mix their records, and it would be for free. I'd help them with the artwork and do it for free. My wife did graphics. I was working my ass off, non-stop. It was nine years of boot camp, but absolutely fantastic.

The label—more by accident than design—focused on artists from outside the Anglophone world, releasing records by jazz and hip-hop fusion act Chilean Como Asesinar A Felipes and Dubioza Kolektiv, the Bosnian political pop ska outfit.

Gould also found time to travel, spending two months in Lapland in Finland, producing the band CMX in 1997, then living in Barcelona for a year at the start of the millennium, and then in Paris for six months. He also wrote music. 'I am blessed or cursed with the fact that when I write music, it sounds like Faith No More,' he says. 'Everything I tried to do outside of that still sounded like that band. I never had the maturity to figure out that who I was wasn't what I did in this band. I saw myself as the same person. It took me ten years to figure it out. I got to a point where I was just going to keep writing music the way I write. I'm just going to record other bands, and learn how to get better at what I do. I let go that Faith No More was going to happen.'

That learning experience saw him producing—as well as CMX and the Russian band Naive in 1997—German bands Think About Mutation and The Beatsteaks, and Kultur Shock, among others.

Mike Bordin went straight into action with Ozzy Osbourne, and, in

1997, found himself double-jobbing during Ozzfest, playing with Ozzy and then filling in for Bill Ward for some shows with Black Sabbath. In total, Bordin would end up playing in the Ozzy Osbourne band for fifteen years—the same length of time he spent in Faith No More 1.0. 'I had been in a band where the music was ours, the responsibility was ours, the T-shirts, artwork, ticket sales, promotional, advertising, interviews, videos, everything you did was related back to us, and it was our responsibility. Going up there, you put Ozzy's name on the thing, and he's got a band who he plays with, and you do your job good and keep your shit together, but it's about him. I loved that, because I could just play the drums. That was so fucking liberating.'

Roddy Bottum's immediate focus, post-breakup, was on Imperial Teen. Second album *What Is Not To Love* was released in September 1998 to widespread critical acclaim, and Roddy also opened for Hole on their subsequent tour, and, in 1999, played a club tour. He told the *Record* that year, 'I love the intimacy of playing small venues. Faith No More started playing some places that were just too big. You felt so removed from everyone.'

Imperial Teen released another album, *On*, on Merge Records in 2002, and later in the 2000s, Roddy moved into television and film scoring. His first film project was the romantic comedy *Adam & Steve* in 2005, and the transition to film composing was an eye-opening experience, as he explained to the *Hollywood Reporter* in 2008.

'I was coming from a band that had sold millions of records, so I assumed that I'd get work quickly,' he admitted. 'I learned that the band cachet gets you a little respect in your first interview, but it doesn't guarantee work. And when you do get work, you have to put your ego aside. You have to get used to people saying, no, that's not right, which you may not have ever heard in a band. My bands have built careers out of doing things on their own terms, but you certainly don't build a career in film composing that way.'

Jon Hudson, meanwhile, embraced writing and composing. Eventually, in 2000, he got together with Gould to start working on music, with Bordin soon invited to join. This Faith No More trio took the name Castro Sinatra, and news broke on fan forums in late November 2000 that three members of the band were working on an album, to be released on Koolarrow. Gould and Hudson spent a total of eighteen months on the project, Bordin a little less, going so far as to record some tracks in Gould's home studio, but the record was shelved, as Gould recalls. 'We got into a little bit of a whirlpool or a wormhole with that one. It just wasn't right. It wasn't good enough.'

Hudson adds, 'With the absence of a vocalist for the ideas to really solidify around, we knew that it was not coming together.'

The Castro Sinatra experience was the nearest Faith No More would come to regenerating for some considerable time. Outside of that project, the band members spent little time together, even socially. They had other priorities. Patton's creativity and curiosity knew no bounds. He released another album with Mr Bungle, three more with Fantômas, three with Tomahawk, and one with Peeping Tom. He appeared on five John Zorn albums, and four more with the Zorn-composed Moonchild Trio. He made a second solo album, the Italian-language, culinary-themed *Pranzo Oltranzista*. He also moved into film composition, producing his first two film scores, *A Perfect Place* and *Crank 2: High Voltage*, in this time. He made his film acting debut in *Firecracker*, and provided the otherworldly alien voices in the film *I Am Legend*. He collaborated with other artists. He worked with Dillinger Escape Plan, Lovage, and Kaada. He worked with Sepultura, he worked with Björk. He worked with The X-Ecutioners. He worked with Praxis, Foetus, and Zu. He worked with Handsome Boy Modeling School and Serj Tankian. He worked with the Dub Trio, too. In 2002, he explained what drove his love of collaboration to Portuguese newspaper *Jornal de Notícias*: 'Curiosity, mere curiosity, the desire to get out of stereotyped routines and scenes, to do something different, and to try to go further.'

Faith No More fans had their appetites occasionally whetted by repeated record company cash-ins on the band's catalogue. The band's sole involvement in the 1998 *Who Cares A Lot?* release was Gould's suggestion that the track list should be based on a 'Faith No More Greatest Hits' bootleg he found at Moscow's Garbushka Market. Promotion included a single release for the band's cover of The Bee Gees' 'I Started A Joke' in September 1998. Billed as the band's final single, it was originally released as a B-side to 'Digging The Grave', and had been recorded in late 1995 in Gould's studio, with Dean Menta on guitar.

❖

It took weddings in 2006 and 2008 to bring the prospect of a Faith No More reunion closer. The band's manager, Warren Entner, was married in Mexico in November 2006. There, Gould and Bottum began to repair their fractured friendship.

'I would say that after what Roddy went through with the drug experience, there was a lack of communication,' says Gould. 'Not quite being honest with each other. And then through the whole thing where he wasn't very transparent on what his plans were with his band, I lost trust a little bit. I definitely didn't feel inclined to want to see him, and I didn't really reconnect back with him until Warren got married. I went to the wedding, and Roddy was there and we hung out the whole weekend. It was really great. We hadn't really spoken like people in a long time, even maybe back since the *King For A Day* time.'

Meanwhile, Bordin, Bottum, and Patton reconnected at Roddy's own wedding, which took place in the back yard of his mother's house in Los Angeles in 2008. Patton and Bordin, who were sat at the same table, had barely seen each other for a decade.

'I talked to Bill very rarely,' Bordin recalls,' and he wasn't so receptive to the contact. If I ever did have occasion for contact, it was polite and fine. And I'd see Mike at the grocery store here or there, and it was fine. Bill wasn't at the wedding. The dynamic very well could've been different if he was. The deal there was that nobody needed anything from anybody, and we just sat there and enjoyed ourselves.'

Roddy told *Rolling Stone*, 'Ten years later, and to sit down in such an environment like that and have it be a comfortable, casual, easy-going place? We're still such a valid part in each other's lives, despite what went on and how difficult things became. Just even the acknowledgment of that, this is an OK thing. Us being in a physical space together. It's doable.'

Things began happening after the initial meeting. Bordin recalls, 'Warren brought up the subject saying, "You know, there's offers. Maybe you should talk about them."'

Gould wasn't at the wedding. He had been invited, but at the time he was travelling throughout the Balkan region with his wife. 'I was driving from Dubrovnik on the Croatian coast and staying in some hotel halfway up the coast,' he recalls. 'I had got there, found it had internet, plugged in my computer, and saw I had an email from Warren saying, *Where are you? Can I call you?* And I gave him the number of the hotel. He said, "Are you sitting down? Patton says he might be up for doing some shows."'

49   WE SERVED YOU WELL, NOW WE'RE COMING BACK

In the previous ten years, Patton had been the most publicly dismissive of the prospect of the band reuniting. In 2006, he said, 'Every four or five years, some Svengali who thinks he can change the world comes with a briefcase full of cash and makes a crazy offer. And it's not easy to refuse. It would be very easy for some of us to rehearse for a couple of days, smile, and cash the cheques. I'm not at that point. I got enough things on my plate. Maybe if he comes with two briefcases full of money.'

But, by January 2008, he had mellowed. Quizzed on the possibility of a reunion to mark the twentieth anniversary of *The Real Thing*, he said, 'I wouldn't rule it out.'

When he heard from Warren Entner in Croatia in 2008, Gould's immediate reaction was reluctance. 'I was very, very sceptical,' he explains. 'I didn't take it that seriously. I wasn't even sure how I felt about it.' So unconvinced was he that, in December 2008, when rumours that club owners in the UK were being sounded out about a possible reunion tour, he publicly shot them down, telling *Kerrang!*, 'If anything like this were to happen, it would have to come from the band, and I haven't spoken with any of them in over a year.'

After hearing more reports of a possible reunion, however, Gould called Patton, and the pair agreed to meet at a nearby coffee shop. Like Robert de Niro and Al Pacino in *Heat*, Gould and Patton, both coffee connoisseurs, faced off at the Samovar café on a street corner in the Castro district—within walking distance of both their homes.

After the pair exchanged pleasantries, Gould launched straight into the matter at hand: 'What are you doing? Everyone tells me this is coming from you. What the fuck is going on?' There was no rancour, though, and Patton, slightly taken aback, explained, 'I don't know what … that's fucked up, somebody said that? There's no way it's coming from me.'

Ice broken, suspicions eased, the pair just started talking. Catching up with things. Patton told Gould about Roddy's wedding, Gould about his travelling. There was no commitment to a reunion, but days later, Warren Entner invited Gould and Patton, and Bordin and Bottum, up to his house in Los Angeles for lunch—salads all round—and to float the possibility of a reunion.

'We went to Warren's house,' Gould recalls, 'and everybody was acting like they were in the band again. Everybody were just the same old guys that they used to be, and everybody went into their Faith No More band member roles. Already the dynamic was like that, while we're sitting and eating lunch. The body language was already, *OK, so this is happening then.*'

Bottum adds, 'Warren saw an opportunity to get us back together, and presented the idea to us. We'd all spent time together recently, and weren't closed to the idea. It felt good to be in the same room, and we moved forward on it.'

❀

Another key driver toward a reunion was the UK's Download Festival, the world's biggest rock and metal festival. Andy Copping had helped create the festival in 2003, and was the event's festival booker and head of UK touring at Live Nation, one of the world's leading events promoters. In early 2008, as he had done on a few previous occasions, he sounded out Patton's management about the prospect of a reunited Faith No More playing at the festival's 2008 edition at Donington Park in the UK Midlands.

Copping explains, 'I was always a big fan of Faith No More, and was lucky enough to promote a number of their shows in the early days of *The Real Thing* and *Angel Dust*. The band hadn't played together for a long time, and I felt that if we could put an attractive proposal together to present to key members of the band, they might consider it.'

According to Copping, the deal to take Faith No More to Download was agreed long before the band officially announced their reunion. 'The whole negotiation from start to finish took about a year, and that was understandable—the band didn't exist at the time of my first enquiry. We probably "inked" the deal in around November 2008.'

Certainly, the financial offer to play Download was the most lucrative of the band's career, although according to Bottum, 'Download wasn't really anything to me. It was more about us getting together musically, revisiting what we'd done that seemed therapeutic and inspiring. At the time, I had no idea we'd make any money off it. I just wanted an opportunity to hang and create, and readdress what had gone sour.'

❧

There was one crucial matter to resolve first: who was the guitarist? The band were torn between Jim Martin, who had played on their first four records, and Jon Hudson, their most recent guitarist. They decided that they would at least sound out Martin, and gauge how he felt.

Bottum called him in early February. 'Jim was approached,' he recalls, 'but it felt like he was into it for the wrong reasons. I could be totally off base here. His decision would have been harder than ours. The whole *fired by fax* thing, and the way that he was let go must have been an incredibly difficult obstacle for him to get over. Maybe, he put his *professional* foot forward in talking to us, and it came across as kind of distasteful, and not where the rest of us were coming from.'

'Jim was not showing any cards,' Gould adds, 'just saying he wanted to do it. Saying that he had no problem playing somebody else's music—it flagged our suspicions. We thought that we've got this really good thing, and it is fragile. And with Jim, it just seems like you're bringing this random energy, and have no idea where you're going. I would rather just have Jon. Jon did a great job before, and he actually played on the last record.'

Naturally, Martin's version of events is slightly different. In 2012, in a fan Q&A, he told the Faith No More blog:

> For some time during 2008, I had been receiving information with increasing frequency that 'we' were booking a reunion

tour, festivals, Europe. I was informed that, yes, the promoters were selling it as the original line-up. In February 2009, Roddy called and said they were just beginning to think of putting something together, and just now feeling out everyone, and what did I think? I said, yes, I was interested. I also told him I knew the tour was already booked, they were on the eve of announcing it, and it was time to sign the deals. I told him to send over the contracts, so I could review them, and started pressing management for details. Several days later, I was able to get management on the phone, who told me they decided to use someone else.

Hudson, meanwhile, was delighted to be asked to be part of the reunion. 'It really was unfinished business for me, because even though we had toured for about a year, I still felt like I was just getting started.'

On February 19, the cat was out of the bag. Metal site *Blabbermouth* reported that rumours of a reunion were mounting, and added, 'A source close to guitarist Jim Martin, who was in the group from 1983 until 1993, has told *Blabbermouth* that the axeman expressed interest in taking part in the reunion after being recently contacted by keyboardist Roddy Bottum and a member of Faith No More's management team, but that the band inexplicably decided to utilise a different guitarist.'

'That was a big flag for us,' says Gould, 'because then we realised that the knife was out of the sheath, it was just under his coat, but we hadn't seen it. And it seemed to confirm to us that we had made the right move.'

The official announcement of the reunion was further pre-empted on February 23 when—in one of the greatest examples of burying the lede in public relations history—a Mike Patton publicist issued a press release to announce that Patton would be scoring *Crank 2: High Voltage*. The 220-word missive ended with details of Patton's forthcoming schedule, and thirteen words that were music to the ears of millions of Faith No More fans: 'The highly anticipated reunion tour with Faith No More in Europe this summer.'

The following day, the band issued their official statement. It concluded, 'We find ourselves at a moment in time with zero label obligations, still young and strong enough to deliver a kick-ass set, with enthusiasm to not only revisit our past but possibly add something to the present. And so with this we've decided to hold our collective breaths and jump off this cliff … back, God forbid, into the monkey cage.'

50   RISE OF THE FALL

The Download Festival may have been a key factor in the reunion, but the first European dates announced, on March 2, were for the twin German festivals of Hurricane and Southside in June. That, and Download's confirmation one day later of its June 14 dates, saw dates fall like dominoes. For the band, the pressure was on.

'The band hadn't performed once in over ten years,' says Hudson. 'After all that time, what were we setting ourselves up for?'

'My take was always, *Let's play in a room and see how it feels*,' says Bordin. '*Let's play the songs and see if we can relate to them. Let's play with each other and see if we're speaking the same language.*'

In late March, Bordin, Hudson, and Gould did just that, going into a rehearsal space, which would later become their Estudio Koolarrow, in Emeryville, across the Bay from San Francisco. In April, they were joined by Bottum, and they started honing their efforts and putting together a twenty-song set for their initial shows. Lessons had been learned, and as part of their collective agreement for the reunion tour, the band decided to limit tour runs to two weeks at a time and to do no press interviews, though they embraced fan sites and social media, especially Twitter, to get information out. It was via Gould's Twitter account in early May that the band announced that their first show would be a return to Brixton Academy on June 10.

The reasoning was not completely sentimental. 'We wanted to do a show before we played this huge stage,' Gould says. 'We needed to do something to get in the groove.'

✦

The streets and pubs around the Brixton Academy were thronged with long-haired and grey-haired and no-haired fans—almost universally clad in black T-shirts—and there was an almost palpable air of expectation allied to apprehension in the hours before that Brixton return. Inside, the support act, local punks Selfish Cunt, were subject to pantomime booing, and the occasional thrown bottle by the impatient and expectant crowd.

About twenty minutes after the support finished their set, Bordin, Bottum, Gould, Hudson, and Patton formed a huddle at the side of the stage as they prepared to make their entrance. A little after 10:30pm, as the lights dimmed, vociferous chants of 'You Fat Bastards' broke out, finally stilled by the first unfamiliar notes on Bottum's keyboards.

Was this a new song? After ninety seconds of darkness and light instrumentation, the lights came up, and Patton—clad in an ill-fitting peach suit, peach shirt, and peach tie, his black hair slicked back—delicately, breathily, and soulfully sang:

> *The breakup we had*
> *Has made me lonesome and sad*
> *I realise I love you 'cause*
> *I miss you bad, hey, hey.*

As Bottum took over vocals for the second verse, screams and cheers rang out; acclamation, relief, and elation urgently needing expression. The cover of Peaches & Herb's 1978 smash 'Reunited' was perfectly judged, as was Patton's greeting to the crowd: 'What's going on, fuckheads?' He then responded to another chorus of 'You Fat Bastards' with 'You say that now, and it's actually true.' The twenty-four-song setlist threw up some other gems, including the rarely played 'Jizzlobber', 'Malpractice', and 'Mark Bowen'.

The band's look also hit home. The coordinated pastel suits, complete with flower buttonholes, evoked a recondite wedding band—a subtle rejoinder to the funereal black-suited attire of the *Album Of The Year* era.

One week before the show, Gould went in search of stage attire. The original quest was to find some zoot suits as a departure from the suits of 1997–98, so Gould headed to Mission Street, to the city's number-one zoot suit store, Spiegels. But something else caught his eye: 'I saw these really cheap suits. Pastel suits, all different colours. There were five different kinds of suits in five different colours. And I said, Oh, we have to do those!'

Gould emailed photos to the rest of the band, and, later that day and the following morning, the rest of the band made their way, one after the other, to the store and picked out their suits. The following afternoon, Patton was the last to go in, and, as he was paying for his clothes, aware that the 2008 crash was killing retail, he politely asked the cashier, 'How's business been?' The sales clerk replied, 'It really hasn't been very good at all, but it's really started picking up in the last twenty-four hours.'

Back in Brixton, the band brought the 5,000 in attendance down gently, with a second encore of 'I Started A Joke', plus 'Pristina' to finish.

'There was tension, there was emotion, it was exciting,' Bordin recalls. '"Reunited" was perfect for us, because it's silly and sappy. It's also heartfelt, and genuine. I loved it, and again, who else could sing it like that?'

'That show was weird for me,' says Gould. 'I think all of us, our minds went blank; we forgot how to play certain things. It was a surreal experience, really strange. I blanked out. Fucking surreal as hell.'

Three days after Brixton, Faith No More headlined Download in front of 40,000 people. The band were coming back to greater interest and acclaim than when they had departed.

They were also surrounded by bands who claimed Faith No More's influence and lineage. Korn and Limp Bizkit were the two bands on the main stage immediately before Faith No More, and Slipknot were the Saturday night headliners. Andy Copping recalls, 'I had been told that Corey Taylor had wanted to come to Download the day before, and hang out and to specifically see Faith No More. Corey came down, hung out, watched loads of bands, and mainly watched Faith No More. Following their performance, Corey came up to me and asked if it would be possible to meet Mike Bordin.'

Copping duly took Taylor to meet the drummer—'Corey was like a young kid meeting his idol'—and then to meet Patton. 'Corey was again in awe at one of his heroes. Following the conversation, Corey came away and over to me, and he was crying. He said to me that he couldn't believe that he had met Mike Bordin and Mike Patton, and he was totally overcome with emotion.'

✹

Faith No More were staying circumspect. 'I was watching, and trying to observe everything to try to find out what the fuck was really going on,' says Gould. 'The next time we came to the UK was three months later [for the Reading Festival], and it was raining, and we weren't headlining the main stage. Our dressing room had three bottles of water, and we had to share a toilet with eighteen bands.'

They were also observing how things had changed since they left the scene in 1998. 'Things were very, very different,' he adds. 'Backstage was completely boring. Completely changed. But, to tell you the truth, I was so worried about having enough energy to make it through an hour and a half with full power, I didn't care. It's all worked out like a business, and even when we do our own shows, it feels like that. But, then again, we're a bunch of fifty-year-old men.'

With forty-six shows in 2009, the band would have some new experiences, playing for the first time in Latvia, Russia, Bulgaria, Romania, Greece, Turkey, and Peru. The Peru date was part of an October and November tour of South America that inevitably included two dates in Chile—including a standalone show at Santiago's Estadio Bicentenario de La Florida in front of 25,000 people.

One year after announcing their reformation, thoughts within the band were turning to new music. 'The discussion first came up in 2010, down in Australia and New Zealand,' says Jon Hudson, referring to the band's ten Antipodean shows in February and March that year. 'After one of the shows, the question came up: what do we do at this point? Because it's been almost a year on the go, just playing the existing material. Is this what it's going to be? There wasn't any talk about doing another record or anything like that. But the seed was planted. Like, *OK, do we put something else out now?* If this is nothing more than an ongoing reunion of the old stuff, then we should start treating it as such. Otherwise, we owe it to ourselves to get what we need from it.'

As much as there were false starts, there were also false endings. The band played thirty shows in 2010, including six of their own in the United States, either side of a headlining appearance at the Coachella Festival, but they announced in September that another Estadio Bicentenario de La Florida show on December 5 would be their last. Two Hollywood Palladium shows a few days earlier had the air of a farewell party, but did also see Sparks joining the band onstage for 'This Town's Not Big Enough For The Both Of Us' (Faith No More having played on a reprise of the song on Sparks' *Plagiarism* album in 1997), while Sparks touring guitarist Dean Menta re-joined Faith No More for a performance of 'Digging The Grave'.

In Santiago, the band played a cover of The Manhattans' 'Kiss And Say Goodbye', the fifty-seventh different song of the Second Coming tour. The song ended with Patton, his shirt already ripped open from an earlier foray into the crowd, singing the final chorus, before diving back onto a beseeching forest of hands, and into the crowd.

❦

It was a mere caesura. The band's creative itch was getting more difficult to ignore. Bill Gould recalls, 'I was like, *This is great that we've all connected, but I need to do creative stuff.* I was always hands-on where this band is concerned. I'm just that guy, and if I'm putting all this energy and effort into it, I need something. I need some oxygen. It was one of those things like, *Don't ask. Don't tell. Don't bring up new music. Don't talk about it.*'

Then, in July 2011, as the band were preparing for the South American dates, Gould broke cover. 'Finally I thought, *Fuck it, man, I'm just going to fucking say it*: I got a song. Do you guys want to hear it? Stop talking about fucking covers all the time and think of doing some fucking music? And everybody was like, *Yeah, sure, great.*'

Gould had worked out most of the song, tentatively called 'Matador', and played it for the rest of the band in Emeryville. Hudson remembers, 'The arrangements weren't there and the vocals weren't there yet, but I mean, he had something pretty specific completely drawn. But the most important part of it was that we got the excitement. We had something new.'

Gould adds, 'The band goes, Let's learn it. If I knew that was going to be that fucking easy, I would have done it a lot earlier.'

When the song was performed for the first time in Buenos Aires on November 8 2011, speculation abounded on what the brooding, piano-led song could be. An *Angel Dust* offcut? An obscure cover? A Tomahawk song re-purposed? Two days later, *Spin* declared it had solved the mystery of the mystery song, as it was then known to Faith No More fans: 'As it turns out, its identity has been revealed as an old, unreleased leftover from the sessions from their underrated 1995 record *King For A Day ... Fool For A Lifetime*, an album they're playing in its entirety tomorrow in Santiago, Chile.'

'We said nothing on purpose,' Bordin recalls. 'Literally, zero. Then *Spin* said they confirmed that it was an outtake from *King For A Day*. We didn't even deny it. There was nothing to say, nothing to sell.'

As much as Faith No More were moving on, they were also taking the time to revisit their past, and repair ruptures and right wrongs. That Santiago *King For A Day* special featured a guest appearance throughout from Trey Spruance. 'Revisiting it twenty years later, doing the show in Chile with him, we set a lot of shit straight,' says Bordin. 'I think that there's a good understanding now. The relationship is healed.'

✽

Even after revealing 'Matador', Gould remained frustrated at the band's inertia. 'It was like, *OK, we did one song; that was enough*. And I was like, *What do you mean, that was enough? That's just the fucking start, man*. But you couldn't talk to anybody about it, because they just wouldn't answer you.'

In April 2012, Gould bit the bullet. He and Bordin went into the band's Emeryville rehearsal space, and starting playing. Gould had miked up Bordin's drums, and the pair starting playing beats and pulses and firing off each other, like they had first done in 1983.

'We didn't go in there wanting to make a record,' says Bordin. 'Bill said, You want to play some drums? I said, OK, fine, I'll play some drums. He had some ideas, and I had a little idea here or there. And it happened that way.'

Soon, the pair had the skeleton of 'Superhero' together, and they got Hudson on board. Then, Bottum also came on board, and sent five tracks from his new base in New York.

The outside world remained oblivious, more focused on the band's handful of live dates in 2012. In Moscow on 2 July, Faith No More arranged for five members of Pussy Riot, the punk protest collective, to take to the stage before the second encore. They chanted anti-government slogans and called for the release of Pussy Riot members Nadezhda Tolokonnikova, Yekaterina Samutsevich, and Maria Alyokhina, who had been imprisoned after their protests against Vladimir Putin protest in Moscow's Christ the Saviour Cathedral earlier that year.

Faith No More decided to invite Pussy Riot just the night before. 'My buddy Sasha Ivanov was in contact with Pussy Riot's "manager", and we invited him to come join us for dinner,' says Gould. 'He broke down their situation, and how there were still six or seven members that had not been arrested. It seemed like a no-brainer to have them do a quick hit and run onstage after our set, to bring attention to their upcoming court case. We also made a pact to keep it secret and not to tell anyone.'

However, at soundcheck the following day, band manager Tim Moss (who had taken over management duties in 2010) informed them that the owner of the venue was aware of their plans, and forbid any political protest, Gould adds:

> That was odd, and raised some alarm bells in our camp. We had some spirited debates on whether to go ahead with it, with some of the guys dead against it. The girls themselves were very young, and it was obvious that they were very smart, and that they were doing everything on their own, with no backup. That's what swayed it for me. The pro-Pussy Riot camp prevailed.
>
> It was not a victory by any means. The audience became angry and abusive, began yelling at the girls, who pushed right back without a trace of fear. It was crazy and intimidating. On

first glance, it felt like this move had the completely opposite effect from what we intended, but then, privately, quite a few people approached us and whispered, 'Thank you.'

✸

Faith No More had a complete break from live shows in 2013. Even as the band were composing and arranging songs, fans were again fearing the worst. Especially when Mike Patton was asked about the reunion in an interview with *The Believer* in January that year: 'There's a lineage of bands that maybe did some nice things, and then needed the cash and got back together, and basically just sprayed diarrhoea over their entire body of work. We're very worried about that. We don't want to overdo it.'

UNCONQUERED
SUN

51

By the middle of 2013, Bordin, Bottum, Gould, and Hudson, if not quite overdoing it, had put together a suite of songs, and were ready for the next step. 'Puffy, Jon, and I, and then Roddy came in, because we were sending stuff back and forth with him, we were still working,' says Gould. 'It sounded really good. We liked what we were getting. And then it got to the point where it was: *Is Mike P. going to do it or not?*'

There was genuine apprehension, according to Gould. 'We didn't want to go there with him, because we didn't know what he thought about us. He never really told us. But, at some point, we had to tell him, because if he wasn't singing, we didn't have a band, and we didn't have a record. We didn't approach him until after most of the stuff was recorded in demo form.

But then Patton came over to the studio, and I played him a bunch of stuff.'

'I was pretty flattered, to be honest,' Patton told *Rolling Stone*. 'Not only did the shit sound fucking great, the amount of work that had already gone into it at that point was touching. It definitely caught me off guard in a great way, in an ass-kicking way. This music is still vital and didn't feel nostalgic at all.'

Gould recalls, 'There was no resistance. He liked it and he was like, *You want me to sing on it?* which was kind of weird. But I said, Yes! Please!'

❋

The band were operating on their own, and in virtual secrecy. With no labels, no managers, no publicists, no producers, no engineers, there was no external pressure, and there were no obligations. As such, the drive to record music was organic. There was a collective creative impulse. Theoretically, the band could have traded on the past, but, practically, that was never a possibility. The band were moving forward, not looking back.

Going it alone meant that Gould found himself in the role of engineer and producer, as well as bassist and songwriter. As always, the band thrived on limitations. The improvised studio space, the fact that the studio console and playing area had no separation, the sounds of trucks going past outside, and the slightly out-of-tune studio piano that had belonged to Bordin's grandmother, were all embraced.

By the end of 2013, the band were ready to record, as Gould explains:

> The demo sounded pretty good, so rather than book studio time and have anybody know that we're doing this, I knew I could probably get some good tones in our space and experiment— and we did. We know each other, let's just play. It's a pleasure working like that. There's no sterile room you're in. There's no so-called professionalism, or outside people judging what you're doing, which effects how you record. We liked it.
>
> I knew it was going to be a lot of work. That was the biggest hesitation going into this, because I felt that last time I didn't get a lot of support from everybody. That's the worst place to be in when you're going to take all the responsibility for the failure.

My life is pretty chaotic, but when it comes to making music, I'm an absolute perfectionist. It's scary to go in a situation like that, where you realise that it's not finished until you're happy with it, and you're your worst critic. I was super-scared about that.

✦

In early May 2014, rumours reached Faith No More fan sites that the band were working on new music in their rehearsal space. Then, on May 30, the band hinted at new music publicly with a tweet from the band account that stated, 'The reunion thing was fun, but now it's time to get a little creative.'

On July 4, Faith No More were in London as support for Black Sabbath at the British Summertime Festival at Hyde Park. They were third on the bill under Sabbath and Soundgarden, they were playing their first concert in two years, and they were playing at the incongruous time of 5:15pm in the evening sun in front of a crowd of tipsy, superannuated metalheads. For Faith No More, there could be no more apposite time to play more new music. And, at a little after 6pm, the band—all, except Puffy, dressed in all-black Catholic priests' garb, complete with collarinos—did just that. They finished their main set with 'Superhero', then kicked off their encore with 'Motherfucker'.

On November 28, 'Motherfucker' was released as a single for Record Store Day, two weeks after the band had made it available for streaming. The song, like the subsequent album, was released on the band's own imprint, Reclamation Recordings, and distributed by Ipecac Recordings. The release was triply audacious. Its title was a swear word; it was not sung by Mike Patton, but by Roddy Bottum; and it was released on Black Friday (also the name of a song on *Sol Invictus*), taking aim at crass consumerism.

Bottum, who wrote the music and lyrics for the song, explains that it was 'one of the first songs we finished, and it summed up in a weird way our career and accountability, and the responsibility of moving forward. It just made sense.' It also 'didn't have Patton, which was kind of contrarian, which we liked,' Gould adds. 'After twelve years, the first song we put out doesn't have Patton on the main vocals. A lot of people reacted like, *Why would you release a song called that, it will never get on commercial radio. Why?* I thought it was an interesting reaction, because we didn't really think we were going to get on commercial radio anyway.'

❋

'Motherfucker' was mixed by Gould at Estudio Koolarow, but he baulked at mixing the rest of the album and instead called in an old friend and professional partner, Matt Wallace. 'I'm engineering the shit, I'm writing the shit, arranging the shit,' Gould says. 'And then hearing every fucking error, because I'm looking at every wave form. Now you can zoom in on wave forms, and you can look at things to a certain amount of detail you never could before. And, once your eyes see the detail, your ears will always hear it. For the mixing, we needed to take it outside, so I took it to Matt.'

Mike Patton had recorded and effectively mixed his own vocals in his own studio—'I did vocals at my house in my pyjamas,' he told *Rolling Stone*—applying his own reverb, compression, and distortion. The Wallace-assisted mixing commenced in February 2015 and, after mastering by Maor Apeelbaum, *Sol Invictus*, Faith No More's first album in eighteen years, was made available for streaming through selected media outlets on May 11, and went on sale on May 13.

The band had set up their own Reclamation Recordings label to self-release the record. 'We did not owe Warner Bros any more releases,' Gould explains, 'so technically we were free agents for *Sol Invictus*. I don't believe *Sol Invictus* would have materialised if we were still under a Slash/Warner contract. We did look at other labels, however. Different members in the band had different opinions on whether self-releasing was the way to go. I supported it for the sake of control and freedom, but also because it is much easier to do on your own in this day and age.'

The album earned rave reviews from metal magazines, *Kerrang!* and *Metal Hammer;* from leading European newspapers such as *Der Spiegel* and *Ouest-France;* and from UK music press, like *NME* and *Q*. The *New York Times* called it 'a rattlingly vital new album'. *Rolling Stone* called it 'as much a triumphant victory lap as it's a comeback record'. *All Music* said it was 'the rare reunion album that truly adds to the strength of the group's legacy rather than diluting it'.

Sol Invictus was also streamed, downloaded, and bought in impressive quantities, with the album debuting at #6 in the UK and on the *Billboard* Album Sales Chart in the USA. It went #1 in Finland and top 5 in Australia, the Czech Republic, Norway, Switzerland, Belgium, Germany, and Poland.

It peaked in the top 10 in New Zealand, Austria, and the Netherlands. And Canada, France, and Ireland.

It is a holistic record, one that harks back to an almost bygone era before shuffle play and playlists, when albums existed as cohesive collections. Thus, it is more than the sum of its parts, but what parts they are. It veers from the insanely catchy in 'Sunny Side Up' to the brutal in 'Separation Anxiety', from bitter in 'Black Friday' to redemptive in 'From The Dead'. It is celebratory in parts, simple and sombre in others. It also subverts, with the opening title track, whose piano opening is the mature uncle to 'Intro' from the band's first show, suggesting death: *'I'm coming lord, I'm on my way'*, and the closing couplet of the final song, 'From The Dead', a return: *'I can see the end / Welcome home my friend.'* *Album Of The Year* evokes a funeral, *Sol Invictus* a wake.

'In our music, there has to be an element of truth of where we are in our lives,' explains Bill Gould. 'There has to be a resonance of truth to reflect our real situation. For *Sol Invictus,* we weren't just creating it and manufacturing the record, we were living it.'

CHUCK MOSLEY

52

After a hectic 2015 of single, video, and album releases; television shows; and tours to Australia and New Zealand, North America, Europe, and South America, Faith No More played a final *Sol Invictus* tour show at the Aftershock festival in Sacramento on October 25.

Ten months later, in August 2016, to mark the band's own reissue of their debut album, *We Care A Lot*, Faith No More teamed up with Chuck

Mosley for two concerts at the Great American Music Hall in San Francisco and the Troubadour in Los Angeles. Billed as Chuck Mosley & Friends, the band, with Mike Patton also in attendance, played a selection of Mosley-era cuts, culminating with Mosley, resplendent in sharp suit complete with dicky bow and in front of Faith No More's original blood-splattered banner, delivered a re-booted version of his finest pop moment, 'Anne's Song'.

❦

On November 9 2017, Chuck Mosley died at the age of fifty-seven. He left behind long-term partner Pip Logan; two daughters, Erica and Sophie; and his grandson, Wolfgang Logan Mosley. He had died 'due to the disease of addiction', his family wrote in a statement.

His passing left his former bandmates devastated, numb, and bereft. Chuck was the voice of Faith No More for most of the 1980s, and personified the raw, untamed, and brash band spirit that set them apart from contemporaries.

Chuck had been struck down just as he was making a creative comeback. He had embarked on a series of Re-Introduce Yourself tours in 2016 and 2017. He teamed up with Matt Wallace to record some tracks in August 2017, and, as part of the band Primitive Race, he released an album, *Soul Pretender*, just one week before his tragic death. His close friend Douglas Esper, from Chuck's adopted home city of Cleveland, had worked tirelessly to ensure that Chuck received recognition in what proved to be his final years. And, with those August 2016 shows and the *We Care A Lot* re-release, there came recognition and redemption.

Chuck—charismatic, boisterous, quickwitted—was a natural frontman. When he joined Faith No More in 1983, the band wanted a presence for live shows rather than a voice for recordings. And Chuck delivered: he was part poet, part punk preacher, part precarious performer, all attitude.

Chuck was also an accomplished lyricist, capable of devastating self-awareness and of expressing delicate and personal emotion. And he was equally adept at penning party anthems and catchy chatter. He hit his lyrical and vocal peak on 'The Crab Song', probably the most personal and romantic song in the Faith No More oeuvre. It is the perfect embodiment of how Chuck's bratty rap could effortlessly complement Faith No More's music.

On the day of Chuck's death, and despite darkness and despair, the band, his band, succeeded in capturing his essence in pitch-perfect fashion in their short tribute, penned by Roddy Bottum, who had remained very close to Chuck:

> It's with a heavy, heavy heart we acknowledge the passing of our friend and bandmate, Chuck Mosley. He was a reckless and caterwauling force of energy who delivered with conviction and helped set us on a track of uniqueness and originality that would not have developed the way it had had he not been a part. How fortunate we are to have been able to perform with him last year in a reunion style when we re-released our very first record. His enthusiasm, his sense of humour, his style and his bravado will be missed by so many. We were a family, an odd and dysfunctional family, and we'll be forever grateful for the time we shared with Chuck.

CONCLUSION: THE SIGILS AND THE SIGNS

53

In thirty-five years as a band, Faith No More succeeded in their quest to do it their own way, to follow the music, and to turn miseries into nursery rhymes. The cankers and medallions of chart hits, album sales, and Grammy hits were incidental.

'What made us special, was that we even went against our own interests sometimes, to go where the music was taking us,' Bill Gould says. 'The way we approached something as conventional as music, we kept going into uncharted territory. We've managed, even with all of our difficulties, to still maintain that course into uncharted territory.'

In that course, they updated the hardcore approach to touring: working relentlessly, travelling everywhere, sleeping anywhere, and overcoming indifference.

They updated the punk approach to performance: making every show an event, subverting expectations, breaking down the barrier between artist and audience. An enraged audience was better than an unengaged audience.

They updated the indie approach to the industry: doing it yourself, but not fearing the mainstream, being in it but not of it, and maintaining artistic integrity even while on a major label.

They updated the concept of a comeback: eschewing nostalgia, alternating group and individual projects, and producing new music neither hostage to the past, nor slave to the present.

A band who had to scrape the money together to record their first album, Faith No More recorded seven albums, and five of them partly or fully on the world's third-biggest major label. A band whose first album sold fewer than six thousand copies in the first twenty years after its release, Faith No More sold more than eleven million albums in total.

A band who billed their first-ever show a 'one-time only performance', Faith No More played over nine hundred concerts. A band who sought to have a different line-up for every show, Faith No More may have had nineteen members in their various guises, but they retained the same core of Mike Bordin, Roddy Bottum, and Bill Gould from 1983 onward, bolstered by Mike Patton since 1988.

'Billy and I had a past from which we could pool,' Bottum says. 'My sister once said Billy could make drinking water exciting. He's a very excitable and inspired artist. Him at the helm of what we did was irreplaceable. We all faltered and drooped, and fell off the band map over the history of our career, but Billy had the tenacious sustainability and belief mechanisms to keep it all exciting and moving forward. He has a crazy knack for musical drama that I trace back to our roots of being independent radical kids.'

Of Bordin, he adds, 'He has a similar tenacity, a similar sense of patience and rock-steady quality that suits him and his craft. He's absolutely the best drummer I've ever heard. His language in his drums is inspired and unique, and scary powerful. He's open-minded and encouraging, and fluid in his drive.'

Bordin says, 'We looked at things the same way. We were driving in the same direction, and we were in agreement with what we were doing. We were up for listening to each other, and up for trying new things. Without that, we would have been like a million other bands.'

As much as Chuck Mosley's hardcore hip-hop style and Jim Martin's reimagining of metal guitar within the confines of a non-metal band helped power the band's early endeavours, the arrival of Mike Patton ensured that Faith No More could never be like a 'million other bands'. 'He has great intuition,' says Gould. 'He's very in touch with his gut instinct. Sometimes I need a minute to digest it, but it always works. He's all intuition, all commitment—which fits in exactly with the way we approach our music.'

'I believe he has a photographic memory,' Bottum adds. 'He has a categorical brain that keeps order and degrees of musical chaos in check. I feel like he never forgets. With that comes a huge sense of confidence. He knows that he's never wrong. He rarely is. His taste is his own, and that helps him. He knows what he wants to hear, and he's really stubborn and focused on what he expects and allows. His independence and bullheadedness propels his vision in a remarkable way.'

✸

By the middle of 2018, Faith No More's bullheadedness and vision was propelling them to create new music. In late November 2017, Bottum, on a visit to the West Coast from New York, entered Faith No More's Estudio Koolarrow rehearsal space in Emeryville with Bordin and Gould. Bordin and Gould locking in together, like they first had almost four decades previously. Bottum teasing out new melodies from an old piano. Over the next few months, they would continue to work together.

The Faith No More *troika* was back in harness. The Faith No More story was not finished.

ACKNOWLEDGEMENTS

This book would not have been possible without the love, patience, and forbearance of Christel Harte. Merci Christel—and Elliott and Eloïse—for putting up with my many physical, mental, and spiritual absences when thinking and writing and promoting this book. For all of this, and everything, I'll be forever grateful.

Eternal gratitude and much love also to my parents, Mary and Jim, for instilling a love of learning and books, and to my siblings Declan, Orla, Seamus, and Elaine for putting up with my Faith No More obsession, and everything else.

Merci also to the Crausazs for allowing me to turn the house in Chêne into a personal writing retreat, and for much more.

Though an independent publication, this book would never have happened without the input and endeavour of Faith No More themselves. I can never repay the generosity of Bill Gould for his time, repeated assistance, and ability to answer queries and help with contacts. For helping, with Margaret, to make me welcome in San Francisco, and for always being available to reply to countless email queries and much, much more.

Equally, my thanks go to Mike Bordin for spending so much time with me in San Francisco, and for his eagerness and enthusiasm to speak at length in many phone interviews. I also thank them both for opening up their photo archives to me.

Thanks to Roddy Bottum for being such an engaging interviewee, and being so quotable. Thanks also to Jon Hudson for spending time to give me his insights in San Francisco.

I cannot thank the band enough for—I think—going against their better judgement and participating so completely. And for their candour, honesty, trust, and understanding. I hope I've given the band the book they deserve.

Mike Patton opted not to be interviewed, but thanks to him in any case for not putting any obstacles in my way, and for his starring role in the story.

It was a great pleasure to get to speak to Chuck Mosley at length before his tragic passing. Sadly, he did not get a chance to answer all my questions, but, nonetheless, Chuck's humour and voice comes through clearly in the book. Thanks also to Anne D'Agnillo, and to Douglas Esper for his help throughout.

Thanks indeed to all the band's former members for agreeing to participate. Especially to Wade Worthington for the many photos and font of knowledge he provided, and also to M. Morris for agreeing to meet and to be interviewed.

Trey Spruance was especially honest and lucid in his insights. Thanks Mark Bowen, Joe Callahan, Paula Frazer, Walter O'Brien, Jim Pasque, and Jake Smith.

Thanks to Jim Martin for replying to my entreaties. He decided against being interviewed, but directed me to his extensive 2012 interview with the Faith No More blog to find answers.

Thanks also to Faith No More's long-time producer Matt Wallace for welcoming me into his studio in Los Angeles, for being so open in sharing his memories and knowledge, and for answering a steady stream of emails.

Thanks to band manager Tim Moss for all his help and feedback. Thanks also to former manager John Vassiliou for his openness and time. Thanks to all in Faith No More past, present, and future for allowing me to tell their stories, and to try to weave a narrative about their lives.

Just as the band might not have ever had the Faith No More name without him, I'm pretty sure this book could not have been done properly without the supreme kindness of Will Carpmill—thanks, Will, for providing the perfect base during my San Francisco sojourn.

The supremely talented and knowledgeable Jim Wirth prodded me into doing this book, and offered invaluable advice on how to proceed. He also made the book immeasurably better with his masterful editing of the draft version.

The brilliant Mark Chaplin's forensic editing skills and music knowledge helped turned a stream of consciousness into a series of properly punctuated sentences. Thanks for everything.

Jim Brown, the man behind Faith No More Followers, has been a constant source of support. His archive of Faith No More interviews was a priceless resource in my research, and I'm indebted to his continued help with promotion, graphic design, video, and more besides.

Equally, Andrew Bowie's FNM Gig Database was an essential research tool, and helped provide a roadmap for the book. As the unofficial FNM historian, Andrew also provided expert feedback as a reader of the draft version.

And sincere thanks to Jardar Tolaas, the curator of early and pre-Faith No More history, for his faithnoman.com site, and for sharing his research and contacts.

Thanks to Nigel Osborne and Tom Seabrook of Jawbone Press for their faith in publishing *Small Victories*. Special thanks to Tom for this patience, thoughtfulness, and expertise in bringing a first-time author's book to fruition.

Thank you to the extensive Faith No More fan community for their support and enthusiasm: Andy Couch; Carol Bargielowski and Daniel Gledhill (Faith No More blog); Bertrand Dessemond, Vanessa Monteiro, and Stevens Drean (Faith No More French Community); Alton Blom (Patton Fanatic); Andrés Morales (FNM 4Ever); Pablo Fernandez (Bungle Weird); Francisco Rodríguez (The Holy Filament), Pogo Lynch (Patton Archivo); and Bruce Paterson (FNM Discography).

Andrés and Pablo also helped considerably with the chapter on Chile, as did Carlos Nunez, Daniel Hidalgo, Juan Luis Trejo Piazza, and Adrián Mazzeo. Gracias.

Thanks also to Alberto Fuguet for sharing his wonderful stories for that chapter, for his support, and his endorsement.

Many thanks to Steven Blush for his endorsement, and for his memories.

Thanks to everyone who agreed to be interviewed and tell their tales. Thanks also to Ben Mitchell, Sean Clancy, Joan Osato, William Winant, Penelope Houston and all at the San Francisco Public Library, Lonnie Readioff, Ben Sullivan, Abbey Konowitch, Matt Welch, Michael Minky, Philco Raves, Doug Moody, Candace D'Andrea, Richard Bradburn, Solana Rehne, Johnny Bartlett, Casey Williams, Dave Brushback, and Bryony Hall and Society of Authors.

Thanks also to David Farrelly, John Harmon, Andy Lockwood, Elodie Masson, Elvira Asensi Monzó, Paul Murphy, plus David Moen and Joe Sullivan and all the lads in Loch Mor and Ballybay, where my Faith No More fire was kindled.

Thanks to everyone who reads this book, and everyone I've inevitably and unforgivably forgotten.

NOTES AND SOURCES

INTERVIEWS

Small Victories includes original material from the author's interviews with the following:

Current and former members: Mike Bordin, Roddy Bottum, Bill Gould, Jon Hudson.

Plus: Mark Bowen, Joe Callahan, Paula Frazer, M. Morris, Chuck Mosley, Walter O'Brien, Jim Pasque, Jake Smith, Trey Spruance, Wade Worthington.

Also: Anne D'Agnillo, Steve Berlin, Steve Blush, Will Carpmill, Seán Clancy, Eddie Chacon, Andy Copping, Ginger Coyote, Tim Dalton, Dick Deluxe, Alberto Fuguet, Pat Hoed, Kent Jolly, Derek Kemp, Kevin Kerslake, Rich Krim, Iris Lettieri, Clif Norrel, Joan Osato, Roderick 'Rodcore' Palmer, Phillip Raves, Solana Rehne, Ruth Schwartz, Anna Statman, Juan Luis Trejo Piazza, John Vassiliou, Matt Wallace, Paul Wims, William Winant, Ralph Ziman.

All quoted material is from original interview sources unless stated below.

BOOKS

Chirazi, Steffan. *Faith No More: The Real Story*. (Castle Communications, 1994)

Schuftan, Craig. *Entertain Us: The Rise And Fall Of Alternative Rock In The Nineties*. (ABC Books, 2012)

VISUAL

Beavis And Butt-Head: 'Close Encounters' MTV, August 9 1995 (directed by Mike Judge and Yvette Kaplan)

Especial De Faith No More: Séptimo Vicio. Vía X, June 8 2009

Mike Patton Interview MTV Brasil, September 1991

MTV Behind The Music: Courtney Love MTV, June 21 2010 (written by Sean Gottlieb)

In The Studio '92 MTV, January 1992

MTV Post-Modern MTV Europe, November 1992

Super Rock MTV, April 29 1995

MAJOR ARTICLES

Arnaud, Charlélie, and Stephane Auzilleau. 'Faith No More sous le soleil exactement.' *Rock Hard*, May 2015.

Barry, Robert. 'A Deathly Plague: Mike Patton Talks About Mondo Cane And Avant Metal.' *The Quietus*, May 5 2010.

Bate, Martin. 'Review and interview.' *Consumable*, April 1995.

Bennett, J. 'Smooth Operator.' *Decibel*, March 2013.

Blush, Steve. 'Jim Martin interview.' *Guitar World*, September 1992.

Carney, Trisha. 'Faith No More.' *Your Flesh*, 1987.

Chirazi, Steffan. 'Faith No More "We're Not Splitting!"' *Kerrang!*, October 14 1995.

Chirazi, Steffan. 'Kalifornia Dreamin`,' *Kerrang!*, October 21 1989.

Chirazi, Steffan. 'Midlife Crisis.' *Kerrang!*, July 17 1993.

Chirazi, Steffan. 'Raw Power.' *BAM*, December 2 1988.

Chirazi, Steffan. 'Rod Against The Machine' *Kerrang!*, July 7 1993.

Chirazi, Steffan. 'Testing The Faith.' *Kerrang!*, June 22 1992.

Chirazi, Steffan. 'The Epic Adventures Of Faith No More.' *BAM*, October 5 1990.

Crigler, Pete. 'Dean Menta.' *Perfect Sound Forever*, April 2016.

Daarke, Amelia. 'My Life Story.' *Metal Hammer*, March 2002.

De Lima, João Gabriel. 'Entrevista Mike Patton.' *Veja*, October 1991.

Dick, Jonathan. 'Faith No More's Mike Patton: "You Create Your Own Freedom."' *The Record*, NPR, May 28 2015.

Elliott, Paul. 'Chucking It All Away.' *Sounds*, June 10 1989.

Fong, Erik. 'Trey Spruance.' *Perfect Pitch Online*, July 2003.

Francone, Vincent. 'Weird Little Cats In A Bag: An Interview with Mike Patton.' Nightimes.com, October 29 2002.

Gold, Jonathan. 'The Most Unlikely Metal Heroes In The Business.' *Los Angeles Times*, April 12 1990.

Gold, Jonathan. 'Where Hip And Headbanging Meet, Faith No More Are The Kings Of Neo-Metal.' *Los Angeles Times*, October 14 1990.

Goldstein, Patrick. 'Warner Records Stays Faithful To Mike Patton's Bungle.' *Los Angeles Times*, February 3 1991.

Hart, Ron. 'Mike Patton.' *Cmj New Music Report*, June 28 1999.

Hobbs, Mary Anne. 'Last In, First Out?' *Select*, August 1993.

Klem, Matthew. 'Interview With Roddy Bottum.' *Vaj*, June 1995.

Kot, Greg. 'How Rock's "Bigfoot" Changed All The Rules.' *Chicago Tribune*, September 22 1991.

Kucera, Pavel. 'Faith No More: Moc Jsme Se S Tim Nes**li.' IDNES.cz, August 14 2008.

Loud, Lance. 'Heavy Metal Homo.' *The Advocate*, June 15 1993.

Mckenna, Kristine. 'Slash Records: After The Punk Revolution.' *Los Angeles Times*, June 21 1987.

Morris, Chris. 'Tour Power Fuels Faith No More: Extensive Roadwork Accompanies New Set.' *Billboard*, July 11 1992.

Morris, Gina. 'Faecal Attraction.' *Nme*, January 3 1993.

Neely, Kim. 'Faith No More: The Real Thing?' *Rolling Stone*, September 6 1990.

Owen, Frank. 'Faith No More: Artists Of The Year.' *Spin*, December 1990.

Peel, John. 'Pop: John Peel Enjoys Faith No More.' *The Observer*, January 31 1988.

Perry, Neil. 'Charge Of The Fright Brigade.' *Melody Maker*, May 5 1990.

Perry, Neil. 'Whistle Down The Wind.' *Sounds,* January 23 1988.

Putterford, Mark. 'A Real Ugly Experience.' *Select*, August 1992.

Redding, Dan. 'Interview With Trey Spruance Of Mr Bungle, Faith No More, Secret Chiefs 3.' *Culture Creature*, February 18 2017.

Selvin, Joel. 'Faith No More Gets Reborn.' *San Francisco Chronicle*, February 16 1997.

Shaw, William. 'Twist Of Faith.' *Details*, September 1992.

Sherman, Lee. 'Get The Funk Out.' *Guitar*, September 1992.

Simonini, Ross. 'Interview With Mike Patton.' *The Believer*, January 1 2013.

Smith, Mat. 'Hell Street Blues.' *Melody Maker*, February 6 1988.

Snyder, Michael. 'Keeping The Faith With A Heavy Metal Punk Band.' *San Francisco Chronicle*, June 26 1986.

Sprague, David. 'Faith No More Seeks Fool's Gold.' *Billboard*, February 4 1995.

Sutcliffe, Phil. 'Faith No More: Regrets, They Have A Few.' *Q*, May 1995.

Uhelszki, Jaan. 'Faith No More's Patton Has New Band' *San Francisco Chronicle*, April 12 1998.

Van Der Vliet, Gina. 'Faith No More's New Vid To Give Viewers "Vertigo".' *Billboard*, June 28 1997.

Wall, Mick. 'Hidden In Plain Sight: Faith No More: Introduce Yourself.' *Mick Wall*, March 24 2015.

Watts, Chris. 'Testing The Faith.' *Kerrang!*, September 9 1992.

Wawzenek, Bryan. '25 Years Ago: The Soundscan Era Rocks The Music Industry.' *Ultimate Classic Rock*, May 25 2016.

Weingarten, Christopher R. 'Faith No More: Rock's Most Contrarian Band Returns.' *Rolling Stone*, May 12 2015.

Weingarten, Christopher R. 'The Real Things: Dillinger Escape Plan Interview Mike Patton.' *Revolver*, June 5 2010.

ONLINE

Alt Music Faith No More (groups.google.com/forum/#!forum/alt.music.faith-no-more)

Alt Music Mr Bungle (groups.google.com/forum/m/#!forum/alt.music.mr-bungle)

Bungle Fever (bunglefever.com)

Bungle Weird (bungleweird.com.br)

Caca Volante (cacavolante.org)

CV Database (negele.org/cvdb2/?b=2)

Faith No Man (faithnoman.com)

Faith No More Blog (faithnomoreblog.com)

Faith No More Gig Database (fnmlive.com)

Faith No More Followers (faithnomorefollowers.com)

Faith No More French Community (facebook.com/groups/105616129472984)

Faith No More 2.0 (newfaithnomore.com)

FNM4EVER (faithnomore4ever.com)

Patton Archivio (zemaraim.blogspot.ch)

Patton Fanatic (pattonfanatic.com)

The Holy Filament (theholyfilament.cl)

ENDNOTES

INTRODUCTION
Author interviews: Mike Bordin, Roddy Bottum, Bill Gould.

CHAPTER 1
Author interviews: Roddy Bottum, Bill Gould, Paul Wims, Chuck Mosley.

'Can you imagine having ...' J. Bennett. 'The Untimely Death And Glorious Rebirth Of Faith No More.' *Noisey*, March 19 2015.
'As soon as me ...' 'Chuck Mosley.' *Fear & Loathing*, November 1 2016.

CHAPTER 2
Author interviews: Bill Gould, Wade Worthington, M. Morris.

CHAPTER 3
Author interviews: Mike Bordin, Eddie Chacon, Wade Worthington.

'By that time we ...' Steve Blush. 'Jim Martin interview.' *Guitar World*, September 1992.

CHAPTER 4
Author interviews: Mike Bordin, Roddy Bottum, Will Carpmill, Bill Gould, M. Morris, Matt Wallace, Wade Worthington.

'Heavy bass- and drum-orientated ...' Jeff Bale. 'Review.' *Maximum Rocknroll*, September 1983.
'The Sound of Music ...' Jeff Vrabel. 'The 5 Best Faith No More Concerts.' *Live Nation TV*, October 7 2015.

CHAPTER 5
Author interviews: Mike Bordin, Roddy Bottum, Bill Gould, Wade Worthington.

CHAPTER 6
Author interviews: Mike Bordin, Roddy Bottum, Joe Callahan, Ginger Coyote, Dick Deluxe, Bill Gould, Jake Smith.

'The live show seems ...' 'Review.' *Unsound*, 1983.

CHAPTER 7
Author interviews: Mike Bordin, Roddy Bottum, Mark Bowen, Paula Frazer, Bill Gould, Walter O'Brien, Jim Pasque.

'It was the summer I was eighteen ...' *MTV Behind The Music: Courtney Love*
'Roddy was an occasional ...' Jardar Tolaas.
'Desmond Shea.' *Faith. No Man.*
'I started jamming on ...' / 'I didn't get into punk ...' / 'I told him not to join ...' Steve Blush. 'Jim Martin Interview.' *Guitar World*, September 1992.
'We had this property ...' 'The death of Cliff Burton.' *Classic Rock*, January 2005.

CHAPTER 8
Author interviews: Mike Bordin, Roddy Bottum, Bill Gould, Phillip Raves.

'Here is a parade ...' 'Review.' *Wiring Department*, 1985.
'On its first Los Angeles visit ...' Terry Atkinson. 'An Act Of Faith.' *Los Angeles Times*, December 24 1984.

CHAPTER 9
Author interviews: Mike Bordin, Roddy Bottum, Mark Bowen, Bill Gould, Chuck Mosley.

'On the twenty-first ...' 'Faith No More.' *Wiring Department*, June 1985.

CHAPTER 10
Author interviews: Mike Bordin, Roddy Bottum, Pat Hoed, Kent Jolly, Chuck Mosley, Joan Osato, Solana Rehne, Ruth Schwartz.

'Oh, yes stay tuned for Faith No More ...' Kent Jolly. 'Northern California.' *Maximum Rocknroll*, November 1985.
'Take the necessary ingredients ...' Martin Sprouse. 'Review.' *Maximum Rocknroll*, December 1985.
'Nihilist rockers from ...' 'Faith No More, We Care A Lot.' *Billboard*, January 18 1986.
'Already the title track ...' PC Hertz. 'Reviews.' *Ward Music Monthly*, February 3 1986.

CHAPTER 11

Author interviews: Steve Berlin, Mike Bordin, Roddy Bottum, Bill Gould, Anna Statman.

'Tucson is a weird scene …' Trisha Carney. 'Faith No More.' *Your Flesh*, 1987.
'We were playing this pop music …' Amy Yates Wuelfing and Steven DiLodovico. *No Slam Dancing, No Stage Diving, No Spikes: An Oral History Of The Legendary City Gardens* (DiWulf Publishing, 2014)
'I've never felt that …' Kristine McKenna. 'Slash Records: After The Punk Revolution.' *Los Angeles Times*, June 21 1987.
'We tend to get …' 'LA's maverick label meets the majors.' *BAM*, February 10 1984.
'Faith No More have officially …' 'Newsreels.' *BAM*, October 31 1986.
'Even major commercial rock …' Michael Snyder. 'Keeping The Faith With A Heavy Metal Punk Band.' *San Francisco Chronicle*, June 26 1986.
'There's no such thing …' Trisha Carney. 'Faith No More.' *Your Flesh*, 1987.

CHAPTER 12

Author interviews: Anne D'Angillo, Steve Berlin, Mike Bordin, Roddy Bottum, Bill Gould, Chuck Mosley, Matt Wallace.

'The title "Chinese Arithmetic" …' Jim Brown. 'Introducing Chuck: Focus On The Song.' faithnomoreblog.com, April 13 2013.
'Everyone was on my …' Brown, Jim. 'Chuck Mosley Interview.' faithnomorefollowers.com, May 2 2017.
'Getting broken up with …' 'Chuck Mosley Q&A: The Answers.' faithnomoreblog.com, May 23 2013.

CHAPTER 13

Author interviews: Mike Bordin, Roddy Bottum, Bill Gould, John Vassiliou.

'The strategy is …' 'Have Faith.' *Billboard*, December 5 1987.
'Faith No More's snide …' Chris Willman. Care Package.' *Los Angeles Times*, August 24 1987.
'Mike's a bitter little …' Neil Perry. 'Whistle Down The Wind …' *Sounds*, January 23 1988.

CHAPTER 14

Author interviews: Anne D'Agnillo, Mike Bordin, Roddy Bottum, Tim Dalton, Bill Gould, Derek Kemp, John Vassiliou.

'Their rhythms are battered …' Chris Watts. 'Review.' *Kerrang!* , February 13 1988.
'Mat Smith from …' Mat Smith. 'Hell Street Blues.' *Melody Maker*, February 6 1988.
'Faith No More have wrung …' John Peel. 'Pop: John Peel Enjoys Faith No More.' *Observer*, January 31 1988.

CHAPTER 15

Author interviews: Mike Bordin, Roddy Bottum, Bill Gould, John Vassiliou.

'This gig was a …' Neil Perry. 'Talk About The Passion.' *Sounds*, May 21 1988.
'I came home early …' Mick Wall. 'Hidden In Plain Sight: Faith No More: Introduce Yourself.' mickwall.com, March 24 2015.
'I was fired. Why? …' 'Chuck Mosley Q&A: The Answers.' faithnomoreblog.com, May 23 2013.
'Faith No More singer …' 'Newsreels.' *BAM*, July 1 1988.
'Auditions are underway …' Sheila Rene. 'Hear And There.' *Gavin Report*, August 8 1988.

CHAPTER 16

Author interviews: Mike Bordin, Roddy Bottum, Joe Callahan, Bill Gould, Roderick 'Rodcore' Palmer, Trey Spruance, John Vassiliou.

'FNM is looking for …' 'Newsreels.' *BAM*, July 1 1988.
'I resisted it. I honestly did …' J. Bennett. 'Smooth Operator.' *Decibel*, March 2013.
'It's a big, giant …' Heidi Lipsanen. 'Mr Bungle.' *Diarium Autopsia* 1992.
'From a young age …' Ross Simonini. 'Interview With Mike Patton.' *The Believer*, January 1 2013.
'I only got into …' Simon Young. 'The Wanderer.' *Kerrang!*, October 13 2001.
'My first gig as …' Jonathan Dick. 'Faith No More's Mike Patton: "You Create Your Own Freedom."' *The Record*, NPR, May 28 2015.
'The idea of an …' J. Bennett. 'Smooth Operator.' *Decibel*, March 2013.

CHAPTER 17

Author interviews: Mike Bordin, Roddy Bottum, Bill Gould, John Vassiliou, Matt Wallace.

'Patton lay waste to …' Steffan Chirazi. 'Raw Power.' *BAM*, December 2 1988.
'The writing certainly isn't …' Steffan Chirazi. 'Faith Healers,' *Kerrang!*, June 10 1989.
'I really don't enjoy …' Ross Simonini. 'Interview With Mike Patton.' *The Believer*, January 1 2013.
'It bothers me …' Ford, Bianka. 'Keeping the Faith.' *Blunt*, May 2015.

CHAPTER 18

Author interviews: Mike Bordin, Roddy Bottum, Bill Gould, Matt Wallace.

CHAPTER 19

Author interviews: Mike Bordin, Roddy Bottum, Bill Gould, Matt Wallace.

'I like creating fictional …' Charlélie Arnaud and Stephane Auzilleau. 'Faith No More sous le soleil exactement.' *Rock Hard*, May 2015.
'"Zombie Eaters" is about…' *Village Noize*, Issue 8, 1988.
'You owe it to …' Judith Thurman. 'My Visit With Balthus.' *The New Yorker*. June 19 2017.
'Fear is a big …' / 'The song "The Morning After" …' / 'There's also the whole …' Mike Gitter. 'Faith No More.' *Thrasher*. April 1990.
'We recorded them on …' 'The Death Of Cliff Burton.' *Classic Rock*, January 2005.
'Living on the margins …' John Hughes. 'Washington Legacy Project: Krist Novoselic: Of Grunge and Grange.' *Washington Legacymakers*, 2008.

CHAPTER 20

Author interviews: Mike Bordin, Roddy Bottum, Bill Gould, Derek Kemp, John Vassiliou, Matt Wallace.

'Let's move on to …' Steffan Chirazi. 'Raw Power.' *BAM*, February 10 1989.
'Faith No More finished its …' Jae-Ha Him. 'Faith No More Defies Pigeonholing.' *Chicago Sun-Times*, January 12 1990.
'You once might have …' Steve Hochman. 'Faith No More Presents Metal With A Twist.' *Los Angeles Times*, June 22 1989.
'Mike Patton is better …' Greg Kot. 'Rave Recordings …' *Chicago Tribune*, August 17 1989.
'Faith No More's second …' Eric McClary. 'Metal.' *Reno Gazette-Journal*, August 20 1989.
'Mike Patton's vinyl performance …' Neil Perry. 'Sauna For The Soul.' *Sounds*, July 15 1989.
'Maybe all it needs …' Paul Elliott. 'Chucking It All Away.' *Sounds*, June 10 1989.
'We had The Cult …' / 'We haven't had a …' Steffan Chirazi. 'Kalifornia Dreamin'.' *Kerrang!*, October 21 1989.
'If Metallica doesn't leap …' Mike Boehm. 'Metallica: A Future Without the Fury?' *Los Angeles Times*, September 23 1989.
'Faith No More members were …' *Gavin Report*, October 13 1989.
'hard rock and heavy …' Jonathan Gold. 'Heavy Metal Looks Like A Hot Commodity Convention Studies The Futures Market.' *Los Angeles Times*, September 21 1989.
'If the last UK …' Phil Alexander. 'Review.' *Raw*, October 1989.

CHAPTER 21

Author interviews: Mike Bordin, Roddy Bottum, Tim Dalton, Bill Gould, Derek Kemp.

'We have decided today …' Laurence Dodds. 'Berlin Wall: How The Wall Came Down, As It Happened 25 Years Ago.' *Telegraph*, November 9 2014.
'We got a surprise …' Jeff Gilbert. 'Big Ugly Truth.' *The Rocket*, March 1990.
'By the time we …' 'Band Interview: Voivod.' *Damnation*. June 2 2016.
'It was pretty weird …' Jim Sullivan. 'Neither Metal Rival Expects A Grammy.' *Boston Globe*, January 19 1990.

CHAPTER 22

Author interviews: Mike Bordin, Roddy Bottum, Bill Gould, Matt Wallace, Ralph Ziman.

'Epic is a mix …' 'New releases.' *Gavin Report*, June 1 1990.
'I was just noodling …' Lee Sherman. 'Get The Funk Out.' *Guitar*, September 1992.

'It was about sexual …' Gary Cee. 'An Epic Year For Faith No More.' *Circus*, October 31 1990.

'The lyrics present a …' Robert Barry. 'A Deathly Plague: Mike Patton Talks About Mondo Cane And Avant Metal.' *The Quietus*, May 5 2010.

CHAPTER 23
Author interviews: Mike Bordin, Roddy Bottum, Bill Gould, Derek Kemp, John Vassiliou.

'"Faith No More have …' Steffan Johnson. 'Review.' *Kerrang!*, February 3 1990.

'The past year has …' Mitch Potter. 'Faith No More Believes In Latest Line-Up.' *Toronto Star*, March 23 1990.

'The biggest band to …' Terri F. Reilly. 'Faith No More Is Faithful To Its Roots.' *St. Louis Post-Dispatch*, March 30 1990.

'The biggest band to …' Jonathan Gold. 'The Most Unlikely Metal Heroes In The Business.' *Los Angeles Times*, April 12 1990.

'There's no common ground …' Neil Perry. 'Charge Of The Fright Brigade.' *Melody Maker*, May 5 1990.

CHAPTER 24
Author interviews: Mike Bordin, Roddy Bottum, Bill Gould, Rich Krim

'It was another universe …' Dave Everley. 'No More Bull.' *Metal Hammer*, July 2015.

'The breakthrough of Faith …' Greg Kot. 'How Rock's "Bigfoot" Changed All The Rules.' *Chicago Tribune*, September 22 1991.

CHAPTER 25
Author interviews: Mike Bordin, Roddy Bottum, Bill Gould, John Vassiliou.

'We basically discovered Faith …' Peter Holmes. 'Disconformity.' *Sydney Morning Herald*, September 7 1990.

'To FNM: The good …' Bill Gould archive

'When they are asked …' Kim Neely. 'Faith No More: The Real Thing?' *Rolling Stone*, September 6 1990.

'Axl Rose sent us …' Steffan Chirazi. 'The Epic Adventures Of Faith No More.' *BAM*, October 5 1990.

'The hard rock group …' Valli Herman. 'Rockers Turn Their Garb Into Garble For Eclectic Awards Night.' *Los Angeles Daily News*, September 8 1990.

'[Idol's] worst break …' John Leland. 'Billy Idol's Surly Punk Lounge Act.' *Newsday*, September 17 1990.

'If the "movement" …' Jonathan Gold. 'Where Hip And Headbanging Meet Faith No More Are The Kings Of Neo-Metal, Which Is Art Music Packaged For Hard-Rock Teens.' *Los Angeles Times*, October 14 1990.

CHAPTER 26
Author interviews: Mike Bordin, Roddy Bottum, Bill Gould.

'He put his foot …' Cary Darling. 'Keeping The Faith In Tough Times.' *Orange County Register*, October 27 1990.

'I think the rumours are …' Mike Gitter. 'Facts Not Fiction.' *Kerrang!*, August 21 1990.

'We heard that …' 'Can You Feel It, See It, Hear It Today? If You Can't, Then It Doesn't Matter Anyway …' *Hot Metal*, August 1990.

'Mike is going to …' Patrick Goldstein. 'Warner Records Stays Faithful To Mike Patton's Bungle.' *Los Angeles Times*, February 3 1991.

'They tried to squash …' Vincent Francone. 'Weird Little Cats In A Bag.' nightimes.com, October 29 2002.

'It was difficult for …' Sylvie Simmons. 'Turn It Down.' *Raw*, June 27 1990.

'Robert Plant was an …' 'Roddy Bottum Fan Q&A: The Answers.' faithnomoreblog.com, January 31 2013.

'Faith No More is the …' Frank Owen. 'Faith No More: Artists Of The Year.' *Spin*, December 1990.

CHAPTER 27
Author interviews: Bill Gould, John Vassiliou.

'I've noticed about a …' 'Faith No More.' *Wiring Department*, June 1985.

'The whole structure of …' Theodor W. Adorno and George Simpson. *On Popular Music* (Institute of Social Research, 1942)

'In the US, cultural …' Matt Neufeld. 'Faith No More Resists Labels With Hybrid Sound.' *Washington Times*, October 18 1992.

'For some reason, all …' Pippa Lang. 'Angelic Upstarts.' *Metal Hammer*, June 1992.

CHAPTER 28
Author interviews: Mike Bordin, Roddy Bottum, Alberto Fuguet, Bill Gould, Daniel Hidalgo, Juan Luis Trejo Piazza.

'Seeing the show, one …' Ivan Valenzuela. 'Rock In Rio II.' *El Mercurio*, January 1991.
'The Festival of Viña …' Brenda Elsey. 'As The World Is My Witness: Transnational Chilean Solidarity And Popular Culture.' In *Human Rights And Transnational Solidarity In Cold War Latin America* (University of Wisconsin Press, 2013)
'When they started their …' Italo Passalacqua. 'Partió La Maratón Para Masoquistas.' *La Segunda*, February 6 1991.
'He kissed Antonio Vodanovic …' *Especial de Faith No More*: *Séptimo Vicio*
'The right people left …' 'Faith No More Aqui Vina.' *Aqui Vina* . TVN, February 5 1991.
'principal spokesman for his …' Nicholas Birns. 'Alberto Fuguet.' In *The Contemporary Spanish-American Novel* (Bloomsbury Academic, 2013)
'It went from 7,500 …' John Lannert. 'ABC's Of Lucrative Touring In S. America.' *Billboard*, September 14 1991.
'Just like the Stones …' Daniel Hidalgo. 'Faith No More: El Final De Un Mito.' *Paniko*, February 28, 2011.
'The best thing that …' Felipe Arratia. 'La Agitada Trastienda De Faith No More En Chile.' *La Tercera*, September 28 2015.

CHAPTER 29
Author interviews: Mike Bordin, Roddy Bottum, Bill Gould.

'It was the biggest …' *Mike Patton interview.* MTV Brasil, September 1991.
'The presentation at Rock …' / 'It feels like being …' João Gabriel de Lima. 'Entrevista Mike Patton.' *Veja*, October 1991.

CHAPTER 30
Author interviews: Mike Bordin, Roddy Bottum, Bill Gould, Matt Wallace.

'Popularity begets popularity …', Bryan Wawzenek. '25 Years Ago: The SoundScan Era Rocks The Music Industry.' *Ultimate Classic Rock*, May 25 2016.
'Like Faith No More …' Gary Graff. 'Nirvana Can Be Found Not Just In Seattle Anymore.' *Detroit Free Press*, October 11 1991.
'One of the country …' / 'I don't think we …' / 'Pretty much the whole …' / 'The only way to …' *In The Studio '92*, MTV, January 1992.

CHAPTER 31
Author interviews: Mike Bordin, Roddy Bottum, Seán Clancy, Bill Gould, Matt Wallace, William Winant.

'Last time they kind …' / 'I don't really know …' / 'It's inevitable that some …' / 'I stayed up for …' *In The Studio '92*, MTV, January 1992.

CHAPTER 32
Author interviews: Mike Bordin, Roddy Bottum, Seán Clancy, Bill Gould, Iris Lettieri, Matt Wallace.

'I get really turned …' Steffan Chirazi. 'Rod Against The Machine.' *Kerrang!*, July 7 1993.
'With the somewhat sizable …' 'Angel Dust Month: A Tale Of One Angry Keyboardist, A Missing Box And One Scared Drum Tech!' faithnomoreblog.com, June 18 2012.
'Throughout our career, the …' Gina Morris. 'Faecal Attraction.' *NME*, January 3 1993
'My parents are very …' Lance Loud. 'Heavy Metal Homo.' *The Advocate*, June 15 1993.
'I found out by …' Phil Sutcliffe. 'Faith No More: Regrets, They Have A Few.' *Q*, May 1995.
'At least one person …' Everett True. *Nirvana: The True Story* (Omnibus, 2006)
'It's romantic. That's why …' Dana Kennedy. 'The Young And The Reckless.' *Entertainment Weekly*, November 26 1993.

CHAPTER 33
Author interviews: Mike Bordin, Roddy Bottum, Seán Clancy, Bill Gould, Matt Wallace.

'The band doesn't really …' Lee Sherman. 'Get The Funk Out.' *Guitar*, September 1992.
'The guitar player has …' *Visions*, May 1997.

'Angel Dust was more …' 'Big Jim Q&A.' faithnomoreblog.com, November 11 2012.

'I just wanted to …' Steve Blush. 'Jim Martin interview.' *Guitar World*, September 1992.

CHAPTER 34

Author interviews: Mike Bordin, Roddy Bottum, Bill Gould, Matt Wallace.

'There are some very …' Rob Andrews. 'Breaking The Rules.' *Hit Parader*, June 1992.

'The record company president …' 'Big Jim Q&A.' faithnomoreblog.com, November 11 2012.

'The record company wanted …' Tony Miller. 'Faith No More.' *Rip It Up*, July 1992.

'There's nothing totally like …' Chris Morris. 'Tour Power Fuels Faith No More: Extensive Roadwork Accompanies New Set.' *Billboard*, July 11 1992.

'This new stuff is …' Paul Rees. 'Strangers In A Strange Land.' *Raw*, May 27 1992.

'We were getting a …' Joe Brown. 'Finding Faith On The Road.' *Washington Post*, July 17 1992.

'Lots of kids bought …' Simon Reynolds. 'Review.' *Melody Maker*, June 1992.

'It's been very unpleasant …' Steffan Chirazi. 'Testing The Faith.' *Kerrang!*, June 22 1992.

CHAPTER 35

Author interviews: Mike Bordin, Roddy Bottum, Bill Gould, Kevin Kerslake, Matt Wallace.

'I had the idea …' 'Big Jim Q&A.' faithnomoreblog.com, November 11 2012.

'"Midlife Crisis' is the band's …' 'Singles.' *Music & Media*, June 6 1992.

'A few spins are required …' 'Single Reviews.' *Billboard*, June 13 1992.

CHAPTER 36

Author interviews: Mike Bordin, Roddy Bottum, Bill Gould.

'To me, the stage …' Christopher R. Weingarten. 'The Real Things: Dillinger Escape Plan Interview Mike Patton.' *Revolver*, June 5 2010.

'They were really curious …' Pavel Kucera. 'Faith No More: Moc Jsme Se S Tim Nes**li.' IDNES.cz, August 14 2008.

'Patton is rampaging …' Pleasant Gehman. 'Epic Journey.' *Spin*, September 1992.

'Afterward, the group sit …' William Shaw. 'Twist Of Faith.' *Details*, September 1992.

'We may not like …' *OOR*, August 8 1992.

'A roiling, musically adventurous …' Tom Sinclair. 'Faith No More: Angel Dust.' *Rolling Stone*, September 3 1992.

'Faith No More broke …' David Wild. 'Angel Dust: Faith No More.' *St. Louis Post-Dispatch*, 26 June 1992.

'Angel Dust would be …' Andy Langer. 'Angel Dust, Faith No More.' *Dallas Morning News,* 21 June 1992.

'While it's easy to …' Greg Kot. 'Home Entertainment.' *Chicago Tribune*, June 25 1992.

'They create what is …' Janiss Garza. 'Angel Dust.' *Entertainment Weekly*, July 10 1992.

'This is tightly constructed …' Simon Reynolds. 'Review.' *Melody Maker*, June 1992.

CHAPTER 37

Author interviews: Mike Bordin, Roddy Bottum, Bill Gould.

'Our manager sent us …' Simon Witter. 'On The Road With Faith No More.' *Sky*, December 1992.

'Vegas with a flannel …' Kim Neely. 'Lollapalooza '92: On The Road With The Chili Peppers, Pearl Jam And Soundgarden.' *Rolling Stone*, September 17 1992.

'A small victory for …' Chris Dafoe. 'A Small Victory For A Gathering Of Tribes.' *Globe & Mail*, July 23 1992.

'I hate the whole …' Mark Putterford. 'A Real Ugly Experience.' *Select*, August 1992.

'We like to watch …' Joe Brown. 'Finding Faith On The Road.' *Washington Post*, July 17 1992.

'I'm getting more and …' Mark Putterford. 'A Real Ugly Experience.' *Select*, August 1992.

'Our job is just …' Chris Watts. 'Testing The Faith.' *Kerrang!*, September 9 1992.

CHAPTER 38

Author interviews: Mike Bordin, Roddy Bottum, Bill Gould, Derek Kemp.

'Eyewitnesses said the group's …' Anthony Violanti. 'Patton Offers No Apologies.' *Buffalo News*, October 5 1992.

'It feels like there's …' Chris Watts. 'Testing The Faith.' *Kerrang!,* September 9 1992.

'We're all pretty much …' *MTV Post-Modern.* MTV Europe, November 1992.

'It's the most radio-friendly …' Nathan Ammons and Tim Newman. 'Talking Music And Zoning With Roddy Bottum Of Faith No More.' *Public News* (Houston), January 27 1993.

'Warners spent the video …' 'Billy Gould Answers Your Questions About Angel Dust.' faithnomoreblog.com, September 8 2012.

CHAPTER 39
Author interviews: Mike Bordin, Roddy Bottum, Bill Gould.

'Sure, anything'S Possible …' 'It Ain't Easy.' *Hot Metal*, January/February 1993.

'We're Not About …' Shane Danielsen. 'Acts Of Faith.' *Sydney Morning Herald*, May 6 1993.

'Mike Patton Is Quitting …' Mary Anne Hobbs. 'Last In, First Out?' *Select*, August 1993.

'There Is An Obvious …' Steffan Chirazi. 'Midlife Crisis.' *Kerrang!*, July 17 1993.

'Everyone Is Tired …' Paul Rees. 'Review.' *Raw*, August 1993.

CHAPTER 40
Author interviews: Mike Bordin, Roddy Bottum, Bill Gould, Clif Norrel.

'Hey Butthead, you know …' 'Close Encounters', *Beavis and Butt-Head*, MTV, August 9 1995.

'The band announced Trey's …' Steffan Chirazi. 'New guitarist revealed.' *Kerrang!,* July 23 1994.

'We all knew that …' Drew Masters. 'Faith No More.' *MEAT*, May 1995.

CHAPTER 41
Author interviews: Mike Bordin, Roddy Bottum, Bill Gould.

'Trey simply didn't want …' Neil Jeffries. 'Humping Axl's Leg.' *Raw*, March 1 1995.

'Patton advised against having …' Gavin Martin. 'Defecation In Venice.' *NME*, February 18 1995.

'I was working at …' Pete Crigler. 'Dean Menta.' *Perfect Sound Forever*, April 2016.

CHAPTER 42
Author interviews: Mike Bordin, Roddy Bottum, Bill Gould, Derek Kemp.

'Some people will get …' David Sprague. 'Faith No More Seeks Fool's Gold.' *Billboard*, February 4 1995.

'The album is almost …' Al Weisel. 'Music Reviews.' *Rolling Stone*, June 1 1995.

'What seems like several …' Jonathan Gold. 'Reviews.' *Spin*, May 1995.

'Archaic progressive-rock fusion …' Dimitri Ehrlich. 'King For A Day, Fool For A Lifetime.' *Entertainment Weekly*, March 17 1995.

'Faith No More are not …' '*Faith No More At Axion Beach special.*' Ka2, July 1995.

'The band's first Brit …' Steffan Chirazi. 'Thanks A Million! Faith No More's Fantastic Return!' *Kerrang!*, February 4 1995.

'Bowel Wow Wow.' *NME*, February 18 1995.

'Royal Flush.' Mike Peake. *Kerrang!*, March 4 1995.

'Tell me about this …' *Super Rock*. MTV, April 29 1995.

'It's a good way …' Martin Bate. 'Review And Interview.' *Consumable*, April 1995.

'Faith No More "We're Not Splitting!"' Steffan Chirazi. *Kerrang!*, October 14 1995.

CHAPTER 43
Author interviews: Mike Bordin, Roddy Bottum, Bill Gould, Jon Hudson.

'Hopefully in the future …' Matthew Klem. 'Interview with Roddy Bottum.' *VAJ*, June 1995.

'This is emphatically not …' Steven Mirkin. 'Slash's Imperial Teen in motion with Seasick.' *Billboard*, March 30 1996.

'I've always thought he …' Joel Selvin. 'Ozzy Marches to Different Drummer.' *San Francisco Chronicle*, May 5 1996.

'Certain members of the …' Pete Crigler. 'Dean Menta.' *Perfect Sound Forever*, April 2016.

CHAPTER 44
Author interviews: Mike Bordin, Roddy Bottum, Bill Gould, Jon Hudson.

'We did about seven …' *Zillo*, May 1997.

'He only liked about …' Lauren Zoric. 'Keeping the Faith.' *Herald-Sun*, May 1997.

'We have another guitarist …' / 'Billy is completely hooked …' 'Faith Renewed.' *Beat*, March 1997.

'Amid rumours of a …' Joel Selvin. 'Faith No More Gets Reborn.' *San Francisco Chronicle*, February 16 1997.

CHAPTER 45
Author interviews: Mike Bordin, Roddy Bottum, Bill Gould, Jon Hudson.

'They had this mask …' *Closure*. BBC Choice. November 25 2002.

'Faith No More are floundering …' Lorraine Ali. 'Album Of The Year.' *Rolling Stone*, June 16 1997.

'In naming its seventh …' Steffan Chirazi. 'Review.' *San Francisco Chronicle*, June 1997.

'For once the tongue-in-cheek …' John Perry. 'Poo! What A Scorcher!' *NME*, June 1997.

'Forget the radio stations …' Justin Seremet. 'Album Of The Year.' *Hartford Courant*, July 3 1997.

'The idea of Mike …' / 'We usually pick the …' Gina Van Der Vliet. 'Faith No More's New Vid To Give Viewers "Vertigo".' *Billboard*, June 28 1997.

CHAPTER 46
Author interviews: Mike Bordin, Roddy Bottum, Bill Gould, Jon Hudson.

'Faith No More made …' *Total Guitar*, March 2006.

'They can both be …' / 'Patton … suggested that the …' Craig Schuftan. *Entertain Us: The Rise And Fall Of Alternative Rock In The Nineties* (ABC Books, 2012)

'Nu-metal makes my …' Amelia Daarke. 'My Life Story.' *Metal Hammer*, March 2002.

CHAPTER 47
Author interviews: Mike Bordin, Roddy Bottum, Bill Gould, Jon Hudson

'Faith No More's Patton has …' Jaan Uhelszki. 'Faith No More's Patton has new band.' *San Francisco Chronicle*, April 12 1998.

'Puffy did not refer …' Neil Strauss. 'Losing Faith.' *New York Times*, April 23 1998.

'I was nervous starting …' Ron Hart. 'Mike Patton.' *CMJ New Music Report*, June 28 1999.

CHAPTER 48
Author interviews: Mike Bordin, Roddy Bottum, Bill Gould, Jon Hudson.

'I love the intimacy …' Ed Condran. 'No More Faith No More Says Teen Keyboardist.' *The Record* (New Jersey), April 2 1999.

'I was coming from …' Chuck Crisafulli. 'New Generation Rockers Trying Their Hand At Film Music.' *Hollywood Reporter*, January 4 2008.

'Curiosity, mere curiosity …' Simões, José Manuel. 'Entrevista Mike Patton "Continuo A Dormir Sem Ninguém Ao Lado".' *Jornal de Notícias*, March 7 2002.

'Ten years later and …' Christopher R. Weingarten. 'Faith No More: Rock's Most Contrarian Band Returns.' *Rolling Stone*, May 12 2015.

CHAPTER 49
Author interviews: Mike Bordin, Roddy Bottum, Andy Copping, Bill Gould, Jon Hudson.

'Every four or five …' Gelu Sulugiuc. 'Ex-Faith No More Singer Rediscovers Melody.' *Reuters*, May 25 2006.

'I wouldn't rule it …' 'Faith No More Reunion Possible?' *Artisan News Service*, January 18 2008.

'If anything like this …' 'Faith No More To Reform?' *Kerrang!*, November 29 2008.

'For some time during …' Big Jim Q&A.' faithnomoreblog.com, November 11 2012.

'A source close to …' 'Guitarist Jim Martin Not Taking Part In Rumoured Faith No More Reunion.' *Blabbermouth*, February 17 2009.

'The highly anticipated reunion …' 'Mike Patton Completes Major Motion Film Score For *Crank 2*.' Ipecac news release, February 24 2009.

CHAPTER 50
Author interviews: Mike Bordin, Roddy Bottum, Andy Copping, Bill Gould, Jon Hudson.

'As it turns out …' 'Hear Faith No More Play Unearthed Song In Argentina.' *Spin*, March 31 2015.

'There's a lineage of …' ' Ross Simonini. 'Interview With Mike Patton.' *The Believer*, January 1 2013.

CHAPTER 51
Author interviews: Mike Bordin, Roddy Bottum, Bill Gould, Jon Hudson.

'I was pretty flattered …' / 'I did vocals at …' Christopher R. Weingarten. 'Faith No More: Rock's Most Contrarian Band Returns.' *Rolling Stone*, May 12 2015.

'a rattlingly vital new …' Nate Chinen. 'Faith No More Brings Reboot To Madison Square Garden.' *New York Times*, July 30 2015.

'as much a triumphant …' Kory Grow. 'Sol Invictus.' *Rolling Stone*, May 19 2015.

'the rare reunion album …' Mark Deming. 'Sol Invictus—Faith No More.' *AllMusic*, May 19 2015.

CHAPTER 52
'It's with a heavy …' 'Faith No More Tribute.' facebook.com/faithnomore, November 11 2017.

CHAPTER 53
Author interviews: Mike Bordin, Roddy Bottum, Bill Gould.

INDEX

ALSO AVAILABLE IN PRINT AND EBOOK EDITIONS FROM JAWBONE PRESS